Ask Those Who Know

Muhammad al-Tijani al-Samawi

IN THE NAME OF ALLAH

THE BENEFICIENT, THE MERCIFUL

CONTENTS

Introduction	1
Open Letter to Sayyid Abul-Hasan Al-Nadawi, an Indian Scholar	7
Ask those Who Know if You do not Know	19
Chapter One:	
Concerning The Creator, The Most Sublime and Majestic	23
Chapter Two:	
Concerning The Prophet (s)	39
Chapter Three:	
Concerning The Ahl al-Bayt (as)	73
Chapter Four:	
Concerning The General Companions	119
Chapter Five:	
Concerning The Three Caliphs, Abu Bakr, 'Umar and 'Uthman	185
Chapter Six:	
Concerning The Caliphate	257
Chapter Seven:	
Concerning The Noble Hadith	279
Chapter Eight:	
Concerning The Two Sahihs of Al-Bukhari and Muslim	321
Conclusion	363

Abbreviations

In keeping with the original Arabic text, I have used the following abbreviations in this translation:

(s)

May Allah's peace and greetings be upon him and his progeny (*Ahl Al-Bayt*). Specifically for Prophet Muhammad (s).

(as)

May Allah's peace and greetings be upon him / them.

(sa)

May Allah's peace and greetings be upon her (used for Hazrat Fatima Zahra (sa))

(r)

May Allah be pleased whith him/her

Where necessary, I have used square brackets [ ] so as facilitate a more meaningful translation into English.

Editor

Introduction

In the name of Allah, the most Merciful, the most Beneficent

All praise is for Allah, the Lord of the universe. May the best of blessings and greetings be upon our leader and master Muhammad (s), who was sent as a mercy to the universe, he is the master of the foremost ones and the last ones; he was purified from all disgraces. May Allah's choicest blessings and greetings also be upon the illustrious and purified *Ahl al-Bayt*, the standards of guidance, light of those in darkness and the Imams of the Muslims.

This work consists of some questions which I prepared for Muslim researchers - especially those Sunnis who maintain that they alone hold fast to the true practice of the Prophet (s). They are severe in their disapproval of other Muslims and call them derogatory names. New organizations have sprung up in several Islamic countries in the name of defending the *Sunnah* of Muhammad (s) and in the name of "the helpers of the *Sunnah*" and "the helpers of the companions". Numerous books have been published to insult and condemn the Shi'as, their Imams and to ridicule their scholars. These ideas have been propagated, by international means of communications, to every part of the world - Muslim and non-Muslim - to the point where people today speak [only] of the Sunnis and the Shi'as.

On many occasions, I meet some young, truthful, Muslim scholars who enquire and ask questions about the Shi'as, i.e., the true and false [notions] about them. They are perplexed in reconciling what they observe while living amongst their Shi'a friends with what they hear and read about them. They do not know where the truth lies. I have spoken to some of them and have presented them with copies of my book "*Then I was Guided*".[1] Praise be to Allah, the majority of them, after researching and debating, are guided to the truth and follow it. This, however, does

---

[1] Available at: https://www.al-islam.org/then-i-was-guided-muhammad-al-tijani-al-samawi

not suffice for those youths whom I meet coincidentally or for those who do not have such opportunities to meet and therefore remain confused regarding the conflicting ideas they are exposed to.

Despite the convincing proofs and irrefutable arguments [cited] in "*Then I was Guided*", and "*To be With the Truthful ones*",[2] these two books are not sufficient to combat the frenzied attacks and crude allegations [instigated] by various means of propaganda that some of the wicked sources have financed by their petro dollars.

Despite all this, however, the voice of truth will emerge in the midst of this discomforting uproar and it will be a glowing light shining in the gloom of darkness since the promise of Allah is true, and it will certainly manifest itself. Allah says: *"They seek to extinguish Allah's light by their mouths, but Allah will perfect this light even though the disbelievers hate that"* *(61:8)*. Allah further explains that their acts will fail and will rebound on them: *"Verily, those who disbelieve spend their wealth in hindering [people from] the path of Allah, they will continue to spend; then they will regret therein. Ultimately, they will be overcome and the disbelievers will be gathered in hell"* *(8:36)*.

Due to this, it is essential for the scholars, writers and thinkers to explain to the lay persons what is difficult for them [to comprehend] and to guide them to the right path. The most exalted says:

"Those who seek to conceal the clear [signs] which We have revealed and guided - after we have clearly explained it for the people in the book - Allah will curse them as will those who are entitled to curse. Except those who repent,

---

[2] Available at: https://www.al-islam.org/be-with-truthful-muhammad-al-tijani-al-samawi

make amends and make clear [that which they sought to hide]. Towards them I shall turn, for I am the Forgiving, the Merciful"(2:160).

Why don't the scholars discuss this topic diligently and sincerely for Allah's sake? Why [should they not do this] when the most Glorious has revealed the clear signs and guidance, perfected His religion and completed His favors on humankind? When the Prophet (s) has fulfilled Allah's mission to him, proclaimed His message and advised the *ummah,* then why this disunity, enmity, hatred and calling derogatory names and each party considering the other to be a disbeliever?

In my role, I have to take an unequivocal position here and to declare to all Muslims, that there can be no salvation, no safety, no unity, no happiness, and no paradise unless we return to the two basic sources: Allah's book and the Prophet's household (peace be upon them). [Nothing can be attained] unless we embark on the ship of salvation, the ship of the *Ahl al-Bayt* (as). This statement is not something that I have conjured up; rather, it is the word of Allah in the noble Qur'an and His Prophet (s) in the honorable Prophetic *Sunnah*. The Muslims today have two options to attain the desired unity:

The first approach: The *Ahl al-Sunnah wa'l -Jama'a* accept the *madhab* (school of thought) of the household of the Prophet which is the *madhab* that the Ithna' Ashari Imami Shi'as follow. This *madhab* would then be classified as a fifth *madhab* to them (the Sunnis), and they could then treat its jurisprudential texts in the same way that they do with the other four Islamic schools. They should not disparage it nor deride those who embrace it. They should give the educated students the freedom to choose the *madhab* which they are satisfied with. And, by the same token, it is incumbent upon every Muslim - Sunni and Shi'a - that they recognize the other Islamic *madhabs,* such as the Ibadiyya and the Zaydiyya. This approach is a remedy for many of the conflicts and differences that affect our *ummah,* but it still does not present a complete cure for the historical discord we have endured for centuries.

The second approach: The Muslims should unite under a common creed as dictated by Allah and His Prophet (s). They should do so in one way and on the right path, which is to follow the Imams of the *Ahl al-Bayt*, [they are] those from whom Allah has removed all filth and has purified them completely. Indeed, all Muslims - Shi'as and Sunnis - agree upon their acts and their superiority in their piety, virtue, asceticism, character, knowledge and good deeds.

Since the Muslims differ regarding the companions, they should leave what they differ on in favor of what they agree upon in compliance with the *hadith* of the Prophet (s): "Keep away from what casts doubt in you in favor of what does not make you doubtful". By doing this, the Muslim *ummah* would come together and unite based on a fundamental rule that forms the pivot around which everything revolves, [a principle] established by the Prophet (s) when he said: "I leave amongst you two weighty things, if you stick to them, you will never go astray: the book of Allah and my *Ahl al-Bayt*" [cited in] *Sahih Muslim*.

Since this *hadith* is accepted by both sects, in fact by all Muslims regardless of their different *madhab*, why is it that a faction amongst them does not act in accordance to it? If all the Muslims were to follow this *hadith*, such strong Islamic unity would be fostered between them that no breeze could shake it, no storm destroy it, no propagation could refute it, and no enemy of Islam could thwart it.

In my view, this is the only solution towards the salvation and safety of the Muslims. Any other approach is futile and [is tantamount to] embellished words. Whoever studies the Qur'an and the Prophet's traditions, as well as studies history and reflects upon it with a sound mind will certainly agree with me.

The first approach has failed since the first day the Prophet (s) left us when the companions differed amongst themselves resulting in the division of the Muslim *ummah* and the destruction of the bonds of solidarity. The *ummah* has failed throughout the centuries to revert to the second approach which is the adherence to the book and the Prophet's household (as). This is due to the propaganda spread earlier by the Umayyad and 'Abbasid dynasties, and, in our times, because of the defamation, misrepresentation and condemnation of the followers of the *Ahl al-Bayt* of the Prophet. There remains for us then nothing else but a clear approach and a disclosure of the truth for all who wish to know it. This can be done in the style of the noble Qur'an in its challenge: *"Come forth with your proof if you are indeed telling the truth"* (2:111).

Clear proof and argument will never be subjugated by force or wealth; neither can they be refuted by warnings and threats. [This is true] for free human beings who have pledged themselves to Allah alone. They have never deviated - and will never do so - from the truth, even if they lose their lives.

If only the modern day scholars of the *ummah* were to organize a conference to examine these matters with open hearts, astute minds, and pure consciences. They would, by doing so, serve the Muslim *ummah,* assemble its scattered fragments, heal its wounds, unite its ranks and bring together its [different] views.

This unity will come, [whether they] like it or not, for Allah, Glory be to Him, has reserved, for that purpose, an Imam from the progeny of al-Mustafa (the chosen one) who will fill the earth with justice and equity, just as it was filled with oppression and tyranny. This Imam is from the purified loins. It is as though Allah, great is His wisdom, tests this *ummah* throughout its life span until, when the time is near, He reveals to it the errors it has committed and gives it an opportunity to return to the truth and follow the original path which Muhammad (s) called to when he supplicated: "O Allah, guide my people for indeed they do not know."

Until that time comes, I present my book, *"Ask those who know"*. It is a collection of questions and answers based on the views and the teachings of the Imams of the *Ahl al-Bayt* (as). Hopefully, the Muslims in every Islamic country will benefit from it and work towards the concordance of views in preparation of the coveted unity.

My success is from Allah. Upon Him I rely and to Him I turn. My Lord, expand my breast and make my affairs easy for me [to handle]. Loosen the knots on my tongue so that my words can be understood. I ask Him, Glory be to Him, the most exalted one, to accept my work and make it [a source of] virtue and blessing, for it is only a stone in the building of a united body.

I say this because the contemporary Muslims are still very far away from realizing basic human rights and working harmoniously with each other. I realized this first hand during my travels and numerous visits to the Muslim countries or in the countries where there are Muslims [residing]. The latest was in the Indian subcontinent which has a population of over 200 million Muslims, a quarter of whom are Shi'as and three quarters are Sunnis. I had heard a lot about them, but what I witnessed really perplexed and astonished me. It also made me fearful. I was saddened and I wept over the path this *ummah* has taken. Were it not for my hope, wishes and faith, despair would have overcome my heart.

Immediately after my return from India, I sent an open letter to an Indian scholar who the *Ahl al-Sunnah wa'l-Jama'a* in that subcontinent refers to, Abul- Hasan 'Ali al-Nadawi. I promised him that I would publish this letter and his reply. So far, however, I have not received a reply. I have published my letter in the introduction to this book in its original form so that it acts as an historical testimony which will bear witness for us in front of Allah and the people that we are amongst those who enjoined unity.

Muhammad al-Tijani al-Samawi

May the blessings and peace of Allah be on the most honorable
of the Messengers and on his purified household.

Open Letter to Sayyid Abul-Hasan Al-Nadawi, an Indian Scholar

Peace, Mercy and Blessings of Allah, the Exalted, be upon you:

I am Muhammad al-Tijani al-Samawi, a Tunisian whom Allah has favored with guidance and success. I have embraced the school of the *Ahl al-Bayt* of the Prophet after lengthy research, having previously been a Maliki. I was a follower of the famous Sufi *tariqa* (path) in North Africa, the Tijaniyya order. I came to recognize the truth during a successful visit to the Shi'i '*ulama*' (scholars); I have written a book about that visit which I called "*Then I was Guided*". It was printed in India by "*al-Majma' al-'ilmi al-Islami*" in different languages and, for the occasion (of publishing), I was invited to visit India.

Dear Sir, I came to India for a short visit. I had hoped to meet your honorable self when I heard about you and learnt that you were a councilor amongst the *Ahl al-Sunnah wa'l-Jama'a*. However, the immense distances (of travelling) and lack of time prevented me from doing that. I had to be content with visiting the cities of Bombay, Poona, Jabal Pur and other cities in Gujarat. I was greatly pained by what I saw in India, i.e., enmity and hatred between the *Ahl al-Sunnah wa'l-Jama'a* and their Shi'a Muslim brothers.

I had heard that they wage war sometimes and fight each other and [even] spill innocent blood on both sides in the name of Islam. However, I did not believe this, thinking that it was slander. What I witnessed and heard during my visit could make [one] perplexed and astonished. I was certain that there are despicable plans and dangerous conspiracies being instigated against Islam and the Muslims so as to destroy all of them, Sunnis and Shi'as. What made this belief of mine even more certain, and my knowledge even more entrenched, was a confrontation which occurred between myself and a group of Sunni scholars. The honorable Shaykh 'Aziz al-

Rahman, the Mufti of *al-Jama'a Islamiyya* was leading them (in this). The meeting was held in their mosque in Bombay and took place after their invitation.

I had just settled down with them when disdain and derision, insults and curses, against the followers of the household of the Prophet began. By this, they wanted to provoke and incite me, since they had known that I had composed a book [in which] I invited people to embrace the school of the *Ahl al-Bayt*, peace be upon them.
I understood their intentions and controlled my temper. I therefore smiled at them saying: "I am your guest, you are the ones who invited me; I came to you in haste responding to your call. Did you invite me to insult and revile me? Are these the manners which Islam has taught you?"

They replied to me in an arrogant manner saying that in my life I had never been a Muslim, even for a day, because I was a Shi'a and the Shi'as have nothing to do with Islam. They swore to that.

I said: "Fear God, O brothers, for our Lord is one, our Prophet is one, our book is one, and our *qibla* is one. The Shi'as believe in one God and they practice Islam in accordance with [the teachings of] the Prophet and his family, they pray, give *zakat* and go for pilgrimage to the house of God. How is it permissible for you to consider them to be infidels?"

They replied: "You do not believe in the Qur'an, you are hypocrites, you dissimulate (*taqiyya*) and your Imam has said: "Dissimulation is [part of] my religion and that of my father." You are a Jewish sect which 'Abd Allah b. Saba' the Jew had founded."

I said to them smiling: "Let us leave the Shi'as [aside] and let us talk about me personally. I was a Maliki like you and I was satisfied, after lengthy research, that the *Ahl al-Bayt* are most right and most worthy of following. Do you have proofs which you can dispute with me? Or do you want to ask me what are my arguments and proofs so that we can understand each other?"

They said: "The *Ahl al-Bayt* are the wives of the Prophet, you do not know anything of the Qur'an."

I said: "*Sahih al-Bukhari* and *Sahih Muslim* report differently from what you mention." They said: "All that is in al-Bukhari and Muslim and other Sunni books which you base your arguments upon are [due to] the Shi'as interpolating and inserting in our books".

I replied to them laughingly: "If the Shi'as can interpolate your books and your *Sahih* works, then there is no importance or value to [your books] nor to your school which is based on [these books]." They kept quiet and were dumbfounded. One of them intended to make fun and to provoke me again. He said: "One who does not believe in the Caliphate of the rightly guided Caliphs of our Sayyid Abu Bakr, Sayyid 'Umar, Sayyid 'Uthman and Sayyid 'Ali and Sayyid Mu'awiyah and Sayyid Yazid, may God be pleased and happy with them, then he is not a Muslim."

I was astonished at this talk which I had never heard in my life, since it meant that anybody who did not believe in the Caliphate of Mu'awiyah and his son Yazid was to be considered an infidel. I said to myself: "It is understandable that the Muslims be pleased with Abu Bakr, 'Umar and 'Uthman, this is a natural thing. As for [being pleased with] Yazid, I have never heard of it except in India." I turned to all of them and asked them: "Do you all agree with his view?" They all replied: "Yes."

At that point, I knew that there was no point in continuing the conversation. I understood that they wanted to provoke me so that they could exact revenge (for conversion), they might perhaps even kill me on the pretext of my having abused the companions, who knows?

I saw evil in their eyes and I asked my friend who had brought me to them to take me away immediately. He took me; he was hurt and apologized to me for what had occurred. This innocent person had wanted to know the truth through this meeting. As a matter of fact, he is a well behaved young man, Sharaf al-Din, owner of an

Islamic printing press and publishing house in Bombay. He was a witness to what had transpired between us in this aforementioned discussion. He did not hide his disappointment with these people who considered themselves to be amongst the prominent scholars.

I left them whilst angry and sorry at the condition which the Muslims had reached, especially by those posing as the centre of preaching and calling themselves scholars. I said to myself: "If the '*ulama* are at this level of blind fanaticism, what will the condition and ignorance of the masses be like?" I knew then how the fighting and wars in which blood was spilled illegally, honor and dignity disgraced, had started in the name of protecting Islam.

I cried over the path taken by this wretched and ill-fated people which Allah, Glory be to Him, has entrusted with the responsibility of guidance. The Prophet of God (s) has also entrusted it with the responsibility of transmitting light into the dark hearts, if they need the glow of light. At any one time, there are in India alone 700 million persons who worship [other gods] apart from God, the most exalted. They consider the cow, statues, and idols to be sacred. Instead of unifying the efforts of Muslims so as to guide and preach to them and to bring them out from darkness to light so that they should submit to the Lord of the universe, we see that the Muslims today, especially in India, are themselves in need of guidance and reformation.

Because of this, sir, I am sending my letter to you asking you in the name of God, who is the most Merciful and Beneficent, and in the name of the noble Prophet and in the name of the greatness of Islam, according to the saying of the most High: *"And hold firmly to the rope of Allah all together and do not become divided." (3:103).*

I ask you to adopt the stance of a brave Muslim who is not scared, for Allah's sake, of the sternest critics and is not swayed by fanaticism or sectarianism, a position which Satan and his friends would like.

I invite you to a stance which is sincere and clear; you are the one whom Allah has entrusted with responsibility as long as you talk in the name of Islam in that region. Allah will not be pleased with you if you adopt the stance of a contented spectator with what is happening here and there, a tragedy the price of which the innocent Shi'a and Sunni Muslims are paying. God is going to ask you on the Day of Judgment about every small or big deed, and you will have to account for every single thing because those who know and those who do not know are not equal.

As long as you consider yourself to be amongst the *'ulama'* of India, there is no doubt that your responsibility is immense. A word from you could be for the betterment of the *ummah* in India just as it could be for the destruction of the future civilization. So have fear of God, O people of understanding!

As Allah, Glory be to Him, gave the scholars an elevated status after the angels, the most High says: *"Allah bears witness that there is no God but He and the angels and those bestowed with knowledge are undertaking their affairs with justice"* **(3:18)**. And if He, Glory be to Him, is instructing us all to *"undertake your measurement with equity and do not defraud the scales"(55:9)* and if the commentators talk of the need to deal justly in material scales, which has limited value, how about dealing justly when creedal issues [are at stake] which can take one between truth and falsehood and on which depends the guidance of mankind and salvation of the whole of humanity?

Allah, the Most High said: *"When you judge, do so in a just manner"* and He also said: *"O David, We have made you a Caliph on earth so judge between people on [the basis of] truth, do not follow desires, for they will take you away from the path of God."(38:26)*

And the Prophet of God (s) said: "Speak the truth even if it be against you; speak the truth even if it is bitter."

My Dear Sir, I invite you to the book of God and to the *Sunnah* of His Prophet. Speak it clearly and loudly, even if it is bitter; it will be a testimony for you in front of Allah. By your Lord, do you consider the Shi'as to be non-Muslims?

Do you truly believe they are infidels? Is the following of the household of the Prophet, who believe in the unity of one God, and glorify Him more than any other sect - because of their belief that He is above any resemblance (with human beings), corporealism and bodily traits, tantamount to disbelief? They believe in His Prophet Muhammad (s) and extol him more than any other sect due to their belief in his complete infallibility even before the call to prophecy - do you consider them to be infidels?

Those who take Allah, His Prophet, and believers as friends and desire what the family of the Prophet desires and accept them as their friends (as Ibn Manzur has introduced them in his "*Lisan al-Arab*" in his [section on] the origins of the Shi'a), do you consider them to be non-Muslims?

Are these Shi'as who undertake prayers as their best undertaking and they pay the *zakat* as well as an additional one fifth of their property in obedience to Allah and His Prophet and fast the month of Ramadan and other [extra] days and go for pilgrimage and glorify the signs of God, who respect the friends of God and dissociate themselves from the enemies of Allah and Islam, do you consider them to be polytheists?

Do those who believe in the Imamate of twelve Imams from the *Ahl al-Bayt* from whom Allah has removed all filth and purified them completely and believe that the Prophet of God (s) has designated them (as al-Bukhari and Muslim and others have reported from the Sunni *Sahih* works), are these, in your view, deviants from Islam?

Were the Muslims ever ignorant of the Imamate and never accepted it whether at the time of the Prophet or after his death so that we should attribute the belief in and origins of the Imamate to the Persians and Zoroastrians?

Do you now say that one who does not accept the Imamate of Yazid b. Mu'awiyah to be an unbeliever, a person whose immorality is known to the rank and file Muslims? Yazid's vileness and debaseness can be discerned from what the Muslims have agreed on, i.e., his allowing his army and soldiers to do as they pleased in al-Medina al-Munawwara so as to extract allegiance to him by force and to admit that they (the people) are his slaves.

They killed 10,000 of the best companions and the followers and defiled the honor of pure women and young Muslim girls so that they bore children from fornication, a number which nobody but Allah knows. It is enough for his eternal shame, dishonor, and disgrace that he killed the master of the youths of paradise and enslaved the children of the Prophet, and hit the teeth of al-Husayn with his cane, composing the famous ode:

"If only my ancestors at Badr would witness..." He also said: "The Banu Hashim played with the kingdom, no news came and no revelation descended."

It is clear that he did not believe in the prophecy of Muhammad nor in the noble Qur'an. Is it proper that you agree to consider as an infidel one who dissociates himself from Yazid and his father Mu'awiyah who was cursing 'Ali and ordered his cursing? He [even] killed any prominent companion who refused (to curse) as he did with Hujr b. 'Adi al-Kindi and his companions. He (Mu'awiyah) established a *Sunnah* [which was] followed for seventy years even though he was aware of the saying of the Prophet (s): "One who curses 'Ali curses me, and one who curses me curses Allah." This has been reported in the *Sahih* works of the *Ahl al-Sunnah*. Additionally, he [performed] acts which opposed [the teachings of] Islam, like his killing of the innocent and upright ones so as to get *bay'a* for his son Yazid by force and coercion, and his killing of al-Hasan b. 'Ali through Ju'da, the daughter of Ash'ash and many other crimes which the Sunni historical works mention and are testified by the followers of 'Ali.

I do not think, dear sir, that you will agree to all this and if you do, then we can bid farewell to Islam and forget the world. There will remain no standards of judging, nor reasoning, nor law, nor logic, nor proof.

Allah, the most Glorious and Exalted, says: *"O you who believe, have fear of God and be with the truthful ones"(9:119)*. By God, the '*alim* of Pakistan may God forgive his sins, Abu'l-A'la al-Mawdudi, may God have mercy on him, has spoken the truth when he says in his book entitled "*al-khilafa wa'l mulk*" on page 106 reporting from al-Hasan al-Basri:

There were four traits in Mu'awiyah, any one of which was enough to disgrace him:

1. His seizing of the matter (Caliphate) without consulting the Muslims although there were, amongst them, eminent companions and overwhelming light.

2. His appointing his son, the drunkard and winebibber who wore silk and played with drums, to be the Caliph after him.

3. His recognizing Ziyad as his brother - the Prophet of God (s) said: "The child belongs to the bed (legal father), the adulterer is to be stoned."

4. His killing of Hujr and the companions of Hujr. Woe unto him for what he did to Hujr and his companions (he repeated this three times).

May God have mercy on Abu'l-A'la al-Mawdudi, for he came out openly with the truth. Had he wished, he would have added forty-four more traits but he, may God have mercy on him, deemed this to be a sufficient crime against Mu'awiyah. The meaning of a sinful word is well known (perishing in fire).

Maybe al-Mawdudi was sensitive to the feelings of the people who had learnt from their predecessors to revere and respect Mu'awiyah and to be pleased with him and even to his son Yazid. I heard that for myself from your scholars in India. There is no power nor strength except in God, the Almighty, the most Great.

I was also sensitive to the feelings of those who had invited me so as to revile me, I did not mention anything of this to them in fear of myself.

I appeal to you, sir, to adopt a clear stance, seeking, through it, the pleasure of Allah, the Most Exalted, for Allah does not shirk from the truth. I do not ask from you that you concede [their wrongdoing] so as to get even with them nor to publish their disgraces, for history will bear witness to that.

What is requested from you is for you to concede and teach your followers that those who do not accept the Imamate of these people nor befriend them are also true Muslims deserving respect, there is no doubt about it. And for you to say that the Shi'as have been oppressed throughout history because they did not follow or accept the Imamate of the troublesome, cursed ones for whom Allah has cited examples in the Qur'an.

By your Lord, what is the crime of the Shi'as? The Prophet of God commanded the Muslims to follow his household after him to the point that he likened them to Noah's ark, one who climbs in it is saved and one who stays behind is destroyed. What is the sin of the Shi'as if they obey the order of the Prophet when he said: "I leave behind me two weighty things, the book of God and my family, the *Ahl al-Bayt*: if you cling to them you will never be led astray after me." In addition to the Shi'a books, the *Sihah* of the *Ahl al-Sunnah* testify to that.

Instead of thanking them and giving them preference, precedence, and deeming them to be superior over others we insult them and label them as infidels and dissociate ourselves from them, due to their compliance to the Prophet's (s) commands, which is neither fair nor logical.

Let us cast aside, sir, the foolish and false talk which is based neither on proof nor evidence and does not deceive the educated children of our community. The claims that the Shi'as have a special Qur'an or that the bearer of the message is 'Ali or that 'Abd

Allah b. Saba', the Jew, is the founder of Shi'ism or other absurd and prejudiced allegations, which Allah bears witness to, are due to the imaginations of the enemies of Islam and the enemies of the *Ahl al-Bayt* and their Shi'as, which only blind fanaticism and complete ignorance have invented.

I am asking you, honorable sir, where do the scholars of India stand compared to the scholars of al-Azhar who issued a ruling allowing [people] to embrace the *madhab* of Imami Shi'as thirty years ago? Among the prominent notable *'ulama'* of al-Azhar are those who view the Ja'ffari legal school, which the Shi'as practice, as being more inclusive, rich and more close to the soul of Islam than the other Islamic schools which are actually dependent upon it.

Among the leaders of these nobles is al-Shaykh Muhammad Shaltut, may God have mercy on him. He was the head of al-Azhar during his time. Don't the *'ulama'* of his caliber know Islam and Muslims? Are the Indian scholars more knowledgeable and cognizant than them? I do not know what you will say to that.

My noble Sir, I have strong hopes in you and my heart is open to you with love, kindness, and yearning. I was, like you, veiled from the truth and from the *Ahl al-Bayt* and their Shi'as in the past. Allah, Glory be to Him, guided me to the truth against which there is nothing but going astray. I freed myself from the chains of fanaticism and blind imitation and I knew that most Muslims are still covered with rumors and false (claims). The allegations prevent them from reaching the truth so as to enable all of them to climb to the ship of salvation and to cling firmly to the rope of Allah. There is, as you know, no difference between the Sunnis and the Shi'as except what arose after the Prophet due to the Caliphate. The basis of the difference was their belief in the companions, may God be pleased with them. They differed amongst themselves until they cursed some; they even waged war and killed each other.

If differences concerning them [warrants] being cast out of the fold of Islam then the companions are most guilty of this crime, God forbid. I do not believe that you would be happy with that. Justice therefore dictates that you should not be happy with the out casting of the Shi'as from Islam. Just as the Shi'as devoted themselves to revere and respect the *Ahl al-Bayt*, similarly, the Sunnis devoted themselves to the respect of the *sahaba* and to revere all of them. What a difference between the two positions. If the Shi'as are in error (due to that), then the Sunnis are more in error since all the companions prefer the *Ahl al-Bayt* over themselves and send blessings on them as they send blessings on the Prophet. We do not know of any companion (r) who either preferred himself or saw himself superior, whether in knowledge or in actions, over the *Ahl al-Bayt* of the chosen one.

The time has come to lift the darkness of history over the Shi'as of *Ahl al-Bayt* and to get close to them and to accept them as brothers and to co-operate with each other towards virtue and piety. Enough blood has been shed and sedition instigated in this community.

Sir, maybe Allah, Glory be to Him, will unite the different views through you and will gather the diverse traits, mend the cracks and will cure the wounds. Maybe, because of you, He will extinguish the flames of *fitna* and will disgrace Satan and his party. You will become triumphant in God's eyes especially as, according to what I hear, you are amongst the descendants of the pure family. Act so that you may be gathered with them ("Indeed, this is a single community and I am your Lord, so worship Me"). *"And say: 'Act and Allah and His prophet and the believers will see your actions'."(9:105).* May God grant you and us success. May God make you and us among the sincere workers towards His noble path.

With this letter, sir, I am enclosing a copy of my book '*Then I was Guided*', which I wrote especially on this topic, as a gift from me to you, hoping that you will accept it.

May the peace, mercy and blessings of Allah the Almighty be with you.

Yours sincerely,
Muhammad al-Tijani al-Samawi al-Tunisi

Ask Those Who Know If You Do Not Know[1]

This noble verse instructs the Muslims to refer to the people who know in all [things] which perplex them so that they may discern the path to the truth because Allah, having taught them, has nominated them for that [purpose]. Their knowledge is deeply rooted and they know the interpretation of the Qur'an.

This verse was revealed to introduce the *Ahl al-Bayt (as)*. They are Muhammad, 'Ali, Fatima, al-Hasan and al-Husayn. This [occurred] in the time of prophecy, since, after the Prophet and up to the coming of the hour [of reckoning], the [aforementioned] five are the people of the blanket, in addition to them are nine Imams from the progeny of al-Husayn whom the Prophet of God (s) designated on many occasions and he called them the Imams of guidance and light of those in darkness and "the people who know". [He also called them] "those deeply embedded in knowledge and those to whom Allah, Glory be to Him, has bestowed the knowledge of the book."

These narrations are well established, true and repeatedly narrated (*mutawatir*) by the Shi'as since the time of the Prophet (s) and some Sunni scholars and commentators have also reported them, confirming that they were revealed concerning the *Ahl al-Bayt*, (as). I cite from these (Sunni scholars) by way of example:

1. Al-Imam al-Tha'labi in his *Tafsir al-Kabir* on the meaning of chapter 16 (*al-Nahl*).
2. *Tafsir al-Qur'an* of Ibn Kathir in the vol. 2, p. 570.
3. *Tafsir* of al-Tabari in vol. 14, p. 109.
4. *Tafsir* al-Alusi called *Ruh al-Ma'ani* in vol. 14, p. 134.
5. *Tafsir* al-Qurtubi in vol. 11, p. 272.
6. *Tafsir* al-Hakim, called *Shawahid al-Tanzil*, vol. 1, p. 334.
7. *Tafsir* al-Tustari called *Ihqaq al-Haqq*, by Shushtari in vol. 3, p. 482

---

[1] *Qur'an* 16:43, also 21:7.

8. *Yanabi' al-Mawadda* of al-Qunduzi al-Hanafi, p. 51 and p. 140.

The apparent meaning of the verse suggests that the *ahl al-dhikr* refers to the people of the book, i.e. Jews and Christians. It therefore becomes necessary for us to make it clear that they are not [the ones] intended in the noble verse.

Firstly: Because the noble Qur'an has mentioned in a number of verses that they altered the word of God and they wrote the book with their hands, claiming that it was from God so as to purchase a small price. It also bore witness to their lies and turning the truth upside down. Given this state of affairs, it is not possible for the Qur'an to instruct the Muslims to refer to them on issues which they do not know about.

Secondly: Al-Bukhari has reported in his *Sahih* in "The Book of Testimony" under the chapter "The *ahl al-shirk* (polytheists) aren't to be asked", vol. 3, p. 163. Abu Hurayrah narrated, he said: "The Prophet (s) said: 'Do not believe the people of the book and do not consider them as liars but say: 'We believe in God and what was revealed'".

This means we should not to refer questions to them, rather, [we should] abandon and ignore them because [the command] neither to believe them nor to consider them as liars would nullify the goal [of questioning], i.e., awaiting the correct reply.

Thirdly: Al-Bukhari has reported in his *Sahih* in "The Book of Unity" in the chapter: "Everyday He is concerned [with matters]" vol. 8, p. 208,

Ibn Abbas said: "O Muslims! How come you ask the people of the scriptures, although your book which was revealed to His Prophet has the most recent information from Allah and you recite it, a book which has not been distorted? Allah has revealed to you that the people of the scriptures have changed with their own hands what was revealed to them and they have said: 'This is from Allah' in order to get some worldly benefit thereby." Ibn 'Abbas added:

"Isn't the knowledge revealed to you sufficient to prevent you from asking them? By Allah, I have never seen any one of them asking (Muslims) about what has been revealed to you."

Fourthly: Among the people of the book, if we ask the Christians today they will claim that Jesus is God whilst the Jews will consider them to be liars and will not accept him even as a Prophet. Both of them belie Islam and the Prophet of Islam and they call him a liar and an antichrist. Bearing this in mind, it is incomprehensible that Allah would command us to ask them if we accept that the *ahl al-dhikr* from the apparent [meaning] of the verse refers to the people of the book amongst the Jews and Christians.

This does not contradict [the view] that it was revealed for the household of the Prophet as is established amongst the Shi'as and Sunnis from authentic reports. It is understood from this that Allah, Glory be to Him, the Most Exalted, bestowed the knowledge of the book, which does not neglect anything in it, to these Imams whom He has chosen among His slaves so that people can refer to them on the commentary and interpretation [of the Qur'an]. Therein lies their guidance - if they obey God and His Messenger.

As Allah, Glory be to Him, and sublime is His wisdom, wished the people to submit to the selected ones amongst them, He chose them and taught them the knowledge of the book so that the leadership could be facilitated and the affairs of the people organized due to that. If they were absent from the lives of the people, the opportunity would be open for (false) claimants and ignorant ones. Everyone would then follow his vain desires and the matter would be confusing for the people since everyone could claim to be the most learned.

I will prove this view because I am satisfied that the *Ahl al-Bayt* are the *Ahl al-Dhikr*. I shall pose some questions for which there are no answers for the *Ahl al-Sunnah wa'l-Jama'a* or if there are answers, they are contrived ones, not based on any sound proof acceptable to a researcher. As for their true replies, these are with the pure Imams who have filled the earth with knowledge and cognition, actions and uprightness.

Chapter One

Concerning the Creator, the most Sublime and Majestic

First, the question about the seeing of Allah, Glory be to Him, and His corporealism. Allah, Glory be to Him, says in His noble book: *"The eyes cannot perceive Him"* (6:103); *"And there is nothing like Him"* (42:11); And He says to Moses when he asked to see Him: *"You will never see Me"* (7:143).

How can you accept traditions narrated in *Sahih al-Bukhari* and *Sahih Muslim* that Allah, Glory be to Him, will manifest Himself to His creatures and that they will see Him as they see the moon on the night of a full moon[1] and that He descends to the sky every night[2] and He puts His foot in hell until it becomes filled[3] and that He reveals his thighs so that the believers can recognize Him?[4] He laughs and is pleased. Other narrations make Him a body which moves and changes [positions]. [They report] He has two hands, two legs and five fingers. He puts the first of these on the skies, on the second finger the earth, the trees on the third, and on the fourth He puts water and milk and the rest of the creatures on the fifth finger.[5] He has a house which he resides in and Muhammad seeks permission to enter into the house three times[6]. God is above that, He is the Most Exalted and Great, Glory be to Your Lord, the Lord of power, far is He from how they describe Him.

---

[1] *Sahih, al-Bukhari,* 7/205, *Sahih Muslim,* 1/112.

[2] *Sahih, al-Bukhari,* 2/47

[3] *Sahih, al-Bukhari,* 8/178, and 8/187

[4] *Sahih, al-Bukhari,* 8/182, *Sahih Muslim,* 1/115.

[5] *Sahih, al-Bukhari,* 6/33

[6] *Sahih, al-Bukhari,* 8/183, *Sahih Muslim,* 1/124.

The answer to this lies with the Imams of guidance and lights of those in darkness, i.e., the complete dissociation of Allah, Glory be to Him, the most Exalted from anthropomorphism, resemblance, forms and corporealism (*tajsim*), comparison, (*tashbih*) and limitations (*tahdid*).

Imam 'Ali (as) says about it: "*All praise be to Allah, whose praise cannot be described by those who speak, whose blessings cannot be enumerated by those who count, those who try to cannot give Him His due rights, the height of the intellects cannot reach Him, the depths of perception cannot comprehend Him; for His description, no limit has been laid down, no eulogy exists, no time counted and no duration fixed.*

Whoever has described Allah has linked Him [with something]; whoever links Him [with something] has seen Him as two; whoever has seen Him as two has apportioned Him [into parts]; whoever apportions Him is ignorant of Him; whoever is ignorant of Him has pointed at Him and whoever points at Him has limited Him [to a place]; whoever limits Him has numbered Him.

Whoever has said what is He in, has contained Him [in a place]; whoever says what He is on, believes that He is not on something else. He is a being but not through creation, He exists but not from non-existence. He is with everything but not [in the sense of] physical nearness; He is different from everything but not in a physical sense. He acts but not in the sense of movement and tools [of movement], He sees even when there is no creation of His to be seen."[7]

I draw attention of the young erudite researchers to the treasures which Imam 'Ali (as) has left and which have been compiled in the *Nahj al-Balaghah*, that invaluable journey which is excelled only by the Qur'an, and which has, unfortunately, remained unknown to the majority of the people due to the propaganda, threats and obstacles imposed by the Umayyads and 'Abbasids against whoever was connected to 'Ali b. Abi Talib.

---

[7] *Nahj al-Balagha, Sharh* Muhammad 'Abduh, 1st sermon.

Chapter 1: Concerning the Creator

I would not be exaggerating if I said that the *Nahj al-Balaghah* contains many sciences and admonitions which the people require with the passing of time. The *Nahj al-Balaghah* contains the science of ethics and sociology, economics and valuable indications to space and technology, in addition to philosophy and mode of conduct, politics, and wisdom.

I proved that personally in a doctoral thesis which I presented to the University of Sorbonne and which discussed four subjects which I chose from the *Nahj al-Balaghah*. If only the Muslims were to accord the *Nahj al-Balaghah* a special affection and were to research it in their thesis and theories, for it is a deep sea. Every time a researcher dwells into it he extracts pearls and corals from it.

Remarks

There is a clear difference between the two creeds. The views of the *Ahl al-Sunnah wa'l-Jama'a* which maintain [the belief in] corporealism and claim that Allah, Glory be to Him, has a body, form [which is] seen and His shape is in human form. He walks and descends, and He bends His body and does other abominable things. God is above and exalted over these things.

The beliefs of the Shi'as, who dissociate Allah from forms, bodily traits, and corporealism, maintaining the impossibility of seeing Him in this world and in the next, I personally believe that the traditions which the *Ahl al-Sunnah wa'l-Jama'a* base their arguments upon are all [the result of] interpolation of Jews in the time of the companions because Ka'b al-Ahbar, the Jew who became a Muslim in the time of 'Umar b. al-Khattab, inserted these beliefs which the Jews maintain, using some naive companions like Abu Hurayrah and Wahb b. Munabbih. Most of these are reported in al-Bukhari and Muslim by Abu Hurayrah.

It was stated in a previous discussion how Abu Hurayrah did not differentiate between the traditions of the Prophet and the traditions of Ka'b al-Ahbar until 'Umar hit and banned him from reporting on the question of the creation of Allah and of the [creation of the] heavens and the earth in seven days.

As long as the *Ahl al-Sunnah wa'l-Jama'a* rely on al-Bukhari and Muslim and consider them as the most correct books, and as long as they depend on Abu Hurayrah to the extent that he has become for the *Ahl al-Sunnah wa'l-Jama'a* the chief narrator of Islam, it is not possible, given this situation, for the *Ahl al-Sunnah wa'l-Jama'a* to alter their beliefs unless they free themselves from blind imitation and return to the Imams of guidance and the family of the chosen one (al-Mustafa) and to the door of the city of knowledge from which knowledge can be attained.

This invitation is not confined to the elders and the teachers but is also [extended to] the erudite youths from the *Ahl al-Sunnah wa'l-Jama'a* and also to [one upon] whom it is incumbent to free himself from blind imitation and to follow proof, proper reasoning and evidence.

Second Question on the Justice of God and Predestination

Allah, Glory be to Him, says in His noble book: *"And say the truth has come from your Lord, whosoever wishes, let him believe, whosoever wishes, let him disbelieve." "There is no compulsion in religion; truth stands out clearly from error"* (2:256). *"One who does an atom's weight of good will see it, one who does an atom's weight of evil will see it"* (99:7-8). *"You are only an admonisher, you do not watch over them"* (88:22).

How can you then accept traditions, reported in *Sahih al-Bukhari* and *Sahih Muslim*, that Allah has preordained the actions of His slaves before He [even] created them? Al-Bukhari has reported in his *Sahih*: [8]"Adam and Moses argued with each other. Moses said to Adam: 'O Adam! You are our father who disappointed us and turned us out of paradise'. Then Adam said to him: 'O Moses! Allah

---

[8] *Sahih, al-Bukhari*, 7/214. Al-Qadr, "The Chapter on the Discussion between Adam and Moses", *Sahih Muslim*, 8/49.

Chapter 1: Concerning the Creator

favored you with His talk (talked to you directly) and He wrote [the Torah] for you with His Own Hand. Do you blame me for an act which Allah had written in my fate forty years before my creation?' So Adam confuted Moses, Adam confuted Moses, the Prophet added, repeating the statement three times."

Muslim reported a similar tradition in his *Sahih*. He reported the Prophet said: "The constituents of one of you are collected for forty days in his mother's womb, after which it becomes a clot of blood in another period of forty days. Then it becomes a lump of flesh, then Allah sends His angels to breath in it the spirit and with instructions concerning four things. The angel writes down his livelihood, his death, his actions, his happiness and misfortunes. By Him, besides Whom there is no God, if one of you acts like the people of paradise to the extent that between him and paradise remains the distance of a cubit and then the book (of destiny) overcomes him, he begins to act like the people of hell until he enters it. Another one of you performs the acts of the people of hell to the extent that there remains between him and hell the distance of a cubit and then the book (of destiny) overcomes him, he begins to act like the people of heaven and enters it"[9].

Similarly, Muslim has narrated in his *Sahih* from 'A'isha, the mother of the believers. She said: "The Prophet of Allah was invited to a funeral of a child from the Ansar. I said to him: 'There is happiness for this child who is a bird from the birds of heaven, for it committed no sin nor did he reach the age (of committing sin)'. He said: 'The opposite is the case, O 'A'isha. Indeed Allah has created for paradise its people while they were in their father's loins and He created for hell its people while they were in their father's loins'"[10].

Al-Bukhari has reported in his *Sahih* that a person asked: "'O Prophet of God, can the people of paradise be known from the

---

[9] *Sahih Muslim*, 8/44. al-Qadr, "The Chapter on the growth of a child in his mother's womb", *Sahih, al-Bukhari*, 7/210.

[10] *Sahih Muslim*, 8/55, Kitab al-Qadr, "The Chapter on every child is born in the state of *fitra*".

people of hell?' He replied: 'Yes'. He said: 'Even if he didn't work (for it)?' He replied: 'Everyone does what he is created for or what is decreed for him to do'"[11].

Glory and praise be to You, O Our Lord, You are more sublime and more exalted than this tyranny. How can we believe these traditions [which] contradict your dear book in which You have stated, and Your words are true:

"Indeed, God does not do injustice to the people in any way, but the people do injustice to themselves" (10:44); "Indeed, Allah does not do an atom's weight of injustice" (4:40); "Your Lord does no injustice to anyone" (18:49); "God did not do any injustice to them, but they did injustice to themselves" (3:117); "It was not God who did injustice to them, but they did injustice to themselves" (9:70, 29: 40, 30:9); "We did no injustice to them but they did injustice to themselves" (43:76); "That is because of what their hands have brought forth, indeed, Allah does no injustice to the slaves" (8:51); "Whoever does good, does so for his own self, whoever does evil, [does so] against his (self), your Lord does not do injustice to the servants" (41:46).

Just as He has said in the *hadith qudsi*, (sacred tradition) "O My slaves, I have forbidden injustice for Myself, [as] I have also forbidden it upon you, so do not be unjust to yourselves". How can a Muslim who believes in God, His justice and mercy [also believe] that Allah, Glory be to Him, created the creation, and decreed upon some of them heaven and upon others the fire according to His wishes?

[How can a Muslim believe] that He [also] decreed their acts, everyone proceeding towards what he is created for? [How can he

---

[11] *Sahih, al-Bukhari*, 7/210 Kitab *al-Qadr*, "The Chapter on The Pen is dried up by the knowledge of God"

Chapter 1: Concerning the Creator

accept] these traditions which oppose the noble Qur'an, [and] the state of *fitra* (natural disposition) which God has created the people in, and which oppose sound reasoning and human intuition and basic human rights?

How can we believe in this religion which petrifies human reasoning, [teaching] the human being is a puppet which the hand of fate moves according to its wishes, only to put it into an oven later on? This belief which prevents the human mind from creation, discovery, invention, progress and competition which have brought about such wonderful things; and leaves a person stagnant and contented with the state he is in and with what he has, claiming that he is proceeding towards what has been decreed for him?

How can we accept these traditions which conflict with sound reason and portray a picture that Allah, Glory be to Him, is the Creator, Almighty, Strong and Overpowering and it is up to Him to create weak slaves so as to put them into the hell fire simply because He does what He wills? Do the intelligent beings call this Lord a wise, merciful or just God?

What would happen if we discuss this with non-Muslim erudite scholars and they know that our Lord has these attributes and that our religion has decreed misery upon the people before they were born, will they then accept Islam and enter into the religion in great numbers?

Glory be to You, O Lord, this is false speech which was imprinted by the Umayyads and recorded by them for their own interests, it is up to the researcher to know the secret of that. This is falsified speech because it contradicts Your speech. Far be it from You that Your Prophet should fabricate anything against You which would contradict Your revelation that You sent to him. It is established that he (s) said: "If a tradition comes to you from me, then compare it with the book of God. Accept whatever agrees with the book of God and reject whatever contradicts it".

Traditions of this genre are many; they oppose the book of God and reason. They must be rejected, no attention should be paid to them even if al-Bukhari and Muslim have reported them, and they were not infallible persons.

One proof is sufficient for us to refute these invalid claims; this is the sending of the Prophets and Apostles from Allah to His creatures during the entire course of human history so as to rectify the misdeeds of the servants and to explain to them the right path. [It was also done] to teach them the book and wisdom and to give them the good tidings of heaven if they are upright and to warn them of the punishment of God in the fire if they are corrupt.

Amongst the justice and mercy of Allah, Glory be to Him, to His creatures is that He doesn't punish [anyone] until He sends to them a Prophet and establishes for them proofs. The most High has said: *"One who is guided, is guided for His own self; one who goes astray does so for his own loss, no one bears the burden of another (soul); We do not punish anyone until we send a Prophet"* **(17:15)**.

If the traditions which al-Bukhari and Muslim transmit indicate that Allah has prescribed the acts of His slaves before He created them and He decreed for some of them heaven and for others hell as we have previously indicated and as the *Ahl al-Sunnah wa'l-Jama'a* believe, I say that, if this is true, then the sending of Messengers and the revealing of books is a futile exercise. Allah, the most High and Great, is above all that. They have not credited Allah with His due worth. We should not speak like this about Allah, Glory be to Him, this is a great accusation [against Him].

"Those are the signs of Allah We reveal to You with the truth, Allah does not wish injustice to the universe" **(3:108)**. The answer to this lies with the Imams of guidance and lanterns of those in darkness and the light houses of the *ummah*, i.e., the removal of injustice and futility from Allah, the most Glorious.

Let us hear from the door of knowledge, the commander of believers, 'Ali b. Abi Talib (as). He explains to the people this belief which has remained a puzzle to some Muslims who have

Chapter 1: Concerning the Creator

abandoned the door [of knowledge]. He said (when one of his companions asked him): "Is our journey to Syria by the decree of God and by predestination?"

"Woe to you, Perhaps you take the decree as inevitable and unavoidable destiny. If this was so, then reward and punishment would be in vain, promises and warnings would be meaningless. Indeed, Allah, Glory be to Him, ordered His servants to act according to their free will and prohibited them through warnings. He has made obligations easy, not difficult for them.

For a few good [works], he gives much [reward]. If he is disobeyed, it is not by being overpowered; if he is obeyed, it is not by force. He did not send Prophets for sport; neither did he reveal the book without purpose. He did not create the heavens and the earth and what is between them in vain, *'that is the thinking of those who disbelieve, woe to those who disbelieve due to the fire'" (38:27)*[12]. The Imam (as) has spoken the truth, woe to those who ascribe futility and injustice to Allah, [we seek refuge] from His painful chastisement.

It is noteworthy, and the truth dictates, that the *Ahl al-Sunnah wa'l-Jama'a* should dissociate Allah from futility and injustice. If you were to ask one of them he will never attribute injustice to the Majesty of Allah, Glory be to Him. However, he will find himself at a loss to reject the traditions reported by al-Bukhari and Muslim. So he believes at the same time that they are correct.

Because of that, you will find that when you argue with them logically, he will claim that this is not called injustice on God's part since He is the creator. The creator has the right to do as He wishes to His creatures. He is not asked what He does; [on the contrary] they are to be questioned. If you ask him: "How can God decree on a slave the hell fire before creating him because He has prescribed a wretched state for him, and how can He decree on another heaven before creating him since He has prescribed happiness for him?

---

[12] *Nahj al-Balagha, Sharh* Muhammad 'Abduh, p.673-4, part four.

Isn't that injustice on the two of them? [This is] because the one who enters heaven does not do so by his deeds but because of Allah choosing it for him, similarly, the one entering hell, he does not enter it because of the sins he committed but because of what Allah has decreed. Isn't this injustice, does it not contradict the Qur'an?" He will answer you: "Indeed God does what He wishes". You do not understand the contradiction in his position. This is clear since he has raised al-Bukhari and Muslim to the level of the Qur'an and he says the most correct books after the book of God are al-Bukhari and Muslim. In al-Bukhari and Muslim are [to be found] astonishing, strange and unfortunate things through which the Muslims have been confused. The Umayyads, and after them the 'Abbasids, have greatly succeeded in spreading their innovations and beliefs, which were in agreement with their barren politics. Their effects remain until today since the Muslims believe that it is the best and greatest legacy they have got because, according to their understanding, it is the collection of the correct traditions of the Prophet. If only the Muslims know the extent to which they lied against the Prophet (s) due to their political goals, they (the Muslims) will not believe the traditions especially those which contradict the book of God.

As Allah has guaranteed the protection of the noble Qur'an and as it was preserved by the companions who would present it to the Prophet (for checking), they (the Umayyads) could not change or alter it so they turned to the pure *Sunnah* and they fabricated what they wished and [attributed] to whoever they wished. As they were the enemies of the *Ahl al-Bayt* [who were] the protectors of the Qur'an and the *Sunnah*, they invented, for every event, a tradition which they attributed to the Prophet (s). They presented these to the Muslims, maintaining that these traditions are the most correct, to the exclusion of others, so the people accepted them with confidence. They transmitted these, generation after generation inheriting them.

To be impartial, I admit that the Shi'as too became victims of interpolation and misrepresentation of many traditions which are attributed to the Prophet (s) or to one of the pure Imams (as), and with the passing of time, the Muslims, whether Sunnis or Shi'as, were not safe from this interpolation and fabrication. However, the Shi'as are to be distinguished from the *Ahl al-Sunnah wa'l-Jama'a* by three things which also distinguish them from other Islamic sects. Their beliefs remain sound and are in agreement with the Qur'an and the *Sunnah* and reasoning. These three things are:

Firstly: Their devotion to the *Ahl al-Bayt* of the Prophet. They do not prefer anyone to them and we all know who are the *Ahl al-Bayt*. [They are those] from whom Allah has removed all filth and purified them completely.

Secondly: The number of Imams of the *Ahl al-Bayt*. They are twelve in number, their lives and influences remained for three centuries. They agree with each other in all the rulings and traditions. They do not differ in anything which they have transmitted to their partisans and learned followers in all fields of knowledge and information. [They have done so] with proper clarification and with no contradiction in beliefs or in other fields.

Thirdly: Their acknowledgment and acceptance that their books could contain mistakes and correct [things], they do not have a *sahih* book except the book of God which cannot be afflicted by falsehood from any side. It is sufficient for you to know, for example, that the greatest book for them is the "*Usul al-Kafi*".

They say that in it are thousands of false traditions. Due to that, you will find that their scholars and researchers are devoted to research and criticism, they do not accept [anything] except that which is proven by the text and the chain of narrators (*isnad*) and that which does not oppose the Qur'an and reasoning.

As for the *Ahl al-Sunnah wa'l-Jama'a,* they have restricted themselves to books which they call the *Sihah Sitta* (the six correct books). They argue on the basis that whatever is in them is correct; most of them hereditarily transmit this view without discussing or examining it. If they did so, most of the traditions reported in these books do not stand up to academic inquiry, for in (some) of them is clear blasphemy as they contradict the Qur'an, the etiquettes and actions of the Prophet and degrade his nobility. For a researcher, it is sufficient for him to read the book of the Egyptian scholar al-Shaykh Mahmud Abu Ra'y "Light on the Muhammadan *Sunnah* to discern the value of the six *Sihah*. Praise be to Allah that many young researchers today are freed from those shackles, they have begun to sift between the thick and thin. Even many zealous teachers of the *Sihah* today have come to deny them, not because they are sure of the weaknesses of some traditions but because they find in the [books] arguments which the Shi'as present whether it be in the jurisprudential rulings or in the belief in the unseen. There is no ruling or belief which the Shi'as maintain except it being actually present in one of the six *Sihahs* which belong to the *Ahl al-Sunnah wa'l-Jama'a*.

According to this, some zealous person told me that as long as you believe that the traditions of al-Bukhari are not correct, why do you argue against us by using these traditions? I said: "Not everything in al-Bukhari is correct, neither is everything in it forged, for the truth is true and falsehood is false, it is up to us to sift and choose."

He said: "Do you have a special microscope to distinguish between the correct and false [traditions]?" I said: "I do not have [anything] more than what you have, however, what both the Sunnis and Shi'is agree upon is correct since its authenticity is established by both sides and we make them abide by it as they have accepted it themselves. That which they differ upon, even if it is considered correct by one side, cannot be imposed on the opposite party. The neutral researcher is not expected to accept it and argue based on it since this would be a circular [argument]."

I cite one example so that no problem can remain on this subject and so that the same criticism is not levelled through different means.

The Shi'as claim that the Prophet of God (s) appointed 'Ali as the *khalifa* of the Muslims at Ghadir Khum on the 18th day of *Dhu'l Hijja* after the farewell pilgrimage. He said at that occasion: "Of whomsoever I am the master, this 'Ali is the master. O God,

Chapter 1: Concerning the Creator 35

befriend one who befriends him, and be an enemy to one who shows enmity towards him."[13] This tradition has been narrated by many scholars of the *Ahl al-Sunnah wa'l-Jama'a* in their *Sihah* and *Masanid* and historical works. It is possible for the Shi'as to argue, based on this, with the *Ahl al-Sunnah wa'l-Jama'a*.

The *Ahl al-Sunnah wa'l-Jama'a* claim that the Messenger of God (s) appointed Abu Bakr to lead the people in prayers during the sickness [which led] to his death. He said on that occasion: "God and His Prophet and the believers refuse [anyone to lead] except Abu Bakr."

This tradition is not to be found in the Shi'a books. They merely relate that the Prophet of Allah sent for 'Ali, whereupon 'A'isha sent for her father. When the Prophet of God came to know that, he said to 'A'isha: "You are among the females [who tempted] Joseph." He came out to lead the prayer and moved Abu Bakr.

It is neither possible nor fair that the *Ahl al-Sunnah wa'l-Jama'a* argue against the Shi'as based on what only they accept, especially if the traditions are contradictory and distort reality and history. This is because the Prophet (s) appointed Abu Bakr to be amongst the army of Usama and to be under his command and leadership. It is well known that the commander of the army in an expedition is the leader of the prayer. It has been historically established that Abu Bakr was not present in Medina at the time of the death of the Prophet. He was at al-Sanh, preparing to leave with his commander and leader Usama b. Zayd who was hardly 17 years old. Given this situation, how can we believe that the Prophet of God (s) appointed him to be the leader of the prayer? Unless we believe the saying of 'Umar b. Khattab that the Prophet was crazy and did not know what he did or said. There is no solution to this impossible [issue]; neither do the Shi'as accept it.

Here the researcher should fear God in his research and should not let his sentiments overcome him so as to deviate from the truth

---

[13] For detailed account of this event and chains of narrators of this tradition from Sunni sources, pls see: https://www.al-islam.org/ghadir/

and to follow his desires thereby being led astray from the path of God. It is obligatory for him to accept the truth, even if the truth lies with somebody else. He has to free himself from sediments [of feelings], sentiments and egoism. He should be among those for whom Allah, the most Powerful and Glorious, has praised in His saying: *"Give glad tidings to My slaves who listen to the speech and follow the best of it. These are the ones whom Allah has guided; these are the people of understanding"* (39:18).

It is not correct for the Jew to say that we have the truth and the Christians to claim that the truth lies with us and for the Muslims also to say that the truth is with us whilst they differ in beliefs and practices. It is necessary for a researcher to examine the claims of the three religions and to compare them with each other until the truth becomes clear to him.

It is not proper either for the *Ahl al-Sunnah* to say that the truth lies with them and the Shi'as to claim that the truth is with them alone, whereas they differ in some concepts and rulings. The truth is one and is not divisible.

It is also essential for the researcher to isolate and examine the claims of the two sides and to compare one against the other and for him to rely on his reasoning so that the truth should become clear for him. That is the call of Allah, Glory be to Him, to every sect which lays claim to the truth, for He says: *"Say, bring your proof if you are truthful"* (2:111).

Being in a majority [status] is not an indication of the truth; on the contrary, the opposite is the case. The Most High says: *"If you obey most of those who are on earth, they will mislead you from the path of God"* (6:116). He also said: *"Most of the people will not have faith, however hard you try"* (12:103).

Just as the advancement of civilization and technology and wealth is not a proof for the west to be on the truth and the east to be on falsehood, the Most High has said: *"Do not let their wealth and children dazzle you, for through these, Allah wishes to punish them in this life so that their souls may perish whilst they deny God"* (9:55).

The belief of the Ahl al-Dhikr about Allah, the Most High

Imam 'Ali says: "Praise be to Allah who knows the hidden secrets of things, and clear signs point to Him. He cannot be seen by the eye of an onlooker, yet the eye of one who does not see Him does not deny Him. The mind that proves His existence cannot perceive Him. He has preceded everything in sublimity; nothing is more sublime than He. He is so close nothing is closer than Him. His sublimity does not alienate Him from His creation nor does His closeness bring them on an equal level to Him. He has not informed the intellect about the restrictions to His attributes, and He has not prevented it from knowing what is essential to know about Him. The signs of existence bear testimony to Him to the extent that the mind which denies Him also believes in Him. Allah is beyond what those who liken Him to other things or those who deny Him, say about Him.

Praise be to Allah, for whom one condition does not precede another so that He may be the first before being the Last or that He may be manifest before being hidden. Apart from Him, everything called unique is [actually] little. Apart from Him, everything honorable is meek, everything powerful is weak, and every owner is a slave.

Apart from Him, every scholar is a student, everyone with ability is disabled and weak, every listener other than Him is deaf to light voices while loud voices make him deaf and distant voices are remote from him.

Apart from Him, everyone that sees is blind to hidden colors and delicate bodies. Apart from Him, every manifest thing is hidden; every inner thing apart from Him is manifest. He did not create what He did to strengthen His authority nor due to fear of time nor to seek help against an equally aggressive partner or hateful opponent. Rather, all creatures are nurtured by Him and are His humble slaves. He does not enter into anything so that it can be said that He exists therein, nor is He separated from anything so that it can be said that He is away from it. The creation that He created or the administration of what He controls did not tire Him. No disability overtook Him for what He created. No misgivings ever occurred to Him in what He ordained and resolved. His verdict is certain, His knowledge definite, His governance overwhelming. Even in distress, He is the centre of Hope and, despite all the bounties, He is to be feared."

Chapter Two

Concerning the Prophet (s)

The second question: On the infallibility of the Prophet

Allah, Glory be to Him, the Most High, says concerning the rights of His apostle Muhammad, (s): *"God will protect you from the people"* (5:67). He also says: *"He does not speak from his desires, it is nothing but a revelation revealed to him"* (53:3). He further says: *"What the Prophet brings to you accept it; what he prohibits you, refrain from it"* (59:7). These verses clearly point to his complete infallibility under all circumstances. You say that the Prophet of God (s) is infallible only in proclaiming the Qur'an. Apart from that, he is like other human beings, he errs and does right. You derive proofs of his mistakes at different occasions by traditions which you report in your *Sahih* works.

If that is the case, what is the proof and evidence in your claim to adhere to the book of God and the *Sunnah* of His prophet as long as this *Sunnah* is, in your view, not infallible and there is a possibility of error in it?

On this basis, then, clinging to the book of God and the *Sunnah*, according to your belief, does not guarantee one from not being led astray especially as we know that the whole Qur'an is explained and made clear by the Prophetic *Sunnah*.. What is your proof that the commentary and explanations are not contrary to the book of Allah, the most exalted?

One of them expressed this opinion to me: "The Prophet of God certainly opposed the Qur'an in many rulings according to the demands of the occasion." I said in a surprised manner: "Cite me one example of this opposition."

He said: *"The Qur'an says: 'The adulteress and the*

adulterer, lash both of them with one hundred lashings' (24:2). Whereas the Prophet ordered the stoning of the adulterer and adulteress, this [ruling] is not found in the Qur'an."

I said: "The stoning is for the married person who fornicates, whether male or female, whereas lashing is for the unmarried person if he/she fornicates, whether male or female".

He said: "In the Qur'an, there is no [mention of] unmarried or married [person] as Allah does not specify it, rather, He uses the term adulterer and adulteress without qualifying it."

I said: "Then, on this basis, does this mean that every general ruling in the Qur'an which was specified by the Prophet is thereby contradictory to the Qur'an? Then, do you say that the Prophet opposed the Qur'an in most of his rulings?" He replied diffidently: "The Qur'an is only infallible because Allah has guaranteed its protection. As for the Prophet, he is a man. He errs and does right. As the Qur'an says about him: *'Say I am nothing but a man like you'"(41:6).*

I said: "Why do you pray the morning, midday, afternoon evening and night prayer whereas the Qur'an used the general word, prayer, without specifying its timings?" He replied: "In the Qur'an, it says: *'Indeed the prayer was a prescribed time for the believers' (4:103).* The Prophet explained the timings of the prayers." I said: "Why do you believe him in the timings of the prayers and you refute him in the rulings on stoning the adulterer?"

He tried his best to satisfy me with contradictory, barren philosophies which do not stand against intellectual or logical proofs. For example, he said: "One cannot doubt about the prayer because the Prophet of Allah performed it during the whole of his life, five times every day. However, we cannot be so sure about stoning since he did it only once or twice during his lifetime." Similarly, he claims that the Prophet does not err when God commands him on an issue. However, when he judges by his own reasoning, then he is not infallible. Due to that, the companions

Chapter 2: Concerning the Prophet (s)

would ask him in every case, is this from himself or from God? If he said: "This is from Allah," they obeyed him without any argument. If he said: "This is from me," then they would argue, dispute and advise him. He would accept their advices and views. The Qur'an was at times revealed in agreement with the views of some companions and opposed his (the Prophet's) views as [happened] in the question of the prisoners of Badr and other famous incidents.

I tried my best to persuade him but without any success because the scholars of the *Ahl al-Sunnah wa'l-Jama'a* are convinced by this [view] and the *Sihah* are full of such traditions which destroy the infallibility of the Prophet. It makes him [appear as] a person lower in status than a pious person or a military leader or lower than a Sufi *shaykh* of the path. I would not be exaggerating if I said that he is lower in status than an ordinary person. If we read some of the traditions in the *Sihah* of the *Ahl al-Sunnah wa'l-Jama'a*, it would be absolutely clear to us the degree of influence that the Umayyads, from their times, have had on the thinking of the Muslims, and that their vestiges have remained with the people even today.

If we searched for the aim or goal for that, we would reach a certain and bitter conclusion, which is; those who ruled the Muslims during the Umayyad dynasty, the chief of whom was Mu'awiyah b. Abu Sufyan, did not believe, for a day, that Muhammad b. 'Abd Allah was sent with God's message or that he was truly God's Messenger. Most probably, they believed that he was a magician who overwhelmed the people and built a kingdom at the cost of the downtrodden people, especially the slaves who supported and helped him in his claims. This is not mere conjecture, since some conjectures can be sinful. When we read the historical works to study the character of Mu'awiyah and those around him, and what he did during his lifespan, especially when he ruled, the conjecture becomes a reality; there is no escape from it.

All of us know who Mu'awiyah is and who his father Abu Sufyan and his mother Hind are. He is the freed slave, son of a freed slave, who spent his youth in the circle of his father mobilizing an army to fight the Prophet of God and to opposing his mission with all effort. When all his attempts failed and when the Prophet of God (s) emerged victorious over him and his father, he accepted Islam for pragmatic reasons without any conviction. The Prophet, due to his nobility and great character, forgave him and called him the freed man (*al-taleeq*). After the death of the bearer of the message, his (Mu'awiyah's) father tried to instigate discord and sedition in Islam. That was when, at night, he came to Imam 'Ali to incite him to rise against Abu Bakr and 'Umar and tempting him with property and men. Imam 'Ali (as) knew his aim and so ignored him. He remained living in rancor against Islam and Muslims for the whole of his life until the Caliphate came to his cousin 'Uthman. At that time, the disbelief and hypocrisy lying within him surfaced and he said: "Seize it, seize it again, by what Abu Sufyan swears, there is neither heaven nor hell."[1]

Ibn Asakir has reported in his historical work[2] in the vol. 6, p. 407, from Anas, that Abu Sufyan visited 'Uthman after he had become blind. He asked him: "Is there anyone around?" They said: "No." He said: "O God, make the matters [as they were] at the time of the *Jahiliyyah* and the kingdom [belong] to the usurpers and make the Banu Umayyads the tent pegs (*awtad*) of the earth."

As for his son Mu'awiyah, what do you know about Mu'awiyah? There are no bounds as to what one can say concerning what he did to the *ummah* of Muhammad (s) during his governorship in Syria and after gaining control of the Caliphate through force and power. The historians have mentioned [his acts] concerning his defiling the Qur'an and *Sunnah* and transgressing all the boundaries of the *shari'a*. His actions are those which even the pen cannot write and the tongue cannot mention, due to their evil and corrupt nature. Bearing in mind the feelings of our brothers amongst the *Ahl al-Sunnah wa'l-Jama'a*, we have devoted pages for those who have instilled the love of Mu'awiyah in their hearts and defend him.

It would not be out of place for us to mention the mentality of the man and his belief in the bearer of the message. His belief is not too

---

[1] *Tarikh Tabari*, 11/357, Mas'udi, *Muruj al-Dhahab*, 1/440.

[2] *Tarikh Dimashq* aka *Tarikh Ibn 'Asakir*

Chapter 2: Concerning the Prophet (s) 43

different from the belief of his father. He was fed by the milk of the one who ate human liver[3]. She was well known as a prostitute and an adulterer[4]. Similarly, he inherited [the character of] his father, the leader of the hypocrites. Islam did not find a place in his heart even for a day. Just as we know the character of the father, the son is expressing the same thing but in a more subtle and hypocritical way.

Al-Zubayr b. Bakar reported from Mutawwaf b. al-Mughira b. Shu'ba al-Thaqafi. He said: "I visited Mu'awiyah with my father. My father would [often] visit him and narrate from him. Thereafter, he would come to me and mention Mu'awiyah and his mentality and would [often] be surprised at what he saw. He came to me one evening. However, he did not have dinner and appeared aggrieved. I waited for a while thinking that something had happened between us or [it was due to] what we did. I then said to him: 'What is the matter, I see you are distressed since the evening?' He said: 'O my son, I have come from the most evil of people.' I said to him: 'How can that be?' He said: 'I said to Mu'awiyah when I was alone with him: 'O Commander of the Faithful, you have attained your goal, if only you were to demonstrate justice and spread virtue. You have become old of age. If only you were to look after your brothers, the Banu Hashim, and were to re-establish ties with them. By God, they do not have anything today which you should be scared of. In that there will be [something] for which you will be remembered and will receive reward'. He said to me: 'Far be from it, far be from it. What remembrance do I wish to leave behind me? The brother of Taym (Abu Bakr) ruled and spread justice and did what he did. As soon as he died so did his remembrance except that a person [while mentioning him], would say "Abu Bakr". Then the brother of 'Adi ('Umar) ruled, persevered, and he remained active for ten years. As soon as he died, so did his remembrance, except a person [while mentioning him] would say "'Umar". Then our brother 'Uthman ruled. Here was a man the like of whom there was nobody. He did

---

[3] A reference to Hind's eating Hamza's liver at the battle of Uhud [Editor's note]

[4] Zamakhshari in *Rabi'al-Abrar*, vol.3 *Bab al-Qarabat wa'l-Ansab, Nahj al-Balagha, Sharh* Ibn Abi'l-Hadid, 1/111.

what he did and they did to him what they did. By God, as soon as he died, they forgot his remembrance and forgot what was done to him. The brothers of Hashim shout every day five times: 'I bear witness that Muhammad is the Prophet of God'. What action and what remembrance will remain with this, O motherless one, by God, except [for one] to die and be buried?"[5]

May God debase, disappoint and disgrace you (Mu'awiyah), O one who wanted to bury the remembrance of the Prophet of God with all efforts. You spent everything you owned for that cause but all your efforts met with failure. Allah, Glory be to Him, is observing you and He says to His Prophet: *"We have raised your remembrance."* You (Mu'awiyah) can never erase his remembrance which the Lord of power and might has raised. Plot your schemes and gather your group, you will not be able to extinguish the light of God with your mouth. God will perfect His light despite your hypocrisy and jealousy. Look here, you ruled the world east and west, as soon as you died, so did your remembrance, except that one who remembers you does so due to your evil deeds, through which you had hoped to destroy Islam, just as it has been reported from the tongue of the Prophet of God (s).[6] The remembrance of Muhammad b. 'Abd Allah, the brother of Banu Hashim, has remained during the course of centuries and generations, until God establishes his rule on earth and on the people inhabiting it. Whenever someone mentions him, they do so by sending greetings to him and his family. [This is] despite your plots and the plots of the Banu Umayya who tried, through your guidance and leadership, to prevail over them and their excellences. That only enhanced their status and eminence. You will meet Allah on the Day of Judgment, when He will be angry with you due to what you innovated in His law and He will give you what you deserve.

---

[5] *al-Mufaqiyyat*, p.576, al-Mas'udi, *Muruj al-Dhahab*, 2/341.

Nahj al-Balagha, Sharh Ibn Abi'l-Hadid, 5/130, *al-Ghadir*, 'Allama al-Amini, 10/283.

[6] *al-Siffin*, p.44.

Chapter 2: Concerning the Prophet (s)

If we add to this their offspring, Yazid b. Mu'awiyah, the shameless, corrupt one and wine drinker, the one who openly indulged in sins and debauchery, we find him to be having the same belief, which he inherited from his father Mu'awiyah and grandfather Abu Sufyan. He inherited from them vileness, baseness, wine drinking, fornicating with prostitutes and gambling. If he had not inherited these evil characteristics, his father, Mu'awiyah, would not have appointed him for the Caliphate and imposed him over the neck of the Muslims. All of them knew him the way he should be known, while they were alive. Amongst them were prominent companions like al-Husayn b. 'Ali, the master of the youths of paradise. I do not doubt that Mu'awiyah passed his life and spent his money which he earned through illegal ways, in the path of destroying Islam and the true Muslims. We have seen how he wished to bury the remembrance of Muhammad (s). He was not able to do that, so he initiated a war against his cousin 'Ali, the legatee of the Prophet, until it ended. He then attained the Caliphate with force, deception and hypocrisy. He established an inauspicious *Sunnah* and ordered his governors in all regions to curse 'Ali and the Prophetic household from all the pulpits and in all prayers.

By doing that, he wanted to curse the Prophet of God.[7] When all his plans failed and his destined time arrived and he had did not attain his purpose, he appointed his son as a ruler over the *ummah* to continue along the plan which he and his father Abu Sufyan had established, i.e., the destruction of Islam and returning to the Jahili era. That mad and corrupted person accepted the Caliphate and prepared his entourage to destroy Islam according to the desires of his father. He began by seizing the city of the Prophet of God (s) with his disbelieving army. He did what he did in three days. He killed 10,000 of the most virtuous companions in it and proceeded, after that, to kill the master of the youths of paradise and the delight

---

[7] Ibn'Abd Rabbih reported in *al-'Iqd al-Farid* 2/301. He said that Mu'awiyah cursed 'Ali from pulpit and wrote to his governors asking them to curse him from pulpits. They did that. Umm Salama, the wife of Prophet (s), wrote to Mu'awiyah: "You are cursing Allah and His Prophet from your pulpits. That is because you are cursing 'Ali b. Abi Talib and those who love him". Mu'awiyah, however, paid no attention to her words.

of the Prophet (s) and to kill the Prophetic household. They were the moons of the *ummah.* He [even] enslaved the free persons of the *Ahl al-Bayt.* From Allah do we come, and to Him we shall return.

If Allah had not cut short his life, that wretched, evil person would have destroyed Islam and Muslims. What we are concerned with in our discussion is to unveil his beliefs, just as we unveiled the belief of his father and grandfather.

Historians[8] have narrated that after the terrible event of al-Harrah and the killing of 10,000 of the best Muslims (except women or children) and raping of 1,000 virgins, about 1,000 women became pregnant in those days without being married.

Then the remaining people paid allegiance and agreed that they were to be slaves to Yazid. Whoever refused was killed. When Yazid was informed of all these crimes and vile deeds, which the cowards had perpetrated and which history has never witnessed the like of (even by the Mongols or Tartars or the Isra'ilis), Yazid was happy by that and insulted the Prophet of Islam. He exemplified the speech of Ibn al-Zubara who composed a poem after the battle of Uhud saying:

"If only my ancestors [who died at] Badr, had seen the wailing of the Khazraj from the attacks of spears and of the sword, they would have shouted and cried with joy and would have said: 'O Yazid, your hands should not be paralyzed.'

We killed the master of their leaders, and we extracted revenge of Badr.

I would not be from the progeny of Khandaf if I did not take revenge from the progeny of Ahmad for what he has done.

The Hashimites played with the Kingdom, no news came nor any revelation revealed."

---

[8] Baladhuri *Ansab al- Ashraf,* 5/42, *Lisan al-Mizan,* 6/294, Ibn al-Kathir, *Tarikh,* 8/221, *al-Isaba* 3/473.

The grandfather, Abu Sufyan, the first enemy of God and His Prophet, says loudly "Seize it, O Banu Umayya, seize it again, by that which Abu Sufyan swears, there is neither heaven nor hell."

And the father, Mu'awiyah, the second enemy of Allah and His Prophet, said clearly (when he heard the caller to prayer bearing witness that Muhammad is the Prophet of God) "What actions and what remembrance will remain with this, O motherless one?"

The son Yazid, the third enemy of God and His Prophet, says loudly: "The Hashimites played with the Kingdom, no news came, nor any revelation revealed."

We have known their beliefs about God and His Prophet and about Islam, and we know of their disgraceful acts, through which they wanted to destroy the pillars of Islam. [We have known of] their vileness towards the Prophet of Islam, of which we have mentioned a few details for the sake of brevity. If we wanted to expand on this, we could have filled a huge volume on the actions of Mu'awiyah alone which would have remained a shame and disgrace forever, although some evil scholars have tried to conceal and hide [these]. The Banu Umayya would give them perks and gifts which would make their eyes blind. They sold their hereafter for this world and they confused truth with falsehood whilst fully knowing this. Most of the Muslims remained victims of these lies and falsehoods. If only they knew the true victims, they would remember Abu Sufyan, Mu'awiyah and Yazid with nothing but curses and disapproval.

In this short discussion, what is important for us is to discern the degree of influence these people, their partisans and followers, who ruled the Muslims for 100 years, had. That influence is still at the first stages.

There is no doubt that the influence of these hypocrites on the Muslims was immense. They changed their beliefs, lives, etiquettes and dealings and even their [forms of] worship. Otherwise, how can we explain the desisting of the community from aiding the truth and the abandoning of the friends of God and the siding with the enemies of God and His Prophet?

How can we comprehend [the fact that] Mu'awiyah, the freed man, son of a freed man and accursed son of the accursed one, ascending the Caliphate, [a position] which represented the status and the Caliphate of the Prophet of Allah, (s)? Keeping in view what the historians want us to believe, that the people would tell 'Umar b. al-Khattab: "If we see any deviation in you, we will straighten you with our swords", yet we see them narrating from Mu'awiyah when he ascended the throne of the Caliphate by force and power. The first sermon which he delivered to all the companions was: "I did not fight you so that you should pray and fast but so as to rule over you, I am now your commander". Yet no one moved a finger or opposed him, on the contrary, they accompanied him and they named the year which Mu'awiyah came to power "the year of unity" whereas, in reality, it was "the year of dissension".

Then we see them, after that, accepting his son Yazid, the corrupt one, to rule over them, one who was well known by all of them. They did not revolt nor move, except some upright ones whom Yazid killed at the battle of al-Harrah. Among those who survived, he extracted a pledge that they were to be his slaves. How can we interpret all that?

We find after, that in the name of leading the believers, the corrupt ones amongst the Banu Umayyads like Marwan b. al-Hakam and al-Walid b. 'Uqba and others attained the Caliphate.

The matter of leading the believers reached a level whereby they seized the city of the Prophet, performed evil deeds in it, defiled its sanctity and even burnt the house of God, the sanctuary, and killed prominent companions in it. The matter of the leaders of the faithful reached a stage whereby they spilled the blood of the Prophet of God (s) and that was due to their killing the delight of the Prophet of God and his progeny. They deemed it permissible to enslave his children. No one from the *ummah* moved from the stationary position. The master of the youths of paradise did not find a helper.

Chapter 2: Concerning the Prophet (s)

The matter of leading the believers reached a level whereby they tore up the book of God whilst saying to it: "If you meet your Lord on the day of resurrection, then say: 'O my Lord, al-Walid tore me apart.'" This was what al-Walid, the Umayyad leader, did.

The matter of leading the believers reached a level whereby they cursed 'Ali b. Abi Talib from the pulpits and instructed the people in all regions to curse him. By that, they meant to curse the Prophet of God. Nobody moved from his stationary position. Whoever refused to comply was either killed, crucified or maimed.

The matter of leading the believers reached a level whereby they openly drank wine, fornicated, amused themselves with pleasure, songs, dances and there is no limit to what one can relate. If the matter of the Islamic *ummah* had reached this level of decay of morals, meekness and resignation, there must have been factors which had influenced its beliefs. This is what will concern us in this discussion, since it is connected with the question of the infallibility and character of the noble Prophet (s).

The first thing which deserves our attention here is that the three Caliphs, Abu Bakr, 'Umar and 'Uthman, prohibited the writing and even the discussion of the traditions of the Prophet (s).

Abu Bakr gathered the people during his Caliphate and said to them: "You relate traditions from the Prophet of God and differ about it. The people after you will differ even more, [therefore] do not relate anything from the Prophet. If anyone asks you, say: 'Between us there is the book, so consider as lawful what is lawful in it, and prohibit what is forbidden in it'".[9]

Similarly, 'Umar was another one who forbade the people from narrating traditions from the Prophet. Qarza b. K'ab said: "When 'Umar b. al-Khattab sent us to Iraq, he walked with us and said: 'Do you know why I followed you?' They said: 'To honor us.' He said: 'Besides that, you are going to the villagers. The Qur'an

---

[9] Al-Dhahabi, *Tadhkira al-Huffaz*, vol. 1, p. 2-3.

reverberates in them like the reverberation of a bee. Do not occupy them with traditions. Make them busy and recite the Qur'an, and reduce the narrations from the Prophet and I am an associate to you [in this].'"

This narrator says: "I never narrated a tradition after 'Umar's admonition." When he arrived in Iraq, the people hastened to him asking him about the *hadith*. Qarza said to them: "'Umar prohibited me from that." [10]

Similarly, 'Abd al-Rahman b. 'Awf said that 'Umar b. al-Khattab gathered the companions from remote regions to forbid them from narrating traditions of the Prophet to the people. He said to them: "Stand by me, do not go away from me as long as I live." They did not leave him until he died.[11]

Similarly, al-Khatib al-Baghdadi says, and [so does] al-Dhahabi in *Tadhkira al-Huffaz*, that 'Umar b. al-Khattab imprisoned three companions in Medina. These were Abu Darda, Ibn Mas'ud and Abu Mas'ud al-Ansari due to their excessive narration of traditions. Furthermore, 'Umar commanded the companions to bring the books of traditions at their disposal to him. They thought he wanted to organize them in a way so that there would be no differences between them. They brought their books; he burnt them all in the fire.[12]

Then 'Uthman came after him. He continued the trend and notified all the people that: "It is not permitted for anyone to narrate a tradition which was not heard during the times of Abu Bakr and 'Umar."[13]

After them came the time of Mu'awiyah b. Abu Sufyan, and

---

[10] *Sunan* Ibn Maja, vol. 1, p. 12, *Sunan al-Darimi* vol. 1/85, al-Dhahabi, *Tadhkira al-Huffaz*, volume 1.

[11] Al-Hakim, *Mustadrak*, 1/110, *Kanz al-'Ummal*, 5/239.

[12] Ibn Sa'd, *Tabaqat al-Kubra*, 5/140, al-Baghdadi, *Takyid al-'ilm*.

[13] Commentary of *Muntakhab Kanz al-'Ummal*, Ibn Hanbal, *Musnad*, 4/64.

Chapter 2: Concerning the Prophet (s)

when he attained the position of the Caliphate, he ascended the *minbar* and said: "O people, it is forbidden to speak about *hadith* from the Prophet of Allah (s), except those *hadith* which were mentioned during the Caliphate of 'Umar."[14]

Certainly, there had to be a secret motive behind the proscription of traditions that were uttered by the Prophet of Allah (s), *hadiths* which did not agree with things that were happening at that time. Otherwise, why were the *hadiths* of the Prophet of Allah (s) forbidden for the entire length of this period, and were not permitted to be written except during the Caliphate of 'Umar b. 'Abd al-'Aziz (r)?

We can therefore deduce, based on the events mentioned, especially bearing in mind the clear texts regarding the Caliphate which the Prophet of Allah (s) had declared in the presence of the main witnesses, that Abu Bakr and 'Umar prohibited the narration and transmission of *hadith* from the Prophet, fearing that those *hadiths* would spread to all regions, and even to the neighboring villages. It would then become clear to the people that his Caliphate and the Caliphate of his companion was not [valid] according to the *shari'a*. Rather, it had been usurped from the divinely ordained Caliph, 'Ali b. Abi Talib. We have discussed this topic and uncovered the truth in our book, "So that I may be with the Truthful ones." Whoever wishes further confirmation [of this] can refer to it.

The surprising thing regarding 'Umar b. al-Khattab is his contradictory stance especially in things related to the Caliphate. While we find him to be the one who had urged the allegiance to Abu Bakr and [even] coerced the people to it - at the same time he declares that it was a sudden decision and that Allah had protected [the people] from its disasters. At another time, we find him choosing six people for the Caliphate saying: "If the bald one gets it (meaning 'Ali b. Abi Talib), he will impose severity upon them."

Since he confessed that 'Ali was the only person who could make the people steadfast, then why did he not appoint him and end the

---

[14] al-Baghdadi, al-Khatib, *Sharaf Ashab al-Hadith*, p.91.

matter, thereby giving good advice to the *ummah* of Muhammad (s)? But we see him instead, after this, contradicting himself and preferring the opinion of 'Abd al-Rahman b. 'Awf, then contradicting himself yet again saying: "Were Salim, the slave of Abu Hudhayfa, alive, I would have appointed him over you."[15]

More surprising than that was the issue of Abu Hafs. He forbade him to [transmit] *hadith* from the Prophet (s), and confined the companions in Medina, forbidding them from leaving it. He also forbade the emissaries he sent to other regions to speak of the *Sunnah* of the Prophet (s), and he [also] burnt the books that were in the hands of the companions. In these books were the *hadiths* of the Prophet (s).

Did 'Umar b al-Khattab not understand that the *Sunnah* of the Prophet clarified the Qur'an? Or had he not read the words of Allah, the Glorified and Exalted: *"And we have revealed the remembrance unto you so that you may explain to the people what has been sent down to them"* **(16:44)**. Or did he understand from the Qur'an something which the bearer of the message and the one to whom the Qur'an was revealed, did not understand?

This is what some confused people have tried to do, claiming that the Qur'an on several occasions came to verify the opinions of 'Umar and it opposed the views of the Prophet (s). Grave indeed are the words that come out of their mouths, they do not understand.

I was always perplexed when I read in al-Bukhari of 'Umar's refusal to accept 'Ammar b. Yasir's narration, especially regarding the Prophet's teaching him how to do *tayammum*, just as I was

---

[15] This narration has been taken by Abu Hanifa as proof for the permissibility of the Caliphate of manumitted slaves. In doing so, he goes against a clear *hadith* of the Prophet (s) that Caliphate is to be with the Quraysh only. Because of his position, the Turks espoused the *madhab* of Abu Hanifa when they grabbed the Caliphate, and gave him the title: "The Grand Imam".

Chapter 2: Concerning the Prophet (s)

surprised at 'Ammar's words: "If you wish, I shall not speak of it," in fear of 'Umar. This proves clearly that 'Umar b. al-Khattab was severe on any one who narrated *hadiths* from the Prophet, and would harass him.

If the companions amongst the Quraysh were afraid of the Caliph and would not leave Medina, and even those who did go out desisted from transmitting the Prophetic traditions, and then had their books, in which they had recorded *hadiths,* burnt, yet no one amongst them said anything, then what was the position of 'Ammar b. Yasir, an absolute stranger, despised by the Quraysh for his stand with 'Ali b. Abi Talib, and his love for him?

Let us go back to what we have recently discussed, specifically to the Thursday that preceded the death of the Prophet of Allah (s), a day which was called by Ibn 'Abbas "The day of calamity". [That was] when the Prophet of Allah (s) ordered those who were present to bring paper and ink for him to write a letter so that they would never go astray. We find on that day that 'Umar b. al-Khattab was the one who opposed the Prophet of Allah (s), and accused him of being delirious, i.e., hallucinating and said: "We seek refuge in Allah" and then said: "The book of Allah is sufficient for us." This event has been narrated by al-Bukhari, Muslim, Ibn Maja, al-Nasa'i, Abu Dawud, Imam Ahmad, as well as other historians.

If 'Umar could prevent the Prophet of Allah (s) from writing his own *hadiths*, and could do so in the presence of many companions and the *Ahl al-Bayt*, accusing him of being delirious, with insolence the like of which history has never witnessed, then it is neither strange nor surprising, for him to gather his aides after the death of the Prophet of Allah (s) so as to prevent the people, with all possible effort, from transmitting *hadith* of the Prophet, since he was now the strong Caliph, possessing all power. Either due to greed, fear or hypocrisy, no doubt he had amongst his associates many helpers from the noteworthy Qurayshis, who had influence over the tribes and clans, and who had been companions of the Prophet of Allah (s). We have seen them, despite their large numbers, supporting 'Umar in his statement that the Prophet of Allah (s) was hallucinating. We find them also participating with him in preventing the Prophet from writing the letter. I believe that this was the main reason for the Prophet (s) to refrain from writing [it]; for he knew, through the revelation from his Lord, that the plot was a strong one, and could threaten Islam in its entirety if the letter was written.

This was the letter through which the Prophet of Allah (s) wanted to protect his *ummah* from going astray, but the plotters turned the position around so that the letter became (if it was written), a reason for misguidance and reverting from Islam.

How could the Prophet of Allah (s) not change his stance - may my father and mother be sacrificed for him - for he was ill and on his death bed, receiving revelation from his Lord which resounded in his ears and filled his heart with sadness and suffering for his ill-fated *ummah* which [did not heed to] Allah's words: *"If he dies or is killed, will you then turn back upon your heels?"* (3:144).

This verse was not revealed spontaneously but rather because of Allah's, Glory be to Him, knowledge of their vileness, schemes and plots, for He is aware of the deception of the eyes and what is hidden in the hearts. What consoled the Prophet of Allah (s) was that his Lord had informed him of all this and comforted him. He [also] rewarded him with the best that any Prophet could be given from his *ummah* and did not hold him responsible for the apostasy of the *ummah* nor its turning back upon its heels. For Allah had revealed beforehand: *"On that day the wrongdoer will bite his hands and say: 'If only I had followed the path of the Messenger! Woe unto me! I wish that I had not taken so and so as my sincere friend! Certainly he led me away from the remembrance (of God) after it had come to me. The Satan is a deceiver to man'. Whereupon the Prophet will say: 'O my Lord! My people took this Qur'an as if it was foolish nonsense'. And thus we have made for every Prophet an enemy among the sinners! So sufficient for you is your Lord for guidance and assistance"* (25:27).

Chapter 2: Concerning the Prophet (s)

In this research, we cannot escape from the painful conclusion which we are forced to reach - that Abu Sufyan and Mu'awiyah would not have prevailed over the bearer of the message were it not for the previous position of 'Umar, and his bold conduct in the very presence of the Messenger of Allah (s). This is especially so if we investigate his stance during the entire life of the Prophet (s) and his opposing him on several occasions.

The inescapable conclusion is that there was an extensive plot devised to degrade the eminence of the character of the noble Messenger of Allah (s), to denigrate him, and to present him to the people who did not know him as an ordinary person or of an even lower [status] than that. He could be swayed by sentiments; he could give in to his desires and deviate from the truth.

All of this was done to deceive the people into thinking that he was not sinless. The proof [presented] is that 'Umar confronted him several times and that the Qur'an (allegedly) came down to support Ibn al-Khattab, to the point where Allah threatens His Prophet (s) who weeps and says: "Were Allah to send an affliction unto us, none would be safe except Ibn al-Khattab."[16]

Or [we are also told] that 'Umar used to command the Prophet of Allah (s) to veil his wives and the Prophet of Allah (s) did not do that until [verses of] the Qur'an were revealed in support of 'Umar, ordering the Prophet (s) to veil his wives.[17] Or that Satan was not scared of the Prophet of Allah (s), but that he was scared and fled from 'Umar[18] and several other [such] disgraceful narrations that lower the status of the Prophet of Allah (s), and enhance the status of the companions. 'Umar established records in this objective, to the point where they narrated (May Allah debase them) that the

---

[16] *Al-Bidaya wa al-Nihaya* (The Beginning and the End), Ibn al-Kathir reporting from Muslim, Imam Ahmad, Abu Dawud, al-Tirmidhi. Also *al-Sira al-Halabiya*, and *al-Sira al-Dahlaniya*, volume 1, p.512.

[17] *Sahih al-Bukhari*, 1/46, "The Chapter on "The Women visiting the Toilet".

[18] *Sahih al-Bukhari*, 4/96, 8/161.

Prophet of Allah (s) used to doubt his prophecy. This can be seen in the narration they reported [to the effect] that the Prophet of Allah (s) said: "When Gabriel delayed coming to me, I thought that he was going to 'Umar b. al-Khattab."

I believe that these *hadiths* and other traditions of this genre were fabricated in the time of Mu'awiyah b. Abi Sufyan when the plan to remove 'Ali b. Abi Talib from his rights was beginning to falter. He then resorted to praising Abu Bakr, 'Umar, and 'Uthman and to ascribe excellences to them so that they might be elevated in the eyes of the people over 'Ali, attaining by this, two goals:

The first goal was to degrade the status of the son of Abu Talib (Abu Turab) - as he called him - to degrade him in front of the people and [to lead the people into] considering the three Caliphs who preceded him to be better than him. The second goal, for his fabrication of *hadith*, was [to make] the people accept their neglecting the commands of the Prophet of Allah (s) and his testament that the Caliphate be [confined to] his *Ahl al-Bayt*, especially al-Hasan and al-Husayn, who were the contemporaries of Mu'awiyah. If it was possible for the three previous [Caliphs] to violate the orders of the Prophet of Allah (s) in the [matter of the] Caliphate of 'Ali (as), why was it not possible for Mu'awiyah (the fourth) to disregard the commands of the Prophet of Allah (s) regarding the children of 'Ali?

The son of Hind most certainly succeeded in his plan. The proof is that today, when we speak of the knowledge of 'Ali and his bravery, his closeness [to the Apostle of Allah (s)], and his eminence in Islam over the rest of the Muslims, there is always someone to say to us: "The Prophet of Allah (s) said: 'If the faith of my *ummah* were weighed against the faith of Abu Bakr, the faith of Abu Bakr would prevail.'" And there too is one who confronts us saying: "Umar *al-Faruq* is the one who differentiates the truth from falsehood." And someone confronts us saying: "'Uthman is the possessor of the two lights, and is the one of whom even the angels of the Merciful one were shy."

Anyone who pursues these discussions will find that 'Umar b al-

Chapter 2: Concerning the Prophet (s)

Khattab has taken the lion's share in the chapter on virtue, something which is not accidental, rather, [it is due to] the numerous contradictory positions that he took towards the bearer of the message. The Qurayshis loved him [for that], especially for the role that he played in distancing the Commander of the Faithful, the leader of the legatees, 'Ali b. Abi Talib, from the Caliphate, and reverting the matter (of leadership) to the Qurayshis to rule in the manner they wished, so that the ones who were freed on the day of the conquest of Mecca, and the accursed ones from the Umayyads, could covet it.

All the Qurayshis, the chief of whom was Abu Bakr, knew that the credit in their leadership over the Muslims went to 'Umar. For he was the hero of opposition to the Prophet of Allah (s), he was the one who prevented the Prophet of Allah (s) from writing [a testament of] the Caliphate for 'Ali. And 'Umar was the one who threatened the people and made them doubt the death of their Prophet so that they would not proceed to pay allegiance to 'Ali. 'Umar is also the hero of Saqifa; he is the one who ensured the allegiance to Abu Bakr. He is [also] the one who threatened those who remained in the house of 'Ali, to burn it and all those in it, if they did not pay allegiance to Abu Bakr. And 'Umar is the one who instigated the people into giving their fealty to Abu Bakr, through force and coercion. It was 'Umar who used to appoint the governors and allocate positions during the Caliphate of Abu Bakr. Indeed, we would not be exaggerating if we were to say that he was the actual ruler during the Caliphate of Abu Bakr himself.

Some historians relate that, in accordance with the custom they had [established] with the Prophet of Allah (s), those whose hearts were to be attracted [to Islam] approached Abu Bakr to claim their share which Allah has ordained for them. Abu Bakr wrote it [for them] and they went to 'Umar to collect [their rights], but he tore it up and said: "We have no need of you, for Allah has strengthened Islam and can dispense with you. If you accept Islam it will be better for you, and, if not, then the sword [shall be] between you and us." They returned to Abu Bakr and said to him: "Are you the Caliph or is he?" Abu Bakr replied: "Rather he, if God wishes" and he abided by what 'Umar had done.[19]

On another occasion, Abu Bakr wrote that two companions be given a piece of land, and sent the document to 'Umar to be implemented. The latter spat at it and destroyed it. They insulted him and returned to Abu Bakr and complained to him: "We do not know, are you the Caliph or is 'Umar?" He replied: "Rather he is!" 'Umar then came angrily to Abu Bakr and said to him: "It is not your right to give the land to these two". Whereupon Abu Bakr said: "I told you that you are stronger than me in this affair, however, you overruled me."[20]

From this, we can discern the special status which 'Umar b. al-Khattab enjoyed with the Qurayshis in general and the Umayyads in particular, to the extent that they gave him such titles as "the genius," "the inspired one," "the differentiator [between truth and falsehood]," "the absolute [personification of] Justice," and even to the extent that they preferred him above the Prophet of Allah (s).

We have seen 'Umar's belief regarding the Prophet of Allah (s) from the day of the treaty of al-Hudaybiyya to the day of the calamity. I can add to this that he prevented the companions from paying respect to the relics of the Prophet of Allah (s). He cut down of tree of the pledge of Ridwan. He also sought closeness to al-'Abbas, the uncle of the Prophet, to make the people believe that [since] the Messenger of Allah (s) had died, and his rule had ended, there was no point in remembering him. Therefore, there can be no blame on the Wahhabis who say the same things, for they are not new issues as some [people] wrongly assume.

From this too, the door was opened to the enemies of Islam and the Orientalists, to deduce that Muhammad was a genius who knew that his community was composed of idolaters who had been brought up worshipping idols. Therefore, he removed the idols and replaced for them instead a black stone.

---

[19] *al-Jawhara al-Naira fi fiqh* al-Hanafi, 1/164.

[20] *Al-Isaba fi Ma'rifa al-Sahaba,* al-'Asqalani in the report on 'Uyayna, and also Ibn Abi'l-Hadid in the commentary on *Nahj al-Balagha* 3/108.

Chapter 2: Concerning the Prophet (s)

After all of this, we observe that 'Umar is the hero who rejected the writing of the Prophetic *hadiths*, to the extent that he confined the companions to Medina and prohibited the others from (narrating) *hadith*, burning the *hadith* books, to ensure that the Prophetic traditions did not spread among the people.

We also can deduce from all this why 'Ali remained a prisoner in his home, not going out except when he was summoned to judge a problem that the companions were unable to deal with. 'Umar did not involve him in any office or governorship, nor [did he give him] any responsibility or [send him with] any deputation. In fact, he was also forbidden from Fatima's inheritance, and had nothing which the people could desire from him. As a result, historians relate that he was compelled to pay allegiance after the death of al-Zahra (sa) when he saw the faces of the people turning away from him.

Allah is with you, O Abu'l-Hasan! How could the people not hate you, when you were the one who had killed their heroes, divided their groups and destroyed their dreams. You did not leave for them in the field of merits a single merit whatsoever, nor in the field of good deeds, a single good deed for them. Furthermore, you were the cousin of the chosen one, you were also the nearest of them to him, and you were the husband of Fatima, the leader of the women of the universe, and you were the father of the two *sibtayn*, the two leaders of the youths of paradise, and you were the first person to accept Islam and the foremost of them in knowledge.

Your uncle was Hamza, leader of the martyrs, and Ja'far al-Tayyar was the son of your mother and father. Abu Talib, the master of the elevated places and the protector of the Prophet (s), was your father. And the rightly guided Imams are all from your loin. You were before the foremost ones and most distant from those who came later.

You were the lion of Allah and His Messenger (s) and you were the sword of Allah and His Messenger, and you were the trusted one of Allah and His Prophet, when you were sent by him (s) to dissociate [from the unbelievers], when none could be trusted but you. And you were the most truthful one, after you none can say that of anybody else without lying. You were the great differentiator who accompanied the truth and through whom it was distinguished from falsehood. You were the manifest knowledge and towering light. The faith of a believer is known through the love for you, the hypocrisy of a hypocrite is known by the hatred for you. You were the gate to the city of knowledge, for whoever came to you arrived [at that city]. Whoever claims to have entered [it] and arrived through other means has indeed lied.

Who amongst them has a share like yours O Abu'l-Hasan? And who amongst them has excellences like yours? If there is a proof for honour, then you are it. You are its beginning and end. They envied you due to Allah's bestowal of His grace on you. They distanced [themselves] from you when Allah had chosen you to be close to Him. Surely the oppressors will know their fate.

Indeed the pen has written abundantly the conversations of the Commander of the Faithful, the one who was oppressed in his life and death. In his brother, the Prophet of Allah (s), there was, for him, the best example, for he too was oppressed in life and in death. He spent his life struggling, advising, and seeking to protect the believers, loving and being kind to them. They confronted him at the last moment with evil words, accusing him of delirium, confronting him with disobedience and insolence due to the appointment of Usama [as the leader]. They hastened towards the Saqifa for the sake of the Caliphate, leaving [behind] a forlorn corpse. They were not even concerned about the preparation, bathing or shrouding of his body, may my mother and father be sacrificed for him. After his death, they sought to disparage him in the eyes of people and to denigrate his status, to retract from him the infallibility which the Qur'an, as well as reasoning testifies to.

This was [done] for the sake of [attaining] temporary ruler ship and a transitory world. We can discern, during the course of our investigation, the position [adopted by] some of the companions towards the character of the Prophet of Allah (s) for the sake of attaining the Caliphate.

Chapter 2: Concerning the Prophet (s)

The Umayyad rulers, the chief of whom was Mu'awiyah b. Abi Sufyan, attained the Caliphate by inheriting it. They contented themselves in it and it did not occur to any one of them that one day it would desert them. Why did the Umayyads continue to denigrate the personality of the Messenger of Allah (s), and to concoct narrations that were designed to reduce his status?

I feel that there were two main reasons for this:

The first reason: Behind the denigration of the character of the Prophet of Allah (s) lay their grudges against the Banu Hashim, for they had attained the honor and respect of all the Arab tribes since the Prophet was from them. This becomes more clear when we realize that Umayya used to vie with his brother Hashim and envied him, trying his utmost to destroy him.

Moreover, 'Ali was the leader of the Hashimites after the Prophet of Allah (s), without any doubt. Everyone knew of Mu'awiyah's hatred for 'Ali and the wars that he waged against him to wrest the Caliphate away from him. After his murder, he indulged in insulting and cursing him from the pulpits. As far as Mu'awiyah was concerned, the denigration of the Prophet of Allah (s) lay in destroying the personality of 'Ali, just as the cursing and insulting of 'Ali was, in fact, directed at the Prophet of Allah (s).

The second reason: In the denigration of the character of the Messenger of Allah (s) lay a justification for the vile, evil and heinous acts which the Umayyad rulers perpetrated, [acts which] history has recorded. If the Prophet of Allah (s), as the Umayyads portray him, could follow his lusts and love his wives to the extent that he forgot his obligations, and he inclined to one of them so much so that he could not treat them equally, and they had to send to him [people] requesting equal treatment, then there can be no reproach directed towards ordinary people such as Mu'awiyah, Yazid and those like them.

And the danger hidden in the second reason is that the Umayyads fabricated narrations and *hadiths*, attributing them to the Messenger of Allah (s). These [concoctions] became rules which were acted upon in Islam, the Muslims accepted them as [they were] certain that these were the words and actions of the Prophet of Allah (s). Therefore, these became, for them, the Prophetic *Sunnah*.

I will cite some examples of these disgraceful *hadith* which were falsified to degrade the character of the Prophet of Allah (s), and to lower his status. I do not wish to go into details on this subject, and will therefore restrict myself to what al-Bukhari and Muslim have related in their two *Sahihs* (disgraceful *hadiths* to degrade the Prophet of Allah (s)).

1. Al-Bukhari narrated in "The Book of (ritual) Washing," in "The Chapter on one who has Intercourse and repeats it," "From Anas that the Prophet (s) used to visit his wives in a single hour during the night and day and they were altogether eleven of them." He said: "I said to Anas: 'Did he have the strength for this?' He replied: 'We used to say that he was given the strength of thirty...'" Observe with me, O reader, this filthy *hadith* which portrays for us an image of the Prophet of Allah (s) with this insatiable desire for sex, that he has intercourse with eleven women in one hour, and does so either at night or day with such speed that, without taking a bath after the first one, he approaches the second while he still had the secretions of the first [wife] on him. You have no recourse, O reader, but to form a picture and think: "How can a man throw himself upon his wife like an animal, without any foreplay or greetings?" For we have observed that even among animals, they are engrossed in a sexual act for a long time, since it requires prelude and foreplay. How can this great Prophet conduct himself in this manner? May Allah fight and curse them for their fabrications. The Arabs of that time - and men until today - took pride in their sex drives, reckoning that as a sign of manliness. They attributed this anecdote to the Prophet of Allah (s). Allah forbid, for the Prophet himself used to say: "Do not approach your women like animals, but instead do something that attracts you and them."

From such narrations, the enemies of Islam attack the Prophet (s) describing him as a man of animalistic desires, and accusing him of other things. Can we ask Anas b. Malik, the narrator of this anecdote, as to who informed him? Who told him that the Prophet

Chapter 2: Concerning the Prophet (s) 63

of Allah (s) used to have sex with all his wives in one hour, and that they were altogether eleven in number?

Was it the Prophet who told him this? Is it proper for anyone of us to speak to others about his sexual acts with his wife? Or did the wives of the Prophet inform him of that? Does it behoove a Muslim woman to speak to other men of her sexual acts with her husband? Or did Anas spy upon the Prophet of Allah (s), and accompany him in the private chambers with his wife, spying upon him from the holes of doors? I seek refuge in Allah from the agents of the devil! May Allah's curse be upon the liars!

I do not doubt that the Umayyad and 'Abbasid rulers, notorious for their many wives and slave girls, are the ones who fabricated such stories to justify their deeds.

2. Al-Bukhari reported in vol. 3, p. 132 in his *Sahih*, as well as Muslim in vol. 7, p. 136 of his *Sahih* that 'A'isha said: "The wives of the Prophet (s) sent Fatima, the daughter of the Prophet of Allah (s) to the Prophet.

She sought permission to enter while he was reclining with me in a single garment. He allowed her in and she said: 'O Prophet of Allah! Your wives have sent me to you to ask that you show fairness regarding the daughter of Abu Quhafa'. I remained quiet. He said to Fatima: 'My dear child do you not love what I love'? She said: 'Most certainly.' He said: 'Then love her.....'"

The narration continues to the point where the wives of the Prophet of Allah (s) sent a second message, this time with Zaynab bint Jahsh, wife of the Prophet (s), pleading him to exercise justice regarding the daughter of Abu Quhafa. She went to see him while he was reclining with 'A'isha, covered in her garment, in the same position that he was in when Fatima visited him. She pleaded with the Prophet to observe justice regarding the daughter of Abu Quhafa, speaking on behalf of the other wives of the Prophet, and then resorted to insulting and reviling 'A'isha, who, in turn, retorted and insulted Zaynab until she silenced her. Upon this, the Messenger of Allah (s) smiled and said: "She is the daughter of Abu

Bakr."

What can I say about this loathsome narration which shows the Prophet of Allah (s) to be a man who follows his lusts and does not show justice to his wives, although it is through his tongue that the Qur'an ordered: *"And if you fear that you cannot show fairness, then (marry) one or (resort to) what your right hand possesses."* (4:3)

Furthermore, how can the Prophet of Allah (s) permit his daughter Fatima, the leader of women, to enter when he was reclining with his wife wearing her garment and not to sit up or stand, but rather, remain reclining and say to her: "O my child! Do you not love what I love?" Similarly, when Zaynab came, imploring him to be fair, he smiled and said: "She is the daughter of Abu Bakr." Observe, O noble reader, this despicable [conduct] which they attribute to the Prophet of Allah (s), [who is] the symbol of justice and equality, whereas they say that justice died with 'Umar b. al-Khattab. They portray the Messenger of Allah (s) to be attaching little importance to upright character, not knowing chastity or ideals of manliness. There are many such traditions in the six *Sihah* [works].

The narrators intend to present, behind this, the superior merits of a companion or of 'A'isha, especially as she is the daughter of Abu Bakr. In doing so, they denigrate the Prophet of Allah (s) knowingly or unknowingly, since, as I have shown before in this discussion, these traditions are fabricated to devalue the character of the Prophet. Let us look at a third example [which is] similar to this one:

3. Muslim reported in his *Sahih* in "The Chapter on the Merits of 'Uthman b. 'Affan," on the authority of 'A'isha, the wife of the Prophet (s), and also from 'Uthman, that they both said that Abu Bakr sought permission to visit the Prophet of Allah (s) while he was lying on his bed wearing the garment of 'A'isha. He let him in while he was still in that condition. He fulfilled his needs then Abu Bakr went out. 'Umar then sought permission to enter while the Prophet was still in that state. He also fulfilled his needs and left.

Chapter 2: Concerning the Prophet (s)   65

'Uthman said: "Then I requested permission to enter, whereupon he sat up and said to 'A'isha: 'Gather your clothes around you.' I finished my work with him and left.' A'isha said: 'O Prophet of Allah (s), how come I did not see you scared with Abu Bakr and 'Umar, as you were with 'Uthman?' The Prophet of Allah (s) said: 'Indeed 'Uthman is a very shy man, and I was afraid that if I had granted him permission to enter while I was in that state, he would not have presented his need to me.'"

This narration is similar to another, which al-Bukhari and Muslim narrated, regarding the merits of 'Uthman. The gist [of the report] is that the Prophet of Allah (s) had left his thighs uncovered, had permitted Abu Bakr to enter without covering his thighs. He did the same thing with 'Umar. When 'Uthman sought permission to enter, however, the Prophet of Allah (s) covered his thighs and put his clothes on properly. When 'A'isha asked him about that, he said to her: "Should I not be shy of someone of whom [even] the angels are shy?"

May Allah debase the Banu Umayya, who seek to debase the Messenger of Allah (s) so as to elevate [the status of] their master.

4. Muslim reported in his *Sahih* in "The Chapter on the Injunction to take a Ritual Bath after the Meeting of the Private Parts of the Spouses," on the authority of 'A'isha, the wife of the Prophet (s), that while she was sitting [in his presence]: "A man asked the Prophet of Allah (s), if the bath was obligatory upon both parties when a man has intercourse with his wife, and then he feels lazy [to have a bath]. The Prophet of Allah (s) replied: 'I certainly do it, I and her, then we have a bath.'"

I leave you, O reader, to consider this *hadith* for yourself. It seems now the Messenger's pampering for his wife 'A'isha has reached the level where he can discuss about his sexual relations with her to all people. How many such reports have been transmitted on the authority of 'A'isha, the daughter of Abu Bakr, which demean and disparage the status of the Prophet (s). One time she reports he put his cheek upon her cheek so that she could enjoy the black dancers, and, at another time, carrying her upon his shoulder. At another time, he raced with her and she won against him. The Prophet of Allah (s) then waits, until she gains weight, and races her (and wins) saying: "This is the equalizer." Yet, at another time, he is lying upon his back, with the women beating drums and musical instruments of the devil in his own house, until Abu Bakr rebukes them.

How often, in the *Sahih* works, do such disgraceful traditions occur, traditions whose only aim is to denigrate the Prophet of Islam (s), such as the *hadiths* which state that the Messenger was subjected under a magic spell so he did not know what he did or said. He [even] thought that he had sexual relations with his spouses when, in fact, he had not.[21] And [other] narrations which state that he (s) used to wake up in the mornings of Ramadan in a ritually impure state. (*janaba*[22]), and that he would sleep until he snored, then he would wake up and pray without performing the ablutions (*wudu'*).[23]

[Others state] that he used to forget during his prayer, not remembering how many *rak'ats* (units of prayers) he had performed.[24] And that the Messenger of Allah (s) did not know his fate on the day of resurrection and what would be done to him.[25] [Others state] he used to urinate while standing up, and when his companion went away from him, he would call him back so that he could be near him until he finished urinating.[26]

Yes! The Prophet's (s) pampering of his wife 'A'isha, the daughter of Abu Bakr, reached a point whereby he detained himself and all the Muslims to search for 'A'isha's necklace that had been lost. They had no water with them and the people complained about 'A'isha to Abu Bakr whereupon her father came and reproached and

---

[21] *Sahih al-Bukhari*, 4/68, 7/29.

[22] *Sahih al-Bukhari*, 2/232, 234.

[23] *Sahih al-Bukhari*, 1/44, 171.

[24] *Sahih al-Bukhari*, 1/123, 2/65.

[25] *Ibid*, 2/71.

[26] *Sahih Muslim*, 2/157, in "The Chapter on Wiping over the Shoes".

Chapter 2: Concerning the Prophet (s)

rebuked her. All this happened while Prophet of Allah (s) was asleep on his wife's lap! Here is the narration in detail:

Al-Bukhari in his *Sahih* in "The Chapter on *Tayammum*" and Muslim in his *Sahih*, also in "The Chapter on *Tayammum*," both related on the authority of 'A'isha, who said: "We went out with the Prophet of Allah (s) on one of his journeys. We reached al-Bida or the military encampment when my necklace broke. The Prophet of Allah (s) started searching for it, and the people went along with him. There was no water to be found and they had none with them. The people came to Abu Bakr and said: 'Do you not see what 'A'isha has done? She has caused the Prophet of Allah (s) to busy himself and the people to undertake [this], when they have no water and there is none available in this spot.' Abu Bakr then came whilst the Prophet of Allah (s), having rested his head upon my thigh, had fallen asleep. He said: 'You have detained the Prophet of Allah (s) and the people have no water and cannot find any here.'" She said: "Abu Bakr continued rebuking me for as long as Allah wished him to, then he started hitting me with his hand on my hip. Nothing prevented me from moving except that the Prophet of Allah (s) was on my thigh. The Prophet of Allah (s) slept till the morning. There was still no water to be found so Allah revealed the verses of *tayammum* and they performed it." Asyad b. al-Hudayr, one of the leaders, said: "This is not the first blessing for you, O member of the household of Abu Bakr!" 'A'isha said: "We made the camel, which I was [riding] on, to get up and we found the necklace underneath it."[27]

Can any believer, who is aware of Islam, believe that the Prophet of Allah (s) was lax about the matter of prayer to this extent and that he would detain the Muslims, even though they were in an area where there was no water and they had none with them, to search for his wife's missing necklace?

Then he leaves the Muslims, who are worried about their prayer and complain to Abu Bakr, and instead goes to his wife and falls asleep in her lap, and is so engrossed in his sleep that he is totally

---

[27] *Sahih al-Bukhari*, 1/86, *Sahih Muslim*, 1/191.

unaware of Abu Bakr's entry and his rebuking 'A'isha, and his striking her on her hips? How is it allowable for this Messenger to leave the people who are agitated due to the lack of water and the approaching prayer time, to sleep on his wife's lap?

There is no doubt this narration was fabricated during the Caliphate of Mu'awiyah b. Abi Sufyan and is without foundation. Otherwise, how can we explain [the fact that] an incident like this, at which all the companions were present, was not known to 'Umar b. al-Khattab? He did not know about it when he was asked concerning the *tayammum* as is narrated by both al-Bukhari and Muslim in their *Sahihs* in the chapters on *tayammum*.

The important point in all these discussions is that we realise the plot against the Prophet of Allah (s) was evil and vile, with the goal of belittling the Messenger of Allah (s), and of devaluing his status to the extent where none of us today (in spite of the corruption that has spread to the land and sea) would be personally pleased with these types of conduct and deeds. How can this be [allowed] then for the greatest personality that human history has known, and he whom the Lord of Might and Glory has testified is of the highest character?

In my view, the plots began after the farewell pilgrimage and after the Prophet (s) had appointed Imam 'Ali as his successor on the day of Ghadir Khum. Those who coveted the leadership knew then that in front of them lay only opposition and rebellion due to this appointment, and that these would be at a tremendous cost, even leading to their turning back upon their heels in reversion. Therefore, it seems proper to interpret the events that began with opposing the Prophet of Allah (s) in all his commands. [This started with stopping him] from writing a letter; to his appointment of Usama as [their] leader; to their not joining the army the Prophet of Allah (s) himself had chosen. And so too [is it proper to interpret] the events that followed his death (s) - from forcing the people into pledging fealty by coercion and threatening to burn the dissenters, among whom were 'Ali, Fatima and al-Hasanayn. Similarly, [it seems proper to interpret] forbidding the people from relating the *hadith* of the Messenger of Allah (s), and the burning of books

Chapter 2: Concerning the Prophet (s)

which contained the *Sunnah* of the Prophet of Allah (s), to their detaining the companions so that they may not spread the *hadith* of the Prophet (s).

[It seems proper to interpret] also the killing of companions who refused to pay the *zakat* to Abu Bakr, for he was not the Caliph to whom they had, at the order of their Prophet, pledged fealty. [It seems proper to interpret] their denying the rights of Fatima al-Zahra (sa) to Fadak, her inheritance, and her portion of the *khumus* and to refute her claims. Similarly, the alienation of Imam 'Ali (as) from any position of responsibility, instead granting these [positions] to the corrupt ones and hypocrites from the Banu Umayya over the Muslims; and forbidding the companions from paying respect to the relics of the Prophet of Allah (s), and to attempting to remove his name from the *adhan* and to expose the army of disbelievers to al-Medina al-Munawwara to do therein as they pleased. [This varied] from attacking the sacred house, *bayt al-haram* with fire and razing it, to killing the companions that were within. [It seemed proper] to murder the progeny of the Messenger of Allah (s), to curse and vilify them, and to force the people to do that; to kill and exile those who loved the *Ahl al-Bayt* and followed them - to the point where the religion of Allah became a [source of] amusement and subject to ridicule; the Qur'an [became] something to be shredded and scoffed at.

The plot still persists today, its influences and impact are still prevalent in the Islamic *ummah*. [It will continue] as long as there are those Muslims who are pleased with Mu'awiyah and Yazid, justifying their deeds on the basis that they exercised their personal judgements, and that for them lies a reward from Allah. As long as there are those who write books and articles against the Shi'as of the *Ahl al-Bayt*, hurling all sorts of insults and slander; as long as there are those who allow the murder of the Shi'as of the *Ahl al-Bayt* within the confines of the *bayt al-haram* and the season of the *Hajj* - the plot will continue and will remain continuous until such time as Allah wishes.

I am not able to neither discern the whole [plan] nor comprehend its details and facets, but I will attempt, with my humble efforts, to do my best to distance the Prophet of Allah (s) from the disgraceful narrations that have been attributed to him, and to defend him and his infallibility. I will attempt to convince the educated and free thinking Muslims that this Prophet whom Allah sent for the guidance of all humankind and made him a moon and shining light, is the highest, greatest, most noble, most pure, pious and complete man that Allah has created. It is impossible for us to remain quiet in the face of such narrations. The reporters have no other intention but to denigrate his nobility and devalue his status.

We are not, and never will be, happy with these narrations, even if all the *Ahl al-Sunnah wa'l-Jama'a* agree upon them, and relate them in their *Sahihs* and *Musnads*. Even if all the mortals on earth were to agree with them, Allah's words: *"And you are indeed of the most exalted character"(68:4)* is the final word and decisive judgment. Apart from that, everything else is falsehood and wrong presumption.

This is the position of the Shi'a regarding the leader of human beings, the one who frees them from blindness and misguidance, the one who leads humanity to security and peace. So ponder over it, O you who perceive.

What the Ahl al-Dhikr believe about the Prophet of Allah (s)

Imam 'Ali says: "So that the grace of Allah, Glory be to Him, reach Muhammad (s), Allah brought him out of the best of sources and the most honorable places from which things grow, from the same lineal tree from which He brought forth His Prophets and selected their trustees. Muhammad's progeny is the best progeny, his family the best family and his lineal tree is the best of trees. It grew in sanctity, surpassing all in honor. Its branches are tall and its fruits cannot be reached.

He is the leader of all those who fear Allah, and insight for those who seek guidance. He is a lamp whose flame is burning, a meteor whose light is shining and a flint whose spark is bright. His conduct is upright; his behavior guidance; his speech is the criterion [between right and wrong] and his decision just. Allah sent him,

Chapter 2: Concerning the Prophet (s)

after an interval from the previous Prophets, when people had fallen into errors of action and ignorance....then the Prophet of Allah (s) exerted his utmost in giving sound advice, staying on the right path, calling them towards wisdom and good counsel..., his is the best abode and his origin the noblest of all, coming from the source of honor and the cradles of security. The hearts of the virtuous people incline towards him, and the eyes have focused on him. Through him, Allah buried all rancor and extinguished conflicts. Through him, He brought people together in brotherhood and separated friends. Through him, He elevated the lowly, and humiliated the arrogant and mighty. His speech is clear and even his silence is (indicative) like the tongue. He sent him with sufficient proof and satisfying admonitions. His call eliminates deficiencies, through him; the unknown laws were made manifest, the innovative practices subdued, and the distinctive judgments made clear.

He sent him with light and gave him precedence in purity. He mended all fissures. Through him, those conquering were [themselves] conquered, difficulties were subjugated and hardships alleviated until he wiped out misguidance all around him."

Chapter Three

Concerning the Ahl al-Bayt (as)

The Third Question: Who are the Ahl al-Bayt?

Allah, the most Glorified and High says: *"Allah wishes to remove all impurity from you, O members of the household, and to purify you completely"* (33:33).

The *Ahl al-Sunnah wa'l-Jama'a* maintains that this verse was revealed for the wives of the Prophet (s). They derive their proof from the context of the preceding and following verses. According to their claims, Allah therefore removed impurity from the wives of the Prophet and purified them completely.

Among them are those who add to the [list of the] wives of the Prophet, 'Ali, Fatima, al-Hasan and al-Husayn. But the truth, according to what has been transmitted, as well as according to reasoning, logic and history, refutes this explanation. [This is] because the Ahl al-Sunnah narrate in their *Sahihs* that the verse was revealed regarding five people namely: Muhammad, 'Ali, Fatima, al-Hasan and al-Husayn, and that the Prophet of Allah (s) identified them and his noble self as being referred to by the noble verse when he gathered 'Ali, Fatima, al-Hasan and al-Husayn with him under the cloak. He said: "O Allah! These are my household, so cleanse them of all impurity and purify them completely."

This narration has been reported by a large majority of Sunni scholars. I've listed [some of] them:

1. Muslim in his *Sahih*, in "The Chapter on the Merits of the Prophet's household": Vol. 2, p. 368.
2. Al- Tirmidhi in his *Sahih*, Vol. 5, p. 30.
3. *Al-Musnad*, Imam Ahmad b. Hanbal; Vol. 1, p. 330.
4. *Al-Mustadrak,* al- Hakim; Vol. 3, p. 123.
5. *Al-Khas'ais*, Imam al-Nasa'i; p. 49

6. *Talkhis al-Mustadrak*, al-Dhahabi; Vol. 2, p. 150.
7. *Mu'jam,* al-Tabrani; Vol. 1, p. 65.
8. *Shawahid al-Tanzil*, Hakim al-Haskani; Vol. 2, p. 11.
9. Al-Bukhari in his *Tarikh al-Kabir*, Vol. 1, p. 69.
10. *Al-Isaba*, Ibn Hajar al-Asqalani; Vol. 2, p. 502.
11. *Tadhkira al-Khawas*, Ibn al-Jawzi; p. 233.
12. *Tafsir* of al-Fakhr al-Razi; Vol. 2, p. 700.
13. *Yanabi al-Muwadda*, al-Qanduzi al-Hanafi; p. 107.
14. *Manaqib* of al-Khawarizmi, p. 23.
15. *Al-Sira* of al-Halabi, Vol. 13, p. 212.
16. *Al-Sira* of al-Dihlaniya; Vol. 3, p. 329.
17. *Asad al-Ghaba*, Ibn al-Athir; Vol. 2, p. 12.
18. *Tafsir* of al-Tabari; Vol. 22, p. 6.
19. *Al-Dur al-Manthur*, al-Suyuti; Vol. 5, p. 198.
20. *Tarikh* of Ibn Asakir; Vol. 1, p. 185.
21. *Tafsir al-Kashshaf,* al-Zamakhshari; Vol. 1, p. 193
22. *Ahkam al-Qur'an,* Ibn al-Arabi; Vol. 2, p. 166.
23. *Tafsir* al-Qurtubi, Vol. 14, p. 182.
24. *Al-Sawa'iq al-Muhriqa* of Ibn Hajar, p. 85.
25. *Al-Isti'ab*, Ibn Abd al-Barr; Vol. 3, p. 37.
26. *Al-'Iqd al-Farid,* Ibn 'Abd Rabbih; Vol. 4, p. 311
27. *Muntakhab Kanz al-'Ummal,* Ibn Hanbal; Vol. 5, p. 96.
28. *Masabih al-Sunnah,* al-Baghawi, Vol. 2, p. 278.
29. *Asbab al-Nuzul,* al-Wahidi; p. 203.
30. *Tafsir* of Ibn Kathir; Vol. 3, p. 483.

Other Sunni scholars [who have reported the *hadith*] are numerous, we have not mentioned them [all], being content with these as [the list] was compiled in haste.

If all these scholars admit that the Prophet of Allah (s) had clarified the purport of the verse, of what value are the words of the other companions or the successors of the companions, or commentators who wish to construe its meaning contrary to what Allah and His Prophet desire, seeking instead, to please Mu'awiyah and desiring [to attain] what he has?

Similarly, the Messenger of Allah (s) also identified them on other occasions, specifying that they were the *Ahl al-Bayt*, not

Chapter 3: Concerning the ahl al-bayt (as)

others. This occurred when the verse of Allah, the Glorified and the Highest, was revealed stating: *"Say: 'Come and let us call our children and your children, our women and your women, ourselves and yourselves, and let us take pray, invoking Allah's curse on those who lie'" (3:61).* Thereupon, he called 'Ali, Fatima, al-Hasan, and al-Husayn and said: "These are our children, ourselves, and our women: So now bring yourselves, your children, and your women". According to Muslim's narrative, he said: "O Allah, these are my household."[1]

The *Ahl al-Sunnah wa'l-Jama'a* scholars, whom I referred to in the preceding sources, also agree unanimously that the verse was revealed concerning the five [figures] mentioned above, may Allah's blessings be upon them all.

Moreover, the wives of the Prophet all knew the intent of the noble verse, and, consequently, not one of them claimed to be from the *Ahl al-Bayt*. At the head of these [wives] were Umm Salama and 'A'isha. Every one of them narrated that the verse was specifically for the Prophet of Allah (s), 'Ali, Fatima, al-Hasan and al-Husayn. Muslim, al-Tirmidhi, al-Hakim, al-Tabari, al-Suyuti, al-Dhahabi, Ibn al-Athir and others, have all reported their (the wives') acceptance of this.

I would add to this the fact that the Messenger of Allah (s) removed any confusion and resolved this problem, for he knew that the Muslims might read the Qur'an and construe the [term] *Ahl al-Bayt* in the context of the preceding and following verses, which [actually] warned the wives of the Prophet.

He immediately hastened to teach the *ummah* the meaning of the removal of all impurities and complete purification by continuing, for a period of six months, (after the revelation of the verse) to pass by the door of 'Ali, Fatima, al-Hasan and al-Husayn before starting the prayer and reciting: "Allah wishes to remove all abomination from you, *Ahl al-Bayt* and to completely purify you, so come to the

---

[1] *Sahih Muslim*, 7/121, in "The Chapter on the Merits of Ali b. Abi Talib".

prayer, may Allah have mercy on you."

This immediate action performed by the Messenger of Allah (s) has been reported by:

Al-Sahih, al-Tirmidhi, vol. 5, p. 31
Al-Mustadrak, al-Hakim, vol. 3, p. 158
Al-Talkhis, al-Dhahabi
Al-Musnad, Ahmad b. Hanbal, vol. 3, p. 259
Asad al-Ghaba, Ibn al-Athir, vol. 5, p. 521
Shawahid al-Tanzil, al-Haskani, vol. 2, p. 11
Al-Dur al-Manthur, al-Suyuti, vol. 5, p. 199
Tafsir, al-Tabari, vol. 22, p. 6
Ansab al-Ashraf, al-Baladhuri, vol. 2, p. 104
Tafsir, Ibn al-Kathir, vol. 3, p. 483
Majma' al-Zawa'id, al-Haythami, vol. 9, p. 168

When we add to the above list the Imams of the *Ahl al-Bayt* and the Shi'a scholars, who do not doubt that the noble verse was restricted to Muhammad, 'Ali, Fatima, al-Hasan and al-Husayn, there can remain absolutely no regard for those who disagree with them from the enemies of the *Ahl al-Bayt*, as well followers of Mu'awiyah and the Banu Umayyads who wish to extinguish the light of Allah with their mouths. Allah has perfected His light, even though the disbelievers hate that.

Those who interpret the verse differently to the explanation of the Prophet have shown that, in the past, they were merely the flatterers of the Umayyad and 'Abbasid rulers, and that today they, even though disguised in the garb of jurists and scholars, are amongst those who hate 'Ali.

Furthermore, reasoning shows that the verse (i.e. cleansing of abomination) could not include the wives of the Prophet (s).

1. Let us, by way of example, take the case of the mother of the believers, 'A'isha, who alleged that she was the most beloved wife of the Prophet (s) and the closest one to him, to the extent that the rest of the wives envied her and sent [a delegation] to the Prophet

Chapter 3: Concerning the ahl al-bayt (as)

(s) imploring him to show justice regarding the daughter of Abu Quhafa, as previously discussed. The verse then seems discordant. None of her aides or those who loved her, neither from the earlier generations nor the later ones, can dare to claim that 'A'isha was under the cloak on the day the verse was revealed. How great Muhammad (s) was in his sayings and actions and how truly sagacious he was when he gathered the members of his *Ahl al-Bayt* with him under the cloak, and even when the mother of the believers, Umm Salama, the wife of the Prophet (s), sought to enter with them under the cloak and asked the Prophet of Allah's (s) permission, he prevented her and said: "You are on the right path."

2. The general and specific purport of the verse indicates infallibility. For the removal of abomination covers all sins, [acts of] disobedience, major and minor vices. This is especially so if we add the purification from the Lord of Power and Glory. If Muslims purify themselves with water and dust physically, a purification which does not exceed the outer body, then Allah purified the *Ahl al-Bayt* with a spiritual purity wherein the intellect, hearts, and their minds were cleansed, leaving no room for the insinuations of neither the devil nor any act of disobedience. Their hearts became absolutely clean, pure, sincere, devoted solely to their creator and sustainer in every activity and inactivity.

3. In all cases, every one of these purified souls was an example to all humanity, in [the fields of] asceticism, piety, sincerity, knowledge, forbearance, bravery, manliness, chastity, free from blemishes, shunning the world, seeking nearness to Him, the Glorified and most High. History has not recorded any wrongdoing or sin from any one of them during their entire lives.

This being the case, let us return to the first example, the wife of the Prophet (s), 'A'isha, who attained a lofty and elevated position and [achieved] great popularity which none of the other wives of the Prophet (s) has been accorded. Even if we were to combine all their merits, they would not be able to reach a tenth of the standing of 'A'isha, the daughter of Abu Bakr. This is what the *Ahl al-Sunnah,* and those who claim that half the religion can be learnt from her alone, say regarding her.

If we devote ourselves to the truth without any prejudice or bias, is it reasonable to think that she was purified from sins and disobedience? Or that Allah, Glory be to Him, withdrew His protection from her, after the death of her husband, the Messenger of Allah (s)? Let us examine the reality together.

'A'isha during the life of the Prophet (s)

If we examine her life with her husband, the Prophet of Allah (s), we will find lots of sins and [acts of] disobedience, for she used to frequently conspire with Hafsa against the Apostle until they compelled him to declare as unlawful for himself what Allah had permitted for him, as reported by al-Bukhari and Muslim. They also argued with him, as has been established in all the *Sahihs* and books of *tafsir*, and even Allah has mentioned the two incidents in His glorious Qur'an.

Envy so controlled her heart and her mind that she conducted herself in the presence of the Prophet of Allah (s) without respect or manners. On one occasion, she said to the Prophet (s), when he mentioned Khadija in her presence:

"How can Khadija be compared with me! She was a red cheeked old woman and Allah has given you [someone] better than her." The Prophet of Allah (s) became very angry at this until his hair stood.[2] And, on another occasion, one of the mothers of the believers sent to the Prophet a dish (he was in her house) that he really loved. She destroyed the dish, together with the food in it.[3] On another occasion, she said to the Prophet (s): "You are the one who claims to be Allah's Prophet."[4] Another time, she became angry with him and said: "Be just!" Her father, who was present,

---

[2] *Sahih al-Bukhari*, 4/231, in "The Chapter on the Marriage of the Prophet (s) to Khadija; reported also in *Muslim*".

[3] *Sahih al-Bukhari*, 4/231, in "The Chapter on Envy".

[4] *Ihya' Ulum al-din,* Imam al-Ghazali, 2/29, in "The Book on the Etiquettes of Marriage".

Chapter 3: Concerning the ahl al-bayt (as)

struck her so hard that blood flowed.⁵ Her envy reached a point whereby she lied to Asma' bint al-Nu'man, when she had come as a bride to the Prophet (s). She said to her: "The Prophet (s) loves a woman, who, when he approaches her, says to him: "I seek refuge in Allah from you." Her underlying aim was to have the Prophet (s) divorce this innocent, naive woman, and who the Prophet (s) did divorce due to these words.⁶ Her evil conduct in the presence of the Prophet of Allah (s) reached a point that while he was praying, she would spread her feet towards his direction of prostration. When he prostrated and pinched them, she retracted them. When he stood up for the rest of the prayer, she would spread her feet out again.⁷

On one occasion, she plotted with Hafsa against the Prophet of Allah (s), causing him to isolate himself from his wives for a period of one complete month, and to sleep on a rough straw mat.⁸ When the words of Allah: *"Take back those of them that you please, and leave aside those whom you please."* were revealed, she said to the Prophet unabashedly: "I only see Allah as [one] who hurries to [satisfy] your desires."⁹ If 'A'isha got angry - which she did quite often - she would avoid [uttering] the name of the Prophet (s). She would not mention the name of Muhammad, but would say: "By the Lord of Abraham."¹⁰

'A'isha often used to offend the Prophet (s) and caused him distress, but the Prophet (s) was compassionate and kind, his

---

⁵ *Kanz al-'Ummal* 7/116, also in *Ihya' Ulum al-din*.

⁶ Ibn Sa'd, *Tabaqat al-Kubra,* 8/145, Ibn Hajar, *Al-Isaba*, 4/233, al-Ya'qubi, *Tarikh*, 2/69.

⁷ *Sahih al-Bukhari*, 1/101, in "The Chapter on Prayer on the Mattress".

⁸ *Sahih al-Bukhari*, 3/105, in "The Chapter of The Bed Chamber","The Book of Oppression".

⁹ *Sahih al-Bukhari*, 6/24, 128, in "The Chapter: 'Is it allowed for the women to offer herself (in marriage) to anyone?" *Sahih Muslim*, In "The Chapter of the Permissibility of a Woman to give her turn to her Co-Wife".

¹⁰ *Sahih al-Bukhari*, 6/158, in "The Chapter of the Jealousy and Wiles of Woman".

character lofty, his patience deep, therefore he frequently said to her: "Your Satan has confused you, O 'A'isha." Quite often, he used to be sorry because of Allah's threat to her and Hafsa, the daughter of 'Umar. On many occasions the Qur'an came down regarding her! Allah said to her and to Hafsa: "You two turn in repentance to Allah, your hearts are so inclined," i.e., she had departed and deviated from the truth.[11] His words: *"If you support each other against him, Allah is his protector, as well as Gabriel and the righteous believers, after this, the angels too are his supporters"* (66:4) is a clear threat from the Lord of Power to her and to Hafsa, who used to frequently help her and act according to her commands. Allah also said to both of them: *"Perhaps if he divorces you, his Lord will give him wives who are better than you, who submit and believe."*(66:5) This verse was revealed concerning 'A'isha and Hafsa as testified by 'Umar b. al-Khattab and reported by al-Bukhari.[12] The verse, in itself, indicates that there were believing women among the Muslims who were better than 'A'isha.

Once, when the Prophet of Allah (s) wanted to propose to Sharraf, the sister of Dihya al-Kalbi, he asked 'A'isha to go and look at her. When she returned, her heart was filled with envy, and the Prophet of Allah (s) asked her: "What have you seen O 'A'isha?" She responded: "I did not see anyone worthy." The Prophet of Allah (s) said to her: "You have certainly seen someone worthy. You have seen her and your saliva soured in your mouth." She said: "O Prophet of Allah (s), no secret is unknown to you. Who is able to hide anything from you?"[13]

All of the plots which 'A'isha instigated against the Prophet of Allah (s) were most frequently with the complicity of Hafsa, the daughter of 'Umar. The strange thing is that we find there was

---

[11] *Sahih al-Bukhari*, 3/106, "The Chapter on The Room and Upper Room".

[12] *Sahih al-Bukhari*, 6/69, "The Chapter on When the Prophet (s) confided a secret to some of his wives".

[13] Ibn Sa'd, *Tabaqat*, 8/115, *Kanz al-'Ummal*, 6/294.

mutual understanding and complete harmony between the two women, 'A'isha and Hafsa, like the harmony and mutual understanding between their two fathers, Abu Bakr and 'Umar. The difference was that, with the women, 'A'isha was always the instigator and stronger one and would undertake things and would tug Hafsa, the daughter of 'Umar, behind her in everything. Whereas her father, Abu Bakr, was weaker than 'Umar, the instigator and stronger party and would undertake things. We have observed from the previous discussion that even in [the matter of] the Caliphate, Ibn al-Khattab was the actual ruler. Some historians have reported that when 'A'isha decided to leave for Basra to rise against Imam 'Ali in what has become known as the "battle of the Camel", she sent a message to the wives of the Prophet (s), the mothers of the believers, asking them to go with her. None of them responded except Hafsa bint 'Umar, who prepared herself and decided to leave with her. Her brother, 'Abd Allah b. 'Umar, however, stopped and rebuked her, and she cancelled her trip.[14] Allah, the most Glorious had warned 'A'isha and Hafsa jointly in His words: *"If you two support each other against him, Allah is his protector, as well as Gabriel and the righteous believers, and after that the angels too are his supporters."(66:4)* Allah also said: *"You two turn in repentance to Allah, if your hearts are indeed so inclined."(66:4)* Allah provided for both of them a significant parable in Surah al-Tahrim (66), to teach both of them and the rest of the Muslims who believe that the mother of the believers will enter heaven without any reckoning or punishment, simply because she is the wife of the Prophet of Allah (s). Most certainly not! For Allah has informed His servants, male and female, that mere spousal relationship will neither harm nor benefit [a person], even if the husband is the Prophet of Allah (s). What benefits or harms [a person], in the eyes of Allah, are an individual's deeds. Allah said: *"Allah has set forth an example to the disbelievers, the wife of Noah and the wife of Lot. They were both married to two servants from among our righteous servants. They were deceitful to their*

---

[14] Commentary on *Nahj al-Balagha*, Ibn Abi'l-Hadid, 2/80.

husbands. And they profited nothing before Allah due to that. Instead they were told: 'Enter the Fire with those who enter'" (66:10).

Allah cited an example for the believers, the wife of Pharaoh when she said: "O my Lord, build for me a house in paradise, and save me from Pharaoh and his deeds; and save me from the people who do wrong". And Mary, the daughter of Imran who guarded her chastity and We breathed Our spirit into her. She testified to the truth of the words of her Lord and of His scriptures and she was one of the devout [servants]" (66:11-12).

By this it becomes clear to all that spousal relationship and companionship, even though they both have a lot of merits, do not, in themselves, prevent the punishment of Allah unless they are accompanied by righteous deeds. If they are not, punishment is, in fact, increased. Allah's justice dictates that he does not punish the distant one who does not hear the revelation like [he punishes] the close one in whose house the Qur'an was revealed. A man who knows the truth and yet opposes it is like an ignorant person who does not know the truth.

Now, O reader, we will cite a few narrations in some detail so that you may know the personality of this woman who played the greatest role in distancing 'Ali from the Caliphate, and summoned all strength and resources to rise up in arms against him.

It should be further known that the verse of the removal of filth and purification is as remote from her as the sky is from the earth, and that most of the *Ahl al-Sunnah* are the victims of lies and forgery for they follow the Umayyads without realizing it.

'A'isha, Mother of the Believers, testifies against herself

Let us listen to 'A'isha speak about herself and how, due to

Chapter 3: Concerning the ahl al-bayt (as)

jealousy, she lost her sense of probity and conducted herself in the presence of the Prophet (s) without manners. She said: "Safiyya, the wife of the Prophet (s), sent a dish she had made for him when he was with me. When I saw the maidservant, I trembled with rage and fury, and I took the bowl and hurled it away."

She further said: "The Prophet of Allah (s) then looked at me; I saw the anger in his face and I said: 'I seek refuge from Allah's Apostle cursing me today.'" 'A'isha said: "He said: 'Undo it'. I said: 'What is its expiation, O Prophet of Allah (s)?' He said: 'The food like her food, and a bowl like her bowl.'"[15]

And on another occasion, speaking of herself, she said: "I said to the Prophet (s) 'Enough for you about Safiyya is such and such.'[16] The Prophet of Allah (s) said to me: 'You have uttered words which, if they were mixed with the waters of the sea, would color it.'"[17]

Glory be to Allah! How far was the mother of the believers from the ethics and basic rights which Islam has enjoined concerning forbidding of backbiting and slander? No doubt her speech: "Enough for you about Safiyya is such and such" and the response of the Prophet of Allah (s): "You have uttered words which, if they were mixed with the waters of the sea, would color it" shows what 'A'isha said regarding Safiyya was a grave thing and of immense concern.

I believe that the narrators of the *hadith* found it repulsive, but respected her, and therefore changed the words to "so and so" as is their normal practice in such issues.

And here is 'A'isha, the mother of the believers, narrating, once again, of her envy of the [other] mothers of the believers. She said:

---

[15] *Musnad*, Imam Ahmad b. Hanbal, 6/277 & *Sunan*, al-Nasa'i, 2/148.

[16] By this, 'A'isha was trying to disclose Safiyya's faults.

[17] *Sahih al-Tirmidhi*, and al-Zamakhshari has related the *hadith* from him on p.73. in *Al-Kashshaaf*.

"I have never been as jealous of any woman as I have been of Marya. That was because she had beautiful ringlets and the Prophet of Allah (s) was captivated by her. When he first brought her, she used to stay in the house of Haritha b. al-Nu'man. We frightened her and I became concerned. The Prophet of Allah (s) sent her to a higher place and he would visit her there. That was very hard upon us, and then Allah blessed him with a boy through her and we shunned him."[18]

'A'isha's jealousy went beyond the person of Marya, her co-wife and was directed even against Ibrahim, the innocent, newly born suckling baby. She said: "When Ibrahim was born, the Prophet of Allah (s) brought him to me and said: 'Look how much he resembles me'. I said: 'I do not see any resemblance.' The Prophet of Allah (s) said: 'Don't you see how robust and fair he is?'" 'A'isha said: "I said: 'Whoever is fed with the milk of sheep becomes fair and robust.'"[19]

When she was overcome by suspicion and devilish insinuation, her jealousy crossed all boundaries and was beyond the expression of words, leading her to suspect the Prophet of Allah (s). Quite often, she used to pretend to be asleep when the Prophet stayed the night at her house, but, in fact, she would closely observe her husband, spying upon him in the darkness, following behind where he went. Here is a report, in her own words, which was narrated by Muslim in his *Sahih*, and Imam Ahmad in his *Musnad* and other [scholars].

She said: "When it was the night which the Prophet of Allah (s) spent with me, he came in and put away his upper garment, took off his shoes and put them near his feet, then spread out his lower garment over the bed and lay down. He did not stay long until he assumed that I had fallen asleep, whereupon he took his upper

---

[18] Ibn Sa'd, *Tabaqat*, 8/212, Baladhuri, *Ansab al-Ashraf*, 1/449, on the life of Maria the Copt. She was daughter of Muqawqis, the governor of Alexandria, Egypt.

[19] *Ibid*. 1/37, the account of Ibrahim, son of the Prophet, (s). Also in *Ansab al-Ashraf*.

Chapter 3: Concerning the ahl al-bayt (as)

garment quietly and slowly, put on his shoes, opened the door, went out and closed it behind him quietly. I put the upper garment over my head, covered myself, put on my shawl and veil and I followed his tracks until he came to the Baqi cemetery. He stood there for quite a long time, then raised his hands three times, and then turned back. I also turned back. He quickened his pace and I also quickened my pace. He moved faster and I also moved faster and he reached home and I also arrived there. I preceded him and went into the house. No sooner had he entered the house he said: 'What is the matter O 'A'isha, I see that you are dressed up?'" She said: "I said: 'Nothing is the matter.' He said: 'Either you will tell me or the Gracious and Omniscient Lord will inform me.'" 'A'isha said: "I said: 'O Messenger of Allah (s), my mother and my father be sacrificed for you, and I informed him.' He said: 'You were the black figure which I saw in front of me?' I said: 'Yes'. So he pressed me on my chest and it hurt me. He then said: 'Did you think that Allah and His Messenger will be unjust to you?'"[20]

On another occasion, she said: "I lost track of the Prophet of Allah (s), and I suspected that he had gone to another of his wives. I went looking for him and I found him in prostration, saying: 'O My Lord! Forgive me.'"[21] On another occasion, she said: "One night, when he was with me, the Messenger of Allah (s) went out." She said: "I became jealous. When he came and saw what I had done he said: 'What is the matter, O 'A'isha? Are you jealous?' I replied: 'And why should not those like me be jealous of those like you?' The Prophet of Allah (s) then said: 'Has your devil taken possession of you?'" This last narration proves clearly that when she was jealous, she would exceed her bounds and would do strange things like break dishes or tear clothes. Due to that, she says in this report "When he came and saw what I had done, he said: 'Has your devil taken possession of you?'"[22]

---

[20] *Sahih Muslim*, 3/64, "The Chapter on What is Said when Entering the Grave", *Musnad*, Ahmad b. Hanbal, 6/221.

[21] *Musnad*, Imam Ahmad, 6/147.

[22] *Ibid.* 6/115

This last narration proves clearly that when she was jealous, she would exceed her bounds and would do strange things like break dishes or tear clothes. Due to that, she says in this report "When he came and saw what I had done, he said: 'Has your devil taken possession of you?'"

No doubt 'A'isha was quite often overcome or confused by her devil, for he found a way to her heart through jealousy. It has been narrated that the Prophet (s) said: "Jealousy for a man is faith and for a woman disbelief", meaning that a man may get jealous concerning his wife, for it is not, according to law, allowed for him to share her with anyone else. The woman, however, does not have the right to be jealous of her husband, because Allah, Glory be to Him, has allowed him to marry more than one wife. An upright and believing woman who submits to the rulings of Allah, Glory be to Him, accepts her co-wife whole heartedly, especially if her husband is just, upright and fears Allah. [That being the case] how about the leader of humanity, the symbol of perfection, justice and the most noble character?

Furthermore, we find a clear contradiction in the (alleged) special love of the Prophet (s) for 'A'isha, and what the *Ahl al-Sunnah wa'l-Jama'a* say about her being the most beloved and affectionate wife. They [even] report that some of his wives gave up their turn [of visitation] for her when they came to know that the Prophet (s) loved her and could not wait [for her turn]. This being the case, can we find any justification or explanation for 'A'isha's excessive jealousy? One would have assumed that the opposite would have been the case, i.e., that the rest of the wives of the Prophet (s) would have been jealous of 'A'isha due to his intense love for and inclination towards her, according to what they report and claim. If she was pampered by the Prophet of Allah (s), what was the need for the jealousy?

History reports only her traditions, while the biographical works are replete with her praises, [they report] that she was the beloved of the Prophet of Allah (s), and that he could not be separated from her.

Chapter 3: Concerning the ahl al-bayt (as)

I believe that all these [reports] are from the Umayyads who loved 'A'isha and gave her the highest preference when she served their interests. She narrated for them what they loved [to hear], and she fought against their enemy, 'Ali b. Abi Talib.

I also believe that the Prophet of Allah (s) could not love her when she did [things] which we have reported. How could the Prophet (s) love someone who would lie, backbite, slander and would doubt Allah and his Prophet, suspecting them of injustice? How could the Prophet of Allah (s) love someone who spied upon him, going out of her house without his permission to find out where he had gone? How could the Prophet of Allah (s) love someone who, in his presence, insulted his wives even though they were dead? How could the Prophet of Allah (s) love someone who hated his son Ibrahim, and accused his mother Maria of lying?[23] How could the Prophet of Allah (s) love someone who once came between him and his wives by lying, driven by malice, causing him to divorce her?

How could the Prophet of Allah (s) love someone who hated his daughter, al-Zahra, and who hated his brother and cousin, 'Ali b. Abi Talib, to the extent where she could not mention his name and think any good of him?[24] All this and more [occurred] during the life of the Prophet (s), and after his death, [even] more occurred, discuss it without any restraint.

All these deeds are detested by Allah and His Prophet (s), and they do not love those who perpetrate them, for [with] Allah is the truth, and His Messenger (s) is the personification of truth, so it is not possible for him to love one who is against the truth.

We will learn during the forthcoming discussions that the Prophet of Allah (s) did not love her; indeed, he warned the nation

---

[23] This subject is dealt with in the book *Al-Sahih min sirat al-Nabi al-A'zam* on the life of Prophet Muhammad exposing forged hadithes by 'Allama Ja'far al-Murtada al-'Amili.

[24] *Sahih al-Bukhari*, 3/135, "Chapter on The Gift of a man to his wife" in "The book of Giving Gifts and its Merits".

against her seditions.[25]

I once asked some of our teachers the reason for the Prophet's (s) excessive love for 'A'isha, specifically to the exclusion of the other wives. They came up with numerous answers, all of them false:

One of them said: "Because she was beautiful and young, and she was the only virgin he had, for no man had [taken] her before him". Another said: "Because she was the daughter of Abu Bakr, the truthful one, his companion in the cave."

A third said: "Because she memorized half the religion from the Prophet of Allah (s) and was a learned jurist (*faqiha*)." A fourth said: "Because Gabriel came to him in her form, and he never used to visit the Prophet (s) unless he was in her house."

As you can see, O reader, every one of these claims has no basis and is not acceptable to either the intellect or to reality. We will refute these answers with [indubitable] proofs. If the Prophet loved her because she was beautiful and the only virgin that he had, what prevented him from marrying the beautiful virgins who excelled her in charm and beauty, and were the role models among the Arab tribes, and who were at his beck and call? The historians, on the other hand, also mention 'A'isha's jealousy towards Zaynab bint Jahsh, Safiyya bint Huyayy and Maria the Copt, because they were more beautiful than her.

Ibn Sa'd[26] and Ibn Kathir[27] report that the Prophet (s) married Malika bint Ka'b who was known for her outstanding beauty. 'A'isha went to see her and said to her: "Aren't you ashamed to marry your father's killer?" She then sought refuge from the Prophet of Allah (s), whereupon he divorced her. Her people came to him and said: "O Prophet of Allah, she is young and lacking in

---

[25] *Sahih al-Bukhari*, 4/46, "Chapter on what has been reported about the houses of wives of the Prophet" in "The book of Warfare and Campaigns".

[26] Ibn Sa'd, *Tabaqat*, 8/148.

[27] Ibn Kathir, *Tarikh*, 5/299.

perception. She was deceived, so take her back." The Prophet (s) refused to do so. Her father was killed on the day of the conquest of Mecca; his killer was Khalid b al-Walid al-Khandama.

This narration clearly proves that the Prophet of Allah (s) was not concerned with youth and beauty in his marriages, otherwise, he would not have divorced Malika bint Ka'b when she was young and of outstanding beauty. This narration, and others like it, also shows us the methods which 'A'isha adopted in deceiving the innocent believing women, and prohibited them from marrying the Prophet of Allah (s). We have already discussed [how] she caused the divorce of Asma' bint Nu'man, due to her envy of the latter's beauty. She said to her: "The Prophet (s) loves a woman to say to him when he approaches her: 'I seek refuge in Allah from you.'"

Now we have [the case of] Malika, with ('A'isha) instigating in her feelings for her father's death, and that the killer was the Apostle of Allah (s), saying to her: "Aren't you ashamed to marry your father's killer?" What could this poor woman do but seek refuge against the Prophet of Allah (s)? Perhaps she said more than that, at a time when people still had traits of *jahiliyya* in them, which instigated [people] to retaliation and reproached whoever did not exact revenge against his father's killer.

It is now left for us to ask and it only right that we ask, why did the Prophet of Allah (s) divorce these two innocent women, who both fell victim to the plotting and deception of 'A'isha?

Before anything else, we must realize that the Prophet of Allah (s) was infallible, he would not oppress anyone nor do anything which was not right. In divorcing the two women therefore, there must have been some wisdom known to Allah and His Prophet (s). Similarly, in spite of her deeds, there must have been [some] wisdom in him not divorcing 'A'isha. We shall hopefully touch upon this in the forthcoming discussions.

As far as the first woman is concerned, i.e., Asma' bint al-Nu'man; her [naive] disposition became apparent when 'A'isha's tricks captured her, and the first words that she greeted the Prophet of Allah (s) with, when he stretched out his hand to her were: "I seek refuge in Allah from you." Despite her excessive beauty, the Prophet (s) did not let her remain due to her simple mindedness. Along with some other narrators, Ibn Sa'd, in his *Tabaqat*, vol. 8, p. 145, on the authority of Ibn 'Abbas, said: "The Prophet of Allah (s) married Asma' bint al-Nu'man, and she was among the most beautiful and complete [women] of her time." Perhaps the Prophet of Allah (s) wanted to teach us that the importance of intelligence outweighs that of physical beauty, for how many a pretty woman has been led by her foolishness towards corruption?

As for the second woman, i.e., Malika bint Ka'b, who 'A'isha incited by telling her that her husband was her father's killer, the Prophet (s) did not want this poor girl (who was young and lacked perception as her people testified) to live in fear and terror which would cause great problems for her, especially since 'A'isha would never let her live in peace with the Prophet of Allah (s). No doubt there are other reasons known to the Prophet which are not known to us.

The important thing to realize is that the Prophet of Allah (s) did not crave for beauty or physical and sexual desires, as some ignorant persons and Orientalists assume. They claim that Muhammad was preoccupied with beautiful women. We have observed how the Prophet (s) divorced these two women despite their tender age and beauty. They were the most beautiful and complete women of their times, as documented in the historical and *hadith* books.

The claim of those who say that the Prophet (s) loved 'A'isha for her youth and beauty is baseless and unacceptable. As for those who allege that he loved her because she was the daughter of Abu Bakr, this is also untrue. We can say that he married her for Abu Bakr's sake, because the Prophet of Allah (s) married into several tribes for political reasons so as to placate their hearts and foster affection and feelings of mercy between those tribes, replacing rancor and hatred. The Prophet (s) married Umm Habiba, the sister of Mu'awiyah and the daughter of Abu Sufyan, the foremost enemy of the Prophet (s). That was because he harbored no ill feelings, and

Chapter 3: Concerning the ahl al-bayt (as)

[because] he was a mercy to all the worlds. His compassion and love for the Arab tribes led him to marrying Jews, Christians and Copts so that the people of the scriptures could get closer to each other.

This is especially so if we realize, from our readings of the biographical works, that it was Abu Bakr who asked the Prophet (s) to marry his daughter 'A'isha, just as 'Umar had asked him to marry Hafsa. The Prophet (s) accepted these [proposals] because his heart encompassed all mankind.

Allah, the Exalted, says: *"And if you were harsh and severe of heart, they would have deserted you"* (3:159).

If we return to the narration reported by 'A'isha, she said that the Messenger of Allah (s) did not wait for long before he thought she was asleep, then he took his upper garment, slowly opened the door, went out and then closed it, we can perceive the lie of the claim that he could not do without her.[28]

This deduction is not a spontaneous assumption, which I have conjectured. Most certainly not, for they are supported by proofs from the six *Sahih* works. Muslim, like other Sunni *Sahih* works, has reported in his *Sahih* that 'Umar b. al-Khattab said: "When the Prophet (s) separated himself from his wives, I entered the mosque and the people were scratching the ground with stones and saying: 'The Prophet of Allah (s) has divorced his wives.'"

This was before they had been ordered to wear the *hijab*. 'Umar said: "I said: 'I will certainly know that today.' So I went to 'A'isha and said: 'O daughter of Abu Bakr! Have you reached the point of offending the Prophet of Allah (s)?' She replied: 'My [affair] has got nothing to do with you, O son of Khattab! Look at your own defects.'" He continued: "So I called upon Hafsa bint 'Umar and said to her: 'O Hafsa! Have you reached the point of offending the Prophet of Allah (s)? By Allah! You know that the Prophet of Allah (s) does not love you, had it not been for me, he would have

---

[28] *Sahih Muslim*, 3/64, *Musnad* of Imam Ahmad, 6/221.

divorced you.'[29] Whereupon she wept bitterly...."

This narration clearly illustrates for us, without doubt, that the Prophet's (s) marriage to Hafsa was not due to love, but rather, for the political needs that circumstances dictated.

What makes us certain of our deduction is the fact that 'Umar b. al-Khattab swore by Allah that the Prophet of Allah (s) did not love Hafsa. 'Umar further increases our certitude by saying that his daughter also knew this painful truth, for he said to her: "By Allah! You know that the Prophet of Allah does not love you."

Therefore, not even the slightest of doubt is left in our minds about the marriage to her being for political considerations when he said to her: "Had it not been for me, the Prophet of Allah (s) would have divorced you."

This narration also gives us some idea about the Prophet's (s) marriage to 'A'isha bint Abu Bakr, and that, despite all her troubles, he exercised patience and perseverance for the sake of Abu Bakr. Otherwise, Hafsa was more worthy of the love and affection of the Prophet of Allah (s), for she did not do a tenth of the things that 'A'isha, the daughter of Abu Bakr, did to offend the Prophet (s).

If we study the actual events [which occurred], ignoring the spurious narrations which the Umayyads composed on the merits of 'A'isha, we will observe that the Prophet of Allah (s) was, on many occasions, troubled and angered by her. Here we relate a narration which al-Bukhari and several others of the *Ahl al-Sunnah hadith* transmitters have reported. It speaks of the extent of aversion which 'A'isha felt towards her husband, the Prophet of Allah (s).

Al-Bukhari reports in vol. 7 of his *Sahih*, in "The Chapter on the Expression of a Sick Person: 'I am in pain' or 'my head hurts'". He said: "I heard al-Qasim b. Muhammad say: "A'isha said: 'My head

---

[29] *Sahih Muslim*, 4/188, "The Chapter on the Sepration and being away from them, giving them a choise and Allah's words: 'And if you two support each other against him ....".

Chapter 3: Concerning the ahl al-bayt (as)

hurts.' The Prophet (s) said: 'If that were to happen when I am still alive, I would seek Allah's forgiveness for you and would pray for you'. 'A'isha said: 'A likely story! By Allah, I think you would love to see me die. And that if that occurred, you would spend the other part of the day marrying another of your wives.'"[30] Does this narration indicate that the Prophet of Allah (s) loved 'A'isha?

Lastly, we summarize by pointing out that the Banu Umayya, foremost amongst them Mu'awiyah b. Abi Sufyan, hated the Prophet of Allah (s). From the time the Caliphate fell into their hands, they strove to distort the truth and turn everything head over heels. They thus elevated to the zenith of power people who were, during the life of the Prophet (s), ordinary, with no special standing, while they ignored others who were at the acme of honor and nobility during the lifetime of the Prophet (s).

I believe that their sole criterion in according honor or ignoring, was their intense enmity and excessive hatred for Muhammad and the members of his household, 'Ali, Fatima, al-Hasan and al-Husayn. They (the Umayyads) elevated the status, and fabricated false *hadiths*, on the merits of every person who opposed the Prophet (s) and his *Ahl al-Bayt* whom Allah has purified and from whom He removed all abomination. They sought nearness to them (those who opposed the Prophet), accorded them high positions and grants so that they enjoyed favors and respect among the populace. They sought to denigrate, fabricate defects, falsify reports that denied the superiority and merits of anyone who used to love the Prophet (s) and [would] defend him.

Thus 'Umar b. al-Khattab, who used to dispute every command of the Prophet of Allah (s), even accusing the latter of hallucination in his last days, became the hero of Islam amongst the Muslims during the time of the Umayyad dynasty.

On the other hand, 'Ali b. Abi Talib who was, to him, what Aaron was to Moses, and who loved him, and who was loved by Allah and His Prophet, he who was the guardian of every believer,

---

[30] *Sahih al-Bukhari*, 7/8, in "The Book of Sickness and Medicine".

was cursed from the pulpits for eighty years.

Similarly 'A'isha, who caused the Prophet of Allah (s) much torment and disobeyed his instructions and the instructions of her Lord, rose against the successor of the Messenger of Allah and caused the worst strife known to the Muslims, [a strife] which resulted in the death of thousands of Muslims, became the most famous lady in Islam, with religious rulings being accepted from her.

But Fatima al-Zahra (sa), the leader of the women of this world, she for whom the Lord of Glory gets angry if she becomes angry, and she for whom the Lord is happy when she is happy, became a forgotten woman, and was buried in the secrecy of the night, after they had threatened to burn her, after they forced the door of her house against her stomach, causing her to lose her child. Not one amongst the *Ahl al-Sunnah* Muslims knows a single *hadith* which she reported from her father.

Similarly, Yazid b. Mu'awiyah, Ziyad, the son of his father, Ibn Marjana, Ibn Marwan, al-Hajjaj, Ibn al-'As, and others from the accursed evildoers cursed in the text of the Qur'an and by the tongue of the Prophet (s), they became the commanders of the believers and the guardians of their affairs. As for al-Hasan and al-Husayn, the masters of the youths of paradise, the delights of the Prophet of this nation, the Imams from the progeny of the Prophet (s), the custodians of this *ummah*, they were banished, imprisoned, murdered, and poisoned. In this way, Abu Sufyan the hypocrite, the leader in every battle that was waged against the Prophet, came to be praised and thanked, until it was said that whoever entered his house was secure. As for Abu Talib, the protector and defender of the Prophet (s) with all that he had, [who] passed his life in hostility with his people and relatives for the sake of his nephew's call, so much so that he spent three years in the enclave with the Prophet in the valley of Mecca, keeping his belief secret, for the benefit of Islam, so that some bridges were still open with the Quraysh and so that they would not persecute the Muslims as they wished (he was like the believer from the family of Pharaoh who hid his belief), his (Abu Talib's) [supposed] reward was a pair of slippers in the

Chapter 3: Concerning the ahl al-bayt (as)

hellfire, his feet placed into it and his brains popping out from the pain.

In this way, Mu'awiyah b. Abi Sufyan, who was the freed man, son of the freed man, the accursed one, and the son of an accursed one, he who used to play with the injunctions of Allah and His Prophet, not attaching any importance to it, he who used to murder the upright and innocent [ones] so as to pursue his vile goals and [would] revile the Prophet of Allah (s) whilst the Muslims would see and hear,[31] became known as the scribe of revelation. They say that Allah entrusted His revelation to Gabriel, Muhammad and Mu'awiyah. He came to be described as a man of wisdom, political acumen and reflection.

As for Abu Dharr al-Ghifari, the earth did not carry and the sky did not put its shadow on anyone more truthful in his speech than him; he was treated as a mischief monger. He was beaten, exiled and banished to Rabdha. Salman, Miqdad, 'Ammar and Hudhayfa and all the sincere companions who took 'Ali as their leader and followed him, they met with punishment, banishment and murder.

Similarly, those who followed the school of the Caliphs, the followers of Mu'awiyah and the companions of the schools founded by the tyrannical rulers, they became the *Ahl al-Sunnah wa'l-Jama'a* and they represented Islam. Whoever opposed them was judged to be a disbeliever. If only they had followed the Imams of the *Ahl al-Bayt*, the pure ones.

As for those who followed the school of the *Ahl al-Bayt* and followed the gate to the city of knowledge and the first one to accept Islam, he whom the truth revolved around wherever he was, those who followed the *Ahl al-Bayt* and the infallible Imams came to be [seen as] the people of innovation and misguidance, and

---

[31] The poet says in this regard:"They opposed Ahmad and they reviles Ali
They took as their ruler a hypocrite truly nasty;
Yes! They cursed the Prophet silently
When they abused and cursed his brother 'Ali openly".

whoever opposed and fought against them came to be [seen as] a Muslim. Surely there is no power and no strength except with Allah, the Highest, and the most Powerful. Allah surely spoke the truth when He said: *"If it is said to them: 'Make not any mischief on earth,' they say: 'We are the righteous ones.' Certainly they are indeed the corrupt ones but they do not realize it. And if it is said to them: 'Believe as other people have believed' they say: 'Shall we believe as the stupid ones believe'? They are the stupid ones, though they know it not"* (2:13).

If we return to the subject of the Prophet of Allah's (s) [alleged] love for 'A'isha, as she had memorized half the religion from him, and that he used to say: "Take half your religion from this Humayra," [we realise] that this *hadith* is false, it has no basis of truth. Neither is it consonant with the ridiculous and sorrowful rulings that have been reported from 'A'isha. It is not fitting that the Prophet (s) should have mentioned them. It is sufficient for us to refer to the incident of the suckling of an adult, which she used to report from the Prophet of Allah (s), and which was narrated by Muslim in his *Sahih* and by Malik in his *Muwatta.'* We have fully discussed this matter in our book "*To be With the Truthful ones.*" Whoever wishes a detailed account of the matter should refer to it.

It is sufficient for us [to note] regarding this detestable tradition, that all the [other] wives rejected it and refused to act according to it. Even the reporter of the *hadith* remained [silent for] a complete year, scared to mention it, due to its repulsive and shameless nature.

Let us refer to *Sahih al-Bukhari* in the chapter on: "Whoever Leaves his Place of Residence Must Shorten the Prayer." He narrated: "On the authority of al-Zuhri, from 'Urwa, from 'A'isha (r) [who] said: 'The prayer was first decreed as two *rak'at*. Then this ruling was retained for the prayer on journey, and the prayer in residence was made complete.' Al-Zuhri said: 'I said to 'Urwa: 'So how come 'A'isha completes the prayer [during the journey]?' He replied: 'She interpreted [the ruling] as 'Uthman interpreted it.'"

Chapter 3: Concerning the ahl al-bayt (as)

Muslim also reported it in "The Chapter on The Prayer [recited by] the Travelers and Shortening it" in more explicit words than those [expressed] in al-Bukhari. He narrated on the authority of al-Zuhri from 'Urwa from 'A'isha, that: "The prayer was first decreed as two *rak'ats*. Then this ruling was preserved for the prayer during a journey, and the prayer at [a person's town of] residence was made complete." Al-Zuhri said: "I said to 'Urwa: 'So how come 'A'isha [recites the] complete prayer on a journey?' He replied: 'She interpreted [the ruling] as 'Uthman interpreted it.'"

There is a clear contradiction. For she is the one who reports that the prayer of a traveller was decreed as two *rak'ats*, but she opposes what Allah has made obligatory, and what the Prophet of Allah (s) followed, and instead interpreted it so as to change the ruling of Allah and His Prophet, reviving the practice of 'Uthman. Due to this reason, we see a lot of rulings in the *Sahihs* of the *Ahl al-Sunnah wa'l-Jama'a*, but yet they do not follow them, for, in most cases, they adhere to the interpretation of Abu Bakr, 'Umar, 'Uthman, 'A'isha, Mu'awiyah b. Abu Sufyan and other companions.

If al-Humayra, from whom half the religion is supposedly taken, can interpret the rulings of Allah how she wishes, I do not believe that her husband, the Prophet of Allah (s), would be pleased with her and would order the people to follow her. In fact, it has been related in *Sahih al-Bukhari*, Muslim and the other *Sahihs* of the *Ahl al-Sunnah*, that obedience to her is disobedience to Allah. God willing, we will deal with this at its [proper] time.

As for those who say that the Prophet of Allah (s) loved her because Gabriel used to come to him in her form before he married her, and that he only came to him in her house, these narrations would make a mad person laugh. I do not know whether the form which Gabriel came to him was in photographic or oil paint. In fact, the *Sahihs* of the *Ahl al-Sunnah* relate that Abu Bakr sent 'A'isha with a plate of dates to the Prophet (s) so that he could see her, and that he asked the Prophet (s) to marry his daughter. Was there any need then for Gabriel to come in her form when she lived just a few meters away from the residence of the Prophet of Allah (s)? I believe that Marya, the Copt, used to live in the land of Copts, in

Egypt, far away from the Prophet (s), and since no one expected her to come, it was more appropriate that Gabriel descend in her form and to give the Prophet of Allah (s) the good tidings that Allah would give him Ibrahim from her.

These narrations are from the forgeries of 'A'isha who had nothing with which she could take pride over her co-wives except tales which her imagination created. Alternatively, these are due to the forgeries of the Banu Umayyads, and attributed to her, in order to elevate her standing with those of simple minds.

And as for the allegation that Gabriel did not visit Muhammad (s) when he was reclining except in 'A'isha's house, this is worse than the preceding claim, since it is well known from the Qur'an that Allah threatened her when she demonstrated against His Prophet. Allah threatened her with Gabriel, the righteous believers, and the angels would [also] support [the Prophet].

So the claims of our teachers and scholars are mere conjectures and imaginations. "Indeed, conjectures do not lead to the truth. Say: 'Do you have true knowledge with you? Then bring it forth. You follow nothing but conjecture, you merely guess.'"

'A'isha after the Prophet (s)

If we study the life of the mother of the believers, 'A'isha, daughter of Abu Bakr, after her husband met his Supreme Maker, may my soul be sacrificed for him, we find that after the atmosphere had settled and her father had become the Caliph and leader of the Islamic *ummah*, she became the foremost lady of the Islamic state because her husband was the Prophet of Allah (s) and her father was the Caliph of the Prophet of God.

She believed - or rather, she led herself into believing - that she was the best of the Prophet's (s) wives simply because he had married her when she was a virgin, and that he had not married any other virgin. When the Prophet (s) died, she was in the full splendour of her youth and the prime of her life. According to the best known reports, she was eighteen years old at the most when

Chapter 3: Concerning the ahl al-bayt (as)

her husband passed away. She had not lived with the Prophet of Allah (s) for more than six to eight years, according to different reports. She spent the first years of this period playing games that children play whilst she was the wife of the Prophet (s). She was, as Barira, the slave girl of the Prophet of Allah (s), described her: "A young girl, who sleeps leaving the dough (unguarded) that the goats come and eat."[32]

Yes, eighteen years for a girl who has become a teenager as is said today. She had spent half her life with the bearer of Allah's message with nine or ten other co-wives. Yet there was another woman during the lifetime of 'A'isha, whom we have failed to mention, a woman who was harder for 'A'isha [to accept] than all the wives because the love of the Prophet of Allah (s) for this woman transcended all imagination. This woman was Fatima al-Zahra, the daughter of the Prophet (s) through Khadija and step daughter of 'A'isha. Do you know who is Khadija? Khadija, the foremost believer, to whom Gabriel gave *salaams*, and gave her glad tidings of a house [built] for her in paradise, a house which has no noise or trouble.[33]

The Prophet of Allah (s) never lost an opportunity to mention Khadija. This used to tear apart the liver of 'A'isha. Her heart would burn with jealousy, and she would lose control of herself and forget her manners. She would abuse (Khadija) as she liked, with no respect for her husband's feelings. Let us listen to 'A'isha talk about herself, especially concerning Khadija, as al-Bukhari, Ahmad, al-Tirmidhi, and Ibn Maja report. She said: "I have never been as envious of any wife of the Prophet as I have been of Khadija.[34] That

---

[32] *Sahih al-Bukhari*, 3/156; in "The Chapter on the Fair Treatment of the Women Regarding Each Other".

[33] Ibid. 4/231, and *Sahih Muslim*, in "The Chapter on the Merits of Khadija, Mother of the Believers", 7/133.

[34] We have already seen her statement: "I have never been so envious of anyone as I have been of Safiyya" and "I have never been so jealous as I have been of Marya". May Allah guide you, O' 'A'isha. Were any of the wives spared your jealousy an aggravation?

was because of the Prophet's frequent remembrance and praise of her. I said to him: "Why do you mention that old woman of the Quraysh? She who had reddened cheeks that time had destroyed! Certainly Allah has given you [someone] better than her". She said: "The face of the Apostle of Allah (s) changed. I never saw it change like this except when he was receiving revelation. He said: 'No! Allah did not give me better than her. She believed in me when others rejected me. She believed in me when others disbelieved me. She gave me the wealth she had when others deprived me. Allah gave me children through her whereas he did not through the other women.'"

There is no doubt that the retort of the Prophet of Allah (s) refutes the contention of those who allege that 'A'isha was the most beloved and the best of the Prophet's (s) wives. I am convinced too that 'A'isha's jealousy and hatred increased when the Prophet of Allah (s) scolded her with this reprimand and informed her that His Lord had not given him [someone] better than Khadija. Once again, the Prophet (s) teaches us that he did not have any sort of inclination for base desires, and had no inclination towards beauty and virginity, because Khadija (sa) had been previously married twice and was older than him by fifteen years. Despite this, he loved her and never ceased to praise her. By my life, this is the true character of the Prophet of Allah (s), who loved for Allah's sake and hated for Allah's sake. There is a huge difference between this authentic *hadith* and the forged one which claims the Prophet preferred 'A'isha, so much so that his wives sent to him [someone] imploring him to show fairness with regard to the daughter of Abu Quhafa.

Dare we ask 'A'isha, *Umm al-Mu'minin*, who never saw Khadija for a single day in her life nor ever met her, how did she know that she was an old woman with red cheeks? Is this the conduct of the average believer who is forbidden to speak ill of anyone in their absence if that person is alive? How about if that person is dead and has been taken up to the Lord? And how [severe is the crime] if the person being backbit is the wife of the Prophet (s), the lady in whose house Gabriel came down and gave her the tidings of a house in paradise, a house without noise or trouble?[35]

Certainly, the hatred and envy for Khadija that was kindled in 'A'isha's heart had to have an outlet; otherwise they would have exploded inside her. 'A'isha did not find anyone [on whom to vent her fury] except Fatima, Khadija's daughter, and her ('A'isha's) stepdaughter, who was, according to various reports, about her own age or a little older.

The deep love that the Prophet of Allah (s) felt for Khadija was certainly rooted and strengthened in his daughter, his unique one, Fatima al-Zahra. She was the only one who lived with her father and carried within her the qualities which the Prophet used to love in Khadija; he used to call her "the mother of her father".

'A'isha's envy was further increased when she saw the Messenger of Allah (s) extolling [the virtues of] his daughter, calling her the leader of the women of the world and leader of the women in paradise[36]. Furthermore, Allah bestowed to him, through her, the two masters of the youths of paradise, al-Hasan and al-Husayn. She saw that the Prophet of Allah (s) used to sleep at Fatima's place, watching over the upbringing of his grandchildren. He used to say: "My two children here are my fragrance of this *ummah*," and he used to carry them on his shoulders. This further added to her envy, as she was barren. Her envy increased until it covered Fatima's husband, the father of al-Hasan and al-Husayn. This was for no other reason than the love that the Prophet of Allah (s) showed towards him, preferring him above her father Abu Bakr in all places. There is no doubt that she was living through fateful times.

She saw that the son of Abu Talib way excelled her father on every occasion and that the Prophet (s) continued to love him and preferred him above everyone else. She also knew that her father had returned in defeat with the forces who were with him on the day of Khaybar, and that the Prophet (s) was pained by this and

---

[35] *Sahih al-Bukhari*, 4/231. *Sahih Muslim*, in "The Chapter on the Merits of Khadija, *Umm al-Mu'minin*".

[36] *Sahih al-Bukhari*, 4/209, 7/142.

said: "I will give the standard tomorrow to a man who loves Allah and his Prophet, and who Allah and his Prophet love, [a man] who will be steadfast and will not flee." That man was 'Ali b. Abu Talib, the husband of Fatima. After 'Ali had captured Khaybar, he returned with Safiyya bint Huyayy who the Prophet (s) married. This descended like a flash of lightning upon the heart of 'A'isha.

She also knew that the Prophet of Allah (s) had sent her father to proclaim the *Surah al-Bara'at* (chapter 9) to the pilgrims, but then had sent 'Ali after him, to take [the responsibility] from him. Her father returned in tears and asked the reason for this action, whereupon the Prophet of Allah (s) responded: "Allah commanded me that none should proclaim [this] except me or someone from my *Ahl al-Bayt.*"

She also knew that the Prophet (s) had appointed his cousin, 'Ali, as the Caliph over the Muslims after him and had ordered his companions and his wives to congratulate him for this leadership over the believers. Her father was among the first people to say: "Congratulations, Congratulations to you, O son of Abu Talib. You have become and will remain the guardian of every believing man and woman."

She also knew that the Prophet (s) had put in command over her father a youth with no hair [growing] on his cheek, for he was only seventeen years old, yet he commanded him to go on military expeditions under his leadership and to pray behind him.

There is no doubt that 'A'isha was influenced by these events. Deep inside she was concerned for her father, and his competing for the Caliphate, and the conspiracy that was among the leaders of the Quraysh. Her envy and hatred for 'Ali and Fatima grew; she tried her best to intervene at all costs to change the situation to her father's advantage. We have seen how she sent for her father, supposedly on behalf of her husband, ordering him to lead the people in prayer, after she learnt that the Prophet of Allah (s) had summoned 'Ali for this duty. When the Prophet (s) learnt of this plot, he was forced to come out, remove Abu Bakr from his place and lead the people in prayer while he was sitting. He was angry at

'A'isha and said to her: "You women are like the companions of Yusuf (meaning that their plots were great)."[37]

A researcher of this event will find clear contradictions in several different and discordant reports. The Prophet had called her father to join the army and commanded him to embark under the leadership of Usama b. Zayd three days before that prayer. It is known logically that the leader of the army also leads the prayer. Usama b. Zayd therefore was the Imam of Abu Bakr on that expedition. 'A'isha sensed this disdain and understood the Prophet's motive, especially as he had not drafted 'Ali b. Abi Talib into that army in which even the notable emigrants and Ansars, leaders and people of stature from the Quraysh, had been drafted.

She further perceived, as did most of the companions, from the Prophet (s) that his days were numbered. She possibly shared 'Umar b. al-Khattab's view that the Prophet had now begun to hallucinate, not knowing what he did. Her burning envy incited her to behave in the way she wished, elevating the status and esteem of Abu Bakr against his rival, 'Ali. Because of all this, she denied that the Prophet of Allah (s) had appointed 'Ali as his successor. Therefore she tried to convince the simple minded people that the Prophet (s) had died in her chambers lying between her lungs and chest. She narrated that the Prophet (s) said to her when he was ill: "Call your father and brother to me so that I may write a behest for them, maybe someone might make an allegation which Allah and His Prophet and the believers will refute unless it is [in favor of] Abu Bakr." Did anyone ask her as to what prevented her from summoning them?

'A'isha's position against 'Ali, the Commander of the Faithful

The researcher of her views regarding Abu'l-Hasan finds a strange, surprising thing. There is no explanation for it except her envy and enmity to the household of the Prophet. History has recorded her incomparable hatred and malice towards Imam 'Ali. She reached the point where she was not even able to utter his

---

[37] Commentary on *Nahj al-Balagha*; Ibn Abi'l-Hadid. 9/197, reporting from Imam 'Ali.

name,[38] not able to stand the sight of him. When she heard that the people had paid allegiance to him for the Caliphate after the murder of 'Uthman, she said: "I wished that the skies had become like the earth before 'Ali had attained it." She exerted every effort into causing problems for him, leading troops against him to wage a war of insurrection, and when the news of his death reached her, she prostrated in thanks to Allah.

Like me, are you not surprised at the *Ahl al-Sunnah wa'l-Jama'a* who report in their *Sahihs* that the Prophet of Allah (s) said: "O 'Ali! none but a true believer loves you, and none but a hypocrite hates you".[39] Then they also report in their *Sahihs, Musnads* and history books that 'A'isha hated Imam 'Ali so much that she could not mention his name. Is this not a testimony from them regarding the nature of the woman? Just as al-Bukhari has reported in his *Sahih* that the Prophet of Allah (s) said: "Fatima is a part of me. Whoever angers her angers me, and whoever angers me angers Allah."[40] Then al-Bukhari himself relates that Fatima died whilst she was angry with Abu Bakr, not speaking to him to the time she died.[41]

Are these traditions not [enough] testimony from them that Allah and His Prophet are both angry at Abu Bakr? This is what all intelligent people understand. I always say, therefore, that the truth will surface, no matter how much the falsifiers try to hide it, no matter how much the helpers of the Umayyads try to misrepresent and fabricate it. For the proof of Allah is evident upon His servants from the day of the revelation of the Qur'an until the final hour [of reckoning]. Praise be to Allah, the Lord of all the worlds.

Imam Ahmad reports that Abu Bakr once came to the Prophet of Allah (s), and sought permission to enter. Before he went in, he heard 'A'isha's voice raised, saying to the Prophet (s): "By Allah! I

---

[38] *Sahih al-Bukhari,* 1/162, 3/135, 5/140.

[39] *Sahih Muslim,* 1/61, *Sahih Tirmidhi* 5/306, *Sunan,* al-Nasa'i, 8/116.

[40] *Sahih al-Bukhari,* 4/210.

[41] *Ibid.* 5/82, 8/3.

Chapter 3: Concerning the ahl al-bayt (as)

surely know that 'Ali is dearer to you than me and my father", she repeated this twice or three times."⁴²

'A'isha's hatred for Imam 'Ali was so much that she always tried to distance him from the Prophet (s) whenever she could find the means to do so. The Mu'tazili Ibn Abi al-Hadid, in his commentary on the *Nahj al-Balagha* said the Prophet of Allah (s) beckoned to 'Ali to come close. He came close until he sat between him and 'A'isha, and he and the Prophet (s) were clung together. She said to him: "Can you not find a seat for this one except [on] my thigh?"

He also narrated that one day the Prophet of Allah (s) was walking with Imam 'Ali and the conversation became prolonged. 'A'isha approached as she was walking from behind until she came between them saying: "What is it between you two that you are taking so long?" Upon this the Prophet of Allah (s) became angry.⁴³

It is also reported that she once came upon the Prophet (s) whilst he was conversing quietly with 'Ali. She screamed and said: "What is it with you and me, O son of Abu Talib? I have [just] one day with the Prophet of Allah (s)." Thereupon the Prophet (s) became angry.

How often did she anger the Prophet (s) with her conduct, which arose due to her intense jealousy and furious nature and her offensive words? Would the Prophet (s) be pleased with any believing man or woman whose heart was filled with hatred and malice towards his cousin, the leader of his progeny, he of whom he said: "He loves Allah and His Prophet, and Allah and His Prophet love him?"⁴⁴ He also said about him: "Whoever loves 'Ali has loved me and whoever hates 'Ali has hated me."⁴⁵

---

⁴² *Musnad*, Imam Ahmad b. Hanbal, 4/275.

⁴³ The commentary to *Nahj al-Balaghah*, Ibn Abi'l-Hadid. 9/195.

⁴⁴ *Sahih al-Bukhari* and *Muslim*, in "The merit of 'Ali b. Abi Talib"; 7/130.

⁴⁵ *Al-Mustadrak*, al-Hakim. 3/130. Authenticated according to the standard set by al-Bukhari and Muslim, and tens of other sources.

And remain in your houses and do not venture forth

Allah, Glory be to Him, ordered the wives of the Prophet (s) to remain in their houses and not to go out from them, displaying their ornaments. He also ordered them to read the Qur'an, to undertake the prayer, to pay *zakat* and to obey Allah and His Apostle (s).

All the wives of the Prophet of Allah (s) obeyed the injunctions of Allah, and the commands of His Prophet, who forbade and warned them before he died: "Which one of you will ride the camel and have the dogs of al-Haw'ab bark at her?" All of them [obeyed] with the exception of 'A'isha. She disobeyed all his orders and scoffed at all the warnings. Historians relate that Hafsa bint 'Umar wanted to go with her (for the battle of the Camel). But her brother, 'Abd Allah reproached her and recited the [aforementioned] verse to her. Hafsa then cancelled her plans. 'A'isha, however, rode the camel and the dogs of al-Haw'ab barked at her. Taha Husayn says in his book "*The Great Sedition*" (*al-Fitna al-Kubra*): "On her route, 'A'isha passed by some water and some dogs barked at her. She asked about the water and was told that it was al-Haw'ab. She was greatly shocked and said: 'Take me back! Take me back! I have heard the Prophet of Allah (s) saying while he was with his wives: 'Which one of you will the dogs of al-Haw'ab bark at? 'Abd Allah b. Zubayr came, having been instructed to pacify her, bringing fifty men from the Banu 'Amir who falsely swore that the water was not that of al-Haw'ab."

I believe that this narration was fabricated during the time of the Banu Umayya to reduce the severity of *Umm al-Mu'minin*'s disobedience, thinking that *Umm al-Mu'minin* would be exonerated after her nephew, 'Abd Allah b. al-Zubayr, deceived her, coming with fifty men who swore by God and gave false testimony that the water was not that of al-Haw'ab. It is truly a foolish joke; they wanted to delude, through such reports, those of shallow perception and to convince them that 'A'isha was fooled because, when she passed the water and heard the barking of the dogs, and enquired about the water, it was said that they were at al-Haw'ab. She was distressed and said: "Take me back! Take me back."

Do the idiots who forged this narration search for an excuse for

Chapter 3: Concerning the ahl al-bayt (as)

'A'isha's disobedience of the order of Allah, and what was revealed in the Qur'an regarding the incumbency for her to stay in her house? Or do they seek for an excuse for her disobedience to the order of the Prophet of Allah (s) to stay within her house and the prohibition of riding a camel before arriving at the well of al-Haw'ab, the watering place of the barking dogs? Do they find an excuse for *Umm al-Mu'minin*, after she rejected the advice of *Umm al-Mu'minin* Umm Salama? Historians have recorded the incident in which she said to her: "Do you remember the day the Prophet of Allah (s) proceeded and we were with him and he turned left from [a place called] Qadid and sat alone with 'Ali and whispered to him for a long time? You wanted to force yourself on them; I tried to prevent you, but you disobeyed me and intruded. It wasn't long before you returned in tears. I asked: 'What happened to you?' And you replied: 'I approached them and they were in conversation, so I said to Ali: 'I get with the Prophet of Allah one day out of nine, so can you not, O son of Abu Talib, leave me with him on my day?' The Messenger of Allah came towards me and he was red with anger, and said: 'Go back! By Allah, none except those who have abandoned faith can hate him.' I returned repentant and sad.'" 'A'isha said: "Yes, I remember that."

Umm Salama continued: "I will also remind you too that you and I were with the Prophet of Allah and he said to us: 'Which one of you will be the rider of the trained camel, at whom the dogs of Haw'ab will bark, and she will have deviated from the right path?' We said: 'We seek refuge from Allah and His Prophet from that.' He touched your back and said: 'Don't be that one, O Humayra.'" 'A'isha said: "I remember that." Umm Salama said: "Do you not remember that day when your father came with 'Umar, so we put on our veils. They came in and spoke about what they wanted to, until they said: 'O Prophet of Allah (s) we do not know how long you will be with us. If only you were to tell us who will succeed you as Caliph over us, so that there will be after you a place we can turn to.' He said to them: 'As for me, I have seen his position [infront of you]. Were I to do this, you would all fall into disunity as the Israelites dispersed from Aaron.' They remained quiet and left. After they had departed, we came out to the Prophet of Allah and you said to him, as you were more forthcoming with him than all of us: 'O Messenger of Allah who did you appoint as Caliph over them?' He said: 'The wearer of the mended shoe.' We went out and we saw it was 'Ali. You said: 'O Prophet of Allah, I do not see anyone apart from 'Ali'. He replied: 'He is the one.'" 'A'isha said: "Yes, I remember that." Umm Salama said to her: "So then, 'A'isha, how can you go ahead after this"? She replied: "I venture forth to reconcile the people."[46]

Umm Salama sought to prevent her from the uprising, using strong words, saying: "The pillars of Islam, if they lean, are not set erect by women; and if they crack, are not joined by women. The praiseworthy things for women are lowering their gazes and protecting their chastity. What would you say if the Messenger of Allah (s) appeared before you in one of these deserts and finds you driving your camel from one watering place to another? By Allah, if I were to embark upon this journey of yours, then it was said to me: 'Enter paradise' I would be ashamed to face Muhammad after having thrown off the veils he has placed upon me."[47]

Just as *Umm al-Mu'minin* 'A'isha did not accept the advice of many sincere companions, al-Tabari in his history related that: "Jariya b. Quddama al-Sa'di said to her: 'O mother of the believers, by Allah, the murder of 'Uthman is less despicable than you going out on this accursed camel from your house and bearing arms. Allah has imposed on you the veil and sanctity you have destroyed your cover and defiled your respect. Surely, whoever sees your uprising sees your destruction. If you come to us obeying, then go back to your house. If you have come to us in coercion, then seek the help of the people.'"[48]

The mother of the believers was the leader

Historians have recorded that she was the general leader,

---

[46] Commentary on the *Nahj al-Balaghah*, Ibn Abi'l-Hadid. 2/77.

[47] Ibn Qutayba in *"Kitab al-Musanif fi Gharib al-Hadith"* in *Al-Imama wa al-Siyasa* (The Leadership and Politics).

[48] *Tarikh Tabari*, 6/482.

Chapter 3: Concerning the ahl al-bayt (as)

supervising, separating [people] and issuing commands. Even when Zubayr and Talha argued as to who should lead the prayer, and when both of them wanted to lead, 'A'isha intervened and removed them both and ordered 'Abd Allah b. Zubayr, her nephew, to lead the people in prayer.

She would dispatch messengers with letters which she sent to several regions, requesting their assistance against 'Ali b. Abi Talib and urging them with the *jahili* zeal. She even recruited twenty thousand or more rabble and greedy Arabs to fight and depose the Commander of the Faithful. Her urging resulted in zealous discord, where large numbers of people were killed in the name of defending and aiding the mother of the believers. The historians say that when the companions of 'A'isha came to 'Uthman b. Hanif, the governor of Basra, they took him along with seventy of his officers who were in charge of the public treasury as prisoners. They brought them to 'A'isha who ordered that they be put to death. They were slaughtered as sheep are slaughtered. It is [even] reported there were 400 men in all and that they were the first Muslims whose heads were cut off whilst they were patient.[49]

Al-Sha'bi reported from Muslim b. Abi Bakra from his father: "When Talha and Zubayr reached Basra, I put on my sword as I wanted to help them. I visited 'A'isha, she was ordering, prohibiting; she was in command. I remembered a *hadith* from the Prophet of Allah (s) which I used to hear him say: 'A community which has its affairs administered by a woman will never succeed.' I [therefore] withdrew from them and left them."

Al-Bukhari has reported from Abi Bakra: "Allah benefited me by a word during the days of the [battle of the] Camel. For when the Prophet (s) heard that the Persians had made the daughter of Chosroes their Queen, he said: 'The people that have their affairs administered by a woman will never succeed.'"[50]

---

[49] *Tarikh Tabari*, 5/178, *Sharh Nahj al-Balaghah*, 2/501 and others.

[50] *Sahih al-Bukhari*, 8/97, "The Chapter on Sedition" *Sunan* Al-Nasa'i, 4/305, *al-Mustadrak*, 4/525.

One of the things that makes us laugh and weep at one time is that 'A'isha, *Umm al-Mu'minin,* went out of her residence in disobedience to Allah and His Prophet and then ordered the companions to remain in their houses. This is surely a strange thing. How, dear Lord, could this occur?

The Mu'tazili Ibn Abi'l-Hadid, in the commentary on the *Nahj al-Balagha,* reported, along with historians, that 'A'isha sent a letter when she was in Basra to Zayd b. Sawhan al-'Abdi in which she said to him: "From 'A'isha, the mother of the believers, daughter of Abu Bakr, the truthful one, wife of the Prophet. To her devoted son, Zayd b. Sawhan. Remain at home and make the people abandon the son of Abu Talib. I hope to hear what I would love from you, since you are the most trustworthy of my family...Wasalaam."

This righteous man replied to her thus: "From Zayd b. Sawhan to 'A'isha bint Abi Bakr: Allah issued a commandment to you and He also issued a commandment to us. He ordered you to remain in your residence, and He ordered us to fight. Your letter has come to me instructing me to do contrary to what Allah has ordered me to do, [You have asked me] to do what Allah has ordered you to do and that you do what Allah has asked me to do. Your order to me is [something] that I cannot obey, therefore there is no reply [necessary] to your letter."

From this, it becomes clear to us that 'A'isha was not content with leading the army of the Camel, but rather, she craved for absolute control over the believers in all the corners of the land. In all matters, she would command Talha and al-Zubayr, who had been nominated for the Caliphate by 'Umar. Due to this, she made it lawful for herself to correspond with the chiefs of the tribes and with the governors, enticing them and seeking their help.

Due to this, she attained the status and fame among the Banu Umayyads, to the point where she became the protégé and the source of reverence for all of them, and [she became one] whose power and rebuke they all feared.

If the heroes and men, famous for their courage, abandon and flee from the lines of battle [when] facing 'Ali b. Abi Talib and would not stand in front of him, she stood, inciting, screaming and arousing [the people].

The mind is perplexed at all of this, the historians are bewildered, for they knew her stance in the smaller battle of the Camel before the arrival of Imam 'Ali, and in the greater battle of the Camel after the arrival of Imam 'Ali. [They all know that] he summoned her to the book of Allah and that she refused, obstinately insisting on the battle. There is no explanation [for this], unless we understand the depth and extent of the envy and hatred which the mother of the believers felt towards her children, who were devoted to Allah and his Messenger.

The Prophet's (s) warning against 'A'isha and her sedition

The Prophet (s) sensed the depth and danger of the schemes that revolved around him from all sides. No doubt he knew the influence and discord women could generate on the men, as he also knew that their plot was great enough to almost move mountains. He knew specifically that his wife, 'A'isha, was the instigator of the dangerous role because of the hatred and rancor that she felt towards his successor 'Ali in particular and his family in general. How could he not know, when he lived observing her role and her enmity towards them? He sometimes got angry; sometimes his face would change color and he would try to placate her at all times, informing her that one who loved 'Ali loved Allah, and the one who hated 'Ali was a hypocrite, whom Allah hated. Unfortunately those *hadiths* do not permeate the depth of those souls which never accept the truth to be true, unless it be for her ('A'isha's) benefit, and they do not recognize anything to be correct unless it comes from her.

As a result, the Prophet of Allah (s) was patient when he realised that she was the test that Allah had sent to the *ummah,* to examine it as He had tested the previous nations. *"Do the people think that they will be left alone when they say: 'We believe' and they will not be tested"* (29:2).

The Prophet of Allah (s) warned the *ummah* against her on

several occasions. He even stood one day and pointed towards her house saying: "From there is the mischief, from there is the mischief from where the horns of the devil will rise." Al-Bukhari has reported in his *Sahih*, in "The Book Concerning the Houses of the Wives of the Prophet (s)," on the authority of Nafi' b. 'Abd Allah (r) who said: "The Prophet (s) stood up, addressing [the people] and pointed towards the residence of 'A'isha and said three times: 'From there is mischief from where the horns of the devil will arise.'"[51]

Muslim has also related in his *Sahih* from Ikrima b. 'Ammar from Salim from Ibn 'Umar who said: "The Prophet of Allah (s) emerged from the house of 'A'isha and said: 'The pivot of disbelief is from here, where the horns of Satan will rise.'"[52]

There is no need to pay attention to the additions they have made [to the *hadith*] by their explanation: "That means the east." This is clearly a fabrication to dilute [the accusation against] the mother of the believers and to remove any accusation against her.

Al-Bukhari also reported: "When Talha, al-Zubayr and 'A'isha travelled to Basra, 'Ali sent 'Ammar b. Yasir and al-Hasan b. 'Ali who met us in Kufa. They ascended the pulpit, with al-Hasan ascending to the top while 'Ammar was standing below al-Hasan. We gathered towards him. I heard 'Ammar say: "'A'isha has journeyed to Basra and, by Allah, she is the wife of your Prophet (s) in this life and in the hereafter; but Allah, the most blessed and exalted, is now testing you [to see] whom you obey, Him or her.'"[53]

Allah is the Greatest. This *hadith* also indicates that obedience to her is disobedience to Allah, and to oppose and disobey her is to obey Allah. We can also note in the *hadith*, that the Umayyad narrators have added the phrase "and the hereafter" when saying "she is the wife of your Prophet in this life and the hereafter" so that they may lead the masses into thinking that Allah has forgiven her

---

[51] *Sahih al-Bukhari*, 4/46.

[52] *Sahih Muslim*, 8/181.

[53] *Sahih al-Bukhari*, 8/97.

Chapter 3: Concerning the ahl al-bayt (as)

every sin she committed, and allowed her to enter His heaven, and her husband is His beloved Prophet of Allah (s). Otherwise, how did 'Ammar know that she will be his wife in the hereafter?

This is another trick which the falsifiers of *hadith* narrators resorted to during the time of the Banu Umayya. When they found that a *hadith* was widespread amongst the people, and there was no way to deny or refute it, they decided to add a paragraph or words, or to change some phrases so as to dampen the impact [of the *hadith*] or to [make it] lose its intended meaning. Just as they did with the *hadith*: "I am the city of knowledge and 'Ali is its gate," they added: "and Abu Bakr is its foundation, 'Umar its walls and 'Uthman its roof."

This [trick] is not hidden to the objective researchers who refute these additions which, most of the time, indicate the lack of intelligence of the falsifiers and their lack of wisdom and light of the Prophetic traditions. For they can observe the saying that Abu Bakr is it's foundation means the knowledge of the Prophet (s) is derived from the knowledge of Abu Bakr, and this is disbelief. Likewise, the statement 'Umar is its walls means 'Umar prevents people from entering the city, i.e., prevents them from getting to the knowledge. The saying 'Uthman is its roof is necessarily absurd since there is no city which has a roof, this is impossible. The researchers note too that 'Ammar swore by Allah that 'A'isha is the wife of the Prophet (s) in this world and in the hereafter. This is a shot in the dark. How could 'Ammar take an oath about something he did not know? Did he have a verse from the book of God? Or was it a covenant promised to him by the Prophet (s)?

So we are now left with the true *hadith*, i.e., that 'A'isha travelled to Basra, and that she is the wife of your Prophet, but Allah is testing you through her to know whether you obey Him or her.

All praise is due to the Lord of the Worlds, who has given us intelligence through which we can differentiate between the truth and falsehood, and has made clear to us the [right] path and then tested us by several things so that they can bear witness on the Day of Judgment.

Conclusion

The important thing from what we have covered in our discussion, although in a concise manner, is that 'A'isha, the daughter of Abu Bakr, the mother of the believers and wife of the Prophet of Allah (s), was not counted amongst the *Ahl al-Bayt* from whom Allah removed all abomination and purified completely. He preserved them from all errors and purified them from every kind of filth. Due to this, they became infallible.

Suffice it to say that 'A'isha spent the last days of her life in tears and wailing, sadness and repentance, remembering her acts with her eyes full of tears. Maybe Allah will forgive her errors, for He alone knows the secrets of his servants and knows the truth of their intentions. He knows the deception of the eyes and what is hidden in the hearts. Nothing in the world nor in the sky is hidden from Allah, and it is not for us or for any person to pass the judgement of heaven or hell for His creatures. This is an imposition and intrusion on Allah. The exalted one says: *"All that is in the heavens and the earth belongs to Allah. Whether you exhibit what is in your souls or hide it, Allah will [make you] account for it. He forgives whomsoever He wishes and punishes whomsoever He wishes. Allah has Power over everything"* (2:284).

Based on this, it is not for us to be pleased with her or to curse her. We cannot, however, follow her nor [can we] condone her deeds. We speak of all this so as to enlighten the people about the truth; maybe they will be guided on the right path.

The Commander of the Faithful, Imam 'Ali said: "Do not be amongst those who curse and swear, but rather say: 'They did so and so, for this is more potent as a proof.'"

What the Ahl al-Dhikr believe about the Ahl al-Bayt

The Imam, Commander of the Faithful (as), master of the progeny of the Prophet (s), said: "By Allah! I have learnt the

Chapter 3: Concerning the ahl al-bayt (as)

proclamation of the messages, the fulfillment of promises and perfection of words. With us, the *Ahl al-Bayt*, are the doors of wisdom and the lights of all things.[54] Where are those who claim that they, instead of us, are deeply rooted in knowledge? They do so lying and rebelling against us. Allah has elevated us and degraded them, and has bestowed upon us and deprived them, made us enter and expelled them. It is through us that guidance is sought and blindness removed. Certainly, the Imams will be from the Quraysh, they have been planted in the line of Hashim. The Imamate is not right for others, neither is it for the governors to the exclusion of others."[55]

"We are the close ones and the companions, the treasures and the doors. Houses are not entered except by their doors; whosoever enters them in any other way is called a thief." Then he mentioned the *Ahl al-Bayt* and said: "Within them is the nobility of the Qur'an, and they are the treasures of the Merciful one. When they speak they utter the truth, and when they are silent, none should speak before they do."[56]

"They are the life of knowledge and death of ignorance; their forbearance tells you of their knowledge and their silence the wisdom of their speaking. They do not go against the truth nor do they differ about it. They are the pillars of Islam and the asylums of protection. Through them the truth has returned to its rightful position, falsehood has vanished and its tongue severed from its root. They have understood religion attentively and carefully, not from hearsay or from relaters, because the relaters of knowledge are many, but few observe it.

His progeny is the best of progenies and his family the best of families. His tree is the best of trees, grown in sanctity and excelled in generosity, for them are long branches and fruits that cannot be reached.

---

[54] *Nahj al-Balaghah*, with commentary by Muhammad 'Abduh, p.283.

[55] *Ibid.* p 314.

[56] *Ibid.* p 330.

We are the tree of prophethood, the station of divine message and the place where angels visit. We are the mines of knowledge, the fountain-heads of wisdom. Those who support and love us, can expect mercy, our enemies and one who hates us, await the wrath [of God].[57]

We are the noble ones, and our progeny is the progeny of the Prophets. Our party is the party of Allah, the most Glorious and Majestic. The rebellious group is the party of Satan. Whoever equates us with our enemy is not from us."

"Where do you go and how [much] do you lie? The standards are raised and the signs clear. The minarets have been erected, so where are you wandering? How can you wander blindly, when among you is the progeny of the Prophet (s) and they are the pillars of truth, standards of religion, the truthful tongues? Accord to them the same position as you do to the Qur'an and come to them as thirsty camels approach water springs.

O people take it from the seal of the Prophets (s), that he who dies from amongst us is not dead, and he who decays from amongst us does not really decay. Do not say what you do not understand, because most of the truth lies in what you deny. Accept the argument of one against whom you have no argument. It is me. Did I not act according to the weightier thing (the Qur'an) and did I not leave for you the less weighty thing (the descendants of the Prophet) and did I not fix for you the standard of faith?"[58]

"Examine the *Ahl al-Bayt* of your Prophet and follow their character and footsteps and they will never lead you astray. They will never make you return to destruction; if they lie down, then you lie down, and if they arise, then you arise. Do not precede them otherwise you will go astray. Do not lag behind them as you will be ruined."[59]

---

[57] *Ibid.* 2/213.

[58] *Nahj al-Balagha*, 1/155.

[59] *Nahj al-Balagha*, 1/190.

Chapter 3: Concerning the ahl al-bayt (as)

These are the words of Imam 'Ali (as), especially regarding the purified household from whom Allah has removed all filth and purified thoroughly.

If we followed the speech of his progeny (as) who delivered the sermons to the people, for example Imam al-Hasan, Imam al-Husayn, Zayn al-'Abidin, Ja'far al-Sadiq, and Imam al-Rida (as), we find them all saying the same thing and rejecting the same object, guiding the people at every time and place to the book of Allah and to the family of the Prophet of Allah (s) so as to save them from error and to bring them towards guidance.

I would add that history is the best witness to the infallibility of the *Ahl al-Bayt*. Nothing but knowledge, piety, virtue, asceticism, generosity, nobility, forbearance and forgiveness has been recorded about them. [They were also known] for every deed that Allah and His Prophet love.

History is also the best witness that the righteous ones from this *ummah* and the Sufi ascetics and shaykhs of the different paths, the Imams of the different schools and the upright past and contemporary scholars all profess to their excellence and superiority in knowledge and deeds, and place them closest to the Prophet of Allah (s) in nearness and honor.

Therefore, it is not proper for a Muslim to mix the wives of the Prophet (s) with the *Ahl al-Bayt*, those from whom Allah has removed all filth and purified them thoroughly, and those whom the Prophet gathered under his cloak.

Do you not see that the Imams of the *hadith*, scholars like Muslim and al-Bukhari, al-Tirmidhi, Imam Ahmad, al-Nasa'i and others, when relating *hadiths* of merits in their books and their *Sahih* works, differentiate between the merits of the *Ahl al-Bayt* and [those of] the wives of the Prophet?[60]

Muslim reports in his *Sahih*, on the merits of 'Ali b. Abi Talib,

---

[60] *Sahih Muslim*, 7/130.

from Zayd b. Arqam that the Prophet of Allah (s) said: "I am leaving behind [me] two weighty things among you. One of them is the book of Allah, Glorified and Honored be He. It is the rope of Allah and whoever follows it is guided right and whoever abandons it is misguided".

Then he said: "And my *Ahl al-Bayt.* I remind you in Allah's name of my *Ahl al-Bayt.* I remind you in Allah's name of my *Ahl al-Bayt,* I remind you in Allah's name of my *Ahl al-Bayt.*" We asked: "Are his wives amongst the *Ahl al-Bayt?*" He (Zayd b. Arqam) replied: "No! By Allah, a woman remains with a man for a while then [when] he divorces her, she returns to her father and her people. The *Ahl al-Bayt* are his roots, his group to whom *sadaqa* is forbidden after him".[61]

Similarly, the testimony of al-Bukhari and Muslim has come to us that 'A'isha is from the family of Abu Bakr and not from the family of the Prophet, in the incident of the verse of *tayammum.*[62]

So why this persistence by some obstinate persons who attempt to revive discord at any price and to distort the truth of which there is no doubt? They curse the Shi'as only because they do not accord this distinguished position to *Umm al-Mu'minin* 'A'isha. Why don't they curse their own *Sahihs* and scholars who exclude the wives of the Prophet from the *Ahl al-Bayt?* **"O You who believe! Fear Allah and say that which is correct, so that He may make your deeds pure and forgive your sins. Whoever obeys Allah and His Prophet has surely succeeded" (33:71).**

---

[61] *Ibid.* 7/123. "The Chapter on The Merits of Ali b. Abi Talib".

[62] *Sahih al-Bukhari,* 6/86; *Muslim* 1/191.

Chapter Four

Concerning the General Companions

All the jurisprudential rulings and Islamic beliefs have been transmitted to us by the companions. No one can claim that he worships Allah based upon the Qur'an and the *Sunnah* without the companions acting as the intermediaries to reach these two fundamental sources for the Muslims the world over.

Yet the companions disagreed and differed among themselves after the Prophet of Allah (s), reviling and cursing each other, fighting and eventually killing each other. It is not possible for us then, given these circumstances, to accept rulings from them without discussion, critique, examination and opposition. Likewise, it is not possible to judge for or against them without knowing their status and without reading their biographies concerning what they did during the life of the Prophet (s) and after his death. This is [necessary so as] to distinguish the trustworthy from the falsifier, the believer from the corrupt one, the sincere one from the hypocrite, and to know those who turned back upon their heels, from those who remained devoted.

Regrettably, the *Ahl al-Sunnah* in general do not allow this and vehemently prevent criticism of the companions or finding [any] fault with them. They are pleased with all of them and send blessings upon them, as they send blessings upon Muhammad and the family of Muhammad, without the exception of any of them.

The question that must be posed to the *Ahl al-Sunnah wa'l-Jama'a* is this: Does criticizing and finding fault with the companions deserve banishment from Islam? Or does this [act] conflict with the Qur'an and the *Sunnah?*

To answer this question, it is necessary for me to examine the deeds and sayings of some of the companions during the life of the

Prophet (s) and after his death, referring to what has been mentioned by the scholars of the *Ahl al-Sunnah* in their *Sahihs*, *Musnads* and their historical works. I shall do this in a concise manner without referring to any Shi'i book, since their views on some of the companions are well known and require no further elucidation.

To remove any confusion, and so as not to leave any proofs for an opponent to use in arguing against me, I must state that when we mention the companions in this chapter, we refer to some, not to all of them. Those [whom we refer to] may be the majority or the minority; we will discover this during the course of our research, if Allah wishes.

[I say this] because many trouble makers accuse us of being against the companions. They say that we revile and curse the companions so as to influence those who listen [to us] and to block the path to research. On the contrary, we refrain from insulting and reviling the companions. We are pleased with the sincere companions whom the Qur'an calls "the thankful ones". We dissociate ourselves from those who turned back upon their heels, those who reverted after the Prophet (s) and caused most Muslims to be misguided. Yet, even these we do not malign nor insult them. We merely expose their deeds, which have been chronicled by the historians and the *hadith* scholars, so that the truth may become manifest for the researchers. Our brothers from the *Ahl al-Sunnah* do not like this, they consider it as [an act of] cursing an insulting.

The noble Qur'an and it is Allah's word, [which] does not shy away from the truth, has opened this door for us and has informed us that amongst the companions were hypocrites, corrupts ones, tyrants, liars, polytheists, reverts, and amongst them were those who troubled Allah and His Messenger.

The Prophet of Allah (s), who did not speak from desire and, in Allah's name, cannot be reproached, has opened this door for us and has taught us that among the companions were apostates, heretics, those who broke oaths and dissenters; [amongst them were] those who will enter the fire without their companionship benefiting

Chapter 4: Concerning the General Companions 121

them. On the contrary, it (companionship) will work against him, causing an increase in punishment on the day when no wealth or progeny can be of any benefit.

Allah, the most wise, in his book, as well as the great *Sunnah* of His Prophet bears witness that the situation is so, but, in spite of this, the *Ahl al-Sunnah* want to prevent the Muslims from speaking or debating about the companions, so that the truth may not be known. [They do this so that] the Muslims may not know the friends of Allah [whom] they can befriend. [They do this also] as the Muslims might know the enemies of Allah and His Prophet and would oppose them.

One day, I was in the capital of Tunisia in one of its largest mosques. Having completed the obligatory prayer, the Imam sat in the middle of a circle of those who had prayed and he began the session disparaging and labeling as infidels, those who speak against the companions of the Prophet (s). He talked at length saying: "Beware of those who, under the pretext of academic research and a desire to reach the truth, speak against the honor of the companions. The curse of Allah, the angels and all mankind are upon them. They wish to create doubt in people about their religion. The Prophet of Allah (s) said: 'If there comes to you a *hadith* from my companion, accept it, for, by Allah, even if you were to spend to the extent of Uhud in gold, you would not reach the standing of even a one tenth of them.'"

One of the enlightened members who was accompanying me interrupted him and said: "This *hadith* is false and a lie against the Prophet of Allah." The Imam and some of the audience became furious and turned to us in disbelief and aversion. Realizing that the situation called for diplomacy with the Imam, I said to him: "O Sir, eminent teacher, what is the sin of the Muslim, who reads in the Qur'an: *'Muhammad is just a Messenger. Other Messengers have gone before him. If he dies or is killed, will you turn back upon your heels? Whosoever turns back upon his heels will not harm Allah. And Allah will reward those who are thankful'* (3:144).

And what is the sin of the Muslim who reads in *Sahih al-Bukhari* and Muslim the saying of the Messenger of Allah (s) to his companions: 'On the day of resurrection you will be grabbed from the left, and I will say: 'Where are they [being taken] to?' It will be said: 'To hell, by God.' I will say: 'My Lord! These are my companions.' It will be said: 'You do not know what they did after you. From the time you left them they never ceased to apostatize.' I will say: 'Away with him, away with him, woe to him who changed things after me. And I do not see anyone of them being saved except that he will be like a forlorn sheep.'"[1]

Everyone listened to me in silence, alarmed. Some of them asked me if I was sure the *hadith* is to be found in al-Bukhari? I responded: "Yes, just as I am sure that Allah is one, He has no companion and that Muhammad is His slave and Prophet."

When the Imam realized the effect I had on those present, due to my memorizing the *hadith* which I related, he said calmly: "We learnt from our shaykhs, may Allah have mercy on them, that sedition always lies dormant. May Allah curse one who awakens it."

I said to him: "O Sir, the discord in its lifetime has not been dormant. But we are sleeping. The one amongst us who wakes up and opens his eyes to know the truth you accuse him of reviving discord. In any case, Muslims claim to follow the book of Allah and the *Sunnah* of His Prophet (s), not the sayings of the shaykhs who are pleased with Mu'awiyah, Yazid, and 'Amr b. al-'As."

The Imam interjected saying: "Are you not pleased with our master Mu'awiyah (r), the scribe of the revelation?" I said: "This matter will take a long time to explain. If you wish to know my view regarding this [subject], I give you my book "*Then I was Guided.*" Perhaps it will awaken you from your sleep and open your eyes to some realities."

---

[1] *Sahih al-Bukhari*, 7/209, 4/94, 4/156. *Sahih Muslim* 7/66.

Chapter 4: Concerning the General Companions

The Imam accepted my talk and my gift with some reluctance. After a month, however, he wrote a wonderful letter to me, praising Allah for having guided him to the right path and showing affection and love for the *Ahl al-Bayt*, peace be upon them. I sought his permission to print his letter in the third edition [of the book], as it contains sublime affection and sincerity of the soul which, when it recognizes the truth, adheres to it. This reflects the reality of most of the *Ahl al-Sunnah*, who lean towards the truth as soon as the veils are lifted.

However, he requested me to keep his letter secret and not publish it since it was necessary for him to have adequate time to convince the congregation who prayed behind him. He also wished his conversion to be peaceful, without any commotion or confusion, according to what he said.

Let us return to the subject of the discussion on the companions so that we may reveal the bitter truth which the Qur'an, the wisest book, has recorded and [which] the noble Prophetic *Sunnah* has mentioned.

Let us begin with the words of Allah, through which no falsehood comes, neither from the front nor from behind. It is the [final] ruling, the just and it is the criterion (between truth and falsehood). The most exalted says, regarding some of the companions:

"And of the people of Medina are those who are bent on hypocrisy. You know them not, but We know them. Twice will We punish them, and then they will be cast into severe punishment" (9:101).

"They swear in Allah's name that they did not speak [evil]. They have certainly spoken words of disbelief. They disbelieved after submitting. And they contemplated that which they could not attain" (9:74).

"And among them are those who took a covenant with Allah saying: "If He gives us of His bounty, we will surely spend in charity and be among the righteous people". But when He gave them of His bounty, they were miserly with it and turned back aversively. So He filled their hearts with hypocrisy until the day they meet Him due to their breaking the promise with God which they gave, and because they lied" (9:77).

"The desert Arabs are the most disbelieving, hypocritical and most deserving to be ignorant of the ordinances sent down by Allah unto His Messenger. And Allah is the All Knowing, the Wise" (9:97).

"And of the people are those who say: 'We believe in Allah and the last day'. They believe not and seek to deceive Allah and those who believe. Instead they fool only themselves, though they do not perceive this. In their hearts is sickness, and Allah increases their sickness. For them is a painful chastisement due to their lies" (2:10).

"When the hypocrites come to you they say: 'We bear witness that you are the Messenger of Allah'. Allah knows that you are His Messenger, and Allah bears witness that the hypocrites are liars. They have made their oaths as a shield and turn [people] away from Allah. Evil indeed is that which they do! That is because they believed and then disbelieved. Their hearts were sealed and they do not understand" (63:3).

"Do you not see those who claim to believe in what was revealed unto you and what was revealed before you? They seek judgment from the evil ones even though they were

Chapter 4: Concerning the General Companions

ordered to disbelieve in them. Satan wishes to lead them astray completely. When it is said to them: 'Come to what Allah has revealed and [come] to the Messenger,' you see the hypocrites turn away from you in aversion. Yet when misfortune befalls them due to what their own hands have earned, they come to you swearing by Allah, saying: 'We merely wished goodness and success'" (4:62).

"The hypocrites [seek to] deceive Allah, but He deceives them. When they stand to prayer, they do so in a lazy manner, they [seek to] show off to the people, they do not remember Allah but for a little [while]" (4:142).

"If you see them, their appearances will please you, and if they speak, you will listen to them. They are as blocks of wood propped up. They believe that every cry is against them. They are the enemy, so beware of them. Allah will destroy them [as] they forge lies" (63:4).

"Allah knows those from among you that hinder people and those who say to their brothers: 'Come to us and you will not have to fight except for a little while'. Covetous they are over you. When fear comes, you will see them looking towards you, their eyes rolling as though death hovers upon them. And when the fear is gone, they assail you with sharp tongues, desiring good. They do not believe and Allah has made their deeds of no avail, that is easy for Allah" (33:19).

"And among them are those who listen to you until, when they leave you, they say to those who have been given knowledge: 'What did he just say?' They are those whose hearts Allah has sealed and they follow their own desires"

(47:16).

"Do those in whose hearts is sickness think that Allah will not expose their rancor? Had we so wished, we would have shown them to you, you would have recognized them by their signs. Surely you shall know them by the tone of their speech. Allah is aware of your deeds" (47: 30).

"Those who lagged behind from among the desert Arabs will say to you: 'We were busy with our properties and our families. So seek forgiveness for us'. They utter with their tongues what is not in their hearts" (48:11).

These clear verses from Allah's glorious book explain clearly the hypocrisy of some of them who infiltrated the ranks of the sincere companions so much so that, had it not been for Allah's revelation, their realities would have been hidden from the bearer of the message himself.

However, the *Ahl al-Sunnah* always argue with us concerning this. They say: "What have we to do with the hypocrites? May Allah curse them. The companions are not from them, or these hypocrites were not amongst the companions". If you ask them: "Who are these hypocrites [concerning] whom more than 150 verses were revealed in chapters 9 and 63?" They will respond: "They are 'Abd Allah b. 'Ubayy and 'Abd Allah b. Salul." Besides these two people, they do not find any other [people].

Glory be to Allah! If the Prophet (s) himself did not know most of them, how can the hypocrisy be restricted to Ibn Ubayy and Ibn Abi Salul, those two who were known to the Muslims?

The Prophet of Allah (s) knew a few of them and told their names to Hudhayfa b. al-Yamani, as you say, and ordered him to conceal their matters to the point where 'Umar bin al-Khattab, during the days of his Caliphate, used to ask Hudhayfa about himself: "Was he ('Umar) from among the hypocrites? Had the Prophet (s) mentioned his name?" This is [in accordance with] what

Chapter 4: Concerning the General Companions

you report in your books.[2] The Prophet (s) had given a clear indicator by which the hypocrites would be known, i.e., hatred towards 'Ali b. Abi Talib, as you report in your *Sahihs*.[3]

Most of these companions, whom you are pleased with and accord top [positions] to, hated 'Ali, they waged wars against him, they murdered and cursed him when he was alive and dead. [They did this] to him, his family and those who loved him. You consider all of them to be amongst the eminent companions.

The wisdom of the Prophet of Allah (s) necessitated that he informs Hudhayfa of their names sometimes, and [inform] the Muslims of their signs at other times. [This was done] so that he fulfills his obligation to the people and no one could [then] claim: "We were not aware of this."

What the *Ahl al-Sunnah* say nowadays is of no value, [they say]: "We love Imam 'Ali (r), may Allah brighten his face". We say to them: "There cannot exist in the heart of a believer, love for the friend and enemy of Allah." Imam 'Ali himself said: "One who equates us with our enemies is not from us."[4]

Furthermore, when the noble Qur'an speaks of the companions, it speaks of them in numerous descriptions and distinctive signs. If we exempt the sincere, grateful companions, then the rest of them have been described in the wise book as being corrupt, deceivers, forsakers, breakers of oaths or they turn back, they [express] doubt in Allah and His Prophet, flee from battle, oppose the truth, disobey the orders of Allah and His Messenger, prevent others from *jihad*, hasten to vain things and business, abandoning the prayer, saying what they do not practice, claim to do favors to the Prophet due to their Islam, having hard hearts and not being humble in the remembrance of Allah and the truth that was revealed, raising their voices above the Prophet's, troubling the Prophet of Allah (s), or listening to the hypocrites.

---

[2] *Kanz al-'Ummal* 7/24 ; *Tarikh Ibn 'Asakir* 4/97 ; *Ihya' 'Ulum al-Din* 1/129

[3] *Sahih Muslim* 1/61; *Tirmidhi* 5/306; *al-Nasa'i* 8/116, *Kanz al-'Ummal* 15/105.

[4] *Nahj al-Balagha*, 1/155.

Let us be satisfied with this brief [description], for there are many verses which we have not cited for the sake of brevity. For the benefit of all, however, it is necessary to mention some verses that were revealed to criticize the companions who were described by those attributes but who, due to politics, were all regarded, after the Prophet of Allah (s) and after the cessation of revelation, as upright, trustworthy and just. It was not possible for any Muslim to speak against them or criticize or find faults with them.

The Qur'an reveals the truth about some companions

In order that an obdurate person may not think that the verses on the hypocrites do not pertain to the companions, as the *Ahl al-Sunnah* claim, we have decided to present some of the verses that refer specifically to the believers.

In the wise book, Allah's says: *"O You who believe! What is it with you that when it is said to you to go forth in the cause of Allah you cling heavily to where you are? Do you prefer the life of this world to that of the hereafter? Little is the comfort of this life when compared to that of the hereafter. If you do not go forth, He will inflict a grievous punishment upon you and substitute another people in your place. You cannot harm Him in the least. And Allah has power over all things"* (9:34).

"O you who believe! whoever of you reverts after having believed, Allah will bring a people whom He loves and who love him, humble with the believers, powerful over the disbelievers, struggling in the way of Allah, not afraid of the sternest critics. That is the grace of Allah. He bestows it upon whom He wills. Allah's knowledge encompasses [everything]" (5:54).

"O you who believe! Do not be treacherous to Allah and His Prophet. Do not knowingly betray your trust. And know that your property and your children are a test and that with Allah lies great reward." (8:28).

"O You who believe! Respond to Allah and His Prophet when they call you to what enlivens you. And know that Allah comes between a man and his heart and that to Him you shall be gathered. Beware of discord that it should not affect especially those of you who do wrong; know that Allah is severe in punishment" (8:25).

"O You who believe! Remember the bounties of Allah when armies came against you but we sent against them winds and forces that you could not see. Allah saw clearly all that you did. They came to you from above and from below. And behold! The eyes became dim and the hearts gaped up to the throats and you imagined various things about Allah. Then the believers were tested and they were shaken tremendously. The hypocrites and those in whose hearts there is sickness say: "Allah and His Messenger have promised us nothing but delusions" (33:12).

"O You who believe, why do you say what you do not practice, grievous is the sin in the eyes of Allah that you say what you do not do" (61:3).

"Has the time not now arrived for those who believe that their hearts should humbly be engaged in the remembrance of Allah and the truth which has been revealed." (57:16)

*"They seek to impress upon you that they accepted Islam

as a favor to you: Say: 'Do not count your Islam as a favor to me. Allah has done you a favor by guiding you to the faith, if you are truthful.'" (49:17).

"*Say: If your fathers, your sons, your brothers, your mates and your kins or the wealth that you have gained, or the business in which you fear a decline, or the dwellings in which you delight are dearer to you than Allah and His Prophet or struggling in His path then wait until Allah brings about His decision and Allah does not guide those who are corrupt.*" (9:14).

"*The desert Arabs say: 'We believe'. Say: 'You have not believed. Rather, say: 'We have submitted ourselves to Allah' for faith has not yet entered your hearts.*" (49:14).

"*Those who do not believe in Allah and the last day seek to be excused. Their hearts are in doubt and in their doubt they hesitate.*" (9:45).

"*Had they come out with you they would have only added disorder, hurrying to and fro in your midst and sowing sedition among you. And there are some amongst you who would have listened to them. Allah is well aware of the wrongdoers.*" (9:47).

"*Those who stayed behind rejoiced in their inactivity, [doing so] behind the Messenger of Allah. They hated to struggle with their property and their lives in the path of Allah. They said: 'Do not go forth in the heat.' Say: 'The fire of Hell is more hot', if only they understood.*" (9:81).

Chapter 4: Concerning the General Companions

"That was because they followed what brought forth the wrath of Allah. And they hated Allah's pleasure. So He made their deeds of no value. Or do those in whose hearts there is sickness reckon that Allah will not bring their wickedness to light? Had We so wished, We would have shown them to you, you would have recognized them by their marks. Surely, you will know them by the tone of their speech. And Allah knows your deeds." (47:30).

"And a group from the believers disliked it. They dispute with you about the truth after it was made clear, as if they were being driven to death whilst they were watching it." (8:6).

"Here you are invited to spend in the way of Allah! Amongst you are some who are misers. And whoever is miserly is only miserly to his own soul. Allah is free from all wants and you are needy. If you turn back He will substitute another people and they will not be like you." (47:38).

"And among them are those who slander you in [the distribution of] alms. If they are given from it, they are pleased. If they are not, they become angry." (9:58).

"And among them are those who listen to you until, when they leave you, they say to those who have been given knowledge: 'What did he say just now?' They are those upon whose hearts Allah has placed a seal. They follow their desires." (47:16).

"And among them are those who trouble the Prophet and say: 'He is all ears'. Say: 'He listens to what is best for you.

He believes in Allah and has faith in the believers. And he is a mercy to those of you who believe'. But those who trouble the Prophet will have a grievous punishment." (9:61).

These clear verses are sufficient to satisfy the researchers that the companions can be divided into two groups:

1. One group believed in Allah and His Prophet (s), submitting its affairs and leadership to them. It obeyed Allah and His Prophet, dedicating [itself] whole heartedly to them, sacrificing for their cause. This [group] was the successful one. It represented a minority. The Qur'an called these [people] the 'grateful ones'.

2. Another group outwardly believed in Allah and His Prophet, but had sickness in its heart. It did not submit its affairs except for personal interests and worldly benefits. It opposed the Prophet in his rulings and commands, and preferred itself over Allah and His Prophet. This group was amongst the losers and represented the majority. The Qur'an referred to it succinctly when Allah, the Glorified and Honored, said: *"We have come to you with the truth, but most of you hate the truth" (43:78).*

The researcher discovers that this "majority", during the life of the Prophet (s), lived with him, prayed behind him and accompanied him when he travelled. They sought, by any means possible, to get close to him so that their [true] state may not be revealed to the sincere believers. They tried their best to put up a show, making the believers envious due to their excessive worship and piety in the eyes of the people.[5]

---

[5] Imam Ahmad reported in his *Musnad*, and Ibn Hajar in his *Al Isaba*, in the report of Dhi Thadya from Anas b. Malik: During the time of Prophet of Allah (s) there was a man at whose worship and thinking we used to marvel. We related this to Prophet of Allah (s) as well as the name of the man, but he did not know him. We described him, but still he did not know him. While we were speaking about him, the man appeared. We said:"There he is!"The Massenger of Allah (s) said: "You have informed me about a man. But verily on his face is a sign of the devil. This person and

If this was their state during the life of the Prophet (s), what were they like after his death? No doubt they were energetic; they multiplied in numbers, spread and increased, as did their cover-ups and representatives (in the community). There was no Prophet who could recognize them and no revelation to disgrace them. Especially as, with his death, appeared the early signs of dissension and fragmentation amongst the people of Medina, who were inclined towards hypocrisy. The Arabs in the peninsula apostatized for they were severe in their disbelief and hypocrisy. Among them were those who claimed prophethood such as Musaylima the liar, Tulayha, Sajjah bint al-Harth and their followers. All of them were among the companions.

If we leave aside all of them and concentrate solely on the Medinan companions of the Prophet of Allah (s), we can certainly state that the thorns of hypocrisy appeared in them too. Most of the believers amongst them turned back upon their heels for the [sake of the] Caliphate.

In the previous discussion, we learnt that they plotted against the Prophet (s) and his successor; they disobeyed the commands that the Prophet of Allah (s) had issued to them when he was on his deathbed.

This reality is something from which there is no escape for the researchers, seeking the truth, for they are confronted with it when reading the historical texts and the biographical accounts of the Prophet. Allah's most glorified book has recorded it in the most clear expression and the wisest verses when it said: *"Muhammad is just a Messenger. Other Messengers have gone before him. If he dies or is killed, will you then turn back upon your heels? And whosoever turns back upon his heels will not hurt Allah in any way. Allah will reward those who are grateful."*

---

his comapanions recite the Qur'an, but it does not go beyond their collarbone. They penetrate religion as an arrow goes through game. Kill them, for they are the worst of men"

(3:144).

The grateful ones are a minority amongst the companions, who did not turn back, they were steadfast to the covenant they gave to the Prophet of Allah (s) and did not change in any way.

This noble verse, with its clear implications, refutes the claim of the *Ahl al-Sunnah,* i.e., that the companions have no relation to the hypocrites. Even if we, for argument's sake, accept this, then this noble verse is addressed to the sincere companions who were not hypocrites during the life of the Prophet (s), but instead reverted upon their heels immediately after his death.

The reality of them will become clear when we examine their status during the life of the Prophet (s), and after his death, and what the Prophet of Allah said regarding them. This is abundantly clear in the *hadith,* biographical and historical works.

The Prophet's *Sunnah* reveals the truth about some of the companions

In order that no obstinate person may allege that the Prophetic *hadiths,* which relate to the companions, have any defect and so judge them as being weak, we have relied solely upon the *hadiths* [cited] in al-Bukhari, which is the most authentic book for the *Ahl al-Sunnah.* In keeping with his well known approach, al-Bukhari has concealed many of these *hadiths* in order to protect the reputation of the companions. Although the other *Sahihs* of the *Ahl al-Sunnah* have recorded other numerous traditions and in more explicit terms, we shall be contented with this concise [number of traditions] which al-Bukhari has reported, so that our argument may be complete.

In vol. 1, in the chapter entitled: "The Fear of the Believer of His Acts being made Futile without him Realizing It," in "The Book of Faith," al-Bukhari reported: "Ibrahim al-Tayyimi said: 'Whenever I compare my words with my deeds, I fear I [may] have lied.' Ibn Abi Mulayka said: 'I met thirty companions of the Prophet (s) and each one of them feared hypocrisy within himself. Not one of them

Chapter 4: Concerning the General Companions

could claim to believe in Gabriel or Michael (vol. 1, p. 97).'"

If Abu Mulayka met thirty companions of the Prophet (s) and each one felt that he was a hypocrite and could not claim to have proper belief, how can the *Ahl al-Sunnah* raise them to the level of Prophets, and not accept criticism of any of them?

In vol. 4, in "The Chapter on Spies and Spying," in "The Book of *Jihad* and Campaigns," al-Bukhari reports: "Hatib b. Abi Balta'a (he was amongst the companions of the Prophet (s)) sent [someone] to the polytheists of Mecca informing them of some of the plans of the Prophet of Allah (s). His letter was brought to the Prophet (s). The Prophet of Allah (s) said to him: 'What is this, O Hatib?' He apologised to the Prophet saying that all he wanted was to protect his relatives in Mecca. The Prophet of Allah (s) believed him but 'Umar (r) said: 'O Prophet of Allah (s) let me chop off the head of this hypocrite.' The Prophet (s) replied: 'He witnessed [the battle of] Badr. How do you know, perhaps Allah looked upon the people of Badr and said: 'Do as you wish, for I have forgiven you (vol. 4, p. 19).'"

If Hatib, who was among the first companions at Badr, could divulge the secrets of the Prophet (s) to his idolatrous enemies of Mecca and could betray Allah and His Prophet (s) with the excuse of protecting his relatives, and if 'Umar himself testifies to his hypocrisy, what can be said of the companions who converted after the conquest of Mecca? Or after Khaybar, or after Hunayn? And what [can be said] of those who were freed after they had surrendered, without accepting Islam?

As to what has been quoted in the last paragraph, i.e., the words attributed to the Prophet (s), that Allah said to the people of Badr: "Do as you wish for Allah has forgiven you." We will leave the remarks to the perceptive reader.

In vol. 6, in "The Book on the Merits of the Qur'an, *Surah al-Munafiqun*," al-Bukhari reported in his *Sahih* in "The Chapter on Allah's words: *'It is the same whether you seek forgiveness for them or you do not. Allah will never forgive them, for Allah will not guide the corrupt ones:'"* "A man from the Muhajirun hit an Ansari man. The Ansari said: 'O Ansar, help [me].' And the Muhajir said: 'O emigrants help [me].' The Prophet of Allah (s) heard this and said: 'What is this argument which is characteristic to the claims of the period of ignorance?' They said: 'O Apostle of Allah! A Muhajir hit an Ansari.' He said: 'Leave that alone for it is a detestable [act].' 'Abd Allah b. 'Ubayy heard that and said: 'They have done it? By Allah, if we returned to Medina, those who are powerful will expel the weaker!' This reached the Prophet (s) and 'Umar got up and said: 'O Apostle of Allah (s) let me cut off the head of this hypocrite.' The Prophet (s) said: 'Leave him alone. Let the people not say that Muhammad kills his companions (*Sahih al-Bukhari*, vol. 6, p 65).'"

The *hadith* clearly shows that hypocrites were among the companions. For the Prophet of Allah accepted 'Umar's words, that the man was a hypocrite, but prevented him from killing him, lest it be said that Muhammad killed his companions. Perhaps the Prophet (s) knew that most of the companions were hypocrites and that if every hypocrite was killed, not many of his companions would remain [alive]. Where are the *Ahl al-Sunnah* with regards to this painful reality which refutes their claims?

In vol. 3, al-Bukhari reported in "The Chapter on Traditions of Fabrications," from "The Book of Testimony:" "The Apostle of Allah (s) said: 'Who will help me against a man who has hurt me by harming my family?' Sa'd b. Mu'adh got up and said: 'O Apostle of Allah (s), I will relieve you from him. If he is from the Aws, we will be head him. And if he is from our brothers, the Khazraj, we will do as you order.' Sa'd b. 'Ubada got up, and he was the chief of the Khazraj, and before this he was a righteous man but he was filled with zeal (for his tribe) and said: 'By Allah! You have lied. You will not kill him for you are not capable of doing it.' Usayd b. al-Hudayr rose and said: 'By Allah, you have lied! By Allah, we will certainly kill him for you are a hypocrite and argue on behalf of the hypocrites.'"

The argument between the Aws and the Khazraj became so heated that they were about to fight each other. The Prophet of

Chapter 4: Concerning the General Companions

Allah (s) was on the pulpit, and he kept on placating them until they finally kept quiet, whereupon he also kept quiet *(Sahih al-Bukhari,* vol. 5 p. 156, and vol. 6, p. 8)."

Sa'd b. 'Ubada, the chief of the Ansar, is accused of hypocrisy, having been, as the report testifies, a righteous man, and he is called a hypocrite in the presence of the Prophet (s) who did not defend him. The Ansar, whom Allah has praised so much in His book, instigated the 'Aws and Khazraj who were prepared to fight [each other] for a hypocrite who had annoyed the Prophet (s) concerning his family and [they were prepared] to defend him and had raised their voices in the presence of the Prophet (s). [Knowing all this] how can we be surprised by the hypocrisy of others, those who had dedicated their lives to fighting against the Prophet (s) and his message, or those who intended to burn the house of his daughter after his death, for the sake of the Caliphate?

Al-Bukhari has reported in his *Sahih,* in vol. 8, in "The Book of Unity," in "The Chapter on Allah's words: *'The angels and the holy spirit ascend to Him...'*" "'Ali b. Abi Talib sent some pieces of gold from Yemen to the Prophet of Allah (s). The Prophet (s) distributed it among some people.

The Quraysh and the Ansar became angry and said: 'He has given to the notables of the Najd and forsaken us.' The Apostle of Allah (s) said: 'Rather, I was placating them.' A man came to him and said: 'O Muhammad! Fear Allah!' The Prophet (s) said: 'Who will obey Allah if I were to disobey him? He entrusts me to the people of the earth, don't you trust me?'

Khalid b. al-Walid asked him if he could kill him, but the Prophet (s) prevented him from that. When he went away, the Prophet (s) said: 'From the offspring of this man will come a people who will recite the Qur'an but it will not go past their throats. They will pierce Islam as an arrow pierces the game. They will kill the Muslims but will spare the idolaters. Were I to meet them, I would kill them as 'Ad was killed *(Sahih al-Bukhari,* vol. 8 p. 178).'"

This is another hypocrite among the companions, accusing the

Prophet of Allah (s) of injustice in distribution, and then confronts him in total disrespect with the words: "O Muhammad, fear Allah". Although the Apostle of Allah (s) knew of his hypocrisy, and that from his descendants would emerge a people who would pierce Islam as an arrow pierces the game, killing the Muslims and sparing the idolaters, despite all of this, the Messenger of Allah (s) prevented Khalid from killing him.

In this is an answer to the *Ahl al-Sunnah,* who always argue with me saying: "If the Prophet of Allah knew that there were hypocrites among his companions who would be the cause for leading the Muslims astray, it would have been obligatory upon him to kill them so as to protect his *ummah* and to protect his religion."

In vol. 3, in "The Chapter if the Imam urges for a Treaty" in "The Book of Treaties," al-Bukhari relates:

"Al-Zubayr reported that he argued against a man from the Ansar who had participated at [the battle of] Badr, and that he presented the matter to the Prophet of Allah (s) about a stream which both used for irrigation. The Prophet of Allah (s) said to al-Zubayr: 'Irrigate from it, O Zubayr, and then let [the water] flow to your neighbor.'

The Ansari became angry and said: 'O Apostle of Allah (s) is it because he is your cousin?' The face of the Apostle of Allah (s) changed (with anger) and he said: 'Irrigate and then hold it (the water) until it reaches the walls (vol. 3 p. 171).'"

This is another group of the hypocritical companions who believed that the Prophet of Allah (s) was influenced by sentiments and would favor his cousin. They said it impudently until the Prophet's face changed color due to intense anger.

Al-Bukhari reported in his *Sahih,* in vol. 4, "The Chapter on What the Prophet used to give to those whose Hearts were to be Placated"; in "The Book of "*Jihad* and Campaigns;" "From 'Abd Allah (r), who said: 'On the day of the battle of Hunayn, the Prophet (s) favoured [some] people in the distribution (of booty). He gave

Chapter 4: Concerning the General Companions 139

al-Aqra b. Habis one hundred camels, and he gave 'Uyayna the same amount. He also granted some to the eminent Arabs, giving them preference in the distribution that day. A man said: 'By Allah! There is no justice in this distribution and the pleasure of Allah is not sought in it'. I said: 'By Allah, most certainly I will inform the Prophet (s)'. So I came and informed him. He said: 'And who will be just if Allah and His Prophet are not just? May Allah bless Moses. He was troubled more than this, and yet he remained patient *(Sahih al-Bukhari* vol. 4, p. 61).'"

This is another hypocrite amongst the companions of the Prophet of Allah (s) and perhaps he was amongst the prominent Qurayshis. As a result, the narrator refrained from mentioning his name, afraid of the repercussions from the rulers of the time. You observe that the hypocrite is certain in his belief and swears that Muhammad was not just, and that he (the Prophet) did not wish to please Allah in his distribution. May Allah have mercy on Muhammad for he was troubled more than this, yet he was patient.

In vol. 4, in "The Chapter on the Signs of Prophethood in Islam," in "The Book of the Beginning of Creation," al-Bukhari recorded: "Abu Sa'id al-Khudri (r) said: 'We were with the Prophet of Allah (s) and he was distributing portions. Dhu'l-Khuwaysira came to him. He was from the Banu Tamim. He said: 'O Apostle of Allah (s). Be just.' He said: 'Woe be to you! Who will be just if I am not just? You would be disappointed and at a loss if I were not just.' 'Umar said: 'O Prophet of Allah give me permission to smite his neck.' He said: 'Leave him alone. He has companions whose prayers and fasts, when compared with one of yours, makes it appear insignificant. They recite the Qur'an but it does not go past their throats. They pierce [through] the religion as an arrow pierces through the game *(Sahih al-Bukhari,* vol. 4, p. 179).'"

This is another group of hypocritical companions who outwardly exhibited such an abundance of piety and humility that even the Prophet (s) said to 'Umar: "The prayers and fasts of one of you seems little compared to their prayers and fasts". There is no doubt that they would memorize the Qur'an completely, but it did not go past their throats. The words of the Prophet of Allah (s): "Leave him alone for he has companions" indicates the presence of the hypocrites in huge numbers among the companions.

In vol. 7, in "The Chapter on He who does not Face The People with Reprimand," in "The Book of Ettiquettes," al-Bukhari reported: "'A'isha said: 'The Prophet of Allah (s) did something and allowed it, but some people kept away from it. This reached the Prophet (s). He delivered a sermon, wherein, after praising Allah, he said: 'Why is it that a group of you refrain from doing something that I do? By Allah, I am the most knowledgeable of them concerning Him, and I fear Him most *(Sahih al-Bukhari*, vol. 7, p. 96).'"

This is another type of companions who kept away from the practice of the Prophet (s). No doubt they mocked at his actions and, as a result, we see him (s) delivering a sermon and swearing by Allah that he was the most knowledgeable of them regarding Allah, and that he was the most God fearing.

Al-Bukhari in vol. 3, in "The Chapter on Sharing Together in Sacrifice and the Sacrificial Animals", in "The Book of Oppression" stated: "'Ibn 'Abbas said that on the fourth morning of *Dhu'l-hijja*, the Prophet of Allah (s) came, having declared the intention to make the pilgrimage, and not anything else. When we came forth, he ordered us to make '*umra* and then go to our wives (there was a lot of things that the people said against that). 'Ata said: "Jabir said: 'If one of us goes to Mina, the semen would still be dripping from his penis.' That reached the Prophet of Allah (s) and he addressed the people saying: 'It has reached me that some people say so and so. By Allah, I am the most pious and God fearing amongst you *(Sahih al-Bukhari* vol. 3, p. 114).'"

Here is another group of companions who disobeyed the commands of the Prophet in the *shari'a* rulings. The saying of the Apostle of Allah (s): "It has reached me that some people say so and so" indicates that a lot of them had refused to free [themselves] from the state of *ihram* for their wives, on the pretext that they did not wish to go to Mina with semen dripping from their penises. It did not occur to these ignorant ones that Allah had enjoined a ritual

Chapter 4: Concerning the General Companions

bath and purification upon them after every physical union. How could they proceed to Mina with semen dripping from their penises? Were they more versed than the Prophet of Allah himself in the rulings of Allah? Or were they more virtuous and God fearing than him?

No doubt the *mut'a* marriage, or temporary union with women, was proscribed after the Prophet (s) by 'Umar, following the [same] pattern [as above]. For if, during the life of the Prophet (s), they rejected his commands concerning the cohabitation with their wives during the days of the pilgrimage, then it is not surprising to find them prohibiting temporary marriage after his death, denying for themselves what the Prophet (s) ordered and considering the marriage of *mut'a* as fornication, as the *Ahl al-Sunnah* say today.

In vol. 4, in "The Chapter What the Prophet used to give to Those whose Hearts were to be won Over," in "The Book Of *Jihad And Campaigns*," al-Bukhari reported from Anas b. Malik that when Allah had given the Prophet some property of Hawazin, he gave it to Qurayshi men. The Ansar said: "May Allah forgive the Apostle of Allah, he gives the Quraysh and neglects us when our swords are still dripping with their blood." The Prophet of Allah (s) gathered them in Quba, summoning only them, not leaving any one of them aside and said: "What is this that has reached me about you?" When they repeated their words to him, he said: "I have given it to men who recently converted from disbelief. Aren't you happy that the people go away with wealth, and that you return to your homes with the Prophet of Allah? By Allah, what you return with is better than what they return with."They said: "Certainly, O Prophet of Allah we are pleased." He said: "After me you will see a lot of egoism, so be patient until you meet Allah and His Prophet at the pond." Anas said: "But we were not patient (*Sahih*, al-Bukhari vol. 4 p. 60)."

Now we ask ourselves: "Was there amongst all the Ansar [even] one man [who was] guided and convinced by what the Prophet of Allah (s) did? Did he believe that he (the Prophet) did not follow his own desires and inclination? Did he understand Allah's words in this regard: *'Nay! By your Lord, they cannot believe until they appoint you as a judge in their disputes and [until] they do not find in their souls, resistance against your decisions and they totally submit'* (4:65).

Was there anyone amongst them defending the Apostle of Allah (s) when they said: 'May Allah forgive the Apostle of Allah?' Certainly not! There was no one who had the level of belief which the noble verse demanded. Their words after that: 'Certainly, O Prophet of Allah, we are pleased' were not out of conviction. The testimony of Anas b. Malik, who was amongst them, was appropriate when he said: 'He advised us to be patient, but we were not patient'".

In vol. 5, in "The Chapter on the Battle of al-Hudaybiyya," in "The Book of Wars," al-Bukhari reported from Ahmad b. Ishkab, who said: "Muhammad b. Fudayl informed us from 'Ala b. Musayyab, from his father who said: 'I met al-Bara' b. Azib (r) and said: 'You are honored, you accompanied the Prophet (s) You [also] paid allegiance to him under the tree'. He said: 'O nephew! You do not know what we innovated after him *(Sahih al-Bukhari,* vol. 5, p. 66).'"

Al-Bara' b. Azib spoke the truth. Most people do not know what the companions did after the death of their Prophet (s), who oppressed his successor, his cousin and distanced him from the Caliphate. [Nor do they know] who oppressed his daughter al-Zahra and threatened to burn her. Nor do they know of the usurping of her rights to the gifts from her father, her inheritance and the *khumus.* [Nor do they know of] their opposing the successors of the Prophet (s) and the changing of the *shari'a* rulings, of the burning of the Prophetic *Sunnah,* or placing restrictions upon it. [Nor do they know] of the injury done to him due to the cursing and killing of his family, and their banishment and exile and granting power to hypocrites and corrupt ones, the enemies of Allah and His Prophet.

Yes, all these and more they did after his death. These [things] remain unknown to the masses who do not know the facts except what has been dictated to them by the Caliphs' schools, who specialized in changing the rulings of Allah and His Prophet, doing

Chapter 4: Concerning the General Companions

so by personal judgments which they called good innovations (*bida' hasana*).

Due to this, we say to the *ahl al-sunna*: "Do not take pride, O our brothers, in the companionship and the companions. For here is al-Bara' b. 'Azib, and he is amongst the foremost who pledged fealty to the Prophet (s) under the tree, saying to his nephew in the present tense: "Do not take pride in my companionship or my pledge under the tree, for you do not know what I did after him."

Allah said: *"Those who pay allegiance to you in fact pay allegiance to Allah. The hand of Allah is over their hands. And whoever violates that oath has done so against his own [self]" (48:10).*

How [great] was the number of companions who violated the pledge, so much so that the Prophet (s) took a pledge from his cousin 'Ali to fight them as has been documented in the historical texts.

In vol. 1 and 3 of his *Sahih*, in "The Chapter on if People who leave the Imam in the Friday prayer," in "The Book of the Friday prayer," al-Bukhari reported from Jabir b. 'Abd Allah (r), who said: "A caravan came from Syria bringing foodstuffs. We were praying the Friday prayer with the Prophet of Allah (s). All the people left except twelve men. This verse was then revealed: *'And if they see trade or vain [things], they hurry away and leave you standing (Sahih al-Bukhari*, vol. 1, p. 225: vol. 3, p. 6, 7).'"

This is another group of hypocritical companions who observed no piety or humility. They fled from the Friday prayer to inspect the caravan and trade, leaving the Prophet of Allah standing in front of Allah, fulfilling his obligation in humility and awe.

Was the belief of these Muslims complete? Or were these the hypocrites who scoffed at the prayers and when they stood to observe it, did so in a lackluster manner? None [of them] is exempted from this except those who stood with the Prophet (s) to complete the Friday prayer; they were twelve men in all.

Whoever studies their status and investigates their reports will be appalled by their actions. No doubt their flight from the Friday prayer occurred several times and, as a result, the book of Allah, the most Glorified, has recorded it by stating: *"Say that which is with Allah is better than vain pleasures and trade."*

So that you may realize, O dear reader, the extent of their respect for the prayer (the contemporary Muslims show more [respect] than they did) I present the following narration to you:

Al-Bukhari reported in vol. 3, in "The Chapter on what has been [narrated] Regarding Plants" in "The Book of Deputyship:" "From Sahl b. Sa'id (r) who said: 'We used to rejoice on Fridays for there was an old woman who used to cut some roots of the *silq* (a kind of vegetable) which we used to plant on the banks of our water streams. She would cook them in her pot adding some barley on it; I do not know the amount of it except that there was no fat or melted fat on it. When we finished the Friday prayers, we would go to her and she would serve it to us. Due to that, we used to be happy on Fridays. We would neither eat nor take the midday nap until after the prayer (*Sahih al-Bukhari* vol. 3 p.73).'"

Good for those companions who rejoiced on Fridays, not because they would meet the Prophet of Allah (s) or listen to his sermons and his exhortations or would pray behind him, nor because they would meet each other, or [would rejoice] due to the day's blessings and mercy; they rejoiced on Fridays because of a special dish that an old woman would prepare for them. If a contemporary Muslim were to say that he rejoiced on Fridays for food, he would be regarded as dimwitted and negligent (of the importance of the day).

If we wish to research and investigate more, we would find that the grateful ones, whom the Qur'an praised, were a minority; they did not exceed twelve in number. These were the devoted ones who did not hurry towards vain pleasures and trade, abandoning their prayer. They were steadfast with the Prophet (s) in wars on a number of occasions when the rest of the companions turned their

Chapter 4: Concerning the General Companions

backs and fled.

In vol. 4, in "The Chapter on what is Detested in Argument and Disagreement in War," in "The Book of War and Campaigns," al-Bukhari reported from al-Bara' b. 'Azib who said: "The Prophet (s) appointed an infantry of fifty men on the day of Uhud, and appointed 'Abd Allah b. Jubayr as the leader. He said to them: 'Even if you see birds snatching us, do not leave your positions until I send for you.' They were defeating them. He said: 'And I saw, by Allah, the women fleeing with their anklets and legs visible as they had raised their dresses. The companions of 'Abd Allah b. Jubayr said: 'The booty! O people, the booty! Your companions have prevailed so what are you waiting for?' 'Abd Allah b. Jubayr said: 'Have you forgotten what the Apostle of Allah (s) said to you?' They said: 'By Allah! We will go to them and take [something] from the booty.' When they came to them, their faces were turned away and they started to retreat. At that time, the Prophet of Allah (s) called them from behind. Only twelve men remained with him whilst seventy of us fell (*Sahih al-Bukhari* vol. 4, p. 26)."

We know from what the historians relate of this battle that the Prophet of Allah (s) left with one thousand companions, each one desiring to fight in Allah's path, allured with the help that had come at Badr. However, they disobeyed the commands of the Prophet (s), causing a loathsome, horrible rout in which seventy people were killed, the chief of whom was Hamza, the uncle of the Prophet (s). The remainder fled, and only twelve people remained with the Prophet (s) on the battlefield, according to what al-Bukhari says. The other historians reduce this number to only four. These were 'Ali b. Abi Talib, who resisted the polytheists, thereby protecting the front of the Prophet (s); Abu Dijana who protected the rear, Talha and Zubayr. It is said that Sahl b. Hanif [was also there].

It is in this context that we [can] understand the saying of the Prophet of Allah (s): "I do not see any one amongst them saved except like abandoned livestock (we will discuss this *hadith* presently)."

Allah, Glory be to Him, the Most Exalted, threatened them with hellfire if they fled from battle and said: *"O you who believe! If you meet those who disbelieve in battle, do not turn back! Whosoever flees from them on that day, except as a strategy or to [regroup] with [his] party, has brought upon himself Allah's wrath and his abode is in Hell, it is an evil path"* (8:6).

What, then, is the status of these companions who flee from prayer to pursue vain things and trade, and then flee from battle due to fear of death abandoning the Prophet of Allah (s) alone in the midst of the enemy? In both cases, they all turn their backs and flee; none remain with him except twelve men [according] to the best estimate. Where were the companions, O people of perception?

Perhaps some researchers, when they read of such events and narrations, pay little attention to them and assume that they were occasional happenings which Allah forgave and that the companions did not repeat them afterwards.

Certainly not, the noble Qur'an informs us of startling facts, for Allah, Glory be to Him, has recorded their fleeing on the day of the battle of Uhud[6] in His words: *"Allah fulfilled His promise when you, by His Permission, were about to rout your enemy, yet you failed and fell to arguing about the order and disobeyed it after He brought you in sight of what you coveted. Amongst you are those who desire this world and amongst you are some who desire the hereafter. Then did He divert you from your foes in order to test you. But He forgave you. And Allah is full of grace to the true believers. You were climbing (high ground) without glancing at any one and the Prophet was calling you from behind. Then God gave you one distress after another so that you should not grieve at what [booty]*

---

[6] *Tafsir al-Tahrir wa'l Tanwir*, Thrir b. 'Ashur 4/126, also *Tafsir al-Tabari, Sahih al-Bukhari* 5/29, "The Chapter on the Battle of Uhud".

Chapter 4: Concerning the General Companions

you lost and what has befallen you, and Allah is well aware of what you do" (3:153).

This verse was revealed after the battle of Uhud, wherein the Muslims were routed due to their craving after the worldly goods when they saw the women raising their dresses and showing their legs and their ankles, according to al-Bukhari's report. They disobeyed Allah and His Prophet (s) as is related by the Qur'an. Did the companions pay heed to that event and repent and seek His forgiveness, not repeating such acts afterwards?

Certainly not! They did not repent and perpetrated worse than this at the battle of Hunayn, which occurred in the latter part of the life of the Prophet (s). According to the historians, they were 12,000 in number in that battle.

Despite their larger numbers, they took to flight and turned their backs as usual, leaving the Prophet of Allah (s) amidst the enemies of Allah, the polytheists. He had only 9 or 10 persons from Banu Hashim, at the head of whom was Imam 'Ali b. Abi Talib, according to al-Ya'qubi in his history, as well as according to other [sources].[7]

If their flight on the day of Uhud was disgraceful, then, at Hunayn, it was even more despicable and evil, for the steadfast ones who stayed with him at Uhud were four from out of a thousand companions, a ratio of 1:250.

At Hunayn, there were only ten patient and steadfast ones from 12,000 companions, a ratio of 1:1200. If Uhud occurred at the beginning of the emigration and the people were still few [in number], and only recently converted from the [period of] ignorance, what was their excuse at the battle of Hunayn which occurred at the end of 8 A.H., when only two years of the life of the Prophet remained? Despite their superior numbers and preparedness, they ran away head over heels from the battle, not even looking back at the Prophet of Allah (s).

---

[7] 'Abbas al-'Aqqad in *Abqariyat Khalid*, p.68.

The noble Qur'an clearly explains their feeble stances and their running away from that battle in the following words: *"And on the day of Hunayn when your large numbers elated you but yet availed you naught, the land constrained you despite its width, and you turned in retreat. Allah sent tranquility on the Prophet and on the believers and sent down an army which you did not perceive, and punished those who disbelieved, that is the chastisement for the disbelievers"* (9:26).

Allah explains that He strengthened [the position of] His Prophet (s) and those who persevered with him in the fight, by sending tranquility to them, and then assisted them with an army of angels who fought by their side and helped them against the disbelievers. There was no need of the deserters who fled from the enemy because they were afraid to die, disobeying thereby their Lord and their Prophet. Every time Allah tested them, He found them failing.

For further clarification, it is necessary for us to examine the narration reported by al-Bukhari, especially the routing of the companions in Hunayn. He reported in vol. 5, in "The Chapter on Allah's Words"; 'On the day of Hunayn when you were elated by your numbers, yet it availed you not...'", in "The Book of Military Campaigns," from Abu al-Qatada who said: "On the day of Hunayn, I saw a Muslim fighting a polytheist while another polytheist was coming up from the rear to kill him. I hastened to the one who was coming up from the rear.

He raised his hand to strike me, and I struck his hand and dismembered it. He grabbed me and squeezed me heavily until I feared [for my life]. Then he let up; I broke free and struck him, killing him. The Muslims were routed, and I was defeated with them. 'Umar b. al-Khattab was with the people; I said to him: 'What is the matter with the people?' He said: 'It is by Allah's decree... *(Sahih al-Bukhari*, vol. 5, p. 101).'"

Chapter 4: Concerning the General Companions

By Allah, how amazing is the conduct of 'Umar b. al-Khattab, who is held by the *Ahl al-Sunnah* to be among the bravest of the companions, if not the bravest of them all? They relate that Allah strengthened Islam through him and that the Muslims did not openly preach [Islam] until after his conversion. History informs us of the true events and how he turned his back and fled from battle on the day of Uhud. Just as he turned back on the day of Khaybar, when the Prophet of Allah (s) sent him to the city of Khaybar to conquer it, placing him at the head of an army. He and his companions were routed and they returned accusing him ('Umar) of cowardice, and him accusing them of cowardice.[8] He also retreated and fled on the day of Hunayn with those who fled; perhaps he was the first to flee, and people followed him since he was the bravest of them. As a result, we see Abu Qatada [who was] among the thousands who fled turning and 'Umar b. al-Khattab, as one surprised: "What is the matter with the people?" 'Umar b. al-Khattab was not satisfied with his running away from the battle and leaving the Prophet of Allah (s) in the middle of the polytheists. He [further] pretended to Abu Qatada that it was the decree of Allah!

Did Allah order 'Umar b. al-Khattab to flee from the battle? Or did He command him to remain firm and to persevere in the wars and not to run away? He said to him and his companions: *"O you who believe! If you meet the disbelievers in battle, do not turn upon your heels" (8:1).*

Allah took a covenant from him and his companions about that, as has been related in Allah's wise book: *"They had promised Allah before not to turn upon their heels and the covenant with Allah must be answered for" (33:15).*

How can Abu Hafs ('Umar) turn away from the battle and allege that it is Allah's decree? Where does he stand regarding the injunctions of these clear verses? Or are there seals upon the hearts?

---

[8] *Mustadrak*, al-Hakim, 3/37. Al-Dhahabi in *Talkhis al-Mustadrak*.

We are not here discussing the personality of 'Umar b. al-Khattab, we shall devote a special chapter to him. The *hadith* of al-Bukhari is nonetheless striking and leaves us with no alternative [but] to make quick observations. What concerns us at this point is the testimony of al-Bukhari that the companions, in spite of their large numbers, turned back on the day of Hunayn. Whoever reads the historical texts on those wars and military campaigns will encounter the most surprising things.

If the decree of Allah was not obeyed by most companions, as we realized from the preceding discussions, then their disobedience to the commands of the Prophet of Allah (s) while he was alive and in their midst is not surprising. As for his commands after his death, may my father and mother be sacrificed for him, these were neglected, changed and altered without any concern.

The companions' position regarding the orders of the Prophet during his lifetime

Let us begin with the commands he issued during his lifetime which were countered by the companions with revolt and disobedience.

For the sake of brevity, we shall discuss only those [reports] documented by al-Bukhari in his *Sahih*. We will devote special pages to the rest of the *Sahihs* of the *Ahl al-Sunnah,* they are replete with far more instances, and with far more explicit and challenging reports.

Al-Bukhari reported in vol. 3, in "The Chapter on the Conditions on War and Making Treaties with those who Wage Wars," in "The Book of Conditions," after reporting the episode of the treaty of al-Hudaybiyya and 'Umar b. al-Khattab's opposition to what the Prophet of Allah (s) had agreed to, he doubted him, saying to him openly: "Aren't you really the Prophet of Allah?".. to the end of the story... Al-Bukhari said: "When they finished the matter of writing down the terms [of the treaty], the Prophet of Allah (s) said to his companions: 'Arise and sacrifice the animals and then shave your heads'. He said: 'By Allah! Not a man stood up from them, even

Chapter 4: Concerning the General Companions

after he repeated himself three times. Yet no one amongst them rose. He went to Umm Salama and related to her what he had encountered from the people (*Sahih al-Bukhari*, vol. 3, p. 182).'"

Are you not surprised, O reader, at the insolence and disobedience of the companions with regards to the order of the Prophet (s)? Although it was repeated three times, none of them responded.

It is necessary here to relate a discussion that took place between some scholars and me in Tunis after the publication of my book "Then I Was Guided". In it, they had read my remarks on the treaty of al-Hudaybiyya, and, in turn, had added their comments to mine, saying: "If the companions had disobeyed the order of the Prophet (s) on the sacrifice and shaving, and none of them complied with his order, then 'Ali b. Abi Talib was among them and therefore he [also] did not comply with the order of the Prophet of Allah (s)." I responded to them with the following:

Firstly: 'Ali was not reckoned to be among the companions. He was the brother and cousin of the Prophet of Allah, the husband of his daughter, and the father of his progeny. 'Ali was with the Prophet of Allah on one side, and the rest of the people on the other. If the narrator in *Sahih al-Bukhari* said that the Prophet (s) ordered his companions to slaughter the animals and to shave their heads, then Abu'l-Hasan (as) was not counted among them. He was to him (the Prophet) what Aaron was to Moses. Don't you see that the greetings upon the Prophet are not complete unless the greetings upon his family are added to them? Without doubt he ('Ali) is the leader of the progeny of Muhammad. [As for] Abu Bakr, 'Umar, 'Uthman and other companions, their prayers are not complete unless they mention 'Ali b. Abi Talib along with Muhammad b. 'Abd Allah.

Secondly: The Prophet of Allah (s) always used to share with 'Ali, his brother, his sacrifices, as occurred in the farewell pilgrimage when 'Ali came from Yemen and the Prophet of Allah (s) asked him: "What did you offer [for sacrifice] O 'Ali?" He replied: "What the Prophet of Allah offered." The Prophet shared his sacrifice with him. All the *hadith* reporters and historians have recorded this incident. He must have been his partner at al-Hudaybiyya too. Thirdly: 'Ali b. Abi Talib was the one who wrote the terms of the treaty of al-Hudaybiyya, as dictated by the Prophet of Allah (s), and had never disputed with him in anything throughout his life; not at al-Hudaybiyya, nor at any other occasion. History has not recorded a single instance at which 'Ali (as) delayed [carrying out an order of] the Prophet (s) or disobeyed him even once, God forbid, or that he ever fled from a battle and left his brother and cousin amongst the enemies. Rather, he constantly offered himself [as a sacrifice]. In short, 'Ali b. Abi Talib was like the Prophet (s) himself. As a result, the Prophet (s) used to say: "None is allowed to remain in the mosque while ritually impure (*junub*) except I and 'Ali."[9]

Most of the participants [in the discussion] were convinced by what I had presented and admitted that 'Ali b. Abi Talib never in his life opposed any order of the Prophet of Allah (s).

Al-Bukhari reported in vol. 8, in "The Chapter on Abhorrence of Differences," in "The Book on Adherence to the Qur'an and *Sunnah*," from 'Abd Allah b. 'Abbas who said: "When the time of the Prophet's (s) death drew near, there were people in the house, among them 'Umar b. al-Khattab. He said: 'Come so that I may write for you [something] so that you may never go astray.' 'Umar said: 'Surely the Prophet (s) is overcome by pain; you have with you the Qur'an, and the book of Allah is sufficient for us." The members of the household differed and argued [amongst themselves]. Among them were those who said: 'Come closer, the Prophet of Allah (s) will write for you [something] so you will never go astray afterwards.' Among them were those who said what 'Umar had said. When the noise and differences intensified in the presence of the Prophet (s), he said: 'Go away from me.'"

Ibn 'Abbas used to say: "The calamity of all calamities was the clamour and differences that occurred between the Prophet of Allah

---

[9] *Sahih al-Tirmidhi* 5/303; *History of the Caliphs*, al- Suyuti, p 172; *Al-Sawa'iq al-Muhriqa*, Ibn Hajar, 121.

Chapter 4: Concerning the General Companions

(s) and his writing the dictate for them *(Sahih al-Bukhari*, vol. 8, p. 161; vol. 1, p. 37, and vol. 5, p. 138)."

This is another command of the Prophet of Allah (s) which the companions countered with rejection, disobedience and degradation [of the status of] the Prophet (s).

It must be noted that when he (the Prophet) asked for paper and ink to be brought so that he could write for them a letter which would prevent them from going astray, 'Umar b. al-Khattab said in the presence of the Prophet (s): "The Prophet of Allah is delirious," i.e., hallucinating, God forbid.

Al-Bukhari, however, rectified that expression and changed it to "overcome by pain," because the one who said it was 'Umar b. al-Khattab. You see, he omitted the name of 'Umar in the narration, saying: "and they said the Prophet of Allah is delirious." This is the honesty of al-Bukhari in transmitting *hadith*. (We will, God willing, devote a special chapter to this.)

In any case, most *hadith* scholars and historians relate that 'Umar b. al-Khattab said: "Surely the Prophet of Allah (s) is delirious" and many companions followed him and said what he said in the presence of the Messenger of Allah (s). It is for us to picture the awful event and those raised voices, the intense clamor and dissension in his presence. No matter how the narration expresses it, it can inform us only a little of the actual scene. It is the same if we read a historical book on the life of Moses (as); no matter how vivid the book is, it will not have the effect of a film which we see with our eyes.

In vol. 7, in "The Chapter on What is Allowable in Anger and Intensity for Allah's sake," al-Bukhari reported in "The Book of Morals:" "The Prophet (s) made a small room with a mat from palm leaves. He came out (of his house) and went out to pray on it. The people followed him in this. The [next] night they [also] came, but the Apostle of Allah (s) delayed and did not come out to them. So they raised their voices and threw stones at the door. He came out angrily and said: 'You insisted on it (the prayer), until I thought it would become obligatory upon you. Offer your (optional) prayer in your homes, for surely the best prayer of a man is in his house, except the obligatory prayer (*Sahih al-Bukhari*, vol. 7, p. 99; vol. 2, p. 252; vol. 4, p. 168).'"

Most unfortunately, 'Umar contravened the order of the Prophet (s) and gathered the people for supererogatory prayer during his Caliphate, saying regarding his action: "This is an innovation, a wonderful one."[10] Most of the companions followed his innovation, they espoused his views and supported him in everything he did and said. 'Ali b. Abi Talib, and the *Ahl al-Bayt*, differed with him for they did not act, except [according to] the orders of their master, the Prophet of Allah (s) and did not substitute anything for it. If every innovation leads to error and every error leads to the fire, what about the errors which were invented to oppose the rulings of the Prophet (s)?

In vol. 5, in "The Chapter on the Battle of Zayd b. Haritha," in "The Book of Campaigns," al-Bukhari reported on the authority of Ibn 'Umar (r) who said: "The Apostle of Allah (s) ordered Usama b. Zayd to [lead] a group but they sought to find fault in his leadership. He said: 'If you find fault in his leadership, you [also] sought to find fault in the leadership of his father before him. By Allah, he was created for leadership and was the most beloved of men to me; and now he (Usama) is the most beloved of people to me after him *(Sahih al-Bukhari*, vol. 5, p. 84).'"

This event has been related in detail by the historians; how they angered the Prophet of Allah (s) until he cursed those who stayed behind the expedition of Usama, as he was a young general who had not reached seventeen years of age. The Prophet (s) had put him in charge of an army in which were Abu Bakr, 'Umar, Talha, al-Zubayr, 'Abd al-Rahman b. 'Awf and all the Qurayshi notables; the Prophet (s) did not draft 'Ali b. Abi Talib, nor any of the companions who followed him ('Ali) in that army.

Al-Bukhari always summarizes events and edits the *hadith* to

---

[10] *Sahih al-Bukhari* 2/252, "Book of the *Tarawi* Prayer"

Chapter 4: Concerning the General Companions

protect the honour of the "pious predecessors" amongst the companions. Despite this, what he reports is sufficient for one who wishes to attain the truth.

In vol. 2 of his *Sahih*, in "The Chapter on Reproach of He who Fasted Continuously," in "The Book of Fasting," al-Bukhari reported on the authority of Abu Hurayrah who said: "The Prophet of Allah (s) forbade fasting [two days] continuously without breaking it and a Muslim said to him: 'But you fast continuously, O Prophet of Allah!' He replied: 'And who among you is like me? Verily I stay awake at night and my Lord grants me sustenance and water'. When they refused to stop fasting continuously, he joined them one day's fast with another [day], and then they sighted the crescent. Then He said: 'Had it (the crescent) been delayed, I would have continued [fasting] with you.' It was as a reproach to them for having failed to desist as he had ordered (*Sahih al-Bukhari*, vol. 2, p. 243)."

Well done to these companions who the Prophet of Allah (s) prohibited from doing something but they did not desist from it. He kept on repeating the prohibition, but they would not listen. Did they not read Allah's words: *"Whatever the Prophet gives you, accept it, and whatever he forbids you from, keep away from it, and fear Allah! Indeed Allah is severe in punishment"* (59:7).

Despite the threat of grave punishment by Allah, Glory be to Him, to those who opposed His Messenger, some companions did not attach any importance to His threats and warnings.

If this was their condition, then there can be no doubt about their hypocrisy, even though they outwardly exhibited an abundance of prayer, fasting and strict [adherence to] religion, to the extent that they even forbade themselves from cohabitation with their wives so that they might not travel with their penises dripping with semen. They refrained from what the Prophet of Allah (s) did, as has been discussed previously.

Al-Bukhari, in his *Sahih*, vol. 5, in "The Chapter on the Prophet's (s) sending of Khalid b. al-Walid to Banu Judhayma," in "The Book of Military Campaigns," on the authority of al-Zuhri from Salim from his father, he said: "The Prophet (s) sent Khalid b. al-Walid to Banu Judhayma and he invited them to Islam. It did not seem proper to them to say we have submitted ourselves and so they said [instead]: 'We have left idol worship. We have left idol worship.' Khalid started to kill them and to take captives. He gave each one amongst us his captive. Then, one day, Khalid ordered each man to kill his captive. I said: 'By Allah! I will not kill my prisoner and none of my companions will kill theirs.' [This happened till] we came to the Prophet (s) and we related this to him. The Prophet (s) raised his hands and said twice: 'O Allah! I am innocent of what Khalid has done *(Sahih al-Bukhari* vol. 5, p. 107, vol. 8, p. 118).'"

The historians have chronicled this event in some detail and [shown] how Khalid perpetrated this despicable act of disobedience. He, and some of his companions who obeyed him, did not adhere to the commands of the Prophet of Allah (s) regarding the prohibition of killing anyone who accepted Islam. Certainly, this was one of the worst sins that caused the flowing of innocent blood, and the Prophet (s) had ordered them to invite the people to Islam, not to kill them.

Khaild b. al-Walid was overcome by the urge of the *Jahili* period, and a satanic force overcame him. [This was because] the Banu Judhayma had killed his uncle al-Fakiha b. al-Mughira, during the time of Ignorance. He came upon them and said: "Lay down your arms for the people have accepted Islam." He then ordered that their hands be tied and many of them be killed.

When some of the sincere companions learned of Khalid's intentions, they fled from the army and joined the Prophet (s) and related the news to him. The Prophet of Allah (s) then dissociated himself from his acts and sent 'Ali b. Abi Talib who compensated them for the loss of blood and property.

To know this incident in some detail, there is no harm in reading what 'Abbas Mahmud al-'Aqqad has written in his book: "The

Chapter 4: Concerning the General Companions 157

wonderful [exploits of] Khalid," wherein al-'Aqqad writes on pages 57 & 58 as follows:

"After the conquest of Mecca, his (the Prophet's) concern was directed to the cleansing of the Bedouin tribes surrounding it (Mecca) from idol worship. He sent expeditions to the tribes to invite them and to ascertain their intentions. Amongst the expeditions was that of Khalid b. al-Walid to Banu Judhayma, numbering about 350 emigrants, Ansars and Banu Sulaym. He sent them as missionaries and did not order them to fight. Banu Judhayma was the fiercest tribe during the period of Ignorance and was known as the "spoonful of blood."

Among those that they had killed on one occasion were al-Fakiha b. al-Mughira and his brother, the paternal uncles of Khalid b. al-Walid and the father of 'Abd al-Rahman b. 'Awf and Malik b. al-Sharid and his three brothers from Banu Sulaym in one place, as well as several others from various tribes.

When Khalid came to them and they knew that the Banu Sulaym were with him, they donned their weapons and rode forth for battle, refusing to give in. Khalid asked them: 'Are you Muslims?' It is said that some of them answered in the affirmative and some of them said: 'Saba'na! Saba'na!' i.e., we have left idol worship! We have left idol worship! He then asked them: 'Why are the weapons on you?' They replied: 'There is enmity between us and some Arab tribes and we feared that you might be them, so we donned our weapons.'

He said to them: 'Drop your weapons for the people have accepted Islam'. A man among them who was called Juhdam cried out: 'Woe be unto you O Banu Judhayma! This is Khalid. By Allah, captivity will follow your dropping of weapons. After captivity [he will] behead you. By Allah! I will never give up my weapons'. He was still saying this when his weapons were taken away along with those of others. The other [people] dispersed.

Khalid ordered that they be handcuffed and put to the sword. Banu Sulaym and the other Arabs with them accepted his orders of killing them. The Ansars and Muhajirun, however, refused to kill anyone without being commanded by the Prophet (s) to fight [them]. The news reached the Prophet (s) who raised his hands towards the sky and said three times: 'O Allah! I dissociate myself of what Khalid has done.' He then sent 'Ali b. Abi Talib to Banu Judhayma to compensate them for the blood and property that had been destroyed.

The event appalled the prominent companions, those who had accompanied the expedition as well as those who had not. 'Abd al-Rahman b. 'Awf was so incensed that he accused Khalid of deliberate slaughter to avenge his two uncles."

This is the verbatim quote of what al-'Aqqad reported in his book "The wonderful [exploits of] Khalid." And al-'Aqqad is like the other *Ahl al-Sunnah* thinkers, for, after relating the entire episode, he seeks a cold, fictitious explanation [to defend] what Khalid had done, [an explanation] which is baseless and which no sound reason can accept. There is no excuse for al-'Aqqad except that he wrote "The wonderful [exploits of] Khalid." Everything he presented in defense of Khalid is presumptuous, fragile as a spider's web. Whoever reads it realizes the folly and weakness of his defense.

How can there be any excuse when he himself bore testimony in his own words that the Prophet (s) sent them as missionaries and did not order them to fight? And he admitted that the Banu Judhayma had removed their arms after having donned them when Khalid deceived them by telling his companions: "Remove your weapons, for the people have become Muslims."

He also confessed that Juhdam had refused to lay aside his arms and warned his tribe that Khalid will deceive them by his words: "Woe unto you O Banu Judhayma, he is Khalid! By Allah, there is nothing after the removal of your arms except captivity, and after captivity beheading. By Allah! I will never lay down my arms". Al-'Aqqad said that the Banu Judhayma crowded him until he removed his arms. This shows the submission of the tribe and of their good intentions.

Chapter 4: Concerning the General Companions 159

If the Prophet of Allah (s) sent them as preachers of Islam and had not ordered them to fight, as you yourself testified, O 'Aqqad, then what was Khalid's excuse in opposing the orders of the Prophet (s)? I don't think you can legitimize it, O 'Aqqad!

If the tribe had removed their weapons, declared their Islam, and finally won over their companion, who had sworn that he would not lay aside his weapons until they pacified him, as you have yourself admitted, O 'Aqqad, then what is Khalid's excuse for betraying them and killing them when [they were] passive and were bereft of their weapons?

You have said that Khalid issued orders against them, their hands were tied and they were put to the sword. This is another deed that I do not think you can justify, O 'Aqqad! Did Islam order Muslims to kill those who do not fight them, [even] assuming that they did not declare their Islam? Certainly not, this is the argument that the Orientalists, the enemies of Islam, propagate today.

Then, once again, you admit that the Prophet (s) did not order him to fight the people, for you said that the emigrants and the Ansar rebuked Khalid for having killed anyone without being commanded by the Prophet (s) to fight. What is your excuse, O 'Aqqad, for seeking excuses for Khalid?

In replying to al-'Aqqad, it is sufficient for us [to note] that he completely refuted and destroyed his own excuses by saying: "The revulsion to the event extended to all the prominent companions, those who were present in the expedition and those who were not." If the prominent companions expressed [their] disgust towards Khalid to the extent that they fled from his army and complained to the Prophet (s) and if 'Abd al-Rahman b. 'Awf accused Khalid of deliberately killing the people in revenge for his two uncles, as al-'Aqqad has testified, and if the Prophet of Allah (s) had raised his hands to the sky and said three times: "O Allah, I dissociate [myself] from what Khalid b. al-Walid has done," [and] if the Prophet sent 'Ali with property to compensate the Banu Judhayma for the blood [spilt] and [for the loss] of property so as to appease them, as al-'Aqqad has testified, this [in itself] proves that the community had accepted Islam, but that Khalid had wronged them and committed excesses against them. Can someone ask al-'Aqqad, who tries his best to defend Khalid, is he (al-'Aqqad) more learned than the Prophet of Allah (s) who dissociated [himself] from his acts three times? Or is he more learned than the prominent companions who reproached him? Or more than the companions who were present at the event but escaped from the expedition dismayed by his repulsive acts which they had witnessed? Or [is he more learned] than 'Abd al-Rahman b. 'Awf, who was with him in the expedition and, without doubt, knew Khalid better than al-'Aqqad? He accused him of deliberately killing the people so as to exact revenge for his uncles.

May Allah fight blind fanaticism and *jahili* zeal which changes the truth. Although al-Bukhari summarized the matter in four lines, what he has mentioned is sufficient to convict Khalid, and the other companions who obeyed him in killing innocent Muslims, and whom al-'Aqqad has mentioned by saying: "Banu Sulaym and those Arabs with him obeyed him in killing them." However, al-Bukhari [mentions] only two or three who did not comply with his commands; they fled from the army and returned to the Prophet complaining of Khalid. You cannot convince us, O 'Aqqad, that the emigrants and Ansars who totaled 350, as you have said, did not obey Khalid in killing the people, and that they all fled from the army, no researcher can believe this. This is [merely] an attempt on your part to preserve the nobility of the pious ancestors, the companions, and to hide the realities at any cost. The time has come to remove the veils and to know the truth.

How many despicable massacres of Khalid b. al-Walid has history related to us, especially on the day of al-Battah when Abu Bakr appointed him to be the head of a big army comprising of foremost companions. He deceived Malik b. Nuwayra and his people when they removed their weapons; he ordered that their hands be tied and then beheaded them without a fight. He entered Layla, Umm Tamim, the wife of Malik, on the same night that her husband was killed. When 'Umar b. al-Khattab came to know [what happened], he castigated him and told him: "You killed a Muslim man then sprang on his wife, by Allah, I will stone you with your stones, O enemy of Allah". Abu Bakr stood beside Khalid and said to 'Umar: "Stop [moving] your tongue against Khalid, he used [his reasoning] and erred." This is another issue whose discussion is lengthy and mentioning it is repulsive.

The rights of how many unfortunate people have been usurped because a tyrant is strong and powerful? How [frequently] a tyrant is helped in his tyranny and falsehood because he is rich and close to the apparatus of the rulers. When he examines the story of the Banu Judhayma, al-Bukhari cuts the story short and says: "The Prophet sent Khalid to Banu Judhayma, he invited them to Islam. They did not deem it proper to say 'We have submitted', so they said 'We have turned away from idol worship.'"

Were the Banu Judhayma Persians or Turks or Indians or Germans that they did not deem it proper to say "We have submitted," O Bukhari? Or were they an Arab tribe in whose language the Qur'an was revealed? Blind fanaticism and the major plots which were conspired to protect the nobility of the companions made al-Bukhari utter such statements so as to vindicate the act of Khalid b. al-Walid. Al-'Aqqad also says: "Khalid asked them: 'Are you Muslims?'" Al-'Aqqad then says: "It is said that some of them replied in the affirmative and some of them replied '*saba'na, saba'na* (we have left idolatry).'" The words "it is said" show clearly that the community would accept anything which people conjured up so as to defend Khalid b. al-Walid. [This is] because Khalid b. al-Walid was the raised sword of the ruler and was the defender of the usurping Caliphate. He was its follower, exemplifying overwhelming strength to whoever resolved to rebel or revolt against what had been decided by the heroes of Saqifa on the day that the Prophet (s) passed away. There is no power nor strength except with Allah, the most High, the most Great.

The companions' conduct towards the Prophet's commands after his death.

Their neglecting of the Prophet's *Sunnah*

Al-Bukhari reports in vol. 1 in "The Chapter of Neglecting of the

Salat' from Ghaytan: "Anas b. Malik said: 'I know nothing which is [performed] now that was performed in the time of the Prophet (s)'. It was said: 'The prayer'. He (Anas) responded: 'Have you not neglected it [amongst the things] that you have neglected?'

He said: "I heard al-Zuhri say: 'I visited Anas b. Malik in Damascus and [I found him] crying. I said to him: 'What makes you cry?' He said: 'I do not know of anything which I encountered [during the time of the Prophet] except this *salat* and this has [also] been abandoned *(Sahih al-Bukhari* vol. 1, p. 134).'"

Al-Bukhari has also reported in vol. 1 in "The Chapter of the Superiority of the *Fajr* in Congregation: "Al-A'mash told us: 'I heard Salim saying: 'I heard Umm Darda say: 'Abu Darda came to me whilst he was angry. I said to him: 'What has angered you?' He said: 'By Allah, I do not know from the *ummah* of Muhammad (s) anything else except that they prayed in congregation *(Sahih al-Bukhari* vol. 1, p. 159).'"

In vol. 2 in "The Chapter of going to a Mosque in which there is no *Minbar*" al-Bukhari reports that Abu Sa'id al-Khudri said: "The Prophet of Allah (s) used to go out on the day of *'id al-fitr* and *'id al-duha* to the mosque. The first thing that he used to do was to pray, and then he would exhort the people. The people continued this [practise] until I went out with Marwan when he was the governor of Medina on the day of *'id al-duha* or *'id al-fitr*. He wanted to ascend the pulpit before praying. I caught hold of his clothes but he pushed me away, ascended the *minbar* and delivered the sermon before the prayer. I said to him: 'You have altered [the *sunna*], by God'. He said: 'Abu Sa'id, what you know has gone away'. I said: 'By Allah, it is better than what I do not know.' He responded: 'The people would not remain after the prayer, so I delivered it before the prayer *(Sahih al-Bukhari*, vol. 2, p. 4).'"

The companions during the time of Anas b. Malik and Abu Darda and during the lifetime of Marwan b. al-Hakam, and this was a period [which was] very close to the lifetime of the Prophet (s), changed the *Sunnah* of the Prophet (s) and had discarded everything, even the prayer, as you have heard, and reversed the

Chapter 4: Concerning the General Companions

order of the *Sunnah* of the chosen one (s) for their evil benefits, i.e., the Banu Umayya adopted the practise of reviling and cursing 'Ali and the *Ahl al-Bayt* from the pulpits after every sermon. Most of the people at the *'id al-fitr* and *'id al-duha* had dispersed after prayer was completed, as they did not like to hear the Imam curse 'Ali b. Abi Talib and the *Ahl al-Bayt*, as a result, the Banu Umayya intended to change the *Sunnah* of the Prophet (s), so they delivered the *khutba* before the prayer at the two *'ids*, so that the practise of cursing and abusing 'Ali could be established in the presence of the entire Muslim community, against their will.

At the head of this was Mu'awiyah b. Abi Sufyan, for he established this practice which, for them, became one of the best ways of getting close to Allah. It reached a point where some historians reported that one of their Imams finished his sermon on a Friday and, having forgotten to curse 'Ali started to descend the *minbar* to lead the prayer. The people from every corner started screaming at him: "You have abandoned the *Sunnah*! You have forgotten the *Sunnah*! Where is the *Sunnah*?"

Yes, unfortunately, this innovation which Mu'awiyah b. Abi Sufyan initiated, remained in continuous practice for eighty years on the *minbar* of the Muslims - and even to this day its influences remain. Despite this, the *Ahl al-Sunnah wa'l-Jama'a* are pleased with Mu'awiyah and his followers and they do not accept any reproach or criticism of him, under the pretext of respect for the companions.

Praise be to Allah that the sincere Muslims researchers have begun to differentiate between truth and falsehood. Many of them have begun to distance themselves from the deeds of the companions which Mu'awiyah, his partisans and followers, instituted. Now the *Ahl al-Sunnah wa'l-Jama'a* have begun to wake up to this repulsive inconsistency. They defend all the companions to the extent that they curse one who reviles [even] one of them. If you tell them: "This curse of yours includes Mu'awiyah b. Abi Sufyan, for he reviled and cursed the best of all companions and certainly meant to curse the Apostle of Allah who said: 'He who has cursed 'Ali has cursed me, and he who has cursed me has cursed

Allah;'"[11] at that, they stammer and hesitate in answering. They say things, which if they point to anything, merely indicate the stupidity of their minds and deep, blind fanaticism. Some of them, for example, respond by saying: "These are the lies fabricated by the Shi'as" and others say: "They are the companions of the Prophet of Allah; they can say what they wish to about others. As for us, we are not at their level to criticize them."

Glory and all Praise be to You, my Lord! Your words in the noble Qur'an led me to the realities which were difficult for me to comprehend and believe. Every time I used to read: *"And We have prepared for hell many of the jinn and humankind, they have hearts through which they understand not; they have eyes with which they see not and ears with which they hear not. They are like cattle, nay, worse yet; they are those who are heedless" (7:179).*

I used to be astonished [at this] and would ask myself: "How can this be?" Can a dumb animal be better guided than this human? Is it possible for a person to admire a stone, then worship and seek sustenance and assistance from it? However, praise be to Allah, my astonishment ceased when I dealt with people and travelled to India where I saw astonishing upon astonishing things, doctors in anatomy, well versed in knowledge of the cell structure of human and its formation, yet they worshipped the cow.

Had this sin been committed by the ignorant Hindus, one would have accepted their excuse. But you will see the cream of their intellectuals worshipping cows, stones, the sea, the sun and the moon. After [seeing] this, there remains [no alternative] but for you to submit and to understand the things to which the glorious Qur'an

---

[11] The *hadith* is reported by al-Hakim in his *Mustadrak* 3/121. He said that the tradition is sound, based on the criteria set by two Shaykhs, Muslim and al-Bukhari. It is also reported by al-Dhahabi in his *Talkhis*, who admitted to its veracity. Similarly [the tradition is accepted] by Imam Ahmad b. Hanbal in his *Musnad* vol. 6, p. 323, *al-Nasa'i* and others.

Chapter 4: Concerning the General Companions

points to, especially those human beings who are more misguided than animals.

Abu Dharr al-Ghifari's testimony regarding some of the companions

Al-Bukhari reports in vol. 2 under the heading "That from which *Zakat* is paid is not Buried Treasure" from al-Ahnaf b. Qays [who] said: "I was sitting with the notables from Quraysh, and there came a man of coarse hair, clothes and appearance who stood in front of them, greeted [them] and said: 'Inform those who hoard (wealth) that a stone will be heated in the hell fire and will be put on the nipples of their breasts until it comes out from their shoulder bones, then it will be put on their shoulder bones until it comes from their nipples, it will be moving [inside them]'. Then he went away and sat near a pillar. I followed him and sat near him, although I did not know who he was. I said to him: 'I do not think the people liked what you said.' He replied: 'They do not understand anything. My friend said to me....' I said to him: 'And who is your friend?' He said: 'The Prophet (s)'. He said to me: 'O Abu Dharr, do you see Uhud?' He said: 'I looked at the sun, to see how much of the day remained. I thought that the Prophet wanted to me to go somewhere for a need. So I said: 'Yes.' He said: 'I do not wish to have gold the size of Uhud unless I would spend it all (in charity) except three dinars.' These [people] do not understand, they collect only worldly pleasures. No, by Allah, I will not ask them for worldly possessions nor seek their guidance in religion until I meet Allah the most Honourable, most Majestic *(Sahih al-Bukhari*, vol. 2, p. 12).'"

Al-Bukhari also reports in section seven in "The Chapter [entitled] 'The Fountain and the Saying of Allah, the Most High: *'Indeed I have given you al-kawthar'''*. On the authority of 'Ata b. Yasar, from Abu Hurayrah, that the Prophet (s) said: "While I will be standing, a group of my followers will be brought there and, after I recognise them, a man will come between me and them and will say: 'Come along'. I will ask: 'Where to?' He will say: 'To the fire, by Allah'. I will say: 'What is with them?' He will say: 'They apostatized after you and moved backward'. Then another group will be brought and, as I will recognize them, a man will come between me and them saying: 'Come on'. I will say: 'Whereto?' He will say 'To the fire, by Allah'. I will say: 'What is their case?' He will say: 'They renegated and apostatized after you and I do not see any of them being spared except a few who are like cattle without a shepherd'".

From Abu Sa'id al-Khudri: "It will be said: 'You do not know what they initiated after you'. I will say: 'Woe, woe unto those who changed [things] after me'" (Bukhari vol. 7, p. 209).

Al-Bukhari vol. 5 in "The Chapter of The Battle of al-Hudaybiyya and the Saying of Allah the Almighty: *'And verily Allah was pleased with the believers as they pledged their fealty to you under the tree'" (48:18)*. From 'Ala b. al-Musayyab, who narrated from his father, who said: "I met al-Bara'a b. 'Azib (r) and said to him: 'You are fortunate, you were a companion of the Prophet and paid allegiance to him under the tree'. Whereupon he said: 'My nephew, you do not know what we innovated after him'" *(Sahih al-Bukhari*, vol. 5, p. 66).

This is a major testimony from a prominent companion who was, at least, honest with himself and with the people. His testimony is confirmation of what Allah said regarding them: *"If he dies or is killed, will you then go back on your heels?" (3:144)*

It is [also] a confirmation of the Prophet's (s) statement: "Then it will be said to me: 'They apostatized after you and receded [from Islam]'".

Al-Bara' b. 'Azib was an eminent companion amongst the earliest notables who pledged their allegiances to the Prophet under the tree. He is bearing witness against himself and against other companions that they innovated [practices] after the death of the Prophet (s) so that the people may not take pride in them. He made it clear that being a companion of the Prophet (s) and giving him allegiance under the tree which was called "the pledge of pleasure" did not prevent a companion from going astray and reverting [to unbelief] after the Prophet (s).

Chapter 4: Concerning the General Companions

In vol. 8 al-Bukhari has reported under the heading "The Prophet's (s) words: 'You will surely follow the practices of those who were before you'". "On the authority of 'Ata b. Yasar, from Abu Sa'id al-Khudri, that the Prophet (s) said: 'You will follow the practices of those before you, literally even if they enter a lizard's burrow, you will follow them'. We said: 'O Prophet of Allah, (do you mean) the Jews and the Christians?' He said: 'And who else'" *(Sahih al-Bukhari* vol. 8, p. 151)?

History's testimony about the companions

For us, after the Qur'an and the *Sunnah,* there is another form of testimony which can be more explicit and clear for it was actually lived and felt by the people. They witnessed and interrelated with it, this evolved into history which was recorded and related, memorized and printed.

If we read the *Ahl al-Sunnah wa'l-Jama'a* historical books like the works of al-Tabari, Ibn al-Athir, Ibn Sa'd, Abu'l-Fida, Ibn Qutayba and others, we see the most surprising things; we realise that what the *Ahl al-Sunnah* say regarding the upright conduct of the companions and the absence of blemish in any of them are simply views which are based on no proof, no sound reason will accept them. No one will agree with [these views] except the fanatics, [in them] light has been overcome by darkness. They do not differentiate between the companions and Muhammad, the Prophet (s), the infallible one, who uttered not one word from his own desire and did nothing but what was right. The Qur'an bore witness to their hypocrisy, corruption and lack of uprightness. You find them defending the companions more than they defend the Prophet of Allah (s). I cite some examples of these:

When it is said to any one of them that *Surah 'Abasa* does not refer to the Apostle of God (s) but, rather, refers to one of the prominent companions whom Allah rebuked for his pride and arrogance when he saw a poor blind man, you will not find him accepting this interpretation. He says instead: "Muhammad was nothing but a man, he erred on several occasions and Allah rebuked him more than once. He is not infallible except in proclaiming the Qur'an". This is his view regarding the Prophet of Allah.

If, however, you tell him that 'Umar al-Khattab erred in innovating *salat al-tarawi* which the Prophet of Allah (s) forbade and instead ordered the people to pray in their houses by themselves if a prayer is of a supererogatory nature (i.e., not compulsory), you will see him defending 'Umar b. al-Khattab with defenses which cannot be discussed. He will say: "It is a good *bida*" and he will exert all efforts to find an excuse, despite a clear text from the Prophet (s) forbidding [it]. If you say to him that 'Umar abrogated a share for those whose hearts were to be appeased as [a share] ordained by God in His glorious book, you will find him replying: "Our master 'Umar knew that Islam was strong, therefore he said to them: 'We do not need you.' He is more versed in the Qur'an than everyone else". Are you not surprised at this?

The limit was reached when I said to one of them: "Let us leave aside this "good *bida*" and those whose hearts were to be placated. What is your defense of him when he threatened to burn the house of Fatima al-Zahra (sa) and all who were [residing] in it unless they came out to pledge allegiance"?

He said to me quite candidly: "The truth was with him. Had he not done that, many of the companions would have sided with 'Ali b. Abi Talib and discord would have occurred."

Our conversations with this group of people do not help or benefit us. It is very unfortunate that most of the *Ahl al-Sunnah wa'l-Jama'a* reason in this way for they do not know the truth except according to 'Umar and his actions. They have inverted the rule and know the truth by the men; they are supposed to know the men by the truth (know the truth and you will know it's people as Imam 'Ali has said).

This type of belief spread amongst them and 'Umar surpassed all the *sahaba*. They are all [seen as] upright and it is impossible for anyone to disparage or criticize them. By this method, they built a thick wall and an impenetrable barrier for every researcher who

Chapter 4: Concerning the General Companions 169

seeks to know the truth. You will find that he does not finish one wave but several [others] oppose him; he does not overcome one danger except that several others are put in his path. It is impossible for the poor researcher to arrive at the shore of safety unless he is persevering, patient and brave.

If we return to the topic of history, we find that in the case of some companions, their secrets are exposed, their veils dropped and their true colors are shown, [things] which they had sought to hide from the people. Their helpers, followers and evil judges who sought to be close to them, [also] tried [to hide].

The first thing that grabs the attention is their stance regarding the Prophet (s), the morning after his death, may my soul be sacrificed for him. How could they leave his corpse when they had not prepared, washed it nor shrouded or buried it? Instead, they rushed to their meeting in the hall of Banu Sa'ida, debating and arguing amongst themselves over the Caliphate, whose religiously designated owner they knew. They had pledged allegiance to him during the lifetime of the Prophet (s).

What convinces us that they used the occasion to benefit from the absence of 'Ali and the Banu Hashim, whose morals had prevented them from leaving the Prophet of Allah (s) and rushing to the Saqifa, is that these [companions] wanted to finalize the matter quickly, before they had completed their noble task, and then impose upon them a decided issue. They (the Banu Hashim) were not able to say [anything] or debate since those at the Saqifa had vowed to kill anyone who sought to nullify the matter which they had decided upon, on the pretext of combating those who opposed and [on the pretext] of averting anarchy.

The historians have recorded surprising and strange things, that had occurred in those days, by those companions who later became the Caliphs of the Prophet (s) and commanders of the believers; like their forcing people to pay allegiance by violence, threats and power; their attack on the house of Fatima and opening it, and the pressure on her stomach with the door which she was behind, causing her to miscarry her child. And their coercing 'Ali, with his hands tied, and threats to kill him if he refused to pay allegiance. Similarly, they denied Fatima's rights of gifts, and her inheritance, and her share as a close relative of the Prophet. Up to her death, she was angry with them and she would pray against them in every prayer. She was buried at night in secrecy and no one attended her funeral.

[Another example is] their killing of companions who refused to pay the *zakat* to Abu Bakr in protest until they knew the reason of 'Ali being overlooked for the Caliphate. [This was because] they had pledged to him during the Prophet's time at Ghadir Khum.[12]

Or like their dishonoring the women and transgressing the limits of Allah in their killing of innocent Muslims and forcing themselves upon the women without observing the stipulated waiting period (*'idda*).[13]

[Historians have also recorded] their altering the rulings of Allah and His Prophet (s) which are clear in the book and the *Sunnah* and substituting, instead, judgments based on their personal reasoning that served their personal purposes.[14]

[They have recorded events] like some of them consuming alcohol and continuing to commit fornication when they were governors of Muslims and their judges.[15]

[Events] like the exile and banishment of Abu Dharr al-Ghifari from the city of the Prophet (s) until he died in solitude without

---

[12] The episode of Malik b. Nuwayra and his killing is well known in the books of history.

[13] The story of Khalid b. al-Walid and his sleeping with Layla bint Minhal after the murder of her husband.

[14] Such as the denial of Fatima's inheritance and the share of the Prophet's family and the allotment of those whose heart were to be placated and temporary marriage and *al-hajj al-tamattu'* and other numerous issues.

[15] The story of Mughira b. Shu'ba and his fornication with Umm Jamil – the story is well known in historical books.

Chapter 4: Concerning the General Companions 171

having committed any sin. [Similarly] their beating of 'Ammar b. Yasir until he became unconscious and the beating of 'Abd Allah b. Mas'ud until his limbs broke and their isolating the sincere companions from positions of power which they gave instead to the corrupt ones and hypocrites from the Banu Umayya, [who were] the enemies of Islam.

[Historians have also recorded] the insults and curses directed against the *Ahl al-Bayt*, whom Allah had cleansed and purified completely, and the killing of virtuous companions who followed them.[16]

[Events] like their usurping the Caliphate by force, aggression, murder and threats; and removing anyone who opposed them by different ways like assassination, poisoning and other [means][17] and their seizing the city of the Prophet by the army of Yazid to do in it as they pleased in spite of the saying of the Prophet: "Indeed, my sanctuary [lies] in the city, whoever violates it will have the curse of Allah, the angels and mankind all upon him."

[Historians have also recorded events] like their stoning the house of Allah with [large] catapults and burning the holy sanctuary and their killing some companions who were in it.

[Events] like their waging war against the Commander of the Faithful and the leader of the successors and the master of the pure household at the battles of the Camel, Siffin and al-Nahrwan, due to their despicable greed for this transitory world. He was, to the Prophet of Allah, [the position that] Aaron was to Moses.

[Events] like their killing of the two masters of youths in paradise, Imam al-Hasan by poison and Imam al-Husayn by slaughter and mutilation, and their killing of the whole household of

---

[16] Like Mu'awiyah's killing of Hujr b. 'Adi, the honourable companion and his followers, because he refused to curse 'Ali b. Abi Talib.

[17] Historians report that Mu'awiyah would invite his opponents and feed them with poisoned honey and when they left his presence and later died, he would gloat: "Allah has an army from honey"

the Prophet (s) (apart from 'Ali, b. Husayn, no one was saved). They committed other acts due to which human conscience cries out. I spare my pen from writing about them. The *Ahl al-Sunnah wa'l-Jama'a* are aware of many of these [deeds] and [due to that] try their utmost to prevent the Muslims from reading history or researching the lives of the companions.

All the crimes and acts of violence that I have mentioned [quoting] from the historical books are, without doubt, the actions of the companions. It is not possible for anyone with intelligence, after reading this, to insist on the companions being faultless and to judge them [all] as being virtuous, [not allowing] criticism of any of them.

It must be stressed that we are absolutely aware of the moral probity, uprightness and piety of some of them, of their love for Allah and His Prophet (s) and their remaining true to the covenant [given to] the Prophet (s) until they died and that they did not change in the least. Allah is pleased with them and makes them reside in the proximity of their beloved Prophet Muhammad (s).

They are too great, honored and exalted for any person to ruin their reputation, or to fabricate any lies about them, for the Lord of Glory and Power has Himself praised them on several occasions in His glorious book just as He has acclaimed their companionship and their sincerity to the Prophet of mercy more than once. History has recorded nothing but the most honorable status, filled with chivalry, nobility, bravery, piety and servitude to Allah; congratulations to them, peaceful be their abode and gardens of eternity with doors opened for them, the pleasure of Allah is greatest for those who are grateful. As the book of God reminds us, the grateful ones are a small minority, so do not forget!

As for those who submitted yet no faith entered into their hearts, they accompanied the Prophet of Allah (s) either out of desire, fear or some personal motives which they kept hidden. The Qur'an rebuked and threatened them; the Prophet of Allah warned and cursed them on several occasions. History has recorded some despicable acts and stances...they do not deserve any respect and

Chapter 4: Concerning the General Companions

reverence, let alone that we should be pleased with them and accord them the position of Prophets, martyrs and upright ones.

This, by my life, is the true view for those who weigh things in a just manner and do not transgress the limits imposed by Allah for His slaves, i.e., love for the believers and enmity and dissociation from the corrupt ones. Allah says in His glorious book: *"Do you not see those who befriend a group that has Allah's anger upon it? They are not from you, nor are you from them. They swear falsely, knowingly. Allah has prepared a severe punishment for them. Evil indeed is what they used to do! They used their oaths as a cover to obstruct [men] from the path of Allah; for them is a humiliating chastisement. Neither their wealth nor their progeny will avail them with Allah. They are the inhabitants of the hell fire, they will dwell therein eternally. On the day when Allah will resurrect all of them, they will swear to Him as they swear to you. They will think that they have something, but they are liars. Satan has won them over and caused them to forget the remembrance of Allah. They are the party of Satan. Most certainly, the party of Satan are the losers! Those who resist Allah and His Prophet are the most abased. Allah has written that I and my Prophet will triumph; indeed Allah is most Strong, Powerful. You will not find a people who believe in Allah and the last day loving those who resist Allah and His Prophet, even if they be their fathers, their sons, their brothers or their kinsfolk. For them, Allah has written faith in their hearts and strengthened them with a spirit from Himself. And He will grace them with gardens below which rivers flow to dwell therein forever. Allah is pleased with them and they with Him, they are the party of Allah. Certainly, the party of Allah are the successful ones"*

(58:14-22).

I must not fail to record in this respect that the Shi'as are on the truth for they do not accord love except to Muhammad and his progeny and for the companions who walked on their path and the believers who followed them in goodness until the day of judgment. On the other hand, non-Shi'a Muslims accord love to all the companions paying no heed to those who resisted Allah and His Prophet, and they generally cite as their proof the words of Allah the Exalted: *"O Allah, forgive us and our brothers who preceded us in faith, and cause not in our hearts any rancor for those who believe. O Our Lord, you are most kind, most Merciful" (59:10).*

You will find them being pleased with 'Ali and Mu'awiyah without being concerned with the deeds which the latter committed. The least of what can be said of them is that these are [acts of] disbelief, deviation and fighting against Allah and His Apostle. I have previously mentioned an odd [instance], there is no harm in repeating it. One of the righteous people visited the grave of the eminent companion, Hujr b. 'Adi al-Kindi and found a man crying bitterly. Assuming him to be a Shi'a, he asked him: "Why are you crying?" He replied: "I am weeping over our master Hujr, may Allah be pleased with him."

He said: "What befell him?" He replied: "Our master Mu'awiyah, may Allah be pleased with him, killed him."

He asked: "Why did he kill him?"

He replied: "Because he refused to curse our master 'Ali, may Allah be pleased with him."

Whereupon the righteous man said to him: "And I weep for you, may Allah be pleased with you."

Why this persistence and obsession with the love for every companion? We find that they do not send blessings to Muhammad

Chapter 4: Concerning the General Companions

and his family without adding "and all the companions." The Qur'an did not order them to do this nor did the Prophet (s) demand it nor did any companion say it. The sending of blessings is only for Muhammad and his household, as revealed in the Qur'an and as was taught by the Prophet of Allah (s) to them.

If I ever doubted anything, one thing I do not doubt and never will doubt, is that Allah asked the believers to love the close relatives, they are the *Ahl al-Bayt*. He made this obligatory for them, like a reward for the message of Muhammad. The most High said: **"Say, I do not seek from you any reward except love for [my] kindred" (42:20).**

The Muslims have unanimously agreed upon the need for the love for the *Ahl al-Bayt* (as) and have differed about others. The Prophet of Allah (s) said: "Leave that which causes you doubt, for that which causes you no doubt."

The position of the Shi'as regarding love for the *Ahl al-Bayt* and their followers is indubitable, whereas the view of the *Ahl al-Sunnah wa'l-Jama'a* for the love for all companions presents grave doubts. Otherwise, how can the Muslims accord love to the enemies and murderers of *Ahl al-Bayt* (as) and be happy with them? Isn't there a clear contradiction?

Let us leave aside the talk of those who have gone astray and some Sufis who maintain that a person's heart does not become pure and knows no real faith until there remains not an atom's weight of hatred for all of Allah's servants be they Jews, Christians, heretics and polytheists. They have some incredibly strange sayings about that, agreeing with the Christian church evangelists who deceive men by saying that Allah is love and religion is love. One who loves His creation has no need for prayer, fasting, pilgrimage and other [rituals].

These, by my life, are idle talks, not accepted by the Qur'an, *Sunnah* nor reason. The noble Qur'an says: **"You will not find a community believing in Allah and the last day, loving those** *who resist Allah and His Messenger". He also says: "O you who believe! Do not take Jews and Christians as friends, for they are friends of each other. Whosoever amongst you takes them as friends, they are amongst them, God does not guide the wrongdoing community" (5:51).*

The Most High has said: *"O you who believe! Do not take your fathers and brothers as friends if they prefer disbelief over belief. Whoever amongst you befriends them, they are the wrongdoers" (9:23).* He also said: *"O You who believe, do not take My enemy and your enemy as friends and protectors. You show them love when they have rejected the truth that has come to you" (60:1).*

The Prophet of Allah (s) has said: "The faith of a believer is never complete until his love is for Allah's sake and his hatred is for Allah's sake." And he also said: "Love for Allah and love for His enemy can never co-exist in the heart of a believer."

Traditions of this genre are innumerable. Reason in itself is enough proof that Allah, Glory be to Him, has made believers love faith and adorned it in their hearts. He has made them hate disbelief, corruption and disobedience. For a man may hate his son or his father or his brother for his opposition to the truth and his swaying back and forth to the path of Satan; and he may love a stranger to whom he has no connection, except the brotherhood of Islam.

For all of this, it is incumbent that our love, affection and friendship be to those whom Allah has commanded us to love, just as it is necessary that our animosity, hatred and dissociation be from those whom Allah, Glory be to Him, has ordered us to dissociate from.

As a result of this, our affection is for 'Ali and the Imams from his progeny, even though there was no preceding love for them;

Chapter 4: Concerning the General Companions

[this is] because the Qur'an, *Sunnah*, history and reason have left us no doubt regarding them.

Because of this, we dissociate ourselves from those companions who usurped his rights to the Caliphate, even though there was no preceding hatred for them; [this is] because the Qur'an, *Sunnah*, history and reason have left for us grave doubts regarding them.

Since the Prophet of Allah (s) instructed us: "Abandon that which causes doubt for that which does not cause doubt," a Muslim must not follow any doubtful matter nor neglect the book in which there is no doubt.

Similarly, it is incumbent on every Muslim that he frees himself from the chains and blind imitations and judge according to his reasoning, without any preceding notions nor latent jealousy; because desires and Satan are two very dangerous enemies, they adorn a person's evil deeds so he sees them as beautiful. What a wonderful poetry Imam al-Busayr said in *al-Barda*:

"Deny the soul and the devil. Obey them not
They are foul advisers so refute them".

It is incumbent on Muslims to fear God [in dealing] with His upright servants. As for those who are not pious, there is no sanctity for them. The Prophet of Allah (s) said: "There is no [sin] in slandering a corrupt person." This is allowed so that the Muslims are made aware of his matter and so that they may not be deceived by him nor befriends him.

It is necessary today that Muslims be truthful with themselves and take a good look at their painful, sad, debased reality and do away with praising and taking pride in the greatness of their predecessors and seniors. If our predecessors were on the right path, as we think today, we would not have arrived at this conclusion which is certainly the result of the revolution that occurred in the community after the demise of its Prophet, may my soul and the souls of the entire world be ransomed for him.

"O you who believe, stand firmly for justice and bear witnesses for Allah, even if it be against yourselves, your parents or your kin whether they be rich or poor. For Allah is better than them both. Do not follow desires lest you stray. And if you deviate or decline then verily Allah is well informed what you do" (4:135).

Views of those who know regarding some of the companions

Imam 'Ali (as) said, describing those companions who are seen as among the earliest companions: "When I finally accepted the matter [of leadership], one group broke [their pledge]; the other deviated and others missed the truth as if they did not hear Allah's words when He said: *"That is the abode of the hereafter that we have created for those who do not strive to exalt themselves in the earth nor to create mischief. The best outcome is [for] the pious ones"(28:83).* Nay, indeed, by Allah, they heard and perceived its meaning but alas! The world seemed glittering in their eyes and it's embellishments seduced them (*Nahj al-Balagha*, p. 90)."

And he (as) also said about them: "They chose Satan as their master in their affairs, and he made them partners. He has laid eggs and hatched them in their bosoms. He creeps and crawls in their laps, he sees through their eyes and speaks through their tongues. He has led them to sins and adorned for them what is foul, like the action of one whom Satan has made a partner in his authority and speaks falsehood through his tongue (*Nahj al-Balagha* page 96)."

He said regarding 'Amr b. al-'As, the famous companion: "How strange it is with the son of Nabigha. He has uttered falsehood and sinned with his tongue. Is not the worst of speech, lies? When he speaks, he lies; when he promises, he breaks [it]; when he seeks a favour, he nags; and when he is asked for something, he is miserly. He betrays his pledge, and he ignores kinship... (*Nahj al-Balagha*, page 200)."

Chapter 4: Concerning the General Companions

The Prophet of Allah said: "The signs of a hypocrite are three: When he speaks, he lies; when he promises he breaks [it]; when he is entrusted [with something], he betrays". All these vices, and even more than these were present in 'Amr b. al-'As.

He said, in praise of Abu Dharr al-Ghifari and in criticism of 'Uthman and those with him who had banished him to Rabdha, and exiled him till he died alone: "O Abu Dharr, You were angry for Allah's sake, so place your hopes in Him for whom you were angry. The people were afraid of you for their world, and you feared them for your religion. So leave in their hands that, due to which, they were afraid of you, and flee with that, due to which, you feared them. How badly they need what you have denied them and how little you need what they have denied you. Tomorrow you will know who has profited and you will know the envious ones. Were the skies and the earth a burden for a servant and were he to fear Allah, then Allah would remove his burden. So love nothing but the truth and hate nothing but lies. Had you accepted their world, they would have loved you, had you appropriated to yourself some part of it, they would have given you asylum (*Nahj al-Balagha*, page 299)."

Regarding al-Mughira b. al-Akhnas, who was also a prominent companion, he (as) said: "O son of the accursed one! O tree which has neither root nor branch. By Allah, He will not assist whoever you help and whoever you raise will not stand straight. Go away from us. May Allah distance you from your purpose. Do what you like, and may His mercy be withheld from you if you remain alone (*Nahj al-Balagha*, p. 306)."

He (as) said of Talha and al-Zubayr, the two famous companions who waged war against him after having sworn their oaths of allegiance to him, then they breached it: "By Allah, they did not find any evil in me, they did not do justice between me and them. They are demanding a right which they abandoned and blood which they spilled". This is a rebellious group which contains the near one (Zubayr), the scorpion's venom and doubts which cast veils. The matter is clear and falsehood has been shaken from its foundation, and its tongue has stopped uttering mischief.

You hurried to me shouting allegiance! allegiance! like she camels having delivered newly born young ones, leaping towards their young. I held back my hand but you pulled it towards yourself. I drew back my hand but you dragged it. O Allah, these two have severed all bonds of friendship and wronged me! They broke their oaths and instigated the people against me. My Lord, let what they plot against me fail. Unfasten what they have tied, and do not make strong what they have woven. Show them the evil of what they aimed and acted upon. Before the battle, I gave them a chance to correct their deed and treated them with respect but they belittled the blessing and refused the safety (*Nahj al-Balagha*, p. 306)."

In a letter to them, he said: "O two respected Shaykhs! Revert from your present position for the worst that can befall you now is shame. Later, both shame and hell fire will be combined [against you]. Peace (*Nahj al-Balagha*, p. 626)."

Regarding Marwan b. al-Hakam, who had been taken as captive at the battle of the Camel, then was set free. He was amongst those who had given a pledge and then broke the pledge: "No need have I for his pledge for it is the palm of a Jew. If he swears with his hand, he will violate it after a short while. He will get power for so long as a dog licks its nose, he is the father of four rams who will also rule. The people will face hard days through him and his sons (*Nahj al-Balagha*, p. 176)."

He said of those companions who journeyed with 'A'isha to Basra in the battle of the Camel, amongst them were Talha and Zubayr: "They came out dragging the wife of the Prophet (s) just as a maid slave is dragged for sale. They took her to Basra where they put their women in their houses but exposed the wife of the Prophet (s) to themselves and to others in the army in which there was not a single person who had not offered me his obedience and sworn to me allegiance willingly, without being forced. They approached my officers and treasurers of the public treasury and its other inhabitants. They killed some of them in prison and others by treachery. By Allah, even if they had killed willfully a single Muslim without any fault, it would have been lawful for me to kill the whole of this army because they were present in it but did not disagree with it nor prevented it by tongue or hand, not to say that they killed Muslims of a number equal to that with which had marched on them (*Nahj al-Balagha*, page 370)."

His words regarding 'A'isha and the companions who followed her at the battle of the Camel: "You were the soldiers of a woman and the followers of an animal. The animal snorted and you responded, and when it was killed you fled. Your character is low, your pledge is broken and your religion is hypocritical (*Nahj al-Balagha* p. 98)."

"As for so and so, she is gripped by feminine views while malice is boiling in her bosom like the furnace of a blacksmith. If she were called upon to deal with others as she is dealing with me she would not have done it. Even then she will be given the original respect, while her accounting [of her acts] is with Allah (*Nahj al-Balagha*, p. 334)."

As for the general Quraysh, who were certainly companions, he said about them: "As for the eviction of us from this position, although we were the highest as far as descent was concerned and the strongest in relationship with the Prophet of Allah (s), it was a selfish act towards which the hearts of the people became greedy while some people did not care for it. The arbiter is Allah and to Him is the return on the Day of Judgment. Leave this story of devastation about which there is hue and cry. Come and look at the son of Abu Sufyan. Time has made me laugh after weeping. No wonder, by Allah, what is this affair which surpasses all wonder and which has increased wrong doing? The people have tried to extinguish the light of Allah from His lamp and to close His fountain from its sources. They mix epidemic producing water between me and themselves. If the trying hardships are removed from us, I would take them on the course of the truth; otherwise I do not feel sorry for them. 'Do not let your soul go out vainly, sighing after them. Surely, Allah knows what they are doing (*Nahj al-Balagha*, p. 348).'"

When he buried Fatima al-Zahra, leader of the women of

paradise, he addressed the Prophet thus:"Your daughter will inform you of how the *ummah* joined together to oppress her. Ask her in detail and she will explain the situation. This has happened when you have recently left us and your remembrance has not disappeared (*Nahj-al Balagha*, 460)."

In a letter to Mu'awiyah, 'Ali (as) said:

"You are one whom the devil has taken complete possession of; he has secured his wishes in you and has taken complete control over you like the soul and blood. When were you, O Mu'awiyah, the protector of the subjects and guardian of the affairs of the people, without any forward step or conspicuous distinction? We seek Allah's protection against the befalling of previous misfortunes and I warn you lest you continue getting deceived by desires and your appearance be different from your inner self.

You have called me to war. Leave the people on one side, come out to me [for fighting] and spare both parties from fighting so that it may be known which of us has a rusted heart and covered eyes. I am Abu'l-Hasan, slayer of your father, your uncle and your brother, all in single combat on the day of Badr. That same sword is still with me and I meet my adversary with the same heart. I have not altered the religion nor put up any new Prophet. I am surely heading on that very path which you had willingly forsaken and which you had embraced by force (*Nahj al-Balagha*, 526)."

As for what you say, that "We are of the progeny of 'Abd al-Manaf", so too are we. But Umayya was not like Hashim, nor Harb equal to 'Abd al-Muttalib, nor Abu Sufyan to Abu Talib nor one freed (at the conquest of Mecca) equal to a Muhajir, nor one of clean descent a match for him who has been adopted, nor the truthful one the same as one on falsehood, nor is a believer a match for a hypocrite. How bad are the successors who go on following the predecessors who have fallen in hell.

Besides that, we also have the distinction of Prophethood among us, by virtue of which we subdued the strong and raised up the down trodden. When Allah caused the Arabs to enter his religion in

Chapter 4: Concerning the General Companions 183

overwhelming numbers, and this *ummah* accepted Islam, some did so willingly while others did so forcefully. You were among those who entered Islam due to greed or fear at a time when others had preceded and the first Muhajirs had taken away all the distinction (*Nahj al-Balagha*, page 533)."

"You have called us to follow the judgment of the Qur'an but you are not the people of the Qur'an. We did not accept your proposal but we respond to the Qur'anic injunctions, Peace (*Nahj al-Balagha*, 595)."

"And say: 'Truth has come and falsehood has vanished. Falsehood [is bound] to perish'(17:81).

Chapter Five

Concerning the Three Caliphs, Abu Bakr, 'Umar and 'Uthman

As discussed, the *Ahl al-Sunnah wa'l-Jama'a* permit no criticism or condemnation of any of his companions and maintain the belief in their collective uprightness. If any free thinker writes about them and undertakes to criticize the deeds of some companions, they defame him; in fact, they deem him to be an unbeliever even if he is amongst their own scholars. This is what has happened to some of the free thinking Egyptian and non-Egyptian scholars like Shaykh Mahmud Abu Rayya, author of "The Lights on the *Sunnah* of Muhammad" and "*Shaykh al-Muzayra*", and like Qadi Shaykh Muhammad Amin al-Antaki, author of "Why I chose the school of *Ahl al-Bayt*," and like Sayyid Muhammad b. 'Aqil who composed the book "The complete advice for [he] who befriends Mu'awiyah." Indeed, some Egyptian writers labeled Shaykh Mahmud Shaltut, grand Shaykh of the University of Azhar, an infidel when he issued the ruling that it was permissible to worship according to the Ja'fari *madhab*.

If the grand Shaykh of Azhar, the mufti of all of Egyptian schools, is despised for merely recognizing the Shi'i school which is traced to the teacher of the scholars, Ja'far al-Sadiq (as); then what do you think [they would do] to one who chooses to follow this school after research and conviction, and undertakes to criticize the *madhab* he used to follow, having inherited it from his fathers and forefathers?

This is what the *Ahl al-Sunnah wa'l-Jama'a* will not permit, for they consider it as heresy in religion and going out of [the fold of] Islam; as though Islam is, in their reckoning, the four *madhabs* and everything else is false. These are petrified and stagnant minds resembling those minds which the Qur'an talks of, and that which the Prophet's (s) call encountered. It defied him intensely, for he invited them to monotheism and abandoning the numerous gods. The most High says: *"And they wonder when a warner comes to them from amongst themselves, and the unbelievers say: "This is a lying sorcerer, has he made all the gods as one? This is a surprising thing"* (38:5).

I am safe from the malicious attacks that will be directed against me from those zealous persons who have kept themselves in authority over others. [To them], no one has the right to oppose their writings even if his writings do not take anything away from Islam. Otherwise, how could one who criticizes some of the companions be judged to have gone out of [the fold of] Islam and [become] a disbeliever when the foundations and branches of religion does not have anything [to do] with that?

Some fanatics were propagating amongst themselves that my book "*Then I was Guided*" is like Salman Rushdie's [work], in order to prevent people from reading it and so as to encourage them to curse the book.

This is a plot, forgery and great slander which the Lord of the Worlds will account for. How can they compare "*Then I was Guided*" which calls to the belief in the infallibility of the Messenger (s), his being beyond reproach, and [calls for] the following of the Imams of the *Ahl al-Bayt* from whom Allah has removed all filth and purified completely, with "The Satanic Verses" in which its accursed writer reviles Islam and the Prophet of Islam (s) and considers Islam is [due to] the inspiration of the devils?

Allah says: *"O you who believe! Stand firmly for justice and bear witness for Allah, even if it be against yourselves"* (4:135).

Due to this noble verse, I care not except for the pleasure of Allah, Glorified and Exalted be He, and I fear no criticism as long

Chapter 5: Concerning the Three Caliphs

as I am defending the correct Islam and distancing its noble Prophet from every error, even if that is at the expense of criticizing some close companions, even if they were among "the rightly guided Caliphs," because the Prophet of Allah (s) is more worthy of distancing [from error] than any mortal.

The unbiased, perceptive reader will understand from all my works what is my desired goal for the issue is not to denigrate or degrade the companions, it is to defend the Prophet of Allah (s) and his infallibility, and to defend him against the misconceptions which the Umayyads and the 'Abbasids cultivated about Islam and the Prophet of Islam during the early centuries when they ruled the Muslims with tyranny and force, changing Allah's religion according to what worldly goals, base politics and evil desires dictated.

Their major plots have influenced a large segment of Muslims who followed them out of good intentions towards them and accepted all the distortions and lies they narrated, assuming them to be true and to be a part of Islam; and that it was obligatory on every Muslim to follow them, not to question [them].

Were the Muslims to know the truth of the matter, they would not accord any importance to them or to their narrations. Had history narrated to us that the companions obeyed the commands and prohibitions of the Prophet of Allah (s) and had not argued with him or opposed his judgments, and that they did not disobey him in numerous rulings during the last days of his life, we would have judged all of them to be upright and we would have had no such scope for discussion or speech [against them]. However, amongst them were liars, hypocrites and corrupt ones, according to the Qur'anic text and the authenticated correct *Sunnah*.

They disagreed [with each other] in his presence and disobeyed him in the matter of writing [the testament] to the point that they accused him of hallucination and prevented him from writing. They did not to follow his commands when he appointed Usama over them. They differed on his Caliphate to the extent that they neglected his washing, preparation and burial arguing, instead, about the Caliphate. Some of them were happy about it and others rejected it. Indeed, they differed on everything after him until they accused each other of disbelief, cursed each other, fought and killed each other, and dissociated from each other. [Due to this] Allah's one religion split into different sects with divergent views.

Given this situation, it is necessary, therefore, that we search for the cause and flaws that made the best and most desirable of nations created for man to decay; it became the lowest, most ignorant and debased nation on the face of the earth, it's respect destroyed, sanctity defiled and its people colonized, banished and evicted from their lands; they could not defend [themselves] against the transgressors nor could they remove the shame on its face.

The sole cure for this difficulty, as I see it, is self criticism. Let us forget the praising of our forebears, our false glories which have evaporated and have become ruined museums, empty even of visitors. The reality calls upon us to examine the reasons for our maladies, our remaining behind, our fragmentation and our failures, until we discover the disease and identify a beneficial cure for our well being; before it overcomes us and affects the last one of us. This is the desired goal, Allah is the only one worthy of worship; He is the guide of his servants to the right path.

And as long as our goal is a correct one then there is no value to the opposition of those fanatics who know nothing except insults and slander in their arguments for defending the companions. We will neither rebuke nor hate them after observing their situation, for they are deprived, misguided by their good intention for the companions. This has prevented them from arriving at the truth. They are like the children of the Jews and Christians who have trust in their fathers and grandfathers and do not impose upon themselves [the task of] research in Islam; relying, instead, on the utterances of their predecessors, that Muhammad was a liar and that he was not a Prophet. Allah says:

"The people of the book went astray only after clear signs came to them" (98:3).

Chapter 5: Concerning the Three Caliphs

With the passing of successive centuries, it has become difficult for a Muslim today to convince a Jew or a Christian of the Islamic creed, what if someone tells them that the Bible and Torah in circulation are forgeries and proves that by the Qur'an, will this Muslim find a sympathetic ear amongst them?

Similarly, with a simple Muslim who believes in the uprightness of every companion and is zealous about it with no proof, is it possible for anyone to convince him otherwise?

If they are not able to find fault and criticize Mu'awiyah and his son Yazid, and there are numerous others like them who distorted Islam by their evil deeds - what if they are told about Abu Bakr, 'Umar and 'Uthman, the truthful one, the distinguisher, and one whom the angels are shy of? Or of 'A'isha, mother of the believers, wife of the Prophet (s), daughter of Abu Bakr, whom we have discussed in the preceding chapter of how the reliable authors of the *Sihah* works, according to the *Ahl al-Sunnah*, have narrated from her? Now we have reached the stage of the role of the three Caliphs. Let us discover some of their deeds which the Sunni *Sahih* and *Musnad* and reliable historical works have recorded against them, so that we can illustrate firstly that the concept of collective uprightness of the companions is incorrect and that righteousness was missing even from [some] close companions.

Secondly, we will illustrate for our *Ahl al-Sunnah wa'l-Jama'a* brothers that these criticisms do not amount to insults or slander or denigration, rather, they are means of removing the veils so as to reach the truth, and that they are not inventions or lies of the Rafidis, as most people claim. On the contrary, they are narrations from books that have been judged to be correct and they have obligated themselves to [accept] it.

Abu Bakr during the life of the Prophet (s)

In vol. 6 p. 46 of his *Sahih*, in "The Chapter on the Interpretation of *Surah al-Hujurat* of the Qur'an", al-Bukhari relates that Nafi' b. 'Umar reported from Ibn Abi Malika that "The two pious ones, i.e., Abu Bakr and 'Umar (r) were very nearly destroyed, for they raised their voices in the presence of the Prophet (s) when the delegation from Banu Tamim came to him; one of the two recognized [as their leader] al-Aqra b. Habis, the brother of Banu Majasha, and the other recognized another person. Nafi' said: 'I don't remember his name' whereupon Abu Bakr said to 'Umar: 'You only wish to contradict me.' He replied: 'I did not wish to contradict you.' And their voices rose [in argument] over that matter, and Allah revealed: *'O you, who believe, do not raise your voices...'(49:2)* Ibn Zubayr [later] said: 'After this, 'Umar's voice was not heard by the Prophet to the extent that the Prophet (s) had to ask what he had said. And he ['Umar] didn't mention [the matter] about his father, I mean Abu Bakr.'"

Similarly, in vol. 8, p. 145 in "The Chapter concerning Adherence to the Qur'an and the *Sunnah*" under the heading of "What is Disliked about getting Embroiled [in Argument] and Contention" al-Bukhari relates: "Waki' informed us from Nafi' b. 'Umar from Ibn Abi Malika that: 'The two righteous ones, Abu Bakr and 'Umar, were nearly destroyed when the delegation of Banu Tamim came to the Prophet (s). One of them pointed to al-Aqra b. Habis al-Tamim al-Hanzali, the brother of Banu Majasha, and the other indicated someone else. Then Abu Bakr said to 'Umar: 'Surely, you only wish to contradict me.' 'Umar said: 'I did not wish to contradict you.' And their voices rose in front of the Prophet (s), and the verse was revealed: *'O you who believe, do not raise your voices above the voice of the Prophet nor address him the way you do each other lest your deeds be in vain and you perceive not. Those that lower their voices in the presence of the Prophet, they are those whose hearts Allah has tested for piety; for them is forgiveness and a great reward.'"(49:2)*

Ibn Abi Malika said that Ibn al-Zubayr [later] said: "Thereafter 'Umar didn't mention the matter regarding his father, i.e., Abu Bakr, and whenever he spoke to the Prophet about something, he would do so in a whisper and could not be heard to the extent that the Prophet had to tell him to speak up."

Similarly, in vol. 5, p. 116 in the "Section on Military Campaigns

Chapter 5: Concerning the Three Caliphs 191

(the delegation of Banu Tamim)" al-Bukhari in his *Sahih* relates from Hisham b. Yusuf, on the authority of Ibn Jurayj, who informed them, on the authority of Ibn Abi Malika, who related that 'Abd Allah b. Zubayr informed them that a delegation from Banu Tamim came to the Prophet (s), and Abu Bakr said: Make the chief al-Qa'qa'a b. Ma'bad b. Zuraraî and 'Umar said: "Rather, select al-Aqra b. Habis". Abu Bakr said: "You do only wish to contradict me", and 'Umar said: "I did not wish to contradict you." And they argued until their voices had risen, and the following verse was then revealed: "O you who believe! Do not put yourselves forward between Allah and his Apostle..."

It is apparent from these narrations that Abu Bakr and 'Umar did not behave in a proper way, i.e., in accordance with proper Islamic conduct in the presence of the Prophet (s) and allowed themselves to advance in front of Allah and His Prophet without permission; nor did the Prophet of Allah (s) ask for their views in appointing anyone from Banu Tamim as a leader; then, they were not content until they were arguing in his presence and their voices had risen in front of him (s) with no respect or care for what is customarily decreed by good character and morals, values of which none of the companions could have been ignorant and which they could not have ignored after Allah's Prophet (s) committed his life to their education and upbringing.

Had this event occurred in the early days of Islam, we would have sought to find an excuse for the two shaykhs and would have tried to find some explanation for this. But the reports have been indubitably established that the event occurred in the last days of the Prophet (s), since the delegation from Banu Tamim journeyed to the Prophet (s) in 9 A.H., and he only lived for a few months after that. Every historian and *hadith* scholar who has mentioned the coming of the delegation to the Prophet (s) has testified [to it]. In addition, the noble Qur'an also refers to it in one of the last chapters: *"When help and victory from Allah comes, and you see people entering Islam in large groups..."(110:1-2)*

That being the case, how can the apologists make excuses for the stance of Abu Bakr and 'Umar in the presence of the Prophet (s)? If the account was restricted to the position here exemplified by the two companions only, we would not have the scope for [wide] criticism and objection. However, Allah, who is not shy of the truth, recorded [the incident] and revealed a Qur'anic verse that followed. It contains rebuke and warning for Abu Bakr and 'Umar to the effect that, were they to repeat their deed, Allah would negate their [good] works. Similarly, the narrator of the event began his report with the statement: "The two pious men, Abu Bakr and 'Umar, were almost destroyed..." And the narrator of the incident 'Abd Allah b. al-Zubayr, attempted to convince us that 'Umar, after the revelation of this verse concerning him, whenever he spoke to the Prophet (s), he did so in such a low voice that he had to be asked [to repeat what he said].

In spite of the fact that he didn't mention the [equally reproachable conduct] on the part of his grandfather Abu Bakr, the historical accounts and the *hadith*, preserved by the *hadith* scholars, proves the opposite of it. It suffices to mention the calamity of the Thursday, [just] three days before the death of the Prophet of Allah (s), when we find the very same 'Umar uttering his sinister words: "Surely the Prophet of Allah is hallucinating, the book of Allah is enough for us."

The people were differing between themselves, there being those who said: "Draw near to the Prophet so that he may write [his behest] for you;" and there were those who were saying what 'Umar said.

When the clamor and dissension had increased,[1] the Prophet of Allah (s) said to them: "Go away from me; it is not fitting that the argument should occur near me."[2] It is to be understood from the intensity of the rude talk, clamor, disagreement and contention that they overstepped every limit that Allah had set for them in Surah *al-Hujurat*, as we have already mentioned. There is no possibility of our being convinced that their disagreement, contention and clamor were done quietly in one another's ears; on the contrary, it is to be

---

[1] *Sahih al-Bukhari*, 5/138, "The Chapter on the Sickness and Death of the Prophet".

[2] *Ibid*, 1/37, "The Book of Knowledge".

Chapter 5: Concerning the Three Caliphs

understood from all this that they raised their voices so loudly that even the women, who were behind the curtain and the veil, participated in the argument, saying: "Go close to the Prophet (s) so that the letter may be written." Thereupon 'Umar said to them: "You are indeed the women of Yusuf - if he is ill you squeeze tears from your eyes and if he gets better you ride his neck." The Prophet of Allah (s) then said to him: "Leave them alone, for they are better than you."[3]

Our conclusion from all of this is that they did not carry out Allah's command: *"O you who believe, do not advance before Allah and His Prophet.... and .... do not raise your voices above the voice of the Prophet..."(49:1-2)* nor did they respect the position of the Prophet or behave properly when they slandered him with the term '*yahajar*' (i.e. hallucinating).

Even prior to this, Abu Bakr had uttered abhorrent words in the presence of the Apostle (s) when he said to 'Urwa b. Mas'ud: "Go lick the clitoris of al-Ab."[4] Regarding this expression, al-Qastalin, a commentator on al-Bukhari said: "The expression to 'Lick the clitoris...' is one of the crudest insults among the Arabs..." If such expressions were being uttered in the presence of the Prophet (s), what then is the meaning of "and do not raise your voices over his as you do with each other?"

The Prophet of Allah (s) was of exalted character (as his Lord described him) and more shy than a virgin in her chambers (as is reported by al-Bukhari and Muslim),[5] for both have clearly reported that the Prophet of Allah (s) was neither corrupt nor obscene, and used to say: "The best among you is the one possessing the most

---

[3] *Kanz al-'Ummal*, 3/138.

[4] *Sahih al-Bukhari*, 3/179.

[5] *Sahih al-Bukhari*, "The Book of Merits", "The Chapter on the Attributes of the Prophet", and *Sahih Muslim* in "The Book of Excellences", "The Chapter on His (s) excessive shyness".

upright character;"[6] then how is it that the close companions were not influenced by his exalted character?

I would add to all this that Abu Bakr did not carry out the command of the Prophet of Allah (s) when he appointed Usama b. Zayd over him and made him one of his soldiers, and severely rebuked those who stayed behind till he said: "Allah has cursed whoever stays behind from the army of Usama".[7] This was after he had received the news about people defaming him on the matter of appointing Usama as the leader, an incident reported by most of the historians and biographers.

Similarly, he hurried to Saqifa and participated in the elimination of 'Ali b. Abu Talib from the Caliphate, and left the body of Allah's Apostle (s) a covered corpse, may my father and mother be sacrificed for him. He did not concern himself with bathing, or enshrouding, or preparing him for burial, or burying him; busying himself, instead, with the position of the Caliphate and leadership for which he extended his neck. Where then was the close companionship, the alleged friendship and good character? I am astonished at the attitude of these companions towards their Prophet, who devoted his life to their guidance, nourishment, and advice, these companions to whom the Qur'an advised; "What befalls you concerns him, he is watching you, he is kind and merciful to the believers." Still, [we see them] leaving him [as] a stiffening corpse, and hurrying instead to Saqifa to appoint one among themselves as Caliph! Today, we live in the twentieth century which we claim is the most wretched one, wherein morals have vanished and values have evaporated; yet, in spite of all this, if a neighbor amongst the Muslims dies, they rush to him and busy themselves until they bury him in his grave, in accordance with the saying of the Prophet (s): "Honoring the dead means burying him."

---

[6] *Sahih Muslim* "The Book of Excellences", "The Chapter on His excessive shyness", al-Bukhari "The Book on Virtues", "The Chapter on the Attribute of the Prophet (s)".

[7] *Kitab al-Milal wa al-Nihal (The Book of Sects and Divisions)*, Shahrastani, vol. 4, *Al-Saqifa*, Abu Bakr Ahmad b. al-'Aziz al-Jawhari.

Chapter 5: Concerning the Three Caliphs

'Ali b. Abi Talib (as), the Commander of the Faithful, disclosed these events when he said: "By God, Ibn Abi Qahafa put the shirt [of Caliphate] on himself while he surely knew that my position vies-a-vies the Caliphate was like the position of a pivot to a grinding mill." After this, Abu Bakr allowed the attack upon the house of Fatima al-Zahra, and threatened to burn it unless those who dissented from pledging allegiance to him came out. What happened did happen, historians have mentioned in their books and narrators have transmitted [it] generation after generation. We are not going to mention it here, whoever wants to know more should read the historical books.

Abu Bakr after the death of the Prophet (s), his denial of the truthful and pure Fatima al-Zahra (sa) and his usurpation of her rights

In vol. 5, p. 82 in "The Book of Military Campaigns" in "The Chapter of the Conquest of Khaybar," on the authority of 'Urwa, from 'A'isha, al-Bukhari reports that Fatima (sa), the daughter of the Prophet (s), sent someone to Abu Bakr asking for her inheritance from what Allah's Apostle had left behind. [This included] the *fay* property bestowed on him by Allah, i.e., booty gained without fighting in Medina and Fadak, and from what remained of the *khumus* booty from [the battle of] Khaybar. On that, Abu Bakr said: "Allah's Apostle said: 'Our property is not inherited. Whatever we leave, is *sadaqa*, but the family of Muhammad can eat of this property.' By Allah, I will not make any change in the state of the *sadaqa* of Allah's Apostle and will leave it as it was during the lifetime of Allah's Apostle, and will dispose of it as he used to do." So Abu Bakr refused to give anything of that to Fatima. So she became angry with Abu Bakr and kept away from him, and did not speak to him till she died. She remained alive for six months after the death of the Prophet. When she died her husband 'Ali buried her at night without informing Abu Bakr. When Fatima was alive, the people used to respect 'Ali much, but after her death, 'Ali noticed a change in the people's attitude towards him. So 'Ali sought reconciliation with Abu Bakr and gave him the oath of allegiance.

'Ali had not given the oath of allegiance during those six months..."³

Muslim reports in vol. 2 of his *Sahih*, in "The Book of *Jihad*" in the Chapter "We do not leave Inheritance, but whatever we leave is *Sadaqa*" on the authority of 'A'isha, the mother of the believers (r), that Fatima (sa), the daughter of Allah's Prophet (s), asked Abu Bakr al-Siddiq, after the Prophet's death to apportion to her the inheritance from what the Prophet (s) had left from [his share] of the spoils of war. Thereupon Abu Bakr said to her: "The Prophet of Allah said: 'We do not leave inheritance. What we leave is charity.'" Then Fatima, daughter of the Prophet of God (s), became angry with him and avoided him, continuing thus until she died; she lived for six months after the Prophet's death. 'A'isha said: "Fatima used to ask Abu Bakr for her share from what the Prophet of Allah (s) left behind of [his share] of Khaybar and Fadak, and from his *sadaqa* in Medina. Abu Bakr denied her request and said: 'I will abandon nothing which the Prophet (s) used to do, I will also do it. [This is] because I fear that, should I depart from what he commanded, I would go astray.' As for the Prophet's *sadaqa* of Medina, 'Umar has given it to 'Ali and 'Abbas, and, [as for] the properties of Khaybar and Fadak, 'Umar withheld them, and said: 'These two are charities from the Prophet of Allah (s) his rights fall to his deputies, and their administration is for whosoever is the leader. Thus they are till today.'"⁹

The two Shaykhs (al-Bukhari and Muslim) abridged and shortened these reports so that the truth may not be clear to the researchers. For them, this is a familiar art, which they espoused in order to preserve the honor of the [first] three Caliphs. (We have a separate treatise concerning the two scholars on this issue, and, God willing, we will present it in the near future).

In any case, the narrations they have reported are sufficient to disclose the truth about Abu Bakr, who refuted the claim of Fatima

---

⁸ *Sahih Muslim*, also in "The Book of Jihad", "The Chapter on the saying of the Prophet 'We do not leave an inheritance, what we leave is charity".

⁹ *Sahih al-Bukhari* also narrated this tradition in his book on the incumbency of *khumus*, "The Chapter on the incumbency of *khumus*"

Chapter 5: Concerning the Three Caliphs 197

al-Zahra, which merited her anger upon him and her shunning him unto her death (sa), and necessitated her burial at night in secret by her husband; and, according to her will, Abu Bakr was not being permitted by her to attend. We also learn from these narrations that 'Ali did not pledge allegiance to Abu Bakr for a period of six months, which is the period that Fatima lived after her father and that he was compelled to take this oath when he found that the faces of the people were turning against him, and so he sought to reconcile with Abu Bakr.

What al-Bukhari and Muslim altered was Fatima's (sa) claim that her father, the Prophet of Allah (s), had given her Fadak as a gift during his lifetime; and it (Fadak) was not therefore an inheritance. Even if we were to assume that Prophets do not leave inheritances, as Abu Bakr narrated from the Prophet (s), she refuted his claim and opposed him by [quoting] the text of the Qur'an which states "And Solomon inherited from David." In any case, Fadak was not covered by this alleged *hadith*, since it was a gift to her and was in no way a part of inheritance.

Consequently, one finds that all historians and scholars of *tafsir*, as well as of *hadith*, relate that Fatima (sa) claimed that Fadak was her property and that Abu Baker refuted her, asking her to provide witnesses to support her claim. She brought 'Ali b. Abi Talib and Umm Ayman, but Abu Bakr did not accept their testimony, considering it insufficient. Ibn Hajar admitted this in his *al-Sawa'iq al-Muhriqa* when he reported that Fatima claimed that the Prophet (s) had given her Fadak as a gift but had no witness to her claim except 'Ali and Umm Ayman. Yet their testimony did not meet the stipulated conditions to be considered as sufficient proof.[10]

Imam Fakhr al-Din al-Razi said in his *Tafsir*[11]: "After the death of the Prophet of Allah (s), Fatima claimed that he had given Fadak as a gift to her, whereupon Abu Bakr said to her: 'You are the dearest of people to me in poverty, and the most beloved in richness, but I cannot ascertain the truth of your claim. Therefore, I

---

[10] Ibn Hajar, *al-Sawa'iq al-Muhriqa*, p.21.

[11] *Tafsir al-Kabir* aka *Mafatih al-Ghayb*

am not allowed to rule in your favor.'" Imam al-Razi said: "Umm Ayman testified for her, as did the trustee of the Prophet of Allah (s). Abu Bakr then asked her to bring a witness whose testimony could be accepted according to the *shari'a*, and there was none."[12]

Fatima's claim that Fadak had been given to her as a gift from the Prophet of Allah (s), and Abu Bakr's denial of her claim, are well known to the historians, as well as his rejecting the testimony of 'Ali and Umm Ayman. Indeed all [of them] have mentioned this, from Ibn Taymiyya to the author of *al-Sira al-Halabiyah* and Ibn Qayyim al-Jawziya, and others.

But al-Bukhari and Muslim abridged the narrations, and reported only Fatima's request, specifically relating to the inheritance, so that the reader should assume that Fatima's anger against Abu Bakr was improper and that Abu Bakr had only acted upon what he had heard from the Prophet of Allah (s); and that she was the wrong-doer, Abu Bakr the victim. All this was to protect Abu Bakr's honor. There was no consideration to observe honesty in transmission, nor reliability in *hadith* [transmission], a fact which would have exposed the shortcomings of the Caliphs and [would have] refuted the lies and pretexts composed by the Umayyads and the supporters of the "rightly guided" Caliphate, even though this was at the expense of the Prophet himself (s), or his "part," al-Zahra (sa). Because of this, al-Bukhari and Muslim have won the leadership of the *hadith* scholars among the *Ahl al-Sunnah wa'l-Jama'a* and their books have been regarded as the most authentic books after the book of Allah. This invention is not based on academic proof, and we will, God willing, research the subject in a separate chapter so that we may expose the truth for those who wish to know it.

However, we still [have enough proof to] challenge Muslim and al-Bukhari, who only transmitted a small amount of merits of Fatima al-Zahra (sa). There is enough evidence for the conviction of Abu Bakr who knew al-Zahra and her status with Allah and His Prophet (s) more than al-Bukhari and Muslim did. Despite this, he

---

[12] *Tafsir Mafatih al-Ghayb*, Fakhr al-Din al-Razi, 8/125. Commentary on *Surah al-Hashr*.

Chapter 5: Concerning the Three Caliphs

refuted her, and did not accept her testimony or that of her husband, of whom the Prophet of Allah said: "'Ali is with the truth, and the truth is with 'Ali, hovering about him wherever he goes."[13] Thus, let us compare the testimonies of al-Bukhari and Muslim with what the bearer of the Message (s) confirmed about the merits of his [own] flesh and blood, al-Zahra (sa).

Fatima's impeccability according to the Qur'anic text

In his *Sahih*, vol. 7 in "The Chapter of the Virtues of the *Ahl al-Bayt*" Muslim reports that 'A'isha said: "The Prophet (s) emerged one morning wearing a cloak of black hair. Al-Hasan came and he covered him with the cloak. Then al-Husayn came, and he joined him. Then Fatima came and he brought her within. Then 'Ali came and he covered him too. Then he recited: *'Allah desires to cleanse you from impurities, O Ahl al-Bayt, and purify you completely'(33:33).* Fatima al-Zahra (sa) was the only woman in the *ummah* whom Allah had thus cleansed and purified from every sin and disobedience. I wonder who was Abu Bakr to reject her testimony and ask her for witnesses?

Fatima is the leader of all believing women and the leader of the women of the umma

Al-Bukhari reported in his collection, vol. 7, in "The Book of Seeking Permission" under the section about "One who confides to his Companion in the Presence of others, and does not inform of the secret of his Companions until he dies" and Muslim reports in "The Book Of Merits" that A'isha, the mother of the believers, said: "We, the wives of the Prophet (s), were all together with him, not one of us left, and then Fatima (sa) came walking along, by Allah, her style was similar to that of the Prophet of Allah (s). When he saw her, he welcomed her saying: 'Welcome my daughter' and then he made her seat on either his right or his left and whispered to her. She began to weep bitterly. When he perceived her sadness, he

---

[13] Baghdadi, *Tarikh Baghdad*, 14/321, Ibn 'Asakir, *Tarikh*, 3/119, *Kanz al-'Ummal*, 5/30.

whispered to her a second time whereupon she laughed. I said to her while I was still with his other wives: 'The Prophet of Allah favored you among us with a secret, and then you wept.' When the Prophet of Allah (s) left, I asked her: 'What was the secret he told you?' Fatima said: 'I cannot breach the confidence of the Prophet of Allah.' After he died, I said to her: 'I hold you by whatever right I have over you to tell me'. She said: 'It is alright for me to do so now' and she informed me: 'When he whispered to me the first time, he informed me: 'Gibra'il used to present the Qur'an once every year to me, and this year he had done so twice. There could be no other reason for this except that my time is near. So fear Allah and be patient. For I am the best of those who should go before for you.' Then Fatima (sa) said: 'Then I wept as you saw. And when he saw my grief, he shared a second secret with me. He said: 'O Fatima, are you not happy that you are the leader of the believing women or the leader of the women of this *ummah?*"

If Fatima al-Zahra (sa), is the leader of the believing women, as is affirmed by the Prophet of Allah, and yet Abu Bakr denies her claim to Fadak and rejects her testimony, then what testimony is acceptable after this, I wonder?

Fatima al-Zahra (sa) is the leader of the women of Paradise

In vol. 4 of his collection, al-Bukhari reported in "The Book of the Beginning of Creation" in "The Chapter on The Virtue of Closeness to the Prophet (s)" that the Prophet of Allah (s) said: "Fatima is the leader of the women of paradise". It necessarily means, therefore, that Fatima is the leader of the women of all the worlds, for the dwellers of paradise are not only from the *ummah* of Muhammad, as is obvious. How then could Abu Bakr, "the truthful one" have repudiated her evidence? Don't they allege that he attained the title "al-Siddiq" because he used to believe in everything that his companion Muhammad said to him? Why did he not believe him regarding what he said of own "part",[14] al-Zahra? Or was it that the issue pertained not so much to Fadak, charity and the gifts as it pertained to the Caliphate, which was the right of 'Ali,

---

[14] The word used in the *hadith "bid'a"* means a part of [someone] ED.

the husband of Fatima? His denial of Fatima and her husband, who bore witness on her behalf on the question of the gift, was by far the better choice for him because, in so doing, he closed the doors to any further claims she might make. What a monstrous plot this was, nearly enough to make the mountains disappear.

Fatima is a part of the Prophet (s), and the Prophet (s) is angered when she is angered

In vol. 4, in "The Book of the Beginning of Creation" under "The Chapter of the Virtues of Fatima (sa), the daughter of the Prophet (s)" al-Bukhari reported in his *Sahih* that Abu Walid said that Ibn 'Uyayna reported on the authority of 'Amr b. Dinar on the authority of Ibn Abi Malika, on the authority of al-Miswar b. Mukhrima that the Prophet of Allah (s) said: "Fatima is a part of me, and whoever angers, her angers me". "Fatima is a part of me, and whatever she detests, I detest and what hurts her, hurts me." If the Prophet of Allah (s) becomes angry when his part, al-Zahra, gets angry, and suffers for her suffering, it follows therefore that she is preserved from all errors; otherwise it would not have been permissible for the Prophet (s) to say something like this. This is because it is permissible to cause suffering and to anger anyone who commits a misdemeanor, regardless of his status, as the Islamic *shari'a* does not allow leeway for [special treatment for] ties of kinship, far or near, aristocrat or peon, rich or poor. If the matter is as stated, then who was Abu Bakr to hurt al-Zahra and not heed to her anger? In fact he angered her until she died; she was offended and even shunned him, not speaking to him until she passed away, supplicating against him in every prayer she prayed, as is reported in the history of Ibn Qutayba and other historians.

Indeed these are bitter and painful truths which jolt the pillars and shake our faith. The impartial researcher, devoted to the truth and reality, has no alternative but to admit that Abu Bakr wronged al-Zahra and usurped her rights. It was possible for him, as Caliph of the Muslims, to placate her and give her what she claimed. This is because she was truthful as even Allah, the Prophet and all the Muslims, among who was Abu Bakr, attest to her veracity. But it was politics that overturned everything; the truthful person became a liar and the liar, a truthful person.

Yes, it was a part of a plot instigated to alienate the Prophet's family from the position that Allah had chosen for them. It had started with the alienation of 'Ali from the Caliphate, and the wrongful seizure of the gift and inheritance of al-Zahra; and also the repudiation of her testimony, along with her humiliation, so that there would remain no respect for her in the hearts of the Muslims. It ended with the murders of 'Ali, al-Hasan and al-Husayn, and all their children, their wives, were taken as prisoners of war, whilst their supporters and those who loved and followed them were killed. Perhaps these plots continue even till today; their actions are still being enacted and their fruits are still being reaped.

Certainly any free-thinking, unbiased Muslim will know when he reads the history books and differentiates truth from falsity, that Abu Bakr was the first to wrong the *Ahl al-Bayt*. Reading the collections of al-Bukhari and Muslim suffices to expose the truth, if the researcher is truthful [in his research].

Here we have al-Bukhari as well as Muslim admitting apologetically that Abu Bakr used to believe any ordinary companion who petitioned him. But he denied Fatima, leader of the women of paradise, the one about whom Allah had affirmed [His] cleansing and [His] purifying her; and he (Abu Bakr) repudiated [the testimonies of] 'Ali and Umm Ayman! Let us read what al-Bukhari and Muslim have to say:

It is reported in vol. 3 of Bukhari's *Sahih*, in "The Book of Testimonies," in "The Chapter of one Ordered to Fulfill a Promise," and, likewise, by Muslim in "The Book of Merits" under the heading: "God's Prophet (s) was never asked for something and he denied [the request] and his [generous] giving," that Jabir b. 'Abd Allah (r) said: "After the Prophet (s) died, some property came to Abu Bakr from 'Alaí b. Hadrami, and Abu Bakr said: 'Whoever has given a loan to the Prophet (s), or to whom he had promised anything, let him come to us'". Jabir said: "I said: 'The Prophet of Allah (s) promised to give me this and this..' and he thrice spread his hands.'" Jabir said: "And he counted five hundred [dinars], then

Chapter 5: Concerning the Three Caliphs

another five hundred and another five hundred in my hands."

Did anyone ask Abu Bakr why he believed Jabir b. 'Abd Allah's claim that the Prophet (s) had promised to give him this and this and this, and filled his hands three times to the sum of fifteen hundred [dinars], without asking him to produce a single corroborating witness? Was Jabir b. 'Abd Allah more God-fearing and pious than Fatima, leader of the women of all the worlds? Even more strange than all of the above, is the fact that Abu Bakr repudiated the testimony of her husband 'Ali b. Abi Talib, he whom Allah had cleansed from all impurity and had purified; he upon whom the invocation of blessings is an obligation for each Muslim, just as he invokes on the Prophet (s). The Prophet made love for him [an act of] faith, hatred towards him [an act of] hypocrisy.[15]

Furthermore, al-Bukhari has narrated another incident that gives us a true picture of the oppression on al-Zahra and the *Ahl al-Bayt.* From "The Book of the Gift and its Merits and the Strong Encouragement [to give Gifts]" in the chapter entitled: "It is not lawful for someone to take back his gift or charity," al-Bukhari relates in his *Sahih* that the tribe of Suhayb, which was a client of Ibn Jadh'an, laid claim to two houses and a room that they claimed that the Prophet of Allah (s) had given to Suhayb. Marwan said: "Who will testify as witness on your behalf?" They said: "Ibn 'Umar". So they called him, and he corroborated their claim that the Prophet of Allah (s) gave Suhayb two houses and a room. Marwan based his judgment on Ibn 'Umar's testimony."[16]

Observe, O Muslim, this behavior and the judgments that favor some but not others. Is this not oppression and injustice? If the Caliph of the Muslims could judge in favor of plaintiffs solely on the testimony of Ibn 'Umar, then is it not appropriate for a Muslim to ask himself: "Why were the testimonies of 'Ali b. Abu Talib and Umm Ayman rejected?" The fact is that the [joint] testimony of a

---

[15] *Sahih Muslim* 1/61, "The Chapter on the Proof that love for the Ansar and 'Ali is [a part of] faith, and that hatred towards them in sign of hypocrisy" *Sahih Tirmidhi*, 5/306, *Sunan al-Nasa'i*, 8/116.

[16] *Sahih al-Bukhari*, 3/143.

man and woman is stronger than that of a man only, if we are seeking to fulfill of all the conditions stipulated in the Qur'an [regarding the requisite number of witnesses]. Or is it that the sons of Suhayb were more trustworthy in their petitions than the daughter of the Prophet (s)? Or was it that 'Abd Allah b. 'Umar was reliable in the eyes of the judges while 'Ali was not? As for the claim that the Prophet (s) does not bequeath [an inheritance], the *hadith* that Abu Bakr presented; this was refuted by Fatima al-Zahra (sa), who resorted to the book of Allah, that source of evidence that is never to be rejected, for it has been proven that the Prophet (s) said: "If a *hadith* comes to you from me, compare it with the book of Allah, and, if it agrees with the book of Allah, act upon it, and, if it contradicts the book of Allah, then discard it."

There is no doubt that this *hadith* was contradicted by numerous verses of the noble Qur'an. Was there any one to ask Abu Bakr and the Muslims at large, why was Abu Bakr's single testimony accepted in connection with the narration of this *hadith*, which contradicts [other] narrations, reason and is against Allah's book? And why were the testimonies of Fatima and 'Ali, which were in agreement with [other] transmissions, with reason, and were not against the book of Allah, rejected?

On top of all this, Abu Bakr, however high his status might be, and whatever his supporters and defenders may relate of his merits, cannot attain the station of al-Zahra (sa), the leader of the women of the world, nor the station of 'Ali b. Abi Talib, whom the Prophet of Allah (s) preferred above all the other companions in every field. Let us cite, by way of example, the day when the Prophet of Allah gave the standard and confirmed that he would issue it to one who loved Allah and His Prophet and, in turn, Allah and His Prophet loved him. All the companions longed for it, each wishing it to be given to him but he gave it to none but 'Ali.[17] The Prophet of Allah said of him: "Surely, 'Ali is from me, and I am from him, and he is the guardian of every believer after me."[18]

---

[17] *Sahih al-Bukhari*, 4/5, 4/20.

[18] *Sahih Muslim* 7/121, "The Chapter on the Merits of 'Ali b. Abu Talib".

Chapter 5: Concerning the Three Caliphs

However much the extremists may doubt the authenticity of these *hadiths*, they will not doubt this; that the blessings on 'Ali and Fatima is a part of the blessings upon the Prophet (s), and that the prayers of Abu Bakr, 'Umar, 'Uthman, all those given the glad tidings of heaven, and all the companions along with all the Muslims, would not be accepted if they did not invoke therein blessings upon Muhammad and the family of Muhammad, whom Allah had cleansed of every impurity and has purified, as is reported in the *Sihah* books of the *Ahl al-Sunnah* such as al-Bukhari, Muslim[19], and other *Sihah* works.

[This reached the] point that Imam al-Shafi'i said: "His prayer is invalid who does not invoke blessings on you."

If it is permitted to lie and make spurious claims against these [members of the Prophet's household], then [we can say] good-bye to Islam, and perdition to the world. If you, however, ask why Abu Bakr's testimony was deemed admissible and that of the members of the Prophet's household was rejected, the answer is that he was the judge; and it is up to the judge to rule as he sees fit, for the truth is with him in all cases. Thus, the claim of the strong is akin to the claim of the lion, its proof resulting from the fang and the claw.

Come with me, O reader, so that the veracity of this statement may be made clear for you. See what contradictions al-Bukhari relates in his *Sahih,* especially regarding the matter of the inheritance of the Prophet. Al-Bukhari relates that Abu Bakr reported [the following *hadith*]: "We are the assembly of Prophets; we do not bequeath; whatever we leave is charity." This is the *hadith* that all the Sunnites believe, on which they base their proof for Abu Bakr not responding to Fatima al-Zahra's demand.

What clearly proves that the *hadith* was invalid, and was not known, is that Fatima claimed her inheritance, and so did the wives of the Prophet, the mothers of the believers, for they petitioned Abu

---

[19] *Sahih al-Bukhari*, 6/27, "The Chapter that Allah send and His angels send blessings on the Prophet", *Surah* 33.

Bakr, seeking their inheritance.[20] This is what al-Bukhari reported and what is used as proof that Prophets leave no inheritance. But al-Bukhari contradicted himself by verifying that 'Umar b. al-Khattab distributed the Prophet's inheritance among his wives. For, in "The Book of Deputyship," in "The Chapter of Sharecropping by Division and the Like" al-Bukhari reports on the authority of Nafi' from 'Abd Allah b.

'Umar (r), who informed him that the Prophet concluded a contract with the people of Khaybar to utilize the land on the condition that half the products of fruits or vegetation would be their share. The Prophet used to give his wives one hundred *wasaq* (share of the crops) each, eighty *wasaq* of dates and twenty *wasaq* of barley. (When 'Umar became the Caliph) he gave the wives of the Prophet the option of either having the land and water as their shares, or carrying on the previous practice. Some of them chose the land and some chose the *wasaq*, and 'A'isha chose the land."[21]

This narration clearly demonstrates that Khaybar, from which Fatima claimed her share, was like an inheritance for her from her father. Abu Bakr disallowed her claim on the basis that the Prophet of Allah (s) did not bequeath an inheritance. The narration also clearly shows that 'Umar b. al-Khattab divided Khaybar in the days of his Caliphate among the wives of the Prophet (s) and gave them the option of owning the land or taking the *wasaq* (i.e. share of the crops), with 'A'isha choosing the land. If the Prophet (s) did not bequeath, how is it that 'A'isha, the wife, inherited? And how is it that Fatima, the daughter, did not inherit?

Give us a legal opinion on this, O you of perception, and for you there will be rewards and blessings. In addition, 'A'isha, the daughter of Abu Bakr, appropriated the house of the Prophet of Allah (s) completely and no other wife got what 'A'isha did. She it was who buried her father in that house, and buried 'Umar beside her father, and yet forbade al-Husayn from burying his brother al-

---

[20] *Sahih Muslim* 2/16, "The Book of Prayers", "The Chapter on the Prayer on the Prophet".

[21] *Sahih al-Bukhari*, 3/68.

Chapter 5: Concerning the Three Caliphs

Hasan beside his grandfather, which led Ibn 'Abbas to tell her: "You rode a camel, you rode a donkey, and, if you live, you'll ride an elephant, for the ninth part is from the eighth, and in everything you do what you like." In any case, I do not wish to prolong this subject, for it must be [left] for the researchers to refer to the annals of history. Nonetheless, it does not hurt to mention an excerpt from a speech that Fatima al-Zahra (sa) delivered when Abu Bakr and other prominent companions were present, so that who are destroyed are destroyed after clear signs [come to them] and those who are saved are saved after clear signs [come to them].

"Did you intentionally discard the book of Allah and hurl it behind your backs? It says: 'And Solomon inherited David...' and it says, regarding the story of Zakariyya: 'Grant me from thyself an heir who will inherit me and the family of Ya'qub, and make him, O my Lord, one with whom you are well pleased.'

And Allah says:

'Those who are related by birth are to inherit each other in accordance with Allah's Criterion.'(33:6)

And Allah says:

'Allah dictates to you regarding your [male] children, they get the share of two females' (4:11)

And again:

'It is prescribed for you that, if death approaches, you bequeath property, bequeath it to your parents and your closest kin in the prescribed way. This is a duty on those who are pious.' (2:180)

Did Allah dictate to you a special verse that my father had dismissed? Or are you more knowledgeable than my father and cousin [i.e., 'Ali] regarding the specific and general teachings of the

Qur'an? Or is it that you say people of different faiths cannot inherit each other? What you do is recorded, sealed and waiting for you to stand before it on the day of gathering! Yes, the best judge is Allah; the best leader is Muhammad; and the specified time is the day of resurrection, when all who have lied will be the losers."

Abu Bakr kills the Muslims who refused to pay him the Zakat

Both al-Bukhari, in "The Book of Calling the Apostates to Repent" in "The Chapter on Killing those who Refuse to Accept the Obligatory Laws and those Associated with Apostasy;" and Muslim, in "The Book of Faith" in "The Chapter on the Order to Fight People," report, on the authority of Abu Hurayrah, who said: "After the Prophet had died, and Abu Bakr was made his successor, there were [some] Arabs who turned to disbelief. Umar said: 'O Abu Bakr! How can you fight the people when the Prophet of Allah (s) has said: 'I have been ordered to fight the people until they say: 'There is no God but Allah' and whoever says this, makes himself and his property inviolable except by legal right, and his reckoning is with Allah?' Abu Bakr replied: 'By Allah! I will fight whoever differentiates between *salat* and *zakat*, for *zakat* is a lawful right upon the property! By Allah! Were they to withhold even a single animal that they used to give the Prophet of Allah (s), I will fight them over their withholding it.' Then 'Umar said: 'By Allah! I saw then that Allah had opened the heart of Abu Bakr to [the cause of] fighting, and I realized then that it was correct.'"

This is nothing strange with Abu Bakr and 'Umar, who had threatened to burn the house of Fatima, the leader of the women, along with those companions inside it who withheld the pledge of allegiance [to Abu Bakr].[22] If the burning to death of 'Ali, Fatima, al-Hasan, al-Husayn and a party of the best of companions who had refused the pledge was a trivial thing for them, then the killing of those who refused the *zakat* is just a simple matter. For what is the value of these distant desert tribes, compared to the Prophet's

---

[22] Ibn Qutayba, *al-Imama wa'l Siyasa. Al-'Aqd al-Farid*, vol.2, the *hadith* of saqifa. Al-Tabari, *Tarikh al-Tabari*, al-Mas'udi, *Muruj al-Dhahab*, Abu al-Fida, *Tarikh Abul-Fida*, al-Shahrastani *Kitab al-Milal wa al-Nihal* etc.

Chapter 5: Concerning the Three Caliphs

family and the virtuous companions? I would add to it that those who refused to give their pledge perceived that the Caliphate was their right according to the designation of the Prophet of Allah (s). Even if we assume that there was no appointment on them, then it was still their right to refuse, to criticize and to voice their views if there was consultation, as they claim. The threat of them being burnt to death is established by overwhelmingly numerous reports. Had 'Ali not capitulated and ordered the companions to go out and give their pledge, to prevent the shedding of Muslim blood and to preserve the unity of Islam, there would have been no delay in carrying out the threat of burning them.

Yet the [controversy] subsided and their power grew strong; and there was no more opposition mentioned after the death of al-Zahra and after 'Ali's reconciliation with them. How could they then desist from [acting against] some tribes that refused to pay the *zakat* to them? A refusal based on the argument of waiting until the matters of the Caliphate and what happened after the Prophet's death were clarified, the Caliphate being, as 'Umar himself admitted, a sudden decision.[23]

It is not strange therefore that Abu Bakr and his government should have undertaken the killing of innocent Muslims and the destruction of their sanctity and the enslavement of their women and progeny. Historians have documented that Abu Bakr sent Khalid b. al-Walid, who burnt to death the tribe of Banu Sulaym.[24] He then sent him then to al-Yamama and to Banu Tamim, whom he treacherously killed, having bound them and beheaded them while in captivity. He killed Malik b. Nuwayra, an eminent companion whom the Prophet of Allah (s) had entrusted with charity money of his people, having confidence in him. He [Khalid] then slept with Malikis wife on the same night of her husband's murder. There is no strength and no power except with Allah, the Highest most Powerful.

---

[23] *Sahih al-Bukhari*, "The Book of Waging War against the the infidels and Apostates", "The Chapter on stoning the pregnant woman who fornicated".

[24] Al-*Riyadh al-Nadira*, Muhibb al-Din al-Tabari 1/100.

Malik and his people were guilty of nothing [by way of opposition] except that they had heard of what had transpired after the death of the Prophet (s); the alienation of 'Ali and the oppression of al-Zahra, to the extent that she died still angry at them. Similarly, [they heard] the opposition of the chief of the Ansar, Sa'd b. 'Ubada, and his breaking of the oath, as well as the reports, which the desert tribes had circulated, casting doubt on the validity of the pledge to Abu Bakr. Due to all this, Malik and his people hesitated giving the *zakat*. The [resulting] decree from the Caliph and his supporters was that they be killed; their women and children taken as prisoners of war; their sanctity be defiled and they be subdued, so that the views of the dissidents and the arguments on the Caliphate may not spread to the rest of the Arabs.

Most unfortunately, you will find those who defend Abu Bakr and his government justifying his errors, despite the fact that Abu Bakr himself admitted them.[25] They say what 'Umar did: "By Allah, I perceived that Allah had opened Abu Bakrís heart to fighting and I realized then that it was right."

Can we ask 'Umar the secret of his conviction concerning fighting the Muslims, about whom he himself had said that the Prophet of Allah (s) had forbidden fighting as they had professed [the declaration] "there is no God but Allah?" Indeed, 'Umar himself had opposed Abu Bakr with this *hadith*. How then did he suddenly change his stance and convince [himself] about fighting them and know that it was the right thing simply because he felt Allah had expanded Abu Bakr's heart? How did this operation of expanding his heart occur? And how did 'Umar alone perceive it, to the exclusion of everyone else?

If this "opening of the heart was figurative rather than literal, how would Allah open the hearts of a people to what would make them oppose His rules, which He had dictated through the tongue of

---

[25] When he apologized to the brother of Malik and gave him the blood money for Malik from the public treasury, he said that Khalid had interpreted [things wrongly] and had erred".

Chapter 5: Concerning the Three Caliphs

His Prophet (s)? How could Allah have said to His servants, through His Prophet: "Whosoever says: 'There is no God but God' you are forbidden to kill him, for his accounting lies with me," then He opens the heart of Abu Bakr and 'Umar to fighting them? Did revelation descend upon the two of them after Muhammad (s)? Or was it personal judgment, (*ijtihad*) dictated by political reasons, which discarded the laws of Allah?

As for those apologists who claim that they had reverted from Islam and that it was therefore obligatory to kill them, this allegation is not correct; whoever has read the historical books knows most certainly that those who withheld the *zakat* had not reverted from Islam. How could they have [done so] when they prayed with Khalid and his forces when he came to destroy them? Furthermore, Abu Bakr himself nullified this spurious claim by paying blood money for Malik fom the state treasury and apologized for his death. No apology is needed for the killing of an apostate, nor is any blood money paid from the state treasury. None of the righteous predecessors ever said that those who withheld the *zakat* had reverted from Islam, except in the later periods when there sprang up [different] schools of thought (*madhahib*) and sects. The *Ahl al-Sunnah* then tried their utmost, though unsuccessfully, to justify the actions of Abu Bakr, and found it necessary to formulate the charge of apostasy against them; for they knew that abusing Muslims was wicked and that killing them was [tantamount to] disbelief. This is what has been reported in the *Sahih* literature of the *Ahl al-Sunnah*,[26] and even when al-Bukhari reported the account of Abu Bakr and his speech: "By Allah, I will fight whoever differentiates between *salat* and *zakat*..." he gave the chapter the title, "Whosoever refuses to accept the obligatory commandments, and what is attributed to them with [charges of] apostasy;" this is clear proof that he did not himself believe in the charge of their apostasy (as is obvious).

---

[26] *Sahih al-Bukhari*, "The Book of Faith", "The Chapter on The fear of a believer that his actions will futile whilst he is unaware" and *Sahih* of Muslim "The Book of Faith" "The Chapter on the Prophet's saying: 'The insulting of a Muslim is wicked and killing him is disbelief".

Yet, others have attempted explanations of the *hadith*, as did Abu Bakr, that *zakat* is a right upon property. It is an interpretation taken out of its rightful context.

Firstly: Because the Prophet of Allah (s) forbade the killing of whoever said "*la ilaha illa Allah*;" there are several narrations on this, verified by the *Sihah*, as we will show presently.

Secondly: If *zakat* were a right on property, then the *hadith* allows, in this instance, for the judge to take the *zakat* by force from those who refuse it, without killing them or the spilling their blood.

Thirdly: If this explanation were correct, the Prophet of Allah (s) would have fought Tha'laba, who refused to give the *zakat* to him (the story is well known, and there is no need to repeat it).[27]

Fourthly: We quote what has been authenticated by the *Sihah* regarding the prohibition of killing whoever says "*la ilaha illa Allah*" I shall restrict myself to al-Bukhari and Muslim and to some traditions, for the sake of brevity.

Muslim, in "The Book of Faith" in "The Chapter of Prohibition on the Killing of a *Kafir* after he says "*la ilaha illa Allah*," and al-Bukhari, in "The Book of Military Expeditions" relates: "Khalifa informed me, on the authority of Miqdad b. al-Aswad, that he said to the Prophet of Allah (s): 'What do you think, if I were to meet a man from the disbelievers, and we were to fight, and if he struck one of my hands with his sword and severed it, then fled from me to the shelter of a tree, beseeching: 'I have submitted myself to Allah,' should I, O Prophet of Allah, kill him after he has said this?' The Prophet of Allah (s) said: 'Do not kill him.' So he said: 'But, O Prophet of Allah, he cut off one of my hands, then he said it after severing it.' The Prophet of Allah (s) said: 'Do not kill him. Were you to kill him, he would be in your position before you killed him, and you would be in his position before he had uttered those words.'"

---

[27] Refer to *"Then I Was Guided"*, p. 183.

Chapter 5: Concerning the Three Caliphs

This *hadith* shows us that it is forbidden to kill the *kafir* who professes "There is no God but Allah." even after his attack upon a Muslim and his cutting of his hand. There is no [question here of the] acceptance of Muhammad as a Prophet of Allah (s), nor of the [obligatory] *prayer, zakat,* fast of Ramadan, or pilgrimage. Where, then, do you go and how can you interpret [this]?

Al-Bukhari relates in his *Sahih* in "The Book of Military Campaigns" in the chapter [entitled]: "The Prophet (s) sent Usama b. Zayd to al-Haraqat from Juhayna." and Muslim in "The Book of Faith" in "The Chapter on the Prohibition of the killing of a *kafir* after he has said 'There is no God but Allah,'" on the authority of Usama b. Zayd, who said: "The Prophet of Allah (s) sent us to al-Haraqat and we arrived there at dawn and attacked them; I and an Ansari were in combat with one of their men. After we defeated him, he said: 'There is no God but Allah;' the Ansari turned away from him, but I struck him with my spear until I killed him. When we returned, he informed the Prophet (s) who said: 'O Usama, did you slay him after he said: 'There is no God but Allah?' I said: 'He was seeking to spare himself.' He (the Prophet) kept on repeating this until I wished I had not accepted Islam prior to that day."

This *hadith* proves beyond a shadow of a doubt that it is forbidden to kill whoever says "There is no God but Allah." Because of this, we observe the Prophet of Allah (s) severely rebuking Usama until the latter wished he had not accepted Islam prior to that day, acting in accordance with the *hadith* "Islam cleans whatever was done before it;" and he yearned for Allah's forgiveness for that grave sin.

Al-Bukhari reported in his *Sahih* in "The Book of Clothing" in "The Chapter On White Clothes;" and Muslim narrated in "The Book of Faith" in "The Chapter on Whoever Does not associating anything with Allah will enter heaven" that Abu Dharr al-Ghifari (r) said: "I came to the Prophet (s) and he was clothed in a white outfit and was asleep. I came again and [this time] he was awake. He said: 'Any servant who says 'There is no God but Allah' and then dies in this state, enters paradise.' I said: 'Even if he fornicates and steals?' He said: 'Yes, even if he fornicates and steals'. I said: 'Even if he fornicates and steals?' He said: 'Yes, even if he fornicates and steals'. I said: 'Even if he fornicates and steals?' He said: 'Yes even if he fornicates and steals, despite what Abu Dharr feels.'"

Whenever he used to relate the *hadith,* Abu Dharr used to say: "Despite what Abu Dharr feels." This is another *hadith* which confirms admission to paradise for anyone who says: "There is no God but Allah" and then dies in that state, killing him is forbidden. This is in spite of what Abu Bakr or 'Umar and all their helpers, who interpreted away the realities and turned them upside down, so as to protect the honor of their predecessors and their seniors who changed the rulings of Allah, might have felt.

Most certainly Abu Bakr and 'Umar knew these rulings for they were closer than we are to grasping the rulings, and closer than others to the bearer of the message. However, for the sake of the Caliphate, they reinterpreted the bulk of the rulings of Allah and His Prophet (s), even though they had knowledge and proofs.

Perhaps, when Abu Bakr resolved to fight those who withheld the *zakat,* and 'Umar opposed him with the Prophetic *hadith* forbidding that, he (Abu Bakr) convinced his companion that it was he ('Umar) who had carried the firewood to burn the house of Fatima by himself, and that the least that could be said for Fatima was that she used to testify, "there is no God but Allah". He perhaps also persuaded him that 'Ali and Fatima were still of high standing in the capital city of the Caliphate whereas the tribes withholding the *zakat,* if they were left alone to consult their matters within the Islamic state, they would have a major influence on the centre of the Caliphate. With that, 'Umar perceived that Allah "had opened Abu Bakr's heart" to fighting [such tribes] and admitted that he was right.

Abu Bakr prevents the writing of the Prophet's *Sunnah* as did 'Umar b. al-Khattab and 'Uthman b. 'Affan after him

Whenever the researcher dwells into the history books and acquaints himself with the inner workings of the governments of the three Caliphs, he realizes with absolute certitude that they were

Chapter 5: Concerning the Three Caliphs

the ones who forbade the writing and recording of the noble Prophetic *hadiths*. Indeed, they even prevented [people from] talking about the *hadith* and transmitting it to the people, for they undoubtedly knew that it would not serve their interests or, at the very least, that [the *hadith*] would oppose and contradict a lot of their verdicts; and what they had interpreted was based on their reasoning and according to what their interests dictated. The *hadith* of the Prophet (s) is the second source for law in Islam. In fact it explains and makes clear the primary source, the noble Qur'an, and [this] was left forsaken and forbidden during their reign. For this reason, the *hadith* scholars and historians agree that the collection and recording of the *hadith* started during the time of 'Umar b. 'Abd al-'Aziz (r) or even a little later on. Al-Bukhari reported in "The Book of Knowledge" in "The Chapter on How Knowledge is Acquired" that 'Umar b. 'Abd al-'Aziz wrote to Abu Bakr b. Hazm [and said]: "See what there is of the *hadith* of Allah's Apostle (s) and commit it to writing. I fear the studies of the sciences while the scholars pass away. Nothing should be accepted but the *hadith* of the Prophet (s); so let them [i.e. the learned] spread the knowledge and let them sit together so that the one who is ignorant will learn. Knowledge is not destroyed until it becomes a secret."

Yet, after the death of the Prophet (s), here was Abu Bakr delivering a speech saying: "You relate from the Prophet (s) *hadiths* about which you disagree, and those after you will differ [over them] even more. So don't relate anything from the Prophet of Allah (s) and to whosoever asks you [regarding them], say: "The book of Allah is between us and you; therefore, enjoin whatever is *halal* in it and forbid whatever is *haram* in it." [28]

By Allah, how surprising is this command of Abu Bakr. Here he is, a few days only after that sad day (called "The Calamitous Thursday")[29], agreeing exactly with what his companion 'Umar b. al-Khattab had said: "The Prophet of Allah (s) is hallucinating, and the book of Allah is enough for us."

---

[28] Al-Dhahabi, *Tadhkira al-Huffaz*, 1/3.

[29] *Black Thursday* by the author at: https://www.al-islam.org/black-thursday-muhammad-al-tijani-al-samawi

Here is Abu Bakr saying: "Don't transmit anything from the Prophet. And, to whosoever asks, you say: "The book of Allah is between us; therefore enjoin whatever is *halal* in it and forbid whatever is *haram* in it."

All praise be to Allah for his clear admission that they hurled the *Sunnah* of their Prophet (s) behind them, and it became a forgotten thing for them.

The question that must now be posed to the *Ahl al-Sunnah wa'l-Jama'a*, i.e., the people who defend Abu Bakr and 'Umar and reckon them to be the best of creation after the Prophet of Allah (s), is this:

If your *Sihah* [books] report, as you claim them to do, that the Prophet of Allah (s) said: "I am leaving for you two things after me. If you adhere to them you will never go astray; the book of Allah and my *Sunnah*," and, assuming we accept the authenticity of this tradition, then how is it that the best of your men reject the *Sunnah* and did not accord it any weight, rather, they prevented the people from writing or speaking about it? Did anyone dare ask Abu Bakr from which verse did he deduce the legality of fighting Muslims who withheld the *zakat*, and the taking of their women and children as prisoners of war?

For the book of Allah, which is between us and Abu Bakr, states: *"And among them are those who made a covenant with Allah thus: 'If you bestow your bounty upon us, we will most certainly spend in charity and we will be righteous.' Yet, when Allah showered them with His bounty, they became miserly and turned back from their covenant, and were averse to it. So Allah put hypocrisy into their hearts as a result, until the day they will meet Him because they turned back from what they had promised Allah and because of their lies....."* (9:75-77). This verse, by the consensus of all commentators, was revealed concerning Tha'laba, when he refused

Chapter 5: Concerning the Three Caliphs

to pay the *zakat* during the lifetime of the Prophet (s). I would add that Tha'laba rejected the *zakat* and refused to give it to the Prophet (s), as he said it was *jizya*. Allah, in this verse, showed Tha'laba's hypocrisy, but yet, in spite of this, the Prophet (s) did not fight him nor take his property by force, even though he was capable of doing so. In the case of Malik b. Nuwayra and his people, they did not deny that the *zakat* was an obligatory duty among the injunctions of the religion, but rather, they rejected the one who had usurped the Caliphate after the Prophet, having done so by force, oppression and manipulation of opportunity.

The position that Abu Bakr took [became] even stranger and more astonishing when he discarded the book of Allah behind his back, [even though] Fatima al-Zahra, the leader of the women of the world, argued against him by it, citing to his audience unambiguous clear verses from the book of Allah which confirmed the inheritance of the Prophets. He did not accept it; he nullified it completely with a *hadith* which he brought forth to serve his personal need. If he [truly] said: "You relate from the Prophet of Allah *hadith* about which you differ, and those who come after you will differ even more over them. So do not relate anything from the Prophet's *hadith*. And to anyone who asks you [about it], say: 'The Book of Allah is between us, so enjoin what is *halal* therein, and forbid what is *haram* therein....'", then why did Abu Bakr not do as he preached, when he argued with the truthful, purified one, who was a part of the chosen Messenger (s), regarding the *hadith* of the Prophet: "We Prophets do not bequeath...?" Why did he not judge with her according to the book of Allah, enjoining its *halal* therein and forbidding its *haram*?" The answer is obvious: in this instance, he would have found the book of Allah against him, and Fatima would have triumphed in all her claims over him. If she were to have triumphed against him on that day, she would have later argued on the appointment to the Caliphate for her cousin, 'Ali. It was necessary therefore that Abu Bakr oppose and deny her. Allah says regarding these matters: *"O You who believe! Why do you say what you do not do? It is greatly outrageous to Allah that you should say what you do not do"(61:2-3).*

Due to all this, Abu Bakr could not be comfortable if the *hadiths* of the Prophet (s) were circulating among the people and committed to writing, to memory, to transmission from town to town, village to other [villages]; when those *hadith* were manifest texts that opposed the politics upon which his state was built. There remained no solution for him therefore but to wipe away and conceal the *hadiths*, indeed, to obliterate and burn them.[30] His own daughter, 'A'isha, testified against him. She reported: "My father collected the *hadith* of the Prophet, and they were five hundred in number. He spent the night being undecided [about them]. I said that he was undecided because of a complaint or something that had reached him. In the morning he said: 'O my daughter! Bring me all the *hadiths* that are with you'. I gave them to him, and he burnt them..."[31]

'Umar b. al-Khattab was more severe than his companion on the traditions of the Prophet of Allah and forbade the people from transmitting them

We saw the politics of Abu Bakr in preventing [the preservation of] *hadith* to the extent that he burnt all the *hadiths* that had been collected in his time, all five hundred of them, so that they would not spread to the companions and other Muslims who were thirsty to know the *Sunnah* of their Prophet (s). When 'Umar ascended to the Caliphate, according to Abu Bakr's will, he pursued the same type of politics, though in his own well known severe and harsh manner. He did not limit himself to the forbidding and prevention of the transmission and recording of the *hadith*, but rather, he intimidated and threatened and beat and even imposed [house] arrest.

In vol. 1 of his *Sunan* in "The Chapter on being Honest to the *Hadith*" Ibn Maja narrated on the authority of Qarza b. Ka'b: "'Umar b. al-Khattab sent us to Kufa and accompanied us, walking with us to the mountain passes. He said: 'Do you know why I have walked with you?' Qarza said: 'We said: 'For the right of

---

[30] *Kanz al-'Ummal*, 5/237, Ibn Kathir in *Musnad al-Sadiq*, Al-Dhahabi, *Tadhkira al-Huffaz*, 1/5.

[31] *Kanz al-'Ummal* 5/237.

Chapter 5: Concerning the Three Caliphs

companionship of the Prophet of Allah (s), and for the right of the Ansar.' 'Umar said: "Rather, I did so for something I wish to tell you, and I hope you will remember it as I have walked with you. You will come upon people in whose hearts the Qur'an is vibrating like the vibration of a kettle. When they see you, they will stretch their necks in awe and say: '[These are] the companions of Muhammad.' So reduce the traditions from the Prophet of Allah (s), and I will support you.'" And when Qarza b. Ka'b [later] came to them they said: "Relate [*hadith*] to us". He said: "'Umar forbade us."[32]

Similarly, Muslim related in his *Sahih* in "The Book of Manners" in "The Chapter on Seeking Permission" that 'Umar threatened to beat Abu Musa al-Ash'ari because of a *hadith* he reported from the Prophet of Allah (s). Abu Sa'id al-Khudri said: "We were sitting with Ubay b. Ka'b when Abu Musa al-Ash'ari came to us, upset. He stopped and said: 'I beseech you by Allah! Have any of you heard the Prophet of Allah (s) say: 'Permission is to be sought three times. If it is granted, proceed, if not, return.' Ubay said: 'What about it?' Abu Musa said: 'Yesterday I sought permission three times from 'Umar. He did not grant it, so I went away. I came to him today, and when I entered, I informed him that I had come yesterday, greeted him three times and then left. Then 'Umar said: 'We heard you but at the time we were busy; you should have kept on seeking permission until it was granted to you.'" Abu Musa said: "I sought permission according to what I heard the Prophet of Allah (s) say. He said [to me]: 'By Allah! I'll beat your back and your stomach unless you bring someone to testify to this.' Ubay b. Ka'b said: 'By Allah none will go with you except he who is the youngest amongst us.' Go forth, O Abu Sa'id'. So I went until I came to 'Umar and I said: 'I have heard the Prophet of Allah say this.'"

Al-Bukhari also reported this incident, but, as is his norm, he abridged and edited from it 'Umar's threat to beat Abu Musa, in order to protect 'Umar's honor[33] although Muslim added Ubay's

---

[32] Al-Dhahabi, *Tadhkira*, 1/3-4.

[33] *Sahih al-Bukhari*, "The Book of Seeking Permission", "The Chapter on Greeting and Seeking Permission three times".

address to 'Umar: 'O Ibn al-Khattab! Do not inflict suffering upon the companions of the Prophet of Allah (s).'"

Al-Dhahabi transmitted in his *Tadhkira al-Huffaz* in vol. 1, p. 4 from Abu Salama who said to Abu Hurayrah: "During the time of 'Umar, did you transmit this?" He replied: "Had I narrated in his time as I narrate to you now, he would have whipped me with his whip."

'Umar, after forbidding the [collection of] *hadith* and threatening the people to beat them, burnt the traditions the companions had collected. He addressed the people one day thus: "O People! It has come to my knowledge that certain books have appeared in your hands. I wish, by Allah, that I could change and correct them. Let there not remain anyone amongst you with a book except that he gives it to me so that I may check it." The people assumed that he wished to examine them to correct them on an issue so that there would be no differences in it, and so they brought their books to him whereupon he burnt them in the fire.[34]

In his *Jami' Bayan al-'ilm wa Fadlih*, Ibn 'Abd al-Barr related that 'Umar b. al- Khattab wanted to write down the *Sunnah*, then it seemed better to him not to do so. So he wrote to the cities ordering that anyone in possession of it must destroy it.

In spite of his plan, however, and despite his threats, his proscription, prohibition and his burning of books, some of the companions still persevered in relating what they had heard from the Prophet of Allah (s) whenever they met people on their journeys outside of Medina who asked them about the *hadiths* of the Prophet (s). 'Umar deemed it proper to confine them within Medina, even forcing house arrest on them and undertaking forceful measures. Ibn Ishaq narrated from 'Abd al-Rahman b. 'Awf who said: "'Umar did not die until after he had summoned all the companions of the Prophet of Allah (s) from the farthest places; 'Abd Allah b. Hudhayfa, Abu Darda', Abu Dharr al-Ghifari and 'Uqba b. 'Amir. He said to them: 'What are these *hadiths* that you have related in the

---

[34] Ibn Sa'd, *Tabaqat al-Kubra*, 5/188, Baghdadi, in *Taqyid al-'Ilm*.

Chapter 5: Concerning the Three Caliphs 221

outlying areas from the Prophet of Allah (s)?' They said: 'Are you forbidding us [to do so]?' He responded: 'No! But stay with me. By Allah! You will not leave me as long as I am alive.'"[35]

And after him came the third Caliph, 'Uthman, who followed the same course as his two predecessors. He ascended the *minbar* and declared openly: "It is not permissible for anyone to narrate from the Prophet of Allah (s) any *hadith* that was not heard during the times of Abu Bakr and 'Umar."[36]

In this manner, the restriction continued throughout the rule of the three Caliphs, a period of twenty-five years. If only it had been limited to that period, rather, it continued. When Mu'awiyah grabbed the reins of power, he ascended the pulpit and declared: "I forbid you the *hadith,* except those [accepted] during the time of 'Umar, for he used to make the people fear Allah." This has been reported by Muslim in vol. 3 in "The Book of *Zakat*" in "The Chapter on the Prohibition of Questioning."

Thereafter, the Umayyad Caliphs adopted this path, forbidding authentic *hadiths* of the Prophet while specializing in the fabrication of forged and false *hadiths* against him. It reached to an extent that Muslims of every age have been afflicted by contradictions, myths and legends that do not have any connection whatsoever to Islam. Here is what al-Mada'ini reports in his book, *al-Ahdath*: "Mu'awiyah wrote the same letter to all of his governors after the year of the unity: 'Anyone who reports anything regarding the merits of Abu Turab ('Ali b. Abu Talib) and his family is exempt from [my] protection.' The preachers in every place, every *minbar* then took to cursing 'Ali and dissociating from him, defaming him and his family."

Mu'awiyah then wrote to his governors in all the regions: "Do not accept the testimony of any of those who follow 'Ali and his Family." He further went on: "Seek out from among you those who follow 'Uthman and those who love him, as well as his friends and

---

[35] *Kanz al-'Ummal*, 5/239.

[36] Ahamd b. Hanbal, *Musnad*, 1/363.

protectors and those who relate his merits and praises. Associate with them, frequent their gatherings make them close to you and honor them. Write to me anything that each one of them narrates, and give me his name, his father's name and his progeny."

They did that until the merits and praises of 'Uthman were numerous, all because of the rewards, cloaks, gifts and land grants he sent to them, flowing out to the Arabs and the non-Arab clients. It multiplied in every city and they competed for status and worldly gains. Every man who came to the officials of Mu'awiyah was welcomed when he related praises or merits of 'Uthman; his name was recorded and he was befriended and rewarded. This continued for a while. Then Mu'awiyah wrote to his officials: "The *hadith* of 'Uthman has multiplied and spread to every city. When this letter reaches you ask in favor of various dimensions the people for the *hadiths* regarding the merits of the companions and the first Caliphs. Do not leave any information that any Muslim narrates in favor of Abu Turab, except that you come up with another one that contradicts it from one of the *sahaba*. This is dearer to me and more of a delight to my eye and more of a refutation to the argument of Abu Turab and his party (Shi'a), and more damaging to them than recounting the good deeds and merits of 'Uthman."

His letters were read to the people and many narrations on the merits of the companions were reported, most of them spurious, [there was] no truth in them. And the people really exerted themselves in this until they started doing so from the pulpits. The teachers in the learning circles started doing this and taught the children and youths until they began to narrate and learn them as they learnt the Qur'an. They even taught their daughters and wives and their servants and entourage, they kept on doing this as long as Allah willed.

Then Mu'awiyah sent a common letter to his officials in every region: "Seek out one against whom there is proof that he loves 'Ali and his family, and then erase his name from the national register and cut off whatever [stipend] he is given from the state." He reinforced this with another letter: "Whosoever you accuse of aiding these people, place him in fetters and demolish his home."

Chapter 5: Concerning the Three Caliphs

The affliction was most severe and rampant in Iraq especially in Kufa to the extent that, if a Shi`i was visited by someone whom he trusted, he would bring him to his house and tell him his secrets and thereafter, he would live in fear of his servants and slaves and would not speak until he had taken a severe oath of silence from them. Several spurious and calumnious *hadiths* surfaced; and the jurists and judges and those in authority promoted them. The worst perpetrators of this calamity were those who recited the Qur'an to show off to others and those of weak faith who displayed outward piety and performed rituals while forging *hadith*; so that they could please those in authority and be in their gatherings, thus gaining money, property and positions. This continued until the *hadith* and the reports fell into the hands of the religionists, who could not allow lies and accusations. Rather, they accepted these *hadiths* and transmitted them assuming they were authentic, for, had they known they were spurious, they would not have narrated nor acted upon them.[37]

I say the responsibility of this falls on Abu Bakr, 'Umar and 'Uthman who prevented the recording of the true *hadiths* of the Prophet (s) on the pretext that they were afraid the *hadiths* would be mixed with the Qur'an. This is what their helpers and defenders maintain. This claim amuses even the lunatics. Are the Qur'an and *Sunnah* sugar and salt so that, if they are mixed, they could not be separated from each other? Even sugar and salt do not mix for each is in a specific container. Did it not dawn upon the Caliphs that they could have written the Qur'an on one special scroll and the *Sunnah* of the Prophet in a separate book, as is the situation with us today, and has been since the recording of the traditions from the time of 'Umar b. 'Abd al-'Aziz (r)? Why has the *Sunnah* not been mixed with the Qur'an, even though the *hadith* books exceed hundreds? Moreover, the *Sahih* of al-Bukhari is not mixed with that of Muslim, which in turn is not mixed with Ahmad b. Hanbalis *Musnad* nor the *Muwatta* of Malik b. Anas, let alone being mixed with the noble Qur'an.

This argument is weak like the house of a spider; it cannot stand

---

[37] *Sharh Nahj al-Balagha*, Ibn Abi'l-Hadid, 11/46.

up to the scrutiny of proof. In fact, the proof against it is even clearer. Al-Zuhri reported on the authority of 'Urwa that 'Umar b. al-Khattab wanted to commit the *Sunnah* to writing and sought the counsel of the companions of the Apostle of Allah (s). They advised him to do so; but 'Umar prayed for guidance about this for a month then one morning arose saying: "I had wanted to write the *Sunnah* down then I remembered the people before you that wrote books and chose to follow them, leaving the book of Allah! And By Allah, I will not mix the book of Allah with anything, ever."[38]

Look, O reader, at this narration. The companions of the Prophet (s) advised 'Umar to write down the *Sunnah* and he went against all of them and chose to impose his own view; claiming that the people before them had written books and had chosen to follow these books to the exclusion of Allah's Book. Where was the claim of mutual consultation (*shura*), which the *Ahl al-Sunnah wa'l-Jama'a* invoke? Where are these people who chose to adhere to their books, instead of the book of Allah?

We have not heard of them except in 'Umar b. al-Khattab's imagination. Assuming these people did exist, there is no ground for comparison as they manufactured books from themselves to distort the book of Allah. The Qur'an states: *"Woe unto those who write the book with their own hands then they say 'This is from Allah' to gain thereby a small prize. Woe unto them for what they wrote and for what they gained by their deed"* (2:79). As for books of the *Sunnah,* these are not like that, for they originate from the infallible Prophet who did not utter anything from his own desire but, rather, from the revelation that descended upon him. [The *sunnah*] clarified and explained the book of Allah. The most High stated: *"We have sent unto you the reminder, to explain to the people what has been revealed to them"* (16:44). And the Prophet (s) said: "I was given the Qur'an and with it something similar to it." This is a simple matter for anyone who

---

[38] Ibn 'Abd al-Barr in *Jami' Bayan al-ilm wa fadlih, Kanz al-'Ummal*, 5/239 and Ibn Sa'd from al-Zuhri.

Chapter 5: Concerning the Three Caliphs

knows the Qur'an, for there is no mention in it of five prayers, no specified amount for *zakat* or rules of fasting or *hajj* and various other rulings which the Prophet of Allah (s) has explained. Due to this, Allah said: *"What the Prophet has given you accept it; and from what he has forbidden you, eschew it."(59:7)*

And He says: *"Say! 'If you love Allah, then follow me so that Allah may love you.'"(3:31)*

If only 'Umar knew the book of Allah and paid more attention to it in order to learn from it obedience to the injunctions of the Messenger, and not to argue or refute him.[39] If only he had known the book of Allah and given more attention to it so that he could learn the judgment of al-Kalala[40] which he did not know up to the time he died. During his Caliphate, he issued rulings on it based on various contradictory verdicts. If only he knew the book of Allah and paid more attention to it to learn the rulings of *tayammum* which he did not know even during the days of his Caliphate. He used to rule that he who doesn't find water should not pray.[41] If only he knew the book of Allah and paid due attention to know the laws of divorce of two utterances, after which one should live [with the wife] in accordance with proper forms of behaviour or should separate from her with kindness. Instead, he made all three divorces count as one;[42] and, by following his own view and personal judgment, he opposed Allah's decrees, discarding them.

The truth that cannot be denied is that the Caliphs prevented the spread of *hadiths*. They threatened and exiled whosoever spoke of them. This is because it would have frustrated their plans and exposed their plots and would not have given them any room for

---

[39] *Sahih al-Bukhari*, 1/37, "The Chapter on Writing Knowledge" and 5/138.

[40] *Sunan* al-Bayhaqi, *Kanz-al-'Ummal*, 6/15 and *Sahih Muslim*, Kitab *al-Fara'id* "The Chapter of the Inheritance of *al-Kalala*".

[41] *Sahih al-Bukhari* 1/90, Muslim, 1/193 Bab al-Tayammum.

[42] *Sahih Muslim*, Kitab *al-Talaq*, "The Chapter on Three Divorces", volume one.

interpreting things as they interpreted the Qur'an. This is because Allah's book is silent and multifaceted, whereas the *Sunnah* of the Prophet is comprised of the words and deeds of the Prophet (s), no one can oppose it. Due to this, the Commander of the Faithful, 'Ali (as), said to Ibn 'Abbas when he sent him to debate with the Khawarij: "Do not oppose them with the Qur'an, for the Qur'an has different interpretations. You will say things and they will say [other] things; but debate them by using the *Sunnah,* for they will not find any escape from it."[43]

Abu Bakr bestows the caliphate upon his companion 'Umar and, in doing so, goes against the clear texts

On this matter specifically, Imam 'Ali (as) said: "By Allah! Ibn Abi Quhafa has dressed himself [with the Caliphate]! Yet he knows that my position to it is like that of a pole in relation to the hand mill! The current flows from me and [even] birds cannot aspire to my heights. I put a curtain against the Caliphate and detached myself from it. I began to think whether I should fight [for my rights] with a fettered hand (i.e. unsupported) or endure the blinding darkness of tribulations wherein the old would become feeble, the young would become old, and a believer would strive until he met his Lord.

I perceived being that patience was the wiser course for me. I adopted patience although there was prickling in the eye and suffocation in the throat.

I watched the plundering of my inheritance till the first one passed away; but he handed [the Caliphate] to Ibn al-Khattab after him. (Then 'Ali quoted al-'Asha's verse: 'My days now pass on the camel's back (i.e., with difficulty), while there were days (of ease) in the company of Jabir's brother).'

It is surprising that, during his lifetime, he wished to be released of the Caliphate, yet he confirmed it for the other one after his death. How cleverly the two shared it's udders between themselves.

---

[43] The letter of 'Ali b. Abu Talib to Ibn 'Abbas, *Nahj al-Balagha,* 1/77.

Chapter 5: Concerning the Three Caliphs

This one put the Caliphate in a tough enclosure with harsh speech and a rough touch. Many errors were made, and so many excuses [offered]."[44]

Every researcher and examiner knows that the Prophet of Allah (s) designated and appointed 'Ali b. Abi Talib to the Caliphate before his death. Most of the *sahaba*, amongst whom Abu Bakr and 'Umar were the most prominent, knew of it also.[45] Because of this, Imam 'Ali used to say: "He knows my position to it is like the pole to the hand mill..." Perhaps it was this that caused Abu Bakr and 'Umar to forbid the transmission of *hadiths* from the Prophet (s), as we have shown in the preceding chapter, adhering only to the Qur'an. The Qur'an, even though it contains the verse of successorship, does not clearly mention the name of 'Ali. The *hadiths*, however, specifically mention his name; for example the Prophet's (s) saying: "Of whomsoever I am the master, this 'Ali is his master" and "'Ali is to me as Aaron was to Moses;" and "'Ali is my brother and successor and the Caliph after me;" and "'Ali is from me, and I am from him, and he is the leader of every believer after me."[46]

This helps us understand the extent of success of the step which Abu Bakr and 'Umar took in the proscription and burning of the *hadiths* of the Prophet; thereby muzzling the people to the extent that even the companions did not mention the *hadiths*, as has already been mentioned in the report of Qarza b. Ka'b. This restriction continued for a quarter century, i.e., the period of the first three Caliphs, until the coming of 'Ali to the Caliphate. Now we see he made the companions bear witness, on the day of assembling, to the *hadith* of Ghadir Khum, thirty of them bearing witness, seventeen of whom were veterans of Badr.[47]

This is manifest proof that these companions, and there were

---

[44] *Sharh Nahj al-Balagha*, Muhammad 'Abduh, 1/84-87.

[45] Imam al-Ghazali, in his book *Sirr al-'Alamayn*

[46] All this traditions have been reported by al-Tabari in *al-Riyadh al-Nazara* and al-Nasa'i in his *al-Khasais* and Ahmad b. Hanbal in *Musnad*.

[47] *Musnad*, Ibn Hanbal, 1/119, Ibn 'Asakir, *Tarikh Dimishq*, 2/7.

thirty of them, would not have spoken up had the Commander of the Faithful not asked them to do so. Were 'Ali not the Caliph, with power in his hands, they would have remained silent, fearing to bear witness.

This had actually happened in the case of some companions in whom fear and jealousy prevented them from bearing witness, among them were Anas b. Malik, Bara' b. 'Azib, Zayd b. Arqam, and Jarir b. 'Abd Allah al-Bajli.[48] The claim of 'Ali (as) had reached them however; he was not allowed to manage the Caliphate in peace. His days were filled with trials, mischief and plots. Wars were waged against him from every side; and their jealousy and grudges surfaced by [his showings] at Badr, Hunayn, Khaybar until he fell martyred. Those Prophetic traditions did not find receptive ears among those who broke their pledges, the deviants, those who missed the truth and the opportunists. They indulged in immorality, taking bribes and being fond of the world during the Caliphate of 'Uthman. The son of Abu Talib could not, within three or four years, rectify the corruption and deviation of a quarter century, except by destroying himself, God forbid. 'Ali it was who said: "I know very well what will correct you, but I will not cure you by corrupting myself."

It was not long before Mu'awiyah b. Abu Sufyan ascended the Caliphate and continued the same plan that we have already described, i.e. prohibiting all *hadiths* except those which were prevalent at the time of 'Umar. Indeed, he even went a step further and commissioned a group of the companions and their followers to fabricate traditions. Thus the *Sunnah* of the Prophet of Allah (s) was lost in the web of their lies, tales and their spurious merits.

The Muslims continued thus for a full century during which the *Sunnah* of Mu'awiyah was followed by the general Muslim public. When we say "The *Sunnah* of Mu'awiyah," we mean the *Sunnah* that was pleasing to Mu'awiyah from the acts of the first three Caliphs Abu Bakr, 'Umar and 'Uthman; and also whatever else he

---

[48] Al-Baladhuri, *Ansab al-Ashraf,* 2/156, *Sira al-Halabiyya,* 3/337, *al-Ma'arif* by Ibn Qutayba, 194.

Chapter 5: Concerning the Three Caliphs 229

and his followers added by way of lies, forgeries, curses and insults against 'Ali and the members of his household, and his followers amongst the sincere companions. This is why I reiterate and repeat that Abu Bakr and 'Umar succeeded in their plan to obliterate the *Sunnah* of the Prophet (s), on the pretext of referring to the Qur'an.

For you can clearly see today, after the passing of fourteen centuries, if you argue by the successively transmitted Prophetic texts which prove that the Prophet (s) appointed 'Ali as his successor, it will be said to you: "Let us leave aside the Prophetic *Sunnah* that is differed upon, the book of Allah is sufficient for us; and the book of Allah did not relate that 'Ali is the successor of the Prophet, but instead said: "Your affairs are by mutual consultation." This is their argument, every scholar of the *Ahl al-Sunnah* I talked to, spoke of the *shura* as their slogan and standard practice.

Disregarding the fact that the Caliphate of Abu Bakr was a sudden event, through which Allah shielded the Muslims from evil,[49] it was not done by consultation, as some claim. Rather, it was done by negligence and force, by coercion, intimidation, and beatings.[50] Several of the best companions dissented and opposed it. At the head of this group were 'Ali b. Abu Talib, Sa'd b. 'Ubada, 'Ammar, Salman, Miqdad, al-Zubayr, al-'Abbas and many others, as the eminent historians of this event admitted. Nonetheless, let us leave this matter alone and turn towards Abu Bakr's appointment of 'Umar as successor after him; and let us ask the *Ahl al-Sunnah* who brag about the principle of *shura*: "Why did Abu Bakr appoint 'Umar as his successor and impose it upon the Muslims rather than leaving the matter [open for] mutual consultation, as you claim?"

For further clarification, as is our custom, we depend only on the books of the *Ahl al-Sunnah,* and present to the reader how Abu Bakr appointed his companion as his successor. Ibn Qutayba reported in his *History of the Caliphs* (*Tarikh al-Khulafa'*), in "The Chapter of Abu Bakrís illness and his Designation of 'Umar (r) as

---

[49] *Sahih al-Bukhari* 8/26, Kitab *al-Muharibi min ahl al-Kufr wa'l-ridda,* "The Chapter on stoning the pregnant woman who fornicated".

[50] Ibn Qutayba, *Al-Imama wa al-Siyasa,* the appointment of Abu Bakr.

his successor": "Then he summoned 'Uthman b. 'Affan and said: 'Write my will.' So Abu Bakr dictated and 'Uthman wrote thus: 'In the name of Allah, the Beneficent the Merciful. This is what Abu Bakr b. Quhafa does decide as his last will and testament in this world that he is about to leave, and the first testament to the hereafter that he is about to enter.

I appoint 'Umar b. al-Khattab as my successor, if you perceive him as a just man among you, and this is my opinion of him and hope in him. If he distorts and changes, I only wish for [your] good, and I do not have knowledge of the unseen. And those who do wrong will soon know their fate.'"

He then put his seal upon the document and gave it to 'Uthman. When the news that he had named 'Umar as his successor reached the emigrants and the Ansar, they entered and said: "We see that you have placed 'Umar as the Caliph over us. You know and are aware of his severity with us even while you are among us, how about when you leave us? Now you are going to meet Allah, the Most High and Majestic, and He will ask you about it, what will you say?" Whereupon Abu Bakr replied: "If Allah asks me, I will most certainly say: 'I appointed as Caliph over them he who seemed to me to be the best of them.'"[51]

Some historians, such as al-Tabari and Ibn al-Athir, mention that when Abu Bakr called 'Uthman to write his last testament, he lost consciousness while he was dictating and 'Uthman wrote the name of 'Umar b. al-Khattab. When he regained consciousness, he said: "Read what you have written! So he read it and mentioned 'Umar's name. Abu Bakr asked him: "From where did you get this?" He answered: "You were never wont to oppose him." Abu Bakr replied: "You are right."

When he finished his will, some of the companions, Talha among them, called upon him. Talha said to him: "What will you say to your Lord tomorrow? You have chosen a severe, harsh man to govern us. People run away from him and their hearts beat because

---

[51] Ibn Qutayba, *Tarikh al-Khulafa'*, known as *Al-Imama wa al-Siyasa*, 1/24.

Chapter 5: Concerning the Three Caliphs

of him." Abu Bakr said: "You all helped me, and he was my support. So now support him." He said to Talha: "Do you try to scare me with Allah? If I am asked about it tomorrow I will say: 'I selected the best of your people to rule them.'"[52]

Since the historians all agree that Abu Bakr appointed 'Umar as his successor, without having sought the counsel of the companions, we can only say that he did so despite the wishes of the companions who hated 'Umar. Whether it was Ibn Qutayba who reported that the Muhajirun and Ansar entered and said: "You are fully aware of his severity with us" or Tabari who said: "Some companions, Talha among them, called upon Abu Bakr and Talha said: 'What will you say to your Lord now that you have chosen to rule over us a harsh, severe man from whom people run away and because of whom hearts beat [faster]?'" The end result is still the same: that the companions did not decide their affairs by mutual consultation; and they did not approve the appointment of 'Umar, whom Abu Bakr had imposed upon them without seeking their counsel. The result is that which Imam 'Ali foretold when 'Umar b. al-Khattab treated him so harshly to gain his pledge of allegiance to Abu Bakr; for he said: "He has milked for you milk, half of which will be for you; so enforce his [command] today and he will return it to you tomorrow."

This is exactly what one of the companions said to 'Umar b. al-Khattab when he came out with the letter appointing him as the Caliph. He said to 'Umar: "What is in the document, O Abu Hafs?" 'Umar said: "I don't know, but I shall be the first to hear and obey." Whereupon the man said: "By Allah, I know what is in it. You made him the leader in the first year, and now he has made you the leader."[53]

This clearly proves to us, beyond any doubt, that the principle of *shura*, which the *Ahl al-Sunnah* claim [as their standard], had no basis for Abu Bakr and 'Umar. In other words, Abu Bakr was the

---

[52] Ibn Abi'l-Hadid, *Sharh Nahj al-Balagha*, sermon of *Shaqshaqiyya*.

[53] Ibn Qutayba, *Al-Imama wa al-Siyasa*, "The Chapter on Abu Bakr's appointment of 'Umar".

first to destroy and discard the principle, thereby opening the doors for the Umayyad rulers to follow his action, a Caesar-like dynasty, handed down from father to son. After them, the 'Abbasids did likewise; the idea of *shura* remained a dream which the *Ahl al-Sunnah wa'l-Jama'a* seek but never actualize.

This reminds me of a conversation that took place between a Wahhabi scholar from Saudi Arabia and me in a Nairobi mosque in Kenya concerning the problem of the Caliphate. I was advancing the view that the Caliphate was according to designation and that the entire affair was Allah's to decide as He wished, and that there was no room for people to decide in the matter. He was a proponent of the *shura* and was defending it strongly. He also had with him several of his students who were studying under him and supporting everything he said, on the pretext that his argument was based on the noble Qur'an, wherein Allah said to His Prophet (s): "And seek their counsel in the matter" and also: "Their affairs [are to be decided by] a *shura* between them."

I realized that I was overpowered by them, for they had learnt all the Wahhabi ideas from their teacher and also that they would not listen to the true *hadiths*, but rather, relied on some *hadith* which they had memorized, most of which were false. I therefore surrendered to the principle of *shura* and said to them and to their teacher: "Can you convince the government of His Highness, Your King, of the principle of *shura*, so that he might step down from his throne and follow the example of your pious predecessors? Thereby giving the Muslims in the Arab peninsula the freedom of choice of their ruler? I don't think he will do that, for his father and grandfathers not only ruled the Caliphate, but also the entire Arab peninsula became part of their kingdom. They even called the entire Hijaz 'The Saudi Kingdom.' Upon that, their leader, the scholar, said: "We have no business with politics; we are in the house of Allah wherein we are ordered to remember his name and observe the prayers." I replied: "And also to seek knowledge." He said: "Yes, it is so and we also teach the youth here". I said: "And so we are [engaging] in an academic discussion". He said: "And you have denigrated it by [touching on] politics."

Chapter 5: Concerning the Three Caliphs 233

I left with my companions; I felt sad for the Muslim youths whose minds the Wahhabis had so controlled in every way and declared a war on their fathers. They were all adherents to the Shafi'i *madhhab* which, I think, is the closest to that of the Prophet's family. The Shaykhs used to have respect and piety from the educated and non educated people alike, since most of them came from notable backgrounds of a pure lineage. Then the Wahhabis came and, taking advantage of their poverty, deluded them with money and other material things and they changed their outlook, i.e., [they convinced them] that such respect for the Shaykhs was in fact idolatry because it entailed the veneration of a human being. So the sons turned against their fathers. Regrettably, this is what has happened in many of the Islamic countries in Africa.

Let us return to the topic of the death of Abu Bakr. We find him, just before his death, regretting what he had done, for Ibn Qutayba reported in his "*Al-Imama wa al-Siyasa*"[54] Abu Bakr's words: "Yes, by Allah, I regret only three things that I wish I had not done:

(1) "If only I had left the house of 'Ali." In another narration, that "I had not violated the house of Fatima even if they had declared war upon me;"

(2) "If only, on the day of Saqifa at Banu Sa'ida, I had instead pledged to Abu 'Ubayda or 'Umar and that he were the leader and I the minister;"

(3) "If only, when I came upon Dhi al-Faja'a al-Sulami, while he was a prisoner of war, I had slaughtered him or spared him instead of burning him."[55]

And we add: "If only, O Abu Bakr, you had not oppressed al-Zahra, had not hurt or angered her; and if only you had repented before her death and had pleased her. This is specifically with

---

[54] *Imamate (Leadership) and Politics*

[55] *Tarikh al-Tabari*, 4/52, Ibn 'Abd Rabbih in *al-'Aqd al-Farid*, 2/254, al-Mas'udi in *Muruj al-Dhahab*, 1/414.

regards to the house of 'Ali, which you exposed and allowed to be burnt.

Regarding the Caliphate, if only you had left your two companions and cronies, Abu 'Ubayda and 'Umar, and given the pledge to the divinely prescribed Caliph, who had been named as successor by the bearer of the message, that he would be the leader. Then the world today would be different from what we see and Allah's religion would have spread all over the globe, as Allah had promised and His promise is always true.

With respect to al-Faja'a al-Sulami, whom you burnt to death, if only you had not burnt the Prophetic traditions which you had collected, you would have learnt the correct *shari'a* rulings from them and would not have resorted to personal judgment by your own views.

Lastly, while you were on your death bed, if only you had thought about your appointment of a successor and returned the truth to its owner, he whose position to the Caliphate was like the pole to the millstone. For you were the most aware of his merits, his excellence, his asceticism, his knowledge and his piety; for he was like the Prophet himself (s), especially when he submitted the matter to you and did not rise up against you, for the sake of protecting Islam. You were free to advise the *ummah* of Muhammad (s) and to choose for it one that would have corrected its affairs, governed it properly and taken it to the summit of glory.

We ask Allah, Glorified and Exalted be He, to forgive your sins, and to placate Fatima and her father, as well as her husband and her sons for your sake. For you angered a part of al-Mustafa and God gets angry when she is angry and is happy when she is happy. One who hurts Fatima hurts her father according to the text of his *hadith*; and, according to Allah's words, 'whosoever causes suffering to the Prophet of Allah, and for them is a painful punishment.'"

And we seek Allah's refuge from His anger and we ask Him to be pleased with us and with all the Muslim men and women, the believing men and the believing women.

'Umar b. al-Khattab contravenes the book of Allah with his personal reasoning

The history of 'Umar, the second Caliph, is one filled with his *ijtihad* (personal reasoning) as opposed to the clear texts from the noble Qur'an and the noble *Sunnah* of the Prophet. The *Ahl al-Sunnah* use that as pride and virtue, for which they praise him. The objective ones among them seek excuses and farfetched defenses for him, neither reason nor logic can accept them. How can one who opposes the book of God and the *Sunnah* of His Prophet be one of those who exercises *ijtihad*? Allah says: *"It is not proper for any believing man or believing woman, if Allah and His Prophet have decreed a matter, that they should have any option in their matter. And whosoever disobeys Allah and His Prophet has most manifestly gone astray"* (33:36).

And our Glorious Creator also says: *"Those who do not judge according to what Allah has revealed, they are unbelievers, and those who do not judge by what Allah has revealed they are indeed wrongdoers... and those who do not judge by what Allah has revealed, they are the corrupt ones"* (5:44/45/47).

In "The Book of Adherence to the Qur'an and *Sunnah*" in "The Chapter on what is Mentioned regarding Blameworthy Opinions, Strained Analogies, and Acting and Saying about Things of which you have no Knowledge." al-Bukhari reported that the Prophet (s) said: "Allah does not arbitrarily take away knowledge after having bestowed it, but rather, He takes it away with the passing away of the learned and their knowledge, whereupon the people are left in ignorance, seeking and giving religious opinions from their personal ideas. And in so doing, they are led astray and lead others astray."[56]

Similarly, in the same book, al-Bukhari reports in his *Sahih* in the next chapter: "The Prophet (s), when asked about something for which a revelation had not come, used to say 'I don't know'; or he did not reply until a revelation came to him, he did not speak based on his own opinion or on analogy, in accordance with Allah's words: *'According to that which Allah has shown you.'*"[57] The scholars, old and new, have said one thing: "Whoever exercises his personal judgment in the Qur'an has disbelieved," and this is clear from the unambiguous verses and from the words and deeds of the Prophet of Allah (s).

How then can this rule be forgotten whenever the matter pertains to 'Umar b. al-Khattab or any of the companions or one of the Imams of the four *madhabs*? Indeed, personal interpretation, even in contravention to the judgments of Allah, gets one reward if it is wrong and two if it is right!

One could well say that this point is agreed upon by both the Shi'as and the Sunnis according to Prophetic *hadiths* accepted by both. However, I reply that this is true but they differ on the issue of *ijtihad*. The Shi'a enjoin *ijtihad* in matters where nothing has come down from Allah or His Prophet (s). As for the *Ahl al-Sunnah*, they do not restrict themselves like this. Taking the example of the Caliphs and pious predecessors, they do not see any harm in *ijtihad* even in the face of clear texts. The great scholar, al-Sayyid Sharaf al-Din al-Musawi relates in his book, *al-Nas wa'l-Ijtihad*, more than 100 instances wherein the companions, especially the three Caliphs, contravened the clear texts of the Qur'an and *Sunnah*. The researchers should study this book.

Since we are essentially on this subject, it is necessary to mention some of the instances wherein 'Umar went against clear texts, maybe due to his ignorance of the texts, and this would be astonishing; for he who is ignorant is not fit to judge what is legal

---

[56] *Sahih al-Bukhari*, 8/148.

[57] *Ibid*.

Chapter 5: Concerning the Three Caliphs

and forbidden, from his own volition. Allah says: *"Do not say anything false that your tongues may put forth that this is halal and this is haram, so as to ascribe false things to Allah. Those who ascribe false things to Allah will never prosper"* **(16:116).**

An ignorant person cannot take up the position of Caliph and lead the whole *ummah*. Allah says: *"Is he who leads to the truth more worthy to be followed or he that cannot lead unless he is guided? What is with you? How do you judge"* **(10:35)**

It is also possible that 'Umar was not ignorant of the texts; he knew them yet relied on *ijtihad* due to what the circumstances dictated. The *Ahl al-Sunnah* do not consider this to be *kufr* or deviation; just as [they assume] he must have been ignorant of the presence of one of his contemporaries who knew the correct rulings. [This defense] is baseless since he knew of Imam 'Ali's total command of the Qur'an and *Sunnah*. Otherwise, he would not have sought 'Ali's guidance in many dilemmas, so much so that he said: "Were it not for 'Ali, 'Umar would have perished." Why, I wonder, would Umar then seek 'Ali's guidance in the matters in which he depended on personal reasoning, which he knew had defects?

I believe that the unbiased Muslims will agree on this since this is the type of *ijtihad* that corrupted the creed [of Islam] as well as its legal rulings, nullified them, and caused dissension among the learned of the *ummah* and their fragmentation into numerous sects and schools of thought. And from this spread dissension and opposition, the failure and disappearance of the [Islamic] spirit and the material and spiritual backwardness [of the *ummah*].

We are left to imagine that, even with Abu Bakr and 'Umar in the seat of the Caliphate and the removal of its divinely prescribed person, had the former two collected the Prophetic *Sunnah* and preserved it in a special book, they would have done themselves and the *ummah* general good. Then, no extraneous matter would have entered the Prophetic *Sunnah,* and Islam then, with its Qur'an and *Sunnah,* would have been a one religion, one people, one nation, one creed. Today, we see the opposite.

This is because the *hadiths* were collected, burnt and proscribed from being recorded and transmitted even by word of mouth. This was a great catastrophe, a major calamity. There is no power except with Allah, the Most High, the Most Powerful.

Following are some of the clear texts to show that 'Umar exercised personal reasoning as opposed to [resorting to] the Qur'an:

(1) The Qur'an states: *"And if you have had sexual emission, then purify yourselves. But if you are ill or on a journey, or one of you has passed excrement or have had sexual intercourse, and cannot find water, then make tayammum on clean earth...." (5:6).*

It is well known from the Prophetic *Sunnah* that the Prophet of Allah (s) taught the companions how to make *tayammum,* even in the presence of 'Umar himself.

In "The Book of *Tayammum*" in "The Chapter [entitled] 'The pure earth is the ablution of a Muslim in the absence of water,'" al-Bukhari in his *Sahih* reports the following *hadith* on the authority of Imran: "We were on a journey with the Prophet (s). We journeyed until the last hours of the night then we pitched camp. There is no sweeter camping to the traveler than this. We did not wake up until the sun had risen. The first to arise was so and so, then so and so... whose names were recollected by Abu Raja', but he forgot 'Awf, then 'Umar b. al-Khattab, who was the fourth. When the Prophet (s) slept, he was not awakened by anyone until he himself arose. This was because we did not know what was happening to him in his sleep. When 'Umar woke up and realized what had befallen the people, and he was a very corpulent man, he cited the *takbir* and raised his voice with it. He persisted in saying the *takbir* and raising his voice until it awoke the Prophet (s). When he awoke, the men

Chapter 5: Concerning the Three Caliphs

complained to him about what had befallen them. He said: 'There is no good nor harm here, move from this place.' So they moved, not very far away, then he stopped and called for water with which he made *wudu*, and then, after the call to prayer was pronounced, he led the people in prayer. When he finished the prayer, he saw a man who had separated himself, he had not prayed with the group. He said: 'What prevented you, O so and so, from praying with the people?' He said: 'I am ritually impure and there is no water.' The Prophet (s) said: 'Then use the earth, for that is sufficient for you.'"[58]

However, 'Umar gave a verdict against the book of Allah and the *Sunnah* of his Prophet by saying: "Whoever does not find any water must not pray." This was his opinion which was recorded by most of the *hadith* scholars. In vol. 1 of his *Sahih*, in "The Book of Purification" in "The Chapter on *Tayammum*" Muslim reported that a man came to 'Umar and said: "I have become ritually impure and cannot find water". He said: "Then do not pray." Whereupon 'Ammar said: "Don't you remember, O Commander of the Faithful, when you and I were on an expedition [with the Prophet]? We both became ritually impure and could not find water. You did not pray whereas I rolled over in the dust and prayed. The Prophet (s) said: 'It would have been enough for you to strike the earth with your palms, then blow upon them, then wipe your face and hands.'" 'Umar said: "Fear Allah, O 'Ammar" The latter said: "If you wish, I will not relate it."[59]

Glory be to Allah! 'Umar was not content with opposing the clear texts from the Qur'an and the *Sunnah*, he even tried to prevent the companions from opposing his views. 'Ammar was forced to placate the Caliph by his offer: "If you wish I will not narrate it." How can I and you not be taken aback by this *ijtihad* and opposition and stubbornness on reasoning despite the testimony of a companion of a clear text?

'Umar was not convinced and held this view stubbornly until his death. His view influenced many companions who perceived things

---

[58] *Sahih al-Bukhari*, 1/88.

[59] *Sahih al-Bukhari*, 1/87.

his way. In fact, they sometimes preferred his view over the view of the Prophet of Allah. Muslim reported in "The Book of Purification" in "The Chapter on *Tayammum*," vol. 1, on p. 192 on the authority of Shaqiq who said: "We were seated with 'Abd Allah and Abu Musa when the latter said: 'O Abu 'Abd al-Rahman, what do you think of a man who becomes ritually impure and does not find water for a whole month? What does he do regarding the *salat?*' 'Abd Allah replied: 'He does not make *tayammum* even if cannot find water for a whole month.'

Abu Musa said: 'What about the *ayat* in *Surah al-Maida*: 'And if you do not find water then make *tayammum* on clean earth?" 'Abd Allah said: 'If it were permitted for them, according to this verse, they would seek to make *tayammum* with earth [even] if the water became cold for them'. Then Abu Musa said to 'Abd Allah: 'Did you not hear what 'Ammar said: 'The Prophet of Allah sent me on a mission and I became ritually impure and could not find water, so I rolled in the dust as does an animal. When I met the Prophet (s), I mentioned that to him and he said: 'It would have been enough for you to do with your hands thus: he struck the earth with his hands once then wiped the left over the right hand, over the backs of his hands and face.'" 'Abd Allah said: 'Did you not narrate that 'Umar was not convinced by 'Ammar's story?'"[60]

If we study this narration which has been authenticated by al-Bukhari, Muslim and other *Sihah* [books], we understand how influential the views of 'Umar were among a large number of senior *sahaba*, and from this we also understand the extent of the contradiction in the legal rulings, as well as the erosion and mutual contradiction of the narrations. Perhaps these are what led the Umayyad and the 'Abbasid rulers to devalue Islamic rulings, not according them any importance and permitting numerous discordant rulings on one matter. It is as though they said to Abu Hanifa, Malik, Ahmad and al-Shafi'i: "Say what you wish according to your own views, for if your head and Imam, 'Umar,

---

[60] *Sahih al-Bukhari* 1/91, Kitab *al-Tayammum*, "The Chapter on Tayammum with one strike".

Chapter 5: Concerning the Three Caliphs

said whatever he wished instead of the Qur'an and the *Sunnah*,[61] then there is no blame on you, for you are merely the followers of the followers of the followers, you are not innovators."

Yet more surprising than all of this is what 'Abd Allah b. Mas'ud said to Abu Musa: "Do not make *tayammum* even if you do not find water for a whole month." 'Abd Allah b. Mas'ud, who was among the most prominent companions, felt that one who was ritually impure and could not find water should leave his prayer completely and not perform the *tayammum*. It appears that Abu Musa attempted to convince him [otherwise] by the noble verse which was revealed specifically for this subject in *Surah al-Ma'ida*. 'Abd Allah b. Mas'ud's retort was: "If it was permitted for them by this verse, they would then seek to make *tayammum* with earth if the water got cold for them."

From this we also understand how they used their own *ijtihad* to interpret the Qur'anic texts as they felt appropriate. Regrettably, what they felt was severity and harshness for the *ummah*, even though Allah says: *"Allah desires to make things easy for you and not difficult"* (2:185).

This poor fellow says: "If it were permitted for them by this verse, they would seek to make *tayammum* if the water got cold for them." Did he put himself in the position of conveying the message from Allah and His Prophet? Is he more protective and affectionate over the worshippers than their Creator and Sustainer?

After this, Abu Musa tried to convince him with the *Sunnah* of the Prophet reported by 'Ammar, and how the Prophet taught him to do the *tayammum*. 'Abd Allah rejected this famous *Sunnah* of the Prophet by saying that 'Umar was not convinced by 'Ammar's narration.

---

[61] *Sahih al-Bukhari* 5/158, Kitab *Tafsir al-Qur'an*, "The Chapter on His saying: 'Spend in the path of Allah'".

From this, we understand that 'Umar b. al-Khattab's view was the convincing proof for some companions and that 'Umar's approval of a *hadith* or a Qur'anic verse was the sole criterion for determining the authenticity of a *hadith* or meaning of the verse, even if it contradicted the words and actions of the Prophet (s). As a result, we see today the actions of many people contradicting the Qur'an and *Sunnah*, whether it be in regards to the *halal* or the *haram*. This is because the *ijtihad* of 'Umar, as opposed to the texts, became a *madhab* to be followed. When some of the backsliders, and some who had knowledge, saw that the *hadith* which had been prohibited during the time of the Caliphs, were recorded later by the narrators and scholars and were against 'Umar's *madhab*, they themselves manufactured other false *hadiths* and attributed them to the Prophet of Allah (s), so that they could support the *madhab* of Abu Hafs. Some examples are *mut'a* marriage, *tarawi* prayer, etc. Thus contradictory narrations came into being, and have remained until today a matter of disagreement between the Muslims. This will remain like this as long as there are those who defend 'Umar, just because he is 'Umar, and [as long as] no one desires [to do] any research to find the truth and no one will say to 'Umar: "You erred 'Umar, the *salat* is not forsaken due to lack of water! There is an *ayat* for *tayammum* mentioned in the book of Allah... and that there are *hadiths* of *tayammum* mentioned in every book of the *Sunnah*. Your ignorance of them does not permit you to ascend the position of the Caliphate, nor the leadership of the *ummah*. And your knowledge of them makes you a disbeliever, if you go against these rulings. When Allah and his Prophet have decreed a matter it is not appropriate, if you are a believer, for you to have an opinion in it so that you may judge by what you like and reject what you wish. You are more aware than I am that whoever disobeys Allah and His Prophet has certainly gone completely astray."

(2) Allah says: *"The sadaqa is for the needy, the poor, those who are employed in its collection and those whose hearts need to be placated, for those in bondage and in debt, and [to be spent] in the way of Allah and for the wayfarer. This is a command from Allah and Allah is full of knowledge, full of wisdom..."* (9:60).

Chapter 5: Concerning the Three Caliphs

It was a well known practice of the Prophet of Allah (s) that he would allot a special share for those whose hearts needed to be placated, for their share which Allah had made obligatory for them. However, 'Umar b. al-Khattab nullified this compulsory stipend during his Caliphate and judged contrary to the text, saying to the people: "We have no need for you. Allah has strengthened Islam; it has no need for you". Indeed, he nullified this ruling during the Caliphate of Abu Bakr when the people whose hearts were to be placated came to him, as was their custom with the Prophet. Abu Bakr wrote an authorization for them, and they went to 'Umar to receive their allotment. 'Umar tore up the letter and said: "We have no need for you. Allah has strengthened Islam; it has no need for you. If you accept Islam, it is well; if not, the sword shall judge between us". Thereupon, they returned to Abu Bakr and said to him: "Are you the Caliph or is he?" He replied: "Rather he, if Allah wishes." Abu Bakr rescinded what he had written in agreement with 'Umar, his companion.[62]

The surprising fact is that even today you find those who defend 'Umar on this issue and count it as his merit and ingenuity. Among these is Shaykh Muhammad (known as al-Dawalibi), for he states in his book "*Usul al-Fiqh*" (p. 239), that: "Perhaps the *ijtihad* of 'Umar (R.) in cutting off the stipend which the Qur'an had enjoined for those whose hearts needed to be placated was in the forefront of those rulings he issued which were in accordance with the changing requirements that come with the passage of time, in spite of the fact that the Qur'anic text still stands applicable, and has not been abrogated." Then he further defends 'Umar by saying that the latter looked at the <u>reason</u> for the text, and not at its apparent [or literal] meaning... and he continues to the end, which no sound mind can understand.

We, however, accept his admission that 'Umar changed the Qur'anic rulings as a result of his view that rulings may be changed according to the times. However, we reject his view that 'Umar looked at the reason for the text, rather than its apparent meaning.

---

[62] *Al-Jawhari al-Nayyira fi fiqh al-Hanafi*, 1/164.

We say, instead, to him and to all others, that the text of the Qur'an and the *Sunnah* do not change with the passing of time. The Qur'an explicitly states that even the Prophet (s) himself does not have the right to make any changes. Allah said: *"And when our clear signs are recited unto them, those who do not hope to meet us say: 'Bring us another Qur'an or change it'. Say unto them: 'It is not for me to change it of my own accord; I only follow what is revealed to me. Should I disobey my Lord, I fear the penalty of that great Day'" (10:15).* And the pure *Sunnah* of the Prophet says: "What Muhammad has declared to be *halal* is *halal* until the day of Judgment, and the *haram* is *haram* until the day of Judgment".

However, according to the claim of al-Dawalibi and those who support him concerning *ijtihad*, legal rulings change with the changing times; there is no blame therefore on those rulers who change the rulings of Allah for the rulings dictated by the people, forged rulings necessitated by their needs. Certainly, this is against the judgment of Allah. Among them are those who say: "Break your fast so that you may be strong and overpower your enemy. There is no need for fasting in this age wherein we fight backwardness, poverty and ignorance. Fasting prevents us from production." They [also] prohibit polygamy for they see oppression and abuse of the women's rights in that. There are those who claim that, in the time of Muhammad, the woman was considered "a drop of urine", but now we have emancipated her and given her full rights.

This President has looked at the reason of the text and not at its apparent meaning, the same way as 'Umar looked at it, and has said: "It is necessary now that the inheritance of the male and female be equally divided between them, since Allah gave the man two shares on the grounds that he was the one supporting the family at a time when the woman was inactive. But today, because of stupendous efforts, the woman works and supports the family." He even cites as an example to the people his wife who supports her brother and has become, as a result of her grace and favor, a minister.

He also allowed fornication and said it is a personal right to whoever has reached the age of maturity, as long as it is not done by force or as a profession. He opened child care centers for illegitimate children, claiming that he is merciful towards these illegitimate children, who used to be buried alive for fear of poverty and disgrace. He also had other well known opinions.

The strange thing is that, to some degree, this President admired the personality of 'Umar for he mentions him sometimes with admiration, and then on another occasion he says that he ('Umar) did not bear responsibility, whether alive or dead, for the *ijtihad*, but that he (al-Dawalibi) will bear responsibility whether alive or dead. And yet another time, as if now aware that the Muslims rebutted his interpretations, he said: "'Umar was among the first and greatest of those practicing *ijtihad* in his time. So why then can I not make *ijtihad* in my modern time, for 'Umar was the leader of a nation and I too am the leader of a nation."

Yet stranger still is that, whenever this particular leader mentions Muhammad, the Prophet of Allah (s), one can observe in his speech ridicule and scorn. He said in one of his sermons that Muhammad did not even know geography for he said: "Seek knowledge even if it be in China", assuming that China was the furthermost point on the globe and that Muhammad did not picture that the world would reach this stage wherein crafts of iron would fly in the air! So what do you think would happen if he was told or they related to him about uranium, potassium, nuclear sciences and laser weaponry?

I do not personally blame this poor soul who did not understand a thing from the book of Allah and the *Sunnah* of His Prophet, yet found himself one day ruling a country in the name of Islam, even though he ridiculed Islam and followed Western civilization. He wanted to make his country an advanced European state in keeping with his concept of advancement. He followed the example of many Presidents and kings when he got assistance, praises and accolades from the Western countries and kingdoms. They even gave him the title of "The Greatest Mujahid." Yet I do not reproach him, for what he has brought is not surprising; every cup can only pour out what was poured into it. If I want to be neutral, I would instead blame

Abu Bakr, 'Umar and 'Uthman who opened this door from the day of the Prophet's (s) death and caused every *ijtihad* which the Umayyads and 'Abbasids undertook. Seven centuries followed, and in every one of them, the truths of Islam were wiped out by the texts and legal rulings of *ijtihad,* until matters came to such a point where the leader, Imam of the Muslim people, would deliver a sermon ridiculing the Prophet (s) and no-one would say anything against him, not from within or without the state.

This is what I say now and what I say to some of the brothers from the Islamic movement: "If today you reject the ruler who does not follow the Qur'anic texts and the Prophetic *Sunnah,* then it is necessary that you also reject those who started this innovation of *ijtihad* instead of texts, if you are indeed objective and wish to follow the truth." But they do not accept what I say and criticize me; how can I dare to compare the present day rulers with the rightly guided Caliphs? My response is that the leaders and kings of today are the inevitable result of what has happened in history. For, since the death of the Prophet (s) until today, when have the Muslims ever been free even for a day? They say: "You are of the Shi'as who malign and insult the companions, and if the day comes when we attain power, we'll burn you to death." I say: "Allah will never let you see that day."

(3) Allah says: *"Divorce is permitted twice, after which there must be harmonious cohabitation or separation with kindness. It is not lawful for you (men) to take back anything of what you have given your wives except when both partners fear that they would not be able to keep within the limits ordained by Allah. Then there is no blame on either of them if she gives something for her freedom. Those are limits set by Allah so do not exceed them. And those who exceed the limits of Allah are the wrongdoers. (2:229).*

When a husband divorces her, she is not lawful for him again until she has married another husband and he has

Chapter 5: Concerning the Three Caliphs

divorced her irrevocably. Then there is no blame upon them if they reunite if they feel that they can observe the limits ordered by Allah. Those are the limits of Allah, which He makes clear for those who understand" (2:230).

The Prophet's noble *Sunnah* explained, with no ambiguity, that the wife is not forbidden to her husband except after three divorces. And then, it is not allowed for her husband to reunite with her, except after she has married another man. If this man divorces her also, it is possible for the first spouse to seek her hand in marriage again, the same way as other men; and it is up to the woman to accept or reject, the choice is hers.

'Umar b. al-Khattab however, as usual, transgressed Allah's limits, which He had made clear for people who understand; he changed this ruling with his own judgment by which he pronounced that a 'single effective divorce', if done with three pronouncements, made the wife unlawful for her husband. In this, he contravened the Qur'an and the Prophet's *Sunnah*.

In "The Book of Divorce", in "The Chapter of the Three Divorces" Muslim reported, on the authority of Ibn 'Abbas, that: "The triple divorce during the time of the Prophet of Allah (s) and Abu Bakr, and for two years of the Caliphate of 'Umar, were recognized as one. Then 'Umar b. al-Khattab said: 'The men hasten in a matter wherein they are required to have patience. We should endorse it for them.' And he did so."

By God, how strange that a Caliph could dare to change Allah's judgment in the presence of the companions, and that they agreed with him in everything that he said and did. No one opposed or even questioned him; yet they lead us poor souls into believing that one of the companions said to 'Umar: "By Allah, if we see any crookedness in you, we will straighten you with the sword." This is a lie and fabrication so as to brag that the Caliphs were the best examples in freedom and democracy. History, however, refutes this by the actual events that occurred. There is no importance in claims if the actions are in complete contrast.

Or perhaps they feel that the crookedness was in the Qur'an and *Sunnah,* and that 'Umar b. al-Khattab straightened and corrected them. We seek Allah's protection from this folly.

I was in Qafsa, where often I had to give counsel to those who had declared their wives unlawful by the pronouncement "You are forbidden three times". They rejoiced when I informed them about the correct rulings of Allah in which the Caliphs had not meddled with their personal judgments. However, those who claimed to be knowledgeable scared them by saying that everything is *halal* with the Shi'as. I remember one of them who debated with me in a decent manner saying: "If our master 'Umar b. al-Khattab (r) changed Allah's ruling in this matter and in others, and the companions agreed with him, why did our master 'Ali, may Allah brighten his face and be pleased with him, not refute our master 'Umar?

I replied to him with the reply of Imam 'Ali (as) when the Quraysh said he was a courageous man but knew nothing about warfare:-

"May Allah free their parents from this! Is there anyone among them with more experience in it than me, and more senior to it than me? I was in the battle when I was not yet twenty and here I am now over sixty. But then, no opinion is accorded to him who is not obeyed (*Nahj al-Balagha,* sermon 27)."

Did the Muslims listen to Imam 'Ali except his Shi'as who believed in his Imamate? He opposed him on the prohibition of *mut'a* and the innovation of *tarawi* prayers, and he opposed every ruling which Abu Bakr, 'Umar and 'Uthman changed. But his views remained confined to his partisans and followers. The other Muslims waged war against him, cursed him and tried their utmost to kill him and obliterate his memory.

There is no stronger proof of this opposition than the heroic stand he took on the occasion when 'Abd al-Rahman b. 'Awf called him and nominated him for the Caliphate after the death of 'Umar,

Chapter 5: Concerning the Three Caliphs

stipulating the condition, having chosen him to be the Caliph, that he should rule according to the practice of the two Caliphs, Abu Bakr and 'Umar. 'Ali (as) rejected this condition and said: "I will judge by the book of Allah and the *Sunnah* of His Prophet." For this they abandoned him and chose 'Uthman b. 'Affan who accepted the condition to rule according to the *Sunnah* of the two Caliphs. If 'Ali could not go against Abu Bakr and 'Umar even in their death, how could he have opposed them when they were still living?

So today we see that the gate to the city of knowledge, who was the most knowledgeable of men after the Prophet of Allah (s), the wisest judge, the one who memorized the Qur'an and the *Sunnah* of His Prophet most, abandoned by the *Ahl al-Sunnah wa'l-Jama'a* who prefer instead Malik and Abu Hanifa, al-Shafi'i and Ibn Hanbal. They imitate them in every religious matter from worship to contracts. And they do not refer in anything to Imam 'Ali. Their Imams like al-Bukhari and Muslim did the same thing regarding the *hadith*. For you see them relating hundreds of *hadith* from Abu Hurayrah, Ibn 'Umar, al-Aqra' and al-A'raj and those close and far, and relating only a few *hadiths* from 'Ali which were attributed to him, in which there is a defilement of the honour of the *Ahl al-Bayt*. They were not satisfied with that, they further disclaim and declare as unbeliever any of his sincere Shi'as who imitates and follows him. They call them names like "Rawafid" (rejecters) and [other names] that are disgraceful. The truth is that 'Ali's followers committed no sin except that they followed 'Ali, who was shunned and alienated during the period of the first three Caliphs. Then he was cursed and fought against by the Umayyads and 'Abbasids. Anyone who has any perception and knowledge of history will realize this is the clear, manifest truth and will understand the inner workings and plots that were wrought against him, his family, and his Shi'as.

'Uthman b. 'Affan follows the practice of his two companions in opposing the texts

Perhaps when 'Uthman b. Affan pledged to 'Abd al-Rahman b. 'Awf, on the eve of his being sworn in as the Caliph, that he would govern according to the *Sunnah* of the two Caliphs, Abu Bakr and

'Umar, he really meant that he would use his personal judgment as they had done; and that he would change texts of the Qur'an and the Prophetic *hadith* as they had done. Whoever studies his lifestyle during the period of his Caliphate will find that he went much further in *ijtihad*, to the point where he made people forget the *ijtihad* of his two companions, Abu Bakr and 'Umar. I do not wish to prolong this subject which has provided copious material for the history books, old and new, about the strange things that 'Uthman innovated which caused the people to revolt against him, costing him his life. As usual, I will mention a few instances in order to illustrate for the reader and every researcher what those who supported personal interpretation innovated in the religion of Muhammad (s).

(1) Muslim in his *Sahih* in "The Book of the Prayer of the Traveller", reports that 'A'isha said: "When Allah enjoined the *salat*, He made it two *rak'ats*. Then He finalized it at four for those [praying] at their places of residence, but the prayer of the traveller was fixed to be two *rak'ats* this in accordance with the first injunction."

In the same book, Muslim reported, on the authority of Ya'la b.Umayya, who said: "I said to 'Umar b. al-Khattab: 'There is no harm on you if you shorten the prayer if you fear *fitna* from those who disbelieve but now the people have believed.' 'Umar said: 'I was taken aback by what startles you now, so I asked the Prophet of Allah (s) about it and he replied: 'It is a bounty which Allah has given as a charity to you, so accept Allah's charity.'"

Muslim reported in his *Sahih* in "The Book of Shortening the Prayer of the Travellers" from Ibn 'Abbas who said: "Allah enjoined the prayer through the tongue of the Prophet (s), four *rak'ats* for those in residence, and for those travelling two *rak'ats*, and, in a state of fear, one *rak'at*."

Muslim also reported, on the authority of Anas b. Malik, who said: "Whenever the Apostle of Allah (s) went on a journey of three *amyal* (miles) or three *farsakhs*, he prayed two *rak'ats*." 'Ammar also said: "We journeyed with the Prophet of Allah from Medina to

Chapter 5: Concerning the Three Caliphs

Mecca and he prayed two *rak'ats* until he returned. I said: 'How long did he stay in Mecca? He replied 'Ten [days].'"

From the above *hadiths* reported by Muslim in his *Sahih*, it is clear that the noble verse which was revealed specifically for the shortening of the prayer on a journey, was understood by the Prophet of Allah and explained by word and deed to show that it was a dispensation and charity which Allah had granted to the Muslims, and that it was obligatory on them to accept it. This refutes the claim of al-Dawalibi and those like him who argue in defense of 'Umar and seek to rectify his errors; that he looked at the reasoning of the injunction and not at the apparent meaning. The Prophet of Allah (s) taught him on the occasion of the revelation of the verse to shorten the prayer. 'Umar expressed his surprise that the established texts are not contingent upon the cause(s) for their revelation, and, as a result, the prayer is to be shortened on a journey even if the people may be secure and not afraid of being harassed by the unbelievers. What 'Umar said was different from what al-Dawalibi and the scholars of *Ahl al-Sunnah* said, yet they seek excuses for him because of their high regard for him.

(2) Let us observe 'Uthman b. Affan. It was incumbent that he [also] exercises his personal judgment in the Qur'an and *hadith* texts so that he might be considered as being amongst the "rightly guided Caliphs". He went so far as to make the prayer four *rak'ats* on journey instead of the two as legislated.

Many a time I have asked about the reason for the changing of this injunction and the addition to it, and what are the arguments for it, but I can only perceive that he wished to lead the people, especially the Banu Umayya, into thinking that he was more pious and God-fearing than Muhammad, Abu Bakr, and 'Umar.

Muslim, in "The Chapter on the Prayer of the Traveler and the Shortening of the Prayer at Mina", on the authority of Salim b. 'Abd Allah, who narrated from his father, who reported that the Prophet of Allah (s) prayed the prayer of a traveler at Mina and at other places as two *rak'ats*, as did Abu Bakr, and 'Umar. 'Uthman did the same in the early part of his Caliphate then he finalized it at four."

It is also reported in Muslim that al-Zuhri said: "I said to 'Urwa: 'Why does 'A'isha say the full prayer while on a journey?' He said: 'She interpreted the same way that 'Uthman did'". This is how Allah's religion and its rulings and texts have become subject to the interpretations and explanations of people.

'Uthman also exerted his reasoning to support 'Umar's position regarding the prohibition of the *mut'a hajj* and the *mut'a* marriage. Al-Bukhari reported in his *Sahih* in "The Book of *Hajj*," in "The Chapter of *al-Tamattu'* and *Iqran*," from Marwan b. al-Hakam, who said: "I saw 'Uthman and 'Ali. 'Uthman used to forbid people to perform *hajj al-Tamattu'* and *hajj al-Qiran* (*hajj* and '*umra* together), and when 'Ali saw this, he assumed *ihram* for *hajj* and '*umra* together saying: '*Labbayk* for '*umra* and *hajj*,' and he said: 'I will not leave the tradition of the Prophet for the saying of anyone.'"

Muslim also reported in "The Book of *Hajj*" in "The Chapter on the permissibility of *al-Tamattu*," on the authority of Sa'id b. al-Musayyab who said: "'Uthman and 'Ali met at 'Usfan. 'Uthman had prohibited *mut'a* or the '*umra*, whereupon 'Ali said: 'What do you want to do on a matter which the Prophet of Allah (s) did, and now you prohibit it?' 'Uthman said: 'Leave us alone'. 'Ali said: 'I cannot leave you alone.' When 'Ali saw this, he assumed *ihram* for '*umra* and *hajj* together."

Yes! This is the man 'Ali b. Abi Talib, (as) for he could not abandon the *Sunnah* of the Prophet (s) for the word of any man. The second narration illustrates to us that there were words exchanged between 'Ali and 'Uthman. 'Uthman's words to 'Ali: "Leave us alone" shows us he would go against everything and would not follow him in what he reported from his cousin (s). The narration has been abridged since it says: "And 'Ali said: 'I cannot leave you alone' when he saw that". What is it that 'Ali saw?

There is no doubt that the Caliph, in spite of 'Ali's reminding him of the Prophetic *Sunnah*, insisted on following his own view even though it was in conflict with the *Sunnah*. He forbade the people from *al-tamattu;'* and upon that, 'Ali opposed him and consecrated

Chapter 5: Concerning the Three Caliphs

himself for both, i.e., the '*umra* and the *hajj*.

(3) 'Uthman b. 'Affan exerted his own reasoning in parts of the prayer and did not say the *takbir* before the prostration nor upon rising from it.

In his *Musnad*, vol. 4, p. 440, Imam Ahmad b. Hanbal reported, on the authority of Imran b. al-Husayn, who said: "I once prayed behind 'Ali and was reminded of a prayer that I prayed with the Prophet of Allah (s) and the two Caliphs. He said: "So I went and prayed with him, and he made *takbir* every time he prostrated and when he raised his head from the *ruk'u*." I asked him: "O Abu Najid! Who was the first to depart from this?" He said: "'Uthman (r) when he became old and his voice became weak he stopped doing it."

Yes! In this way the *Sunnah* of the Prophet (s) was discarded and replaced instead by the *Sunnah* of the Caliphs, kings, companions, the Umayyads, and the 'Abbasids; and everything was innovated, introduced into Islam. Every innovation [leads to] misguidance; and every misguidance leads to the fire, as the bearer of the message (s) has said.

As a result, you observe today different modes and types of prayer among the Muslims. You think that they are one, but their hearts are divided. For even though they line up for prayer in one row, you will see one letting his arms hang by his sides, while another will fold his arms. Another holding his folded arms in a specific way, placing his arms above his navel while another places them near his heart. And still another will place his feet together, while another will stand with his feet apart. Each one thinks that he is right. If you ask anyone of them about it, it will be said to you: "My brother, they are all modes; don't pay any attention to them, but pray as you wish, for the important thing is that you pray."

Yes, this is true to a point, for indeed the most important thing is the prayer. However, it is essential that the prayer be [the form of] the prayer of the Prophet of Allah (s); for he said: "Pray as you have seen me pray." It is, therefore, necessary for us to make every effortt to research the prayer of the Prophet (s), for prayer is the pillar of religion.

(4) 'Uthman was the one of whom the angels of the Merciful one were shy. Al-Baladhuri said in vol. 5 p. 54 of his *Ansab al-Ashraf*: "When the news of Abu Dharr's death at al-Rabdha reached 'Uthman, he said: 'May Allah have mercy upon him.' Whereupon 'Ammar b. Yasir said: 'Yes; and Allah has bestowed upon him mercy from our being weary [of him].' 'Uthman said to 'Ammar: 'O one who bites his father's penis! Do you think I am sorry for exiling him?' Whereupon he ordered that he be taken into custody, and said: 'Go to his place as well.'

When they were ready to leave, the Banu Makhzum approached 'Ali and asked him to speak to 'Uthman about him. 'Ali said to him: 'O 'Uthman! Fear Allah. You exiled a righteous Muslim, and he perished in your exile. Now you seek to banish someone like him?' They exchanged words until 'Uthman finally said to 'Ali: 'You deserve to be banished more than 'Ammar.' 'Ali said: 'Then do so if you wish.'

The Muhajirun then went to 'Uthman and said: 'If anytime someone speaks to you, it is highly improper that you exile and banish him.' Whereupon he rescinded [his judgment against] 'Ammar."

And in the *Tarikh* of Ya'qubi vol. 2 p. 147, he reported that 'Ammar b. Yasir recited the funeral prayer over Miqdad and buried him without informing 'Uthman, due to the testament Miqdad had made. 'Uthman became extremely angry with 'Ammar and said: "Woe unto me because of this son of a black woman! I wish I had known this."

Is it possible for someone who is so modest that even the angels are shy of him to be so foul in his speech in respect to the best of the believers?

'Uthman was not satisfied with insulting 'Ammar and swearing at him: "O one who bites his father's penis." Instead he ordered his

Chapter 5: Concerning the Three Caliphs

servant to grab 'Ammar. They stretched his hands and legs whereupon 'Uthman kicked him with his booted feet in the testicles, crushing them. He was weak and old, he lost consciousness. This story is well known amongst the historians,[63] for a group of the companions recorded [many such] events and requested 'Ammar to narrate [his misfortune].

'Uthman did the same to 'Abd Allah b. Mas'ud when he passed him with one of his troopers, 'Abd Allah b. Zam'a. The latter grabbed 'Abd Allah b. Mas'ud and carried him until they came to the door of the mosque, whereupon he hurled him to the ground, breaking one of his ribs[64]. All this was because 'Abd Allah b. Mas'ud had voiced his opposition to 'Uthman's giving the corrupt Banu Umayya the property of the Muslims without accounting for it.

Thus the revolt against 'Uthman began, the events transpired to the extent that he was killed, and they prevented him from being buried for three days. Four people came from the Banu Umayya to recite his funeral prayer, but some of the companions prohibited them from doing so. One of them said: "Bury him, for Allah and his angels have sent blessing upon him." They said: "No! By Allah, he will never be buried in the burial ground of the Muslims!" He was eventually buried in the "Hash Kawkab" - a place where the Jews used to bury their dead. When the Umayyads came to power, they made this place a part of al-Baqi'.

This is a simple account of the history of the three Caliphs - Abu Bakr, 'Umar and 'Uthman. Though it is simple, due to our wish to be brief and to provide only a few examples, it is still sufficient to remove the veil covering the claim of the alleged merits and invented virtues. They never knew such qualities nor did they, for a single day in their lives, dream of exemplifying them. The obvious

---

[63] Al-Baladhuri, *Ansab al-Ashraf*, 5/49, *al-Isti'ab*, 2/422, Ibn Qutayba in *Al-Imama wa al-Siyasa*, 1/29, Ibn Abi'l-Hadid in *Sharh Nahj al-Balagha*, 1/239 *al-'Aqd al-Farid,* Ibn 'Abd al-Rabbih, 2/272.

[64] Al-Baladhuri, *Ansab al-Ashraf;* al-Waqidi, *Tarikh al-Ya'qubi* 2/147. *Sharh Nahj al-Balagha* of Ibn Abi'l-Hadid 1/237.

question that arises is: What do the *Ahl al-Sunnah wa'l-Jama'a* say regarding these facts?

For the people [practicing] the remembrance [of God], the answer is this: "If you know these, then don't deny them, for your own *Sihah* books have verified their veracity despite efforts to obscure them. You have thereby destroyed the myth of the rightly guided Caliphate.

If you deny them and do not agree to their veracity, then you have denied your own "*Sahih*" collections and your reliable books which have reported them. Then you have destroyed all of your beliefs."

Chapter Six

Concerning the Caliphate

The Caliphate! And what do you know of the Caliphate? It was something which Allah sent as a test to this *ummah*. It divided the *umma*; the hungry ones yearned for it. Because of it, innocent blood was shed; for it, Muslims became *kafirs*; it deceived and distanced them from the straight path; it made them enter the hell fire. We have to make a study which, despite its brevity, should cover the inner plots and twists of the Caliphate which were gradually exposed just before and after the death of the Prophet of Allah (s).

The first thing that comes to mind is that leadership among the Arabs was an essential issue in every age. You will see them giving preference to the leader of the tribe or the head of a clan over themselves. They do not decide anything without him; they do not take [a course of action] without his counsel and do not speak before he does.

The head of the clan is usually the oldest of them, the most learned in all matters, and the most noble in terms of personality and lineage. It would appear that this leader, in dealing with his clan, exhibits wisdom, sagacity, bravery, knowledge of current affairs, generosity, kindness towards guests and all the other praiseworthy attributes. Often, the leadership is inherited, not subject to election. We also find that the tribes and clans, despite their independence, all submit to the leadership of a single tribe which may be larger in number and property; and it has heroes in battles that protect the rest of the tribes that are under its sovereignty. An example of that is the [tribe of] Quraysh, which assumed the leadership over the rest of the Arab tribes that submitted to it, based on the rule of chieftaincy and leadership, which entailed responsibility of [looking after] the house of Allah, the sanctuary.

When Islam came, the Prophet of Allah (s), to some extent,

accepted this system of operation. He used to appoint, over the tribes that sent emissaries to him and had accepted Islam, leaders and nobles to be his deputies to lead them in prayer, collect their *zakat* and be the means of communication between he and them.

Then, by Allah's command, Muhammad (s) founded an Islamic State whose laws and regulations were subject to the revelations of Allah. Thus social and individual laws like marriage contracts, divorce, selling and buying, taking, giving, inheritance, *zakat* and everything that concerned the individual and the society as a whole, in war and in peace, transactions and acts of worship came under the laws of Allah. The role of the Apostle (s) was to ensure the implementation and application of those laws.

Naturally, the Prophet of Allah (s) used to think about who he would appoint as his successor for this important role since it involved the leadership of the *ummah*. It is natural that every head of state (if he cares about his people) pay special attention to the person whom he has selected to be his deputy on every occasion that he himself is absent from; he becomes his first minister as well as his close confidant who is present when other people are absent. It is also natural that his deputy be well known to all the ministers, as well as to the people at large.

The intellect cannot believe that the Prophet of Allah (s) was heedless of all this and paid no attention to it. There is no doubt that it was uppermost in his mind, just as there is no doubt that the *hadiths* related to the topic were subjected to the restrictions imposed by the Caliphs who maintained the theory of consultation. They spent all their efforts in contradicting the texts which specified and identified the Caliph. Part of this effort was the denigration of the sanctity of the Prophet (s) and accusing him of hallucination. The denigration was directed to him as well as to the leader whom he had appointed to lead the army, for they claimed that he was not fit to be the leader and *amir* due to his young age. Then they created doubt about the death of the Prophet of Allah (s) so that the matter becomes confusing and the people do not proceed to pledge allegiance to the Caliph who the Prophet of Allah (s) had previously appointed. As a part of that effort, they used the

Chapter 6: Concerning the Caliphate

opportunity, while 'Ali and his helpers were busy with the preparations for the Prophet's burial, to hold an emergency meeting at Saqifa for selecting one whom they were pleased and comfortable with and in whom their hopes lay. They then coerced the people, by threats and promises, into taking the pledge of allegiance and they completely removed any opposition from the political field. Then they took a firm and harsh stance against anyone who resolved to break his allegiance against the Caliph, or had any doubt in the legality of the new Caliphate, even if it be Fatima, the daughter of the Prophet (s).

Then restrictions were placed and people were forbidden to relate the noble *hadiths* of the Prophet in public, so that the clear texts might not become known to the people, thereby causing chaos. [This was enforced] even if it meant the assassination of an individual, or killing of groups so as to stifle any opposition under the pretext of preventing mischief on the one hand and [fighting] apostasy on the other.

We know all this from what the historians have written, even though some of them have attempted to hide the truth by forging some contradictory *hadith*, or making far-fetched explanations and excuses, the secrets of which have been exposed with [the passage of] days, events that occurred, and by research.

Some of the historians can probably be excused as they took their information from the early sources which were written under political and social influences following the great discord and after the events which transpired when the Banu Umayya took over the Caliphate and bestowed wealth and appointments liberally on some companions and followers whom they hired.

Some of the historians reported from these sources because they thought well of them and were unaware of the treachery of the eyes and what is hidden in the hearts. As a result, the authentic narrations got mixed with the spurious ones, and it became difficult for the researcher to know the truth.

To bring the reader and researcher closer to these facts, it is essential to provoke and pose these questions, so that during these questions and answers, some realities will be exposed, or some indicators which lead to the truth, will be known.

Questions and answers which are indispensable for every researcher

Numerous letters have been sent to me from many places, carrying in them important questions which were indicative of the desire of the noble readers for a greater search for and knowledge of the truth. I replied to some of these questions, and left some alone, not with the intention of ignoring them, but because the answers are in my books "*Then I was Guided*" and "*To Be with the Truthful Ones.*"

For general benefit, I will publish them with the answers in this chapter. The reader should note, however, that certain *hadiths* and events have been repeated in one book, or in all three. I have deliberately done this, following the pattern in the dear Qur'an, which repeats events in numerous chapters so that they become embedded in the mind of the believer, and so that it may benefit everyone.

Question 1: If the Prophet knew about the conflict and differences which would afflict the *ummah* because of the Caliphate, why did he not appoint a Caliph?

Answer: He appointed his successor after *hajj al-wida'* (The Farewell Pilgrimage) and this was 'Ali b. Abi Talib. He called to witness his companions who had made the pilgrimage with him. He knew that the *ummah* would ignore it and turn back upon its heels.

Question 2: How is it that none of the companions asked the Messenger about this matter when they used to ask him about everything?

Answer: They did ask him and he replied: *"Allah, the Highest said: 'They say: 'Do we have any choice in the matter?' Say certainly the matter, all of it, is with Allah'"* (3:154). They asked him and he said: *"Indeed Allah and his Prophet are in authority over you and the believers, those who observe the prayer and pay zakat whilst in ruk'u'"* (5:56). They asked and he said: "Certainly this is my brother, my successor and my Caliph after me".[1]

Question 3: Why did some of the companions disagree with the Prophet of Allah when he wanted to write for them a letter which would save them from going astray after him, and instead they said that he was hallucinating?

Answer: Some of the companions went against the Prophet (s) when he wanted to write for them that which would save them from going astray; and they instead claimed that he was hallucinating because they knew that he wanted to appoint 'Ali b. Abi Talib in writing. For he had told them before at the farewell pilgrimage that one who adheres to the book and the household will never go astray. They therefore understood that the contents of the letter would be in the same words, for 'Ali was the master of the household. Instead, they accused the Prophet of hallucinating; to divert him from writing the behest. The discord and disagreement was about the letter before he wrote it. If the Prophet (s) was hallucinating (according to their belief) then his letter would be pointless and common sense dictated that it should not be written.

Question 4: Why did he not insist on writing the letter, specifically as it would prevent the Islamic *ummah* from going astray?

Answer: It was not within his capability to insist on writing; for the prevention from going astray was nullified by the agreement of many companions that the Prophet was hallucinating. The letter then became the source of misguidance rather than preservation against it. Had the Prophet (s) insisted on writing the document, there would have arisen, after his death, false claims which would raise doubts even on Allah's book and the texts of the Qur'an.

---

[1] *Tarikh al-Tabari, Tarikh Ibn al-Athir* in "The Chapter: 'And warm the close relatives of your household'".

Question 5: The Prophet (s) made an oral testament of three things before his death. How is it that only two have reached us, the third one being lost?

Answer: The matter is clear - the first item is the one that was lost because it concerned his designation of 'Ali as his successor. Furthermore, the Caliphate that came into being prohibited *hadith* about it. Otherwise, how can an intelligent person believe that the Prophet would make a behest and his testament would be forgotten as reported by al-Bukhari?

Question 6: Did the Prophet (s) know about the time of his death?

Answer: There is no doubt that he knew beforehand exactly the time of his death. In fact, he knew this before he set out for the farewell pilgrimage. As a result, he named it "The Farewell Pilgrimage" and most of the companions knew of his imminent demise.

Question 7: Why did the Prophet prepare an army, enlisting notable Muhajirun and Ansar among the elderly companions in it, and ordered them to proceed to Mu'ta in Palestine two days before his death?

Answer: When the Prophet (s) became aware of the plots that the Quraysh had planned, and that they had agreed among themselves to discard the agreement after him and to distance 'Ali from the Caliphate; he decided to send them away, to remove them from Medina at the time of his death so that they would not return until the matter of the Caliphate had been settled. After that, they would not be able to implement their plots. There is no [other] acceptable explanation besides this for Usama's expedition. It was not wise for the Prophet to empty the capital of the Caliphate of an army and forces a mere two days before his death.

Question 8: Why did the Prophet not send 'Ali in Usama's army?

Answer: Because it was not fitting for the Prophet of Allah (s) to

Chapter 6: Concerning the Caliphate

depart without leaving a Caliph to administer the affairs after him; and therefore he could not send 'Ali in that army which contained notable Muhajirun and Ansar, like Abu Bakr, 'Umar, 'Uthman and 'Abd al-Rahman b. 'Awf. This astute behavior proved that 'Ali was the Caliph after the Prophet directly. Those whom the Prophet of Allah did not send in the army were not those who coveted the Caliphate, nor those who hated 'Ali, or deceived him.

Question 9: Why did he place at the head of the army a youth who did not even have hair upon his cheeks?

Answer: When those who were envious and against 'Ali sought to disparage him because of his young age, and the Quraysh nobles who had reached sixties would not submit to 'Ali since he was not much past thirty, the Prophet (s) put Usama in charge of them; and he was then seventeen with no hair on his cheeks. He was the [son of] an emancipated slave; [this was done] so as to bend their necks and to break their egos. He wanted to show them firstly, and all the Muslims secondly, that a believer, true to his belief, must listen, obey and accept, even if what the Prophet decides hurts his inner self.

Where is Usama b. Zayd b. Haritha in comparison to 'Ali b. Abi Talib, Commander of the Faithful, master of the successors, the door to the knowledge of the Prophet (s), the all-conquering lion of Allah, and Muhammad's Aaron? As a result, they were upset at the Prophet's handling of affairs and his appointing Usama over them. They found fault in his leadership and refused to rally forth with him, remaining behind. Let us not forget that in this were shrewd persons of whom the noble Qur'an says: *"And they plotted their strategies but their plots were known to Allah even though their plots were of such magnitude that they could destroy mountains" (14:46).*

Question 10: Why did the Prophet's (s) anger over those staying behind become so severe that he cursed them?

Answer: His (s) anger on them intensified when he learnt that they found faults in his appointment. This deprecation was directed towards him, not towards Usama. He realized their lack of faith and sincerity for Allah and His Prophet (s). [It also proved that] they were resolute in carrying out their strategies at whatever cost. Upon that he sent his last curse on the dissidents so that they, their followers and all Muslims may understand that the matter had reached its conclusion; and those who are destroyed are destroyed after clear signs [come to them] and those who are saved are saved after clear signs [come to them].

Question 11: Is it permissible to curse a Muslim, especially when this is from the Prophet (s)?

Answer: If one's Islam is simply the uttering of the two *shahadas*, i.e., a person says: "I bear witness that there is no deity but Allah, and I bear witness that Muhammad is His Prophet" and then he does not submit to their commands nor does he listen to, or obey, Allah and His Prophet (s), then cursing him is allowed. In the noble Qur'an there are many verses [on this]. We quote here Allah's words: *"Those who conceal the clear proofs and guidance that have been sent unto them, after we have explained them for the people in the book, upon them is Allah's curse and those entitled to curse" (2:159).* If Allah curses those who conceal the truth; what do you think about those who oppose the truth and work to nullify it?

Question 12: Did the Prophet of Allah (s) appoint Abu Bakr to lead the people in prayer?

Answer: From the study of contradicting narrations, we understand that the Prophet of Allah (s) did not appoint Abu Bakr to lead the people in prayer, unless we believe what 'Umar b. Khattab said concerning his hallucination, and whoever believes that has committed *kufr*. If not, how can any intelligent person believe that he ordered Abu Bakr to lead the people in prayer at the same time that he had enlisted him in Usama's army and made the latter his leader and Imam? How can he appoint him as an Imam in prayer in Medina when he was not in it? History testifies to the fact that he

Chapter 6: Concerning the Caliphate 265

was not present in Medina the day the Prophet (s) died. The established fact, according to some historians from whom Ibn Abi'l-Hadid reported, is that 'Ali (as) blamed 'A'isha for she was the one who sent for her father to lead the people in prayer, and that, when the Prophet (s) learnt of this, he became angry and said to her: "You (women) are like the women of Yusuf." He then went out to the mosque and removed Abu Bakr, and led the 'emergency' prayer so that there would be no argument left for them afterwards.

Question 13: Why did 'Umar b. al-Khattab swear that the Prophet of Allah had not died and threatened to kill whoever said he had died, not being calm until Abu Bakr intervened?

Answer: 'Umar threatened to kill anyone who attempted to speak of the death of the Prophet (s), to cause doubt and leave the people in difficulties so that they would not complete their pledge to 'Ali and until the heroic plotters could reach Medina. They had agreed to take the reins of power but had not yet reached Medina. He found that he had preceded them and played the role of one mad with grief, and so he drew his sword, intimidating the people. There can be no doubt that he prevented the people from entering the Prophets' room to confirm the matter. If not, then why didn't anyone dare to enter except Abu Bakr? When he arrived, he then entered, uncovered his face and said to them: "Whoever worships Muhammad, surely Muhammad has died. Whoever worships Allah, indeed Allah is the ever living and never dies."

It is necessary for us to attach a small comment to Abu Bakr's address. Did Abu Bakr believe that there was any Muslim who worshipped Muhammad? Most certainly not! Rather, his words were a figurative expression to insult and belittle the Banu Hashim in general, and 'Ali b. Abu Talib in particular, for they used to take pride over the rest of the Arabs that Muhammad, the Messenger of Allah, was from them, that they were his people and his clansmen and the most deserving of the people to him.

This was also an expression uttered by 'Umar b. al-Khattab on the disastrous Thursday when he said: "The Book of Allah is sufficient for us." His tongue was implying: "We have no need of

Muhammad, his term is finished and he has reached his end." This is exactly what Abu Bakr confirmed by his words: "Whoever used to worship Muhammad, indeed Muhammad has died." He meant by that: "O you who used to take pride over us in Muhammad, step back today for his term is ended, and the book of Allah is sufficient for us, for Allah is the ever living and does not die." It must be noted that 'Ali and the Banu Hashim knew more than others the truth about the Prophet (s), and would go great lengths in showing respect and veneration for him and in implementing his commands. The manumitted slaves amongst the companions and those who were not of the Quraysh followed them in this. If the Prophet (s) spat upon the ground, they used to race each other to wipe their faces with it! They also used to vie with each other to get water left over from his *wudu'* or even his hair. All these poor and oppressed people were the followers of 'Ali from the time of the Prophet (s) and he was the one who gave them this name.[2]

On the other hand, 'Umar b. al-Khattab, and some of the companions from the notables of the Quraysh, often disputed the rulings of the Prophet (s), debated with him and disobeyed him. In fact, they even dissociated themselves from his actions.[3] 'Umar chopped down the tree of "*bay'a al-ridwan*" because some of the companions used to take pride in it. The Wahhabis did likewise in this century when they obliterated the relics of the Prophet (s); they did not even leave the house he was born in. They now try, with every effort and wealth, to prevent the Muslims from celebrating his birth and from sending blessings and salutations to him. They even tell the heedless ones that the sending of complete blessing upon him is, in fact, *shirk*.

Question 14: Why did the Ansar secretly get together in the Saqifa of Bani Sa'ida?

Answer: When the Ansar came to know of the plots planned by the

---

[2] *Al-Dar al-Manthur fi Tafsir al-Ma'thur*, Jalal al-Din al-Suyuti, *Surah al-Bayyina*.

[3] *Sahih al-Bukhari*, 3/114 "The Book of Oppression", "The Chapter of Participation in Guidance".

Quraysh to distance 'Ali from the Caliphate, they gathered together on the death of the Prophet (s) and wanted to decide the matter between them so that the Caliph should be from them. If the leaders of the Quraysh, the Muhajirin, [who were] the close ones and clan of the Prophet, had wanted to break the pledge to 'Ali, then the Ansar were more deserving of the Caliphate than others for they believed that Islam was spread by the blades of their swords. The Muhajirin were their dependents. Had it not been for their (the Ansar) opening their city and their houses and their properties, there would not have been any mention left or any merit for the Muhajirun. Had there not been the difference between the Aws and Khazraj who were competing for the leadership - for each wanted it for his own tribe - Abu Bakr and 'Umar would not have found an opportunity to take the Caliphate from them nor to compel them to follow them.

Question 15: Why did Abu Bakr, 'Umar and Abu 'Ubayda hurry to the Saqifa and surprise the Ansar?

Answer: When the Muhajirin, i.e., nobles of the Quraysh, had eyes noting the movement of the Ansar and what was transpiring in their affairs, one of them, Salim, the manumitted slave of Abu Hudhayfa, hurried and informed Abu Bakr, 'Umar and Abu 'Ubayda of the secret meeting. They hurried to the Saqifa to disrupt the plans and decisions of the Ansar and surprise them into believing that they knew everything that went on in their absence.

Question 16: Why was 'Umar b. al-Khattab all along providing words to placate the Ansar?

Answer: No doubt 'Umar b. al-Khattab feared the repercussions of the Ansar's action, as he feared that they might not agree with the distancing of 'Ali. This would cause the destruction of all they had planned and plotted. All their efforts would be in vain, their spirits would have fallen; all this after they had even defied the Prophet himself and thwarted all his plans for the Caliphate. As a result 'Umar, on his way to the Saqifa, was practicing what he would say to them so as to gain their support and agreement on the stratagem.

Question 17: Why did the Muhajirun win over the Ansar and submit the matter to Abu Bakr?

Answer: There are several factors that played [different] roles in the defeat of the Ansar, and the victory of the Muhajirin. The Ansar were, in fact, two tribes; both competing for the leadership since the times of *jahiliyya*. Their struggle had subsided with the coming of the Prophet (s) in their midst. Now that the Prophet (s) was dead and his community wanted to usurp the Caliphate from its divinely ordained person, the Aws rose up under the leadership of Sa'd b. 'Ubada. However, Bashir b. Sa'd, the leader of the Khazraj, was jealous of his cousin. He was certain that he would not attain the Caliphate whilst Sa'd b. 'Ubada was present. He therefore refuted the position of the Ansar and instead joined the ranks of the Muhajirin, pretending to play the role of a trustworthy advisor.

Abu Bakr also stirred up the *jahiliyya* haughtiness in them, and touched on a sensitive spot by his words: "If we were to surrender this matter to the Aws, the Khazraj would never be pleased, and if we surrendered it to the Khazraj, the Aws would never be pleased." Then he tempted them by [offering to] divide the rulership saying: "We are the chiefs, and you are the ministers, and we will never force our views upon you."

Then he astutely played the role of the trusty advisor to the *ummah* by disqualifying himself and showing his distance from the Caliphate and that he would not desire it, by declaring: "Choose whom you wish from these two men, i.e., 'Umar b. al-Khattab and Abu 'Ubayda Amir b. al-Jarrah."

This step was effective and the play successful. Both 'Umar and Abu 'Ubayda said: "It is not fitting that we supersede you when you were the first among us in accepting Islam, you were his companion in the cave, so stretch your hand that we may give our pledge. Upon these words, Abu Bakr stretched his hand and the first to give it was Bashir b. Sa'd, the leader of the Khazraj. All the rest followed with the exception of Sa'd b. 'Ubada.

Question 18: Why did Sa'd b. 'Ubada refuse to give his pledge and

'Umar threaten to kill him?

Answer: When the Ansar rushed to give their pledge to Abu Bakr, so that they might gain thereby fame and closeness to the Caliph, Sa'd b. 'Ubada refused to pay allegiance and tried his utmost to stop his tribe from it, but he was unable to do so because of the severity of his illness as he was bedridden and his voice could not be heard. At that, 'Umar said: "Kill him for he is a mischief monger, so that the root of dissension might be destroyed and so that no one may dissent from the pledge as this would destroy the Muslims and would cause fragmentation of the *ummah* and create discord."

Question 19: Why did they threaten to raze the house of Fatima al-Zahra?

Answer: A large number of those companions who dissented from giving the pledge to Abu Bakr had taken to the house of 'Ali b. Abi Talib. Had 'Umar not hurried and cordoned the house with firewood and threaten to burn it, the matter would have escalated and the *ummah* separated into two parties - the 'Alawis and Bakris. However, 'Umar, in following the dictates of reality, went overboard when he said: "You will come out for the pledge or I will burn the house and everyone in it." By that, he meant 'Ali and Fatima, the daughter of the Prophet of Allah (s). With these words, no one could let himself be seduced into revolting or not entering the pledge of allegiance, for what sanctity was greater than the sanctity of the leader of the women in paradise, and of her husband, leader of the successors?

Question 20: Why did Abu Sufyan stay quiet after having at first threatened and promised them?

Answer: When Abu Sufyan returned to Medina after the death of the Prophet (s) (he had been sent to collect the *sadaqa*), he was surprised by the Caliphate of Abu Bakr and hurried to the house of 'Ali b. Abi Talib. He incited him to revolt and wage war against the community, promising him money and people. 'Ali, however, rejected him for he was aware of his intentions. When Abu Bakr and 'Umar came to know of this, they went to Abu Sufyan and offered him money, promising to give him all the *sadaqa* that he had collected, and to give him some participation in the affair, by appointing his son as the governor in Syria. Abu Sufyan was happy with this and did not speak out against them. They then appointed Yazid b. Abi Sufyan as the governor over al-Sham, and when he died, they appointed his brother, Mu'awiyah b. Abi Sufyan, in his place, thereby enabling him to attain the Caliphate.

Question 21: Was Imam 'Ali pleased with the reality, and did he give them his pledge?

Answer: Never. Imam 'Ali was not happy with the reality and he did not keep quiet. Rather, he argued with them and refused to give his pledge in spite of the threat and warnings. Ibn Qutayba related in his history that 'Ali said to them: "By Allah! I will never give a pledge to you when you should be giving a pledge to me." He came with his wife Fatima al-Zahra (sa) to the assembly of the Ansar. They excused themselves, saying that Abu Bakr preceded them. Al-Bukhari reported that 'Ali did not give his pledge during the lifetime of Fatima (sa). When she died, the people were turning away [from him], he was therefore forced to reconcile with Abu Bakr. Fatima (sa) lived for six months after her father's death. Did Fatima (sa) die without having taken a pledge when her father, the Prophet of Allah (s) said: "Whoever dies without having given a pledge has died the death of *jahiliyya*?" Did 'Ali know that he would live until after Abu Bakr, and delay giving his pledge for those six months? 'Ali, in fact, never stayed quiet and, throughout his life, whenever he found the opportunity, he used to relate of his being oppressed and the usurpation of his rights. There is sufficient proof for this in what he said in his well-known *khutba al-Shaqshaqiyya*.

Question 22: Why did they provoke and anger Fatima when they were in need of reconciliation?

Answer: They deliberately provoked Fatima by taking away her land and property and denying the inheritance from her father. They [also] repudiated all her claims, to undermine her standing and honor among the people, so that they (the people) would no longer believe her. The appointment to the Caliphate had no influence; as a

Chapter 6: Concerning the Caliphate

result, the Ansar apologized to her, for their pledges had already been given to Abu Bakr. Had her husband come before, they would not have turned away from him.

Because of this, her anger intensified towards Abu Bakr and 'Umar until she began to pray against them in every prayer she prayed. She also left a testament to her husband not to let any of them attend her funeral and to keep her away from the faces she detested.

They also deliberately troubled her to inform 'Ali that he was even lesser in their sight than the Prophet's daughter, who was the leader of the women of the world, the one for who Allah would be angered if she became angry, and would be pleased if she was pleased. There was nothing left for 'Ali but silence and acceptance.

Question 23: Why did the notables of the community stay away from the expedition of Usama?

Answer: Once the matter was decided concerning Abu Bakr, and he became the Caliph of the Muslims because of 'Umar's efforts, in defiance of those who opposed him, he asked Usama to leave 'Umar b. al-Khattab to him, so that he could use him in the affairs of the Caliphate. This was because he was not able to complete the strategies alone so it was necessary for him to have active elements that had strength and courage with which they opposed the Prophet of Allah (s). They did not care about Allah's anger nor the curse of the Prophet (s) on one who stayed away from 'Usama's expedition which he himself had selected. There is no doubt that the plotters of this matter stayed back from the expedition in order to execute their plans and to help each other plant their foundations.

Question 24: Why was Imam 'Ali distanced from all responsibility, and they did not involve him in anything?

Answer: They approached a large number of those who were freed (on the conquest of Mecca), and gave them positions in their government and involved them in their affairs. Amongst them they appointed chiefs and governors in every part of the Arabian

Peninsula and every part of the Islamic state. Amongst them were al-Walid b. 'Uqba, Marwan b. al-Hakam, Mu'awiyah and Yazid, the two sons of Abu Sufyan, 'Amr b. al-'As, al-Mughira b. Shu'ba, Abu Hurayrah and several others who used to crowd around the Prophet (s) but they distanced 'Ali b. Abi Talib, abandoning and leaving him a prisoner in his house, not involving him in anything which pertained to their affairs for a quarter of a century, in order to belittle and denigrate him and to alienate the people from him. The people are slaves of the world, inclining towards the rulers, fame and wealth. As long as 'Ali could not find his daily bread except what he earned by his hand and by the sweat of his brows, the people would shun him and not incline towards him. In fact, 'Ali (as) remained in that condition during the Caliphate of Abu Bakr, 'Umar, and 'Uthman, confined at home. Everyone worked to denigrate him and to extinguish his light and to conceal his merits and virtues, for he had no vanities of the world which would attract people towards him.

Question 25: Why did they fight those who withheld the *zakat*, despite the Prophet forbidding that?

Answer: Some of the companions who had been present at the pledge to Imam 'Ali at Ghadir Khum, when they were returning from the farewell pilgrimage in the company of the Prophet (s), refused to give the *zakat* to Abu Bakr; for they were not present at the death of the Prophet (s) nor at the events that followed, i.e., the Caliphate being switched from 'Ali to Abu Bakr, since they did not live in Medina. No doubt some news reached them that Fatima had argued with them and was angry with them, and that 'Ali had refused to give his pledge to them. Because of all this, they refused to give the *zakat* to Abu Bakr until the matter became clear to them.

From here, Abu Bakr, 'Umar and the government apparatus decided to send an army under the leadership of Khalid b. al-Walid, who was their penetrating sword. He crushed their rebellion, silenced their dissent, slew their men and took their women and children as captives, so that it would be a lesson to anyone who contemplated not to obey, or to challenge the authority of the state.

Chapter 6: Concerning the Caliphate

Question 26: Why did they prevent the writing down and transmission of the *hadith* of the Prophet?

Answer: From the very first days, they prevented the narration of the Prophet's *hadiths*, not only because they contained the appointment relating to the Caliphate and the excellences of Imam 'Ali, but because many of them (traditions) contradicted their words and deeds, by which they (the Caliphs) were administering the affairs of the people. These [acts] laid the foundation of the pillars of the new state which they (the Caliphs) had innovated based on their personal views and acts.

Question 27: Was Abu Bakr capable of bearing the mantle of the Caliphate?

Answer: Abu Bakr was not capable of bearing the mantle of the Caliphate, had it not been for 'Umar b. al-Khattab and some shrewd leaders of the Banu Umayya [he would not have got it]. History has recorded that Abu Bakr was always subservient to decisions and opinions of 'Umar al-Khattab [who was] the actual ruler. The proof of that lies in the story of those whose hearts were to be placated. They came to Abu Bakr at the beginning of his Caliphate, and he gave them a letter and sent them to 'Umar who controlled the treasury. 'Umar tore the document and dismissed them. They returned to Abu Bakr asking him: "Are you the Caliph or is he?" He responded: "He is, if Allah wishes."

Similarly, Abu Bakr allotted a plot of land to 'Uyayna b. Hisn and al-Aqra' b. Habis; when 'Umar read the document from Abu Bakr, he rejected and spat at it and erased it. The two people returned to Abu Bakr complaining about what 'Umar had done and said to Abu Bakr: "We do not know, are you the Caliph or is 'Umar?" He said: "Rather, 'Umar is the Caliph." When 'Umar came angrily to Abu Bakr and argued with him using harsh words for giving away the land, Abu Bakr said to him: "Did I not tell you that you are stronger than me in this matter, but you overruled me?"[4]

---

[4] Al-'Asqalani, *al-Isaba fi Ma'rifa al-Sahaba,* profile on 'Uyayna, Ibn Abi'l-Hadid in *Sharh Nahj al-Balagha,* 12/108.

Al-Bukhari reported in his *Sahih* that 'Umar instigated the people to pledge to Abu Bakr, saying to them: "Indeed Abu Bakr is the companion of the Prophet of Allah, the second of the two. He was the best of Muslims to administer your affairs so go forth and pledge to him. Anas b. Malik said: "I heard 'Umar saying to Abu Bakr that day: 'Ascend the pulpit'! Whilst he said this, he (Abu Bakr) climbed up, and the general populace pledged to him."

Question 28: Why did Abu Bakr accept the Caliphate and then give it to 'Umar before his death?

Answer: Because 'Umar b. al-Khattab was the one who played the heroic role in distancing 'Ali from the Caliphate by his fierce opposition to the Prophet (s) initially, and by coercing the Ansar to pledge allegiance to Abu Bakr and by forcing it upon the people by firmness and severity to the point that he threatened to burn the house of Fatima.

And because he was the actual Caliph, as we have already explained, he had the first and last word. There is no doubt that he was amongst the cleverest of the Arabs and knew that the Muslims, especially the Ansar, would not pledge to him due to his harsh nature and hot temper. He therefore strove to promote Abu Bakr to them since he was soft and weak in nature, and he was the earliest among them to convert; his daughter 'A'isha was a bold woman capable of riding through difficulties and changing conditions. He also knew with certainty that Abu Bakr was under his thumb and would be at his beck and call in anything he desired.

That Abu Bakr would hand over the Caliphate to 'Umar was not hidden from many of the companions before he had actually written it. Imam 'Ali had told him from the first day: "He has milked for you milk, half of which will be for you, so enforce his [command] today and he will return it to you tomorrow." Another one of them said to 'Umar when he brought out the document in which Abu Bakr had appointed him: "I know what is in it! You made him Caliph the first year, and he has appointed you the Caliph this year."

Chapter 6: Concerning the Caliphate

So, Abu Bakr's bestowal of the Caliphate upon 'Umar was known to most people, for, during his life, he used to admit in front of all that 'Umar was more powerful than him in this matter; it was therefore not strange that he would hand to him the reins of the Caliphate at his death.

With this, it becomes clear to us once more that what the *Ahl al-Sunnah* say about the Caliphate being based on consultation (*shura*) is unfounded and was not considered by Abu Bakr and 'Umar in their minds. If the Prophet of Allah (s) died and left the matter to consultation [by the people] as they claim; then Abu Bakr was the first to destroy this principle and to contravene the *Sunnah* of the Prophet (s) by bestowing it to 'Umar b. al-Khattab after him.

You always find the *Ahl al-Sunnah* declaring with great pride and glory that they believe in *shura* and that the Caliphate is not proper without this [principle]. They ridicule the statement of the Shi'a who believes that it cannot be except by appointment from Allah and His Prophet (s). You hear most of them criticizing this belief as being an innovation brought into Islam from the Persians, who believed in the transmission of divine ruler ship.

Quite often the *Ahl al-Sunnah* use the verse: *"And their affairs are by shura between them" (42:38)* as proof, saying that it was revealed especially regarding the Caliphate. Thus, we have the right to say that Abu Bakr and 'Umar contravened both the Qur'an and the *Sunnah*, and did not give them any importance in the question of the Caliphate.

Question 29: Why did 'Abd al-Rahman b. 'Awf stipulate the condition on 'Ali b. Abu Talib that he should rule according to the *Sunnah* of the two Caliphs?

Answer: From his preference of this world over Allah, 'Abd al-Rahman b. 'Awf became the one to dictate the course of the *ummah* after 'Umar; he chose for them whoever he wished, and pushed aside whoever he wished; all of this having been planned by 'Umar who preferred his palm rather than the rest of the companions. 'Abd al-Rahman b. 'Awf was the last one amongst the shrewd Arabs and there is no doubt that he was a member of the party plotting for the Caliphate, diverting it away from the divinely legislated person. Even al-Bukhari admitted that 'Abd al-Rahman b. 'Awf was afraid of something in 'Ali;[5] and it was natural therefore that he would also work towards distancing him from the Caliphate as much as possible. 'Abd al-Rahman b. 'Awf knew, as did the other companions, that 'Ali did not agree with the *ijtihad* of Abu Bakr and the rulings of the Qur'an and *Sunnah* that they changed, and he tried his utmost to oppose and refute both of them.

As a result, 'Abd al-Rahman imposed the condition on 'Ali that he must rule according to the *Sunnah* of Abu Bakr and 'Umar. He knew better than others beforehand that 'Ali would not cheat or lie, and would never accept that condition. He also knew that his father-in-law 'Uthman would be the one to whom the Quraysh and all the members of the plot would consent to.

Question 30: The *hadith* pertaining to twelve Imams: Is there any mention of it amongst the *Ahl al-Sunnah*?

Answer: Muslim, al-Bukhari and every *hadith* reporter from the *Ahl al-Sunnah* has reported the *hadith* of the Prophet (s): "The religion will remain [steadfast] until the final hour or until there are 12 Caliphs, all of them from the Quraysh".[6] This *hadith* has remained among the difficult puzzles for which there is no answer amongst the *Ahl al-Sunnah wa'l-Jama'a* and none of their scholars has been able to count after the four rightly guided Caliphs except 'Umar b. 'Abd al-'Aziz; these amount to five. There remain seven which cannot be accounted for.

They have to either admit the Imamate of 'Ali and his progeny, which the Imamiyya ascribe to and, in doing so, become the followers of the Prophet's household, or they refute the *hadith*, the "*Sahihs*" become isolated from the truth, carrying nothing but lies.

---

[5] *Sahih al-Bukhari*, 8/123, "The Chapter on How the Peaple Pay Allegiance to the Imam", "The Book of Laws".

[6] *Sahih al-Bukhari*, 8/127, *Sahih Muslim*, 6/3.

Chapter 6: Concerning the Caliphate

I would add that this *hadith*, which specifically concerns the Caliphate in the Quraysh, alone nullifies the principle of *shura* which they ascribe to. This is because choice and democracy includes every individual in the *ummah*, and is not confined to a specific tribe over others. Indeed, it transcends the Arab tribes to other non-Arab Islamic tribes.

These are quick and concise answers so as to explain to the reader some of the issues that may have perplexed his mind. He can find more detailed answers in the books of history as well as in my two books "*Then I was Guided*' and "*To be with the Truthful ones.*"

It is up to the researcher to refer to the reliable sources, to devote himself to the truth, to sift through the narrations and historical events to discover, in the process, the truths enshrouded in cloaks of falsehood, to uncover them and to look at them in their original garb.

Chapter Seven

Concerning the Noble Hadith

I will prove to the reader that the problem of *hadiths* is among the most difficult of problems the Muslims live with today especially at the present time; because the "Wahhabi Universities" graduate doctors who specialize in the field of *hadiths*. You find them memorizing the *hadiths* that concord with their schools and beliefs. Most of these *hadiths* are [the product] of the fabrications by the Umayyads, their predecessors, whose aims were also to extinguish the light of the message [of Islam] and to portray the Prophet (s) as a feeble-minded clown not knowing what he says, not aware of his contradictory traditions, and deeds which [even] a madman would laugh at.

Despite the efforts of researchers and *Ahl al-Sunnah* scholars to cleanse and sift the traditions, there are still, most unfortunately, in the authentic and reliable books, many [strange] things. Similarly, the Shi'a books are not safe from interpolations and fabrications.

However, they admit that they do not have an authentic book except the book of Allah. Apart from it, they (the books) contain lean and fat. As for the *Ahl al-Sunnah,* they agree that the *Sahihs* of al-Bukhari and Muslim are the most correct books after the book of Allah; in fact, they say that everything in them is correct. Due to that, I will attempt to place in front of the reader some examples of *hadiths* reported in al-Bukhari and Muslim which contain what they contain, i.e., denigration of the sanctity of the great Prophet (s), or the members of his household (as).

I will attempt here to repudiate some of the *hadiths* which were fabricated to justify the actions of the Umayyad and 'Abbasid rulers. They wanted, in reality, to destroy the infallibility of the Prophet (s), so as to justify their crimes and their slaughter of innocent people. Following are some examples:

The Prophet dupes

In "The Book of Seeking Permission" and "The Book of Indemnity" in "The Chapter of Whoever Peeps in the House of People and they Poke his Eyes out, there is no Blood Money upon Them," al-Bukhari, in his *Sahih*, reported the following *hadith*, as did Muslim in his *Sahih* in "The Book of Etiquettes" in "The Chapter of Prohibition to look into Someone's House," from Anas b. Malik: "A man peeped into a part of the Prophet's (s) room. The Prophet (s) stood up holding an arrowhead or arrowheads. It is if I am now looking at him trying to stab the man."

The most exalted character does not accord with this [kind of] behavior, [especially] from the Prophet of mercy who was affectionate and compassionate to the believers. It would be assumed that the Prophet (s) would go to this man who had peeped into his room and would teach him Islamic conduct and make him understand that what he did was forbidden. Not to take an arrowhead and attempt to stab him and poke his eyes. Probably the man could have meant well for the room was not his wives' room. The proof of this is that Anas b. Malik was present in it. What a great accusation this is against the Prophet of Allah (s); as it portrays him as an ill-mannered and hard hearted person who attacks a person without warning, i.e., assaults the man so as to take out his eye.

It is sufficient to note that the commentator of al-Bukhari found it disgraceful and said: "*Yakhtiluhu*", i.e., assaults him by coming upon him from where he cannot see him. This is how they explained it. A surreptitious attack is far from [the acts of] the Prophet (s).

The Prophet inflicts a vile penalty and mutilates Muslims

Al-Bukhari reported in his *Sahih* in "The Book of Medicine" vol.

Chapter 7: Concerning the Noble Hadith

7 p. 13, in "The Chapter on Medications by Camel's Milk" and also in "The Chapter on Medication by Camel's Urine": Thabit informed us, from Anas that some men who were sick said: "O Prophet of Allah! Give us food and shelter". The Prophet (s) ordered them to follow his shepherd, i.e., his camels, and to drink their milk and urine. So they followed the shepherd and drank their milk and urine till their bodies became healthy. Then they killed the shepherd and drove away the camels. When the news reached the Prophet, he sent some people in their pursuit. When they were brought, he cut their hands and feet and their eyes were branded with heated pieces of iron. I saw one of them licking the earth with his tongue until he died".

Can a Muslim believe that the Prophet of Allah (s), who forbade mutilation, himself, mutilates these people, cutting off their hands and feet, and branding their eyes because they slaughtered his herder? Had the narrator said that these people had mutilated the herder, there would have been some justification for the Prophet to punish them in the same way. That was not the case, so how could the Prophet of Allah (s) kill and mutilate them in this way without investigation and cross examination until it became clear who among them was the murderer so that he could kill him for that? Perhaps some would say that they all participated in killing him, could the Prophet of Allah (s) not forgive and pardon them for they were Muslims as proved by their words "O Prophet of Allah?" Did the Prophet of Allah not hear Allah's words: *"And if you punish them, then punish them the way you were punished. And if you are patient then that is better for those who are patient"* *(16:126).*

This verse was revealed to the Prophet of Allah (s) when his heart was burning over his uncle, the master of the martyrs, Hamza b. 'Abd al-Muttalib whose stomach they had slashed open, and eaten his liver and cut his private parts. The Prophet was enraged when he saw his uncle in that condition. He declared: "Should Allah let me prevail over them, I will mutilate seventy [of them]". Whereupon the verse was revealed unto him and he said: "I shall be patient, O my Lord." He then forgave Wahshi, the murderer of his uncle as well as Hind who had mutilated his pure body and ate his liver. This was the [true] character of the Prophet (s).

What proves the repulsive [nature] of the narration and that the narrator himself found it abominable, is that he followed it up by saying: "Qatada said: 'Muhammad b. Sirin informed me that this occurred before legal punishments were revealed...'" to justify, by that, the actions of the Prophet (s). Far removed is the Prophet from judging by himself before his Lord made matters clear to him. If he did not judge in even trivial matters until revelation came to him, what do you think about matters pertaining to blood and penalties?

It is very easy for anyone who reflects upon the matter to realize that it is a narration forged by the Umayyads and their followers to please the rulers who did not hesitate to kill innocent people based on suspicion and accusation, mutilating them in a hideous manner. The proof of this is what came in the end of the report itself which al-Bukhari reported saying: "Salam said: 'I came to know that Hajjaj said to Anas: 'Tell me the severest punishment the Prophet meted out,' and Anas reported this [*hadith*].' When al-Hasan came to know this he said: 'I wish he had not told him this.'"[1]

The *hadith* stinks of the smell of fabrication to please al-Hajjaj al-Thaqafi who caused havoc in the land and murdered thousands of innocent followers of the *Ahl al-Bayt*, mutilating them. He used to cut off their hands and feet and brand out their eyes. He would take out the tongues from the back of the heads and crucify those alive until they were burnt by the sun. Narrations such as these justify his actions for he was simply following the Prophet of Allah: "And you have in the Prophet of Allah a good example." There is no power or strength except with Allah.

As a result, Mu'awiyah became an expert in punishment and mutilation of Muslims who were the followers of 'Ali. How many were burnt to death? How many were buried alive? How many were crucified on branches of date palms? One of the arts which his minister 'Amr b. al-'As invented was that he mutilated Muhammad

---

[1] *Sahih al-Bukhari*, 7/13.

b. Abu Bakr, then clothed him in the skin of an ass and then cast him into the fire.

To justify their craze and great infatuation with maidservants and women, here are some narrations [which they quote].

The Prophet (s) loves intercourse

In "The Book of Bathing," under "The Chapter entitled 'If one has Sexual Intercourse Then repeated [it], and one who Rotates Between his Wives with one Bath only,'" al-Bukhari reported in his *Sahih*, Mu'adh b. Hisham said: "My father reported to me from Qatada, who said: 'Anas b. Malik said: 'The Prophet (s) used to go around all his wives during the night and day in one hour, and there were eleven of them'. He said: 'So I said to Anas: 'Was he able to?' Anas replied: 'We used to say he had the power of thirty...'"

This is a false *hadith* to devalue the greatness of the Prophet (s) so as to vindicate the palaces of al-Rashid and the acts of Mu'awiyah and the deranged Yazid. How did Anas b. Malik know that the Prophet (s) used to copulate with eleven women in one hour? Did the Prophet inform him of that or was he present there? I seek Allah's refuge from lies. How did he know that he had the strength of thirty?

This is an accusation against the Prophet of Allah (s) who spent his life in struggle, worship and in instructing and teaching his *ummah*. What do these ignorant ones think when they narrate such disgraces? It is as if their minds are corrupted by their animalistic lusts. They used to take pride with their mates of their over indulgence in sex and strength of intercourse when, in reality, these are narrations falsified to demean the sanctity of the Prophet (s). Secondly, [these narrations] vindicated the shamelessness of the rulers and Caliphs whose castles were filled with slave girls and women - with no limit, because they were slave girls. What did Anas b. Malik, the reporter of this *hadith,* say when he was confronted by Umm al-Mu'minin 'A'isha, the wife of the Prophet (s) and who used to say that he (s) was like any other man in sex? Muslim reported in his *Sahih*, in "The Book of Purification" in "The

Chapter of Water nullifies [the use of] Water, and the Injunction of Bathing when the Private Parts Meet": "From Abu'l-Zubayr from Jabir b. 'Abd Allah from Umm al-Kulthum from 'A'isha, wife of the Prophet (s) who said: "A man asked the Prophet of Allah (s) about a person who has intercourse with his wife then he feels lazy. Do they have to take a bath?" 'A'isha was sitting, and the Prophet of Allah said: "I do that, I and this one here, then we both bathe."

Then the commentator of the *hadith* added in the margins of *Sahih Muslim*: "Then he feels lazy, the meaning in *al-Misbah* (a famous dictionary) of "*aksala mujami*" is when he withdraws without ejaculation either because of weakness or otherwise". What does this have to do with the claim that he has the strength of thirty [men]?

This is another narration fabricated by the forgers, may Allah destroy them and increase for them a painful punishment. Otherwise, how can reason accept such narrations about the bearer of the messages, he from whom all shyness had gone, he says to men, in the presence of his wife, what an ordinary believer would feel shy to talk of?

To justify songs and dancing which were famous in the time of the Umayyads here are some *hadiths*

The Apostle takes pleasure in dancing and listens to songs:

Al-Bukhari reported in his *Sahih* in "The Book of Marriage," under "The Chapter of Beating the Drum During the Wedding and the Feast": Bishr b. al-Mufaddal told us that Khalid b. Dhikwan said: "Al-Rabi' bint Mu'awwdh b. Afra' said: 'The Prophet came to me after consummating his marriage with me and sat down on my bed as you are sitting now, and small girls were beating the tambourine and singing in lamentation of my fathers who had been killed on the day of the battle of Badr. Then one of the girls said: 'There is a Prophet amongst us who knows what will happen tomorrow'. The Prophet said: 'Leave this talk and say what you were saying before.'"

Chapter 7: Concerning the Noble Hadith

Al-Bukhari also reported in his *Sahih* in "The Book of Struggles," in "The Chapter on Tambourine," as well as Muslim in "The Book of The Two *'id* Prayers" "The Chapter on Permission of Games in which there is no Sin [involved]":

On the authority of 'A'isha who said: "The Prophet of Allah (s) came to my house while two girls were singing beside me the songs of Bu'ath (a story about the war between the two tribes of the Ansar, i.e. Khazraj and Aws). He reclined on the bed and turned his face to the other side. Abu Bakr came and scolded me saying: 'The instrument of Satan in the presence of Allah's Apostle?' The Prophet of Allah (s) turned towards him and said: 'Leave them.' When he became inattentive, I waved the two girls to go away and they left.'"

On the authority of 'A'isha who said: "It was the day of *'id* when Negroes used to play with leather shields and spears. Either I requested the Prophet of Allah or he asked me: 'Would you like to see the display?' I replied: 'Yes.' Then he let me stand behind him and my cheek on his cheek and he was saying: 'Carry on, O Banu Arfida.' When I got tired, he asked me: 'Have you had enough?' I replied: 'Yes.' He said: 'Let us go.'"

Al-Bukhari narrates in his *Sahih* in "The Book of Marriage" in "The Chapter on The woman looking at the Ethiopians and others without any Doubt" that 'A'isha said: "I saw the Prophet (s) covering me with his *rida* (upper garment) while I was looking at the Ethiopians play in the *masjid* until I got bored. Imagine how a young girl desires such entertainment."

Similarly, Muslim narrated in his *Sahih* in "The Book of the *'Id* Prayers," in "The Chapter on The Permission of Entertainment" from 'A'isha who said: "The Ethiopians were playing on the day of *'id* (i.e., they were dancing) in the *masjid*, and the Prophet (s) called me, and I put my head upon his shoulder and I began to look at their games until I had had enough of watching them."

Al-Bukhari also narrated in his *Sahih* in "The Book of Marriage," in "The Chapter of the Women and Children going to a Wedding," from Anas b. Malik who said: "The Prophet (s) saw some women and children coming from a wedding celebration, so he stood hastily and said: 'By Allah! you are the most beloved of people to me.' The commentator of al-Bukhari said: "*Mumatinan*," the meaning is that he stood up quickly and forcefully because of his joy for them."

To justify their addiction to wine and intoxicants, here are some narrations:

The Prophet drinks *nabidh*

In "The Book of Marriage," in "The chapter on The Women Standing And Serving the Men at Wedding Celebrations," and in "The Book of The Dried Fruit and Drinking what does not Intoxicate at Weddings," al-Bukhari reported: From Abu Hazin from Sahl: "When Abu Usayd al-Sa'idi got married, he invited the Prophet (s) and his companions. None prepared the food for them and brought it to them but his wife, Umm Usayd. She soaked some dates in water in a stone pot overnight, and when the Prophet (s) had finished his food, she provided him with that drink (of soaked dates)."

It is clear that they intended [to show] by this narration that the Prophet (s) drank *nabidh*. Possibly, the connotation was not the *nabidh* that is known, rather, it was an Arab custom of soaking dates in water to take away the smell of water. It therefore was not the actual *nabidh*. Some of them deem it proper to use it. Muslim narrated this report under "The Book of Drinks," in "The Chapter on The Permissibility of [drinking] *Nabidh* which has not Fermented nor become an Intoxicant". From here, the drinking of *nabidh* began and the rulers allowed the drinking of wine, claiming it was permissible as long as it did not intoxicate.

To vindicate what the Umayyads and 'Abbasids used to do, here are some narrations:

The Prophet and debasement

In "The Book of *Hajj*," in "The Chapter on Visiting on the Day of Sacrifice," al-Bukhari reported in his *Sahih* that 'A'isha said: "We made *hajj* with the Prophet (s) and went forth in multitudes on the day of sacrifice. Safiyya started her menstruation and the Prophet wanted from her what a man wants from his wife, so I said to him: 'O Prophet of Allah, she is menstruating.'"

How astonishing is this Prophet (s) who wishes to have intercourse with his wife in the presence and knowledge of his other wife who informs him that she (Hafsa) is menstruating, while the one with whom he wanted to sleep knows nothing.

The Prophet does not feel shy

Muslim reported in his *Sahih* in "The Book of Merits," in "The Chapter on The Merits of 'Uthman b. Affan" the following: "From 'A'isha, wife of the Prophet (s) and from 'Uthman. Both of them said: 'Abu Bakr sought permission to visit the Messenger of Allah (s) while he was lying on his bed, wearing the garment of 'A'isha. He let him in, while he was still in that condition. He fulfilled his needs, and then Abu Bakr went out.'" 'Uthman said: "Umar then sought permission to enter while the Prophet was still in that state. He also fulfilled his needs and left." 'Uthman said: "Then I requested permission to enter, whereupon he sat up and said to 'A'isha: 'Gather your clothes around you'. I finished my work with him and left. 'A'isha said: 'O Apostle of Allah (s), how come I did not see you scared with Abu Bakr and 'Umar (r) as you were with 'Uthman?' The Apostle of Allah (s) said: 'Indeed 'Uthman is a shy man, and I was afraid that if I had granted him permission to enter when I was in that state, he would not have presented his need to me.'"

What Prophet is this who meets his companions while reclining with the clothes of his wife on his bed, with her beside him, wearing revealing clothes so that when 'Uthman came, he sat up and ordered her to gather her clothes?

The Prophet displaying his private parts

In "The Book of Salat," in "The Chapter on The Abomination of Praying Undressed," al-Bukhari in his *Sahih* reported a *hadith* which Muslim also did in "The Book of Menses," in "The Chapter on Paying Attention to covering the Private Parts," from Jabir b. 'Abd Allah: "The Prophet of Allah (s) was carrying stones with them for [the building of] the Ka'ba wearing an *Izar* (waist-sheet cover). His uncle al-'Abbas said to him: 'O my nephew! [It would be better] if you take off your *Izar* and put it over your shoulders underneath the stones.' So he took off his *Izar* and put it over his shoulders, but he fell unconscious and since then he was never seen naked."

Look, O reader, at these spurious allegations at the Prophet of Allah (s), the one who made shame one of the tenets of faith. He was shyer than a virgin in her private room. They were not satisfied with their narrations of debasement and his exposing his thighs in front of his companions. Now they accuse him in this false *hadith* of exposing his private parts. In their view, was the Prophet of Allah (s) so simple-minded that he listened to his uncle's advice and exposed his private parts in front of the people?

I seek the refuge of Allah, the most Great, from the allegations of these Satanic devils who lie about Allah and his Prophet (s). Although the law allowed him to disclose his private parts, the wives and the closest of people to the Prophet did not see them. Moreover, the mother of the believers, 'A'isha said: "I did not look at nor ever see a private part of the Prophet of Allah".[2] If this was his conduct with his wives who used to bathe with him in a single vessel and he used to cover himself from them, and they never saw him naked, how then [was his conduct] with his companions and the general public?

Certainly these are all from the fabrications of the Umayyad beetles who did not hesitate from anything. If one of their Caliphs,

---

[2] Ibn Maja, *Sunan*, 1/619.

the Commander of the Faithful, could be so overcome by the verses of a poet who recited a line of a love poem, he got up, exposed himself then kissed his penis; then it should not be surprising after this if they expose the Prophet's private parts. Their inner sickness has spread and has become a common thing today amongst some licentious people who pay no regard to morals and shyness. There are calls and gatherings of nudists in every place where men and women get together with a common verse (O Lord! here we are as you created us).

To justify their playing with religion and the *shari'a* laws, here are some of their narrations:

The Prophet forgets in his prayer

In "The Book of Etiquettes", in "The Chapter of What is Allowed to Remind People" al-Bukhari reported a *hadith* in his *Sahih* as did Muslim in "The Book of The *Masjids* and Places of Prayer" in "The Chapter of Forgetfulness in Prayer and Prostration for it", from Abu Hurayrah who said: "The Prophet (s) led us in *zuhr* prayer and after two *rak'ats*, made the *salam*, then went to a piece of wood in the front of the mosque and placed his hands upon it.

Among the people at that time were Abu Bakr and 'Umar. They were afraid to speak to him, and the people left in a hurry. They said: 'The prayers were shortened'. Amongst the people, there was a man whom the Prophet (s) used to call "Dhu'l-Yadayn." He said: 'O Prophet of Allah! Have you forgotten or was the prayer shortened?' He said: 'I did not forget, nor was the prayer shortened'. They said: 'Then surely you forgot, O Prophet of Allah'. He said: 'Dhu'l-Yadayn has spoken the truth'. He then stood up and prayed two *rak'ats* and then made *salam*, then said "Allahu Akbar" then prostrated like his [normal] prostration or a bit longer then raised his head and said "Allahu Akbar," then made another prostration as he normally did or a bit longer, then raised his head and said "Allahu Akbar."[3]

---

[3] *Sahih al-Bukhari,* and *Sahih Muslim* in "The Book of Pearls and Corals", 1/115.

Allah forbade that the Prophet forgot in his prayer and did not know how many units he prayed, and when it was said to him that he had shortened his prayer, he said: "I did not forget nor was it shortened."

This is a lie to vindicate their Caliphs who used to come to the prayer, often in a drunken state, and would not know how many *rak'ats* they prayed. The story of their leader who led in the Morning Prayer with four *rak'ats* then turned to them and said: "Should I add more or is this enough for you?" is famous in the historical books.

Furthermore, in "The Book of The Call to Prayer" in "The Chapter If a Man Stands to the Left of the Imam," al-Bukhari reported in his *Sahih* from Ibn 'Abbas (r) who said: "I slept at the home of Maymuna, and the Prophet (s) was with her that night. He made *wudu'*, then stood to pray so I stood on his left. He took me and moved me to his right and prayed thirteen *rak'ats*. Then he slept until he snored, for when he slept he used to snore. The *muadhdhin* (one who calls for prayer) then came to him, and he went out and prayed, and he did not make *wudu.*" 'Amr said: "I informed Bukayr about it and he said: 'Kurayb informed me of that.'"

By such spurious narrations against the Prophet of Allah (s), the Umayyad and 'Abbasid Amirs, Sultans and others made mockery of the prayer and *wudu'*, and indeed of every [religious] matter until the saying: "The prayers of leaders are on Fridays and [the days of] *'id*' became widespread.

The Prophet takes an oath then breaks it

In "The Book of Military Expeditions, the story of 'Amman and al-Bahrayn," in "The Chapter on the Arrival of the Ash'aris and the People of Yemen" al-Bukhari reported in his *Sahih* from Abu Qilaba from Zahdam: "When Abu Musa arrived (at Kufa as a governor) he honored this family of Jarm (by paying them a visit). I was sitting near him, and he was eating chicken as his lunch, and there was a man sitting amongst the people. He invited the man to [eat] the lunch, but the latter said: 'I saw chicken eating something [dirty] so I consider them unclean.' Abu Musa said: 'Come on! I saw the Prophet eating it.' The man said: 'I have taken an oath that I will not eat it.' Abu Musa said: 'Come on! I will tell you about your oath. We, a group of al-Ash'ariyin people, went to the Prophet (s) and asked him to give us something to ride but the Prophet refused. Then we asked him for the second time to give us something to ride but the Prophet took an oath that he would not give us anything to ride. After a while, some camels of booty were brought to the Prophet and he ordered that five camels be given to us. When we took them we said: 'We have made the Prophet (s) forget his oath, and we will not be successful after that.' So I went to him and said: 'O Prophet of God! You took an oath that you would not give us anything to ride, but you have given us.' He said: 'Yes, if I take an oath and later I see a better solution than that, I act on what is better.'"

Look at this Prophet, who Allah sent to teach people to respect their oaths and not break them except by [offering an] expiation; but here he is ordering something and not following it. Allah said: *"Allah will not take you to account for thoughtlessness in your oaths, but will call you to account for your deliberate oaths. Its expiation is the feeding of ten poor people, at an average rate for the food of your families or clothing them, or the freeing of a slave. He who cannot do this should fast three days that is the expiation of your oath if you have sworn. So guard your oaths. In this way, Allah makes clear his verses to you so that you may be thankful"* (5:89). Allah also said: *"And do not break oaths after you have confirmed them"* (16:91). But they did not leave even a single merit or virtue for the Prophet of Allah (s) [untouched].

'A'isha frees forty slaves as expiation for her oath

Where does the Prophet (s) stand as opposed to his wife, 'A'isha, who offered expiation for an oath she broke by freeing forty slaves; is she more pious and pure than the Prophet of Allah?

Al-Bukhari reported in his *Sahih* in "The Book of Etiquettes" in "The Chapter of Avoidance and the Saying of the Prophet of Allah (s): 'It is not permissible for a man to avoid his brother for more than three [days].'"vol. 7, p. 90. "'A'isha said that she was told that 'Abd Allah b. al-Zubayr on hearing that she was selling or giving something given to her as a gift, said: 'By Allah, if 'A'isha does not give this up, I will declare her incompetent to dispose [of her wealth].' I said: 'Did he say so?' They said: 'Yes.' She said: 'I vow to Allah that I will never speak to Ibn al-Zubayr.' When this desertion lasted long, 'Abd Allah b. al-Zubayr sought intercession with her, but she said: 'By Allah, I will not accept the intercession of anyone for him, and will not break my vow'. When this was prolonged on Ibn al-Zubayr, he said to al-Miswar b. Makhrama and 'Abd al-Rahman b. al-Aswad b. 'Abu Yaghuth, who were from the tribe of Banu Zahra: 'I beseech you, by Allah, to let me enter upon 'A'isha, for it is unlawful for her to vow to cut relations with me'. So al-Miswar and 'Abd al-Rahman, wrapping their sheets around themselves, asked 'A'isha's permission saying: 'Peace and Allah's Mercy and Blessings be upon you! Shall we come in?' 'A'isha said: 'Come in.' They said: 'All of us?' She said: 'Yes, come in all of you,' not knowing that Ibn al-Zubayr was also with them. So when they entered, Ibn al-Zubayr entered the screened place and got hold of 'A'isha and started requesting her to excuse him and wept. Al-Miswar and 'Abd al-Rahman also started requesting her to speak to him and to accept his repentance. They said: 'The Prophet (s) forbade what you know of avoiding for it is unlawful for any Muslim not to talk to his brother for more than three nights.' So when they continually reminded her and brought her down to a critical situation, she started reminding them, and wept saying: 'I have made a vow and [the question of] vow is a difficult one'. They persisted [in their appeal] till she spoke with 'Abd Allah b. al-Zubayr and she manumitted forty slaves as expiation for her vow. Later on, whenever she remembered her vow, she used to weep so

Chapter 7: Concerning the Noble Hadith

much that her veil used to become wet with her tears."

Even though the vow of 'A'isha was not proper because the Prophet (s) forbade a Muslim to avoid his brother for more than three days, but she refused [to speak] until she gave an expiation for her vow by freeing forty slaves. This is also another proof for us that she had her own property, otherwise how could 'A'isha own forty slaves or their value? That is not an easy thing. History has not recorded that the Prophet (s) freed this large number [of slaves] during his life. They did not leave any evil or defect without attaching it to him, all that [was done] for justifying the acts of their leaders, may Allah destroy them for their fabrications.

To justify their defiling the *shari'a* laws, here are some narrations:

The Prophet plays with the laws of God as he wishes

Al-Bukhari reported in his *Sahih* in "The Book of Fasting", in "The Chapter of The Bath of One who is Fasting" and Muslim in his *Sahih* in "The Book of Fasting," "The Chapter on Severe prohibition of Intercourse during the day in Ramadhan on the one Fasting, and the Incumbency of Major Expiation for it, it is obligatory for the Rich and Poor," on the authority of Abu Hurayrah who said: "While we were sitting with the Prophet (s) a man came and said: 'O Allah's Apostle! I have been ruined.' He asked: 'What happened?' He replied: 'I had sexual intercourse with my wife while I was fasting.' The Prophet of Allah asked him: 'Can you afford to manumit a slave?' He replied: 'No.' He asked him: 'Can you fast for two successive months?' He replied: 'No.' The Prophet asked him: 'Can you afford to feed sixty poor persons?' He replied: 'No.' The Prophet (s) kept silent and while we were in that state, a big basket full of dates was brought to the Prophet. He asked: 'Where is the questioner?' He replied: 'I [am here].' The Prophet said: 'Take this and give it in charity.' The man said: 'Should I give it to a person poorer than I? By Allah, there is no family between Medina's two mountains who are poorer than my family.' The Prophet (s) smiled till his pre-molar teeth became visible and then said: 'Feed your family with it.'"

Observe how the laws and regulations of Allah which He enjoined for his servants regarding the emancipation of a slave for the prosperous are treated. [As for] those unable to free a slave, they only need to feed sixty poor people, and if this is not possible and if he is poor, then nothing [is incumbent] upon him except fasting. This is the stipulated expiation for the poor who do not have enough wealth to free a slave or feed the poor. But this tradition exceeds the bounds of Allah which He legislated for his servants, it is sufficient for this transgressor to say a word that makes the Prophet laugh till his teeth show and for him to be negligent of the law of Allah and to permit him to take the *sadaqa* to his household.

Is there any slander greater than this against Allah and His Prophet (s) that the wrongdoer is allowed to sin willingly instead of being punished? Is there any greater encouragement than this for the disobedient and corrupt ones who will cling on to such false traditions and dance with joy?

Due to such narrations, Allah's religion and His laws have become a [type of] amusement and mockery. Now a fornicator takes pride in his corrupt acts and, calling himself a fornicator, sings songs of praises for it at weddings and parties, just as the one who breaks his fast in the month of *Ramadhan* defies those who fast.

Al-Bukhari has also reported in his *Sahih* in "The Book of Faith and Vows," in "The Chapter If one breaks an Oath through Forgetfulness" from 'Ata on the authority of Ibn 'Abbas (r) who said: "A man said to the Prophet (s): 'I visited before stoning (i.e., I circumambulated the house of Allah, *Tawaf al-Ziyara*).' The Prophet (s) said: 'There is no objection [to it].' Another man said: 'I shaved my head before making the sacrifice.' He said: 'There is no objection [to it]'. Another one said: 'I made the sacrifice before stoning.' The Prophet (s) said: 'There is no objection [to it].'"

From 'Abd Allah b. 'Amr b. al-'As who reported that while the Prophet (s) was delivering a sermon on the day of sacrifice, a man

Chapter 7: Concerning the Noble Hadith

went up to him and said: "O Messenger of Allah, I used to consider this and this before that and that." Thereafter, another person stood up and said: "O Prophet of Allah, I used to consider this and this as part of the three (shaving the head, sacrifice, and stoning)." The Prophet (s) said: "Do it! There is no objection to any of them today." Anything that he was asked about that day he said "Do it! Do it! There is no objection [to it].'"

It is strange that when you read these objectionable narrations, some obstinate people will confront you [saying] that the religion of God means ease and not burden. And that the Prophet (s) said: "Make things easy, do not make things difficult."

It is a true statement intended to [lead to] falsehood. For there is no doubt that Allah desires ease for us and does not desires any hardship upon us, and that he did not impose hardship upon us in religion.

However, the rulings and legislations which He has outlined and imposed on us by way of the noble Qur'an and the pure Prophetic *Sunnah* and has given us necessary concessions when the situation demands like *tayammum* in the absence of water or fear of [using] cold water, or like performing the prayer in a sitting position when required, or breaking the fast and shortening [the prayer] while travelling, all of this is true - but for us to go against His injunctions, Glory be to Him, by, for example, structuring the *wudu'* or *tayammum* as we desire so that we wash the hands before the face, for example, or wipe the feet before the head - this is not permitted.

Nonetheless, the forgers wished that the Prophet of Allah (s) would waive everything so that they could find a loophole, as many people say today (when you argue with them on matters of law): "There is no burden upon you, my brother! The only important thing is to pray! Pray as it pleases you".

It is strange that al-Bukhari himself related, on the same page where there are the words of the Prophet: "Do it! Do it! There is no objection [to it]" an incident where the Prophet demonstrates extreme severity. He reported, on the authority Abu Hurayrah that a man entered the mosque to pray while the Prophet (s) was in a corner of the *masjid.* The man came and greeted him. He said to him: "Return and pray for you have not prayed." So the man went back and prayed then greeted him; the Prophet said "And unto you too. Return and pray for you have not prayed!" The man repeated the prayer three times, and, on every occasion, the Prophet said to him: "Return and pray for you have not prayed." The man said to the Prophet: "Teach me, O Messenger of Allah" so he taught him to be at ease in *ruku',* and in prostration. He said: "Then bow until you are at ease in the bowing position, and then raise your head until you are standing erect, then prostrate until you are at ease in the prostrate position. Then rise until you are balanced and are at ease in the sitting position then prostrate until you are at ease in the prostration, then rise until you are standing erect. Do this in your whole prayer."

In his *Sahih,* al-Bukhari narrated in "The Book of *Tawhid,*" in "The Chapter On Allah's Words: **'Recite from the Qur'an what is easy for you'(73:20)** from 'Umar b. al-Khattab who said: 'I heard Hisham b. Hakim recite *Surah al-Furqan* during the lifetime of the Prophet of Allah (s) so I listened to his recitation and lo! He was reciting in a mode which the Prophet of Allah had not taught me. I almost grabbed him during the prayer, but I waited until he recited the *salam.* Then I took hold of his lower garment and said: 'Who taught you to recite this *Surah* which I heard from you?' He said: 'The Prophet of Allah made me recite [this way].' I said: 'You have lied! He made me recite in a manner different from what you recited.'

So I went out with him and led him to the Prophet of Allah (s), and I said: 'I heard him reciting *Surah al-Furqan* in a mode different from what you have taught me.' He said: 'Let him be. Recite O Hisham'! So he recited the recitation I had heard him whereupon the Prophet of Allah said: 'So it was revealed.' Then the Prophet of Allah (s) said: 'Recite O Umar'! So I recited it in the manner he had made me recite. He said: 'So it was revealed. Indeed this Qur'an was revealed in seven different modes of recitation. So recite it in whichever way is easy for you.'"

Chapter 7: Concerning the Noble Hadith

Does there remain any doubt, after this narration, that the falsifiers were insolent to the sanctity of the Prophet (s) even to the noble Qur'an, and that he taught his companions different recitations, telling each one of them that it was revealed in this manner? Had there not been a big difference in the mode of recitation, 'Umar would not have come close to breaking Hisham's prayer and would not have threatened him. This reminds me of the scholars of the *Ahl al-Sunnah* who insist on a specific recitation and do not allow anyone to recite differently. One day, I was reciting "*Udhkuru ni'mati al-lati an'amtu 'alaykum*" ("Remember my bounty I have bestowed upon you").

One of them scolded me strongly and screamed saying: "Do not destroy the Qur'an if you are ignorant of the recitation." I asked: "How have I destroyed the Qur'an?" He said: "*Udhkuru Ni'matiya and not Ni'mati.*"

Al-Bukhari reported in his *Sahih* in vol. 3 p. 88 in "The Book of Borrowing and the Repayment of Loans," in "The Chapter of Disputes" from 'Abd al-Malik b. Maysara who informed me, he said: "I heard al-Nazzal, I heard 'Abd Allah say: 'I heard a man recite a verse which I had heard the Prophet (s) recite differently. So I took him by the hand and went to the Prophet of Allah (s) who said: 'Both of you are fine.'" Shu'ba said: "I think he said: 'Don't disagree. For those who came before you disagreed and were destroyed.'"

Glory and Praise be to Allah! How can the Prophet of Allah (s) accept their difference and say: "Both of you are fine" and not refer them to a unified [mode of] recitation, thereby eradicating differences?

Then, after that, he says to them: "Do not disagree for you will be destroyed." Is this not contradictory? O Servants of Allah! Give me your opinion, may Allah have mercy upon you! Did they not differ except by his permission, blessings and encouragement? Certainly not! Far be it for the Prophet of Allah (s) [to promote] this contradiction and difference which reason shuns.

Do they not reflect upon the Qur'an which says: *"Were it from other than Allah, they would have found many contradictions in it"* **(4:82)**. Has a greater and more dangerous difference befallen the Islamic *ummah* than numerous modes of recitations which have changed the meaning of the Qur'an to varying interpretations and views so that even the clear verses of *wudu'* have become a matter of dispute?

The Prophet behaves like a child and then disciplines one who does not deserve punishment

Al-Bukhari, in his *Sahih*, in "The Book of Military Campaigns," in "The Chapter On The Illness and Death of the Prophet (s)," and also Muslim in his *Sahih*, in "The Book of Peace," in "The chapter of Aversion to Medication Administered by Force" reported: "From 'A'isha who said: 'We poured medicine in one side of the Prophet's mouth[4] during his illness and he started pointing to us, meaning to say: 'Don't pour medicine in my mouth.' We said: '[It is] a patient's dislike to medicine.' When he recovered he said: 'Didn't I forbid you to pour medicine in my mouth?' We said: '[We thought it was due to] the dislike patients have for medicines.' He said: 'Let everyone present in the house be given medicine by pouring it in his mouth while I am looking at him, except al-'Abbas as he has not witnessed you [doing the same to me].'"

Strange indeed is the case of this slandered Prophet, whom the liars made like a child who is made to swallow bitter medicine which he does not accept. He indicates to them not to administer medicine to him, but yet they force it upon him despite his protests!

When he recovers he says to them: "Didn't I forbid you to pour medicine in my mouth?" They excuse themselves saying they

---

[4] Ibn Manzur says in *"Lisan al-'Arab"* of this process: *"Al-ludd*: It is to take the tongue of child and to force it to one side of mounth, whilst pouring the medicine in the other side of the mouth by inserting the shell between the tongue and the jawbone".

assumed that his prohibition was due to the aversion of a sick person from medicine, then he decrees for all of them that they be given the medicine while he watches to satisfy his rancor, and did not exclude anyone except his uncle al-'Abbas since he was not present when they were administering it.

Lady 'A'isha did not complete the story, was the Prophet's (s) order carried out on them or not, and to whom and how was this done to the men and women present?

The Prophet leaves out some verses of the Qur'an

In the book of "The Merits of the Qur'an," in "The Chapter of Forgetfulness of the Qur'an", as well as in "The Chapter of One Who Sees No Problem in saying *Surah* so and so," al-Bukhari reported the following *hadith* as did Muslim in his *Sahih* in "The Book of The Prayers of Travellers and Shortening it" in "The Chapter of The Order to Abide by the Qur'an and the Hatefulness of saying 'I forgot verse so and so....'": "Abu Usama informed us on the authority of Hisham b. 'Urwa, on the authority of his father from 'A'isha who said: 'One night, the Prophet of Allah (s) heard a man reciting from a chapter [of the Qur'an]. He said: 'May Allah have mercy on him. He has reminded me of verse so and so which I had forgotten from *Surah* so and so.'"

Similarly, in another narration, al-Bukhari related from 'Ali b. Mushiri from Hisham from his father from 'A'isha (r) who said: "The Prophet of Allah (s) heard a reciter at night in the *masjid* and said: 'May Allah have mercy on him. He has reminded me of verse so and so which I left out from *Surah* so and so....'"

This is the Prophet whom Allah, Glory be to Him, sent with the Qur'an, the eternal miracle, which he used to memorize from the day of its revelation upon him, verse by verse, until its complete revelation. Indeed Allah said to him: *"Don't move your tongue to hasten to it"* and He also said: *"It is indeed a revelation of the Lord of all the worlds, sent down through the Faithful Spirit to your heart so that you may be among the warners speaking a clear Arabic tongue and it is indeed in the revealed book of the former Prophets" (26:196).*

But the liars, deceivers and the forgers are not satisfied until they attribute false, nonsensical and legendary things to him which no sane mind or intellect can accept. It is the right of the Muslim researchers to dissociate the Prophet of Allah (s) from such false traditions which fill the *hadith* books, especially those counted amongst the "*Sahihs*".

We have not transmitted [anything] except from the books of al-Bukhari and Muslim which are seen by the *Ahl al-Sunnah* as the most reliable books after the book of Allah. If this is the status of the *Sahihs*, specifically the blemish on the sanctity and infallibility of the Prophet (s), then do not even ask about the other books. All these are [due to the] interpolations of the enemies of Allah; the enemies of His Apostle (s) who sought to flatter the Umayyad rulers during the time of Mu'awiyah and those who succeeded him, until they filled volumes and volumes with spurious *hadiths* through which they desired the denigration of the bearer of the message (s); for they did not believe in everything that he brought from Allah. This is one perspective. The other perspective was to justify the vile and disgraceful deeds of their leaders which Muslim history has recorded. The Prophet of Allah (s) had exposed them from the beginning of his mission, and warned against them, exiling them from Medina, and had cursed them. In his history, al-Tabari says: "The Prophet (s) saw Abu Sufyan was approaching on a donkey, with Mu'awiyah leading him, and Yazid, his son, herding it. He said: "May Allah curse the leader, the rider and the driver."[5] Imam Ahmad in his *Musnad*, on the authority of Ibn 'Abbas, said: "We were on a journey with the Prophet of Allah (s) when he heard two men singing, one of them responding to the other. Whereupon the Prophet (s) said: 'See who they are.' The people said: 'Mu'awiyah and 'Amr b. al-'As'. The Prophet of Allah raised his hands and said: 'O Allah! Debase them and confine them into the fire.'"[6] And from

---

[5] *Tarikh Tabari*, 11/357.

[6] *Musnad*, al-Imam Ahmad, 4/421.

Chapter 7: Concerning the Noble Hadith

Abu Dharr al-Ghifari, who said to Mu'awiyah: "I heard the Prophet of Allah say when you passed by him: 'O Allah! Curse him and make his stomach full of nothing but dust!'"[7] Imam 'Ali (as) said in a letter that he sent to the people of Iraq:

"By Allah! Were I to meet them alone, and they filled the earth, I would not be scared of them. I am sure of their going astray due to what they indulge in; the guided path that we are in is reliable, clear, certain and insightful. I am eager to meet my Lord and am waiting for His bounteous reward. Yet sorrow overtakes me and grief overwhelms me; the matter of this *ummah* will be taken away by the fools and corrupt ones; they will treat the property of Allah as their personal property and the servants of Allah as their slaves; they will fight the upright ones and will make those who have deviated members of their groups."[8]

Since the Prophet of Allah (s) cursed them as you have seen, and they did not find the *hadith* to be distorted since the prominent companions recognized it, they invented other traditions to change truth to falsehood, and to make the Prophet of Allah (s) seem an ordinary person beset by the zeal of the period of *jahiliyya*, subject to severe anger, defaming and cursing those not deserving it. To defend their accursed leaders, they fabricated this *hadith*.

Al-Bukhari reported in his *Sahih* in "The Book of Supplications," in "The Chapter of The Prophet's (s) saying: 'Whoever I have wronged, make it a charity and a blessing for him.'" Muslim also recorded in his *Sahih* under "The Book of Kindness, Kinship and Good Manners," in "The Chapter of Whoever the Prophet (s) Cursed or Insulted or Prayed against, He did not Deserve it, it was made as a Charity, Reward and a Mercy For Him": "From 'A'isha who said: 'Two men called upon the Prophet of Allah (s) and spoke to him about something which I do not know. They angered him and he cursed and insulted them. When they left, I said: 'O Prophet of Allah! Whatever good comes, these two will not receive it.' He said: 'How so?' I said: 'You cursed and insulted them.' He said:

---

[7] *Musnad*, al-Imam Ahmad, 4/421, *Lisan al-'Arab*, 7/404.

[8] Ibn Qutayba, *Al-Imama wa al-Siyasa*, 1/137.

'Don't you know what I have requested from my Lord when I said 'O Allah! I am just a man, so any Muslim that I curse or insult, make it a charity and reward for him.'"

On the authority of Abu Hurayrah, the Prophet (s) said: "O Allah! I have taken a covenant with You which you will never break. For I am only a man so any believer whom I wrong, insult, curse or whip, cause that to be a prayer and a charity for him through which he gets closer to you on the day of resurrection."

Due to such false traditions, the Prophet becomes angry for other than Allah's sake. He insults and abuses. Moreover, he curses and whips one who does not deserve it. What kind of Prophet is this who is so overcome by Satan that he goes beyond the sphere of reason? Is it permitted for an ordinary religious person to behave thus? Or is such a deed by him not detestable? Due to such *hadiths*, the Umayyad rulers, who the Prophet of Allah cursed, supplicated against and whipped a few of them for the vile deeds they committed and exposed them in front of the general populace, came to be [seen as] the oppressed ones! Rather, they became chaste and deprived ones, attaining closeness to Allah.

These spurious narrations are self revealing and disgrace the fabricators. The Prophet of Allah (s) was not an insulter, nor a curser, nor a corrupt person, nor one using obscene language. Allah forbid! Allah forbid! Grave indeed are the words that emerge from their mouths that cause Allah to be angry with them, curse them and prepare for them a painful chastisement!

One narration, which both al-Bukhari and Muslim narrated from 'A'isha, is sufficient for us to refute these false allegations. Al-Bukhari reported in his *Sahih* in "The Book of Etiquettes" in "The Chapter of the Prophet (s) did not commit Vile Deeds or use Foul Language" on the authority of 'A'isha who said: "Some Jews came to the Prophet (s) and said: 'Assaamu 'alaykum! (Death unto you).'" 'A'isha said: "I said: 'And unto you, and May Allah curse and be angry with you.'The Prophet (s) said: 'Go easy O 'A'isha! Be friendly, do not be harsh nor of vile deeds.' I said: 'Did you not hear what they said?' He said: 'Did you not hear what I said? I responded

Chapter 7: Concerning the Noble Hadith

to them and my invocation against them was answered, and their invocation against me went unanswered.'"

Muslim also reported in his *Sahih* in "The Book of Kindness, Kinship and Etiquettes" that the Prophet of Allah (s) prohibited Muslims from cursing. He even prohibited Muslims from cursing beasts and cattle. When it was said to him: "O Prophet, curse the polytheists!" He said: "I have not been sent as a curser, I have been sent as a mercy."

This is what is in concordance with the supreme character and gentle heart that were the special [traits] of the Prophet of Allah (s). He would not curse, abuse or whip those who did not deserve [such treatment]. When he got angry, he did so for Allah's sake; if he cursed, he did so upon one who deserved it; and if he ordered whipping, he did so in order to carry out the penalties [prescribed] by Allah; he did not whip the innocent ones against whom there was no clear proof, or witnesses, or confessions.

They dwindled and their hearts burnt due to the dissemination of narrations which contained curses on Mu'awiyah and the Umayyads. They invented these false traditions to confuse the people and to elevate the status of Mu'awiyah, the forger. As a result, you find that Muslim, in his *Sahih*, after reporting these *hadiths* which make the imprecations of the Prophet on Mu'awiyah a charity, mercy and [a medium for] attaining closeness to Allah, reports a *hadith* from Ibn 'Abbas who says: "I was playing with the boys when the Prophet of Allah (s) came, and I hid behind a door. He came and got me and said: 'Go and call Mu'awiyah for me.' He said: 'I went and said: 'He is eating'". He (Ibn 'Abbas) said: "He then said to me: 'Go and call Mu'awiyah for me.' I went and said: 'He is eating'. He said: 'May Allah not satiate his stomach.'"[9]

We find in the history books that, Imam al-Nasa'i, after writing a book of traits which were special to the Commander of the Faithful, 'Ali b. Abi Talib (as), came to Syria. The people of Syria rebuked and asked him as to why he did not record the excellences of

---

[9] *Sahih Muslim*, 8/27.

Mu'awiyah. He replied: "I do not know of any virtue of him except that Allah does not satiate his stomach." Whereupon they beat him around his private parts until he was martyred. Historians relate that the prayer of the Prophet (s) was effective, for Mu'awiyah used to eat and eat until he would get tired of eating, yet he was not full.

In fact, I was not aware of these narrations which made the curse a blessing and [form of] nearness to Allah, until one of the Shaykhs in Tunis informed me about it. He was reputed for his knowledge and erudition and we were in a gathering engaged in a conversation about *hadith* until the issue of Mu'awiyah b. Abi Sufyan came up. The Shaykh had been speaking of him in profound awe, saying that he was intelligent and famous for his sagacity and astuteness in managing affairs. He started to speak about him and his politics and his victory over our master 'Ali (May Allah brighten his face) in war. I held my patience with anguish but he went to such an extent in his praise and adoration of Mu'awiyah until I could no longer bear it. So I said to him that the Prophet of Allah (s) did not like him and had actually supplicated against him and cursed him. Those who were present were astonished, and there were those who were angered at what I had said. But the Shaykh, with complete tranquility, replied that he believed me, which increased the astonishment of those present. They said to him: "We do not understand anything. On the one hand you praise him and are pleased with him and, on the other hand, you agree that the Prophet cursed him. How can this be correct?" And I too, with them, asked how could this be correct?

The Shaykh responded to us with an answer which was perplexing and difficult to accept. He said: "Whoever the Prophet of Allah has cursed or insulted, it is for him a charity and a blessing, and [a means of] getting closer to Allah, Glory be to Him." Everyone asked in bewilderment: "How is this [possible]?" He replied: "Because the Prophet of Allah (s) said: 'I am a mere mortal like the rest of mankind and I have asked Allah to make my supplications and curses a blessing and a charity'". Then he added saying: "Even he who the Prophet of Allah (s) kills, he goes from this world directly to heaven!"

Chapter 7: Concerning the Noble Hadith

I approached him alone afterwards and questioned him about the source of the *hadith* he had mentioned. He produced *Sahih al-Bukhari* and *Sahih Muslim* and I studied those *hadiths* which only increased my certainty regarding the plots which the Umayyads perpetrated to cover up the realities and to hide their disgraces on the one hand, and to destroy the infallibility of the Prophet (s) on the other.

Subsequently, I found several narrations leading to the same goal. To be appeased, the plotters fabricated even more than that, attributing [them] to the Lord of all the worlds. Al-Bukhari has related in his *Sahih*, in "The book of *Tawhid*" in the Chapter of Allah's saying: "They wish to change Allah's words," from Abu Hurayrah that the Prophet of Allah (s) said: "A man who never did any good deed said that if he died they should burn him and throw half [the ashes] in the earth and the other half in the sea, for, by Allah, if Allah should get hold of him, He would inflict such punishment on him as He would not inflict on anybody else in the world. But Allah ordered the sea to collect what was in it (of his ashes) and similarly ordered the earth to collect what was in it (of his ashes). Then Allah said to him: 'Why did you do so?' The man replied: 'I was afraid of You, and You know it better.' So Allah forgave him."

From Abu Hurayrah also on the same page: "I heard the Prophet saying: 'If somebody commits a sin and then says: 'O my Lord! I have sinned, please forgive me' and his Lord says: 'My slave has known that he has a Lord who forgives sins and punishes for it, I therefore have forgiven my slave (his sins).' Then he remains without committing any sin for a while and then again commits another sin and says: 'O my Lord, I have committed another sin, please forgive me' and Allah says: 'My slave has known that he has a Lord who forgives sins and punishes for it, I therefore have forgiven my slave.' Then he remains without committing any another sin for a while and then commits another sin and says: 'O my Lord, I have committed another sin, please forgive me' and Allah says: 'My slave has known that he has a Lord Who forgives sins and punishes for it. I therefore have forgiven my slave (his sin), he can do whatever he likes.'"

What kind of Lord is this, O servants of Allah? From the first instance, the servant knew that he had a Lord who forgives sins, even though his Lord was not aware of this fact, so that on every occasion he had to ask: "Does my servant know that he has a Lord who forgives sin?"

What kind of Lord is this who, because the repeated perpetration of sins and repeated forgiveness, becomes tired and exhausted and says to his servant: "Do as you wish. Give me rest, Allah will leave you alone."

"Grave indeed are the words that come out of their mouths. They utter not except falsehood, perchance you may kill yourself in their trail, they will still not believe in this speech." Yes, Indeed! They allege that the Prophet of Allah (s) said to 'Uthman: "Do as you wish, for nothing of what you do will harm you after today." This was when 'Uthman helped substantially in preparing the army which was going to Tabuk. According to what they say, it absolved the sins that the monks used to give in exchange for an entry to heaven.

It was not surprising therefore when 'Uthman did those vile deeds that resulted in the uprising against him and his being killed and buried in a non-Muslim graveyard without being washed or [covered with] a shroud. That is their protection [against punishment]. Say: "Bring your proof if you are indeed truthful."

The Prophet contradicts himself in his hadith

In "The Book of Discord", in "The Chapter If Two Muslims meet with their Swords", in vol. 8, p. 92, al-Bukhari recorded in his *Sahih* from 'Abd Allah b. 'Abd al-Wahhab who said: "Hammad informed us on the authority of a man he did not name, that al-Hasan said: 'I went out with my weapons during the nights of sedition, and Abu Bakra met me saying: 'Where are you going?' I replied: 'I wish to assist the cousin of the Prophet of Allah (s).' He said: 'The Prophet of Allah (s) said: 'If two Muslims show up against each other with their swords, both of them are the

Chapter 7: Concerning the Noble Hadith

inhabitants of fire.' It was said: 'This is the killer but how about the one killed?' He replied: 'He wanted to kill his companion.'"

Hammad b. Zayd said: "I mentioned this *hadith* to Ayub and Yunus b. 'Ubayd, for I wanted them to inform me about it. They said: 'Al-Hasan related this *hadith* from al-Ahnaf b. Qays from Abu Bakra.'"

Similarly, Muslim has reported in his *Sahih,* in "The Book of Discord and Signs of the Hour." in "The Chapter if Two Muslims meet each other with their Swords," from the *hadith* of Abu Bakra from al-Ahnaf b. Qays, who said: "I went to assist this man, and Abu Bakra met me and said: 'Where are you going?' I said: 'I am going to help this man.' He said: 'Go back. For I heard the Prophet of Allah say: 'If two Muslims meet with their swords [in combat], the killer and the killed are in the fire.' I said: 'O Prophet of Allah! This [is] the killer, how about the one killed? He said: 'He was intent upon killing his companion.'"[10]

From these false narrations, the reader can clearly understand the reasons for forging them; it indicates Abu Bakra's enmity towards the cousin of al-Mustafa and how he worked towards abandoning the Commander of the Faithful. He was not satisfied with that, however; he even prevented the eminent companions who wanted to aid the truth against falsehood, and so fabricated such *hadiths* which reason cannot accept and which neither the Qur'an nor the true Prophetic *Sunnah* acknowledge. For Allah's words, Glory be to Him, the Most Exalted: *"So fight the party that rebels until it complies with the order of Allah"* **(49:9)** clearly commands to fight rebels and oppressors. As a result, you observe that the commentator of al-Bukhari wrote in the side notes of the *hadith* the following: "Examine this *hadith*, is there any proof for fighting the rebels as per Allah's directive: *"So fight the party that rebels..."* And if a *hadith* contradicts the book of Allah, then it is a lie and is to be discarded." As for the true Prophetic *Sunnah* his words

---

[10] *Al-Bukhari* also reported this *hadith* in "The Book of Faith" in "The Chapter of Disobedience is from the Period of Ignorance".

regarding 'Ali are: "Of whomsoever I am the master, 'Ali is also his master. My Lord! Befriend those who befriend him and oppose those who oppose him and help those who help him. Forsake those who forsake him and let the truth be with him wherever he goes." For friendship of 'Ali is friendship of the Prophet of Allah (s). And helping the Commander of the Faithful is obligatory upon every Muslim and forsaking him is forsaking the truth and is [equivalent to] supporting falsehood.

If you reflect upon the *hadith* of al-Bukhari you will find in the chain of narrators an unknown person whose name he did not mention as he said: "Hammad informed us on the authority of a man he did not name..." This clearly proves that this unknown man was from the hypocrites who hated 'Ali and exerted themselves to erase 'Ali's excellences or, to be exact, to kill him and his memory as much as they were able to. Sa'd b. Abi Waqqas, who also desisted from helping the truth, said: "Come to me with a sword saying this one is on the truth and that one is on falsehood so that I may fight him..." Due to such adulteration, truth is confused with falsehood and the clear path lost, it is replaced with darkness.

We find too in the reliable books of the *Sunnah,* that the Apostle of Allah (s) gave the good tidings of heaven to a lot of his companions especially the ten who became famous among the Muslims as having been assured of paradise.

Ahmad, al-Tirmidhi and Abu Dawud reported that the Prophet (s) said: "Abu Bakr is in heaven, 'Umar is in heaven, 'Uthman is in heaven, 'Ali is in heaven, Talha is in heaven, al-Zubayr is in heaven, 'Abd al-Rahman b. 'Awf is in heaven, Sa'd b. Abi Waqqas is in heaven, Sa'id b. Zayd is in heaven and Abu 'Ubayda b. al-Jarrah is in heaven."[11]

It has been authenticated from the Prophet (s) that he said: "Give good tidings to the family of Yasir for your place is in heaven. And his words: "Heaven yearns for four: 'Ali and 'Ammar, Salman and

---

[11] *Musnad* of Ahmad 1/193, *Sahih al-Tirmidhi* 13/183, *Sunan,* Abu Dawud, 2/264.

Chapter 7: Concerning the Noble Hadith

al-Miqdad." Muslim reported in his *Sahih* that 'Abd Allah b. Salam was given the glad tidings of heaven by the Prophet of Allah and it has been verified that he said: "Al-Hasan and al-Husayn are the two leaders of the youths of paradise."It was verified from him also that Ja'far b. Abi Talib flies with the angels in paradise. And that Fatima al-Zahra (sa) is the leader of the women of paradise and that her mother Khadija was told by Gabriel of a house of gold and silver embroidery in paradise. It was also authenticated that he said: "Suhayb, the foremost of the Romans is in paradise, and Bilal, the foremost of the Ethiopians, is in paradise, and Salman, the foremost of the Persians, is in paradise."

This being the case, why is the *hadith* of the good tidings of paradise restricted to only these ten? You do not find a gathering or an assembly when they discuss heaven, then they mention the ten [who were] given the good tidings of paradise.

We do not envy them in this, nor do we not restrict the wide mercy of Allah which encompasses everything, but we only say that these *hadiths* are at variance and conflict with the *hadith* which says: "If two Muslims meet each other with their swords in combat, then the killer and the one killed are in fire." For if we believe this, then the *hadith* of the ten given the tidings of heaven evaporates since most of them waged war, fought against and killed each other. Talha and Zubayr were killed at the battle of the Camel which was led by the mother of the believers 'A'isha against Imam 'Ali b. Abi Talib. Their swords were raised in combat; indeed, they caused the death of thousands of Muslims.

Similarly, 'Ammar b. Yasir was killed at the battle of Siffin, the flames of which were started by Mu'awiyah b. Abi Sufyan. 'Ammar was present with his sword with 'Ali b. Abi Talib; the rebellious forces slew him. The Prophet of Allah (s) prophesied this. Similarly, the leader of the martyrs, the leader of the youths of Paradise, Imam al-Husayn and the family of al-Mustafa were present with their swords in combat against the army of Yazid b. Mu'awiyah. They killed all of them; no one survived among them except 'Ali b. al-Husayn.

According to the view of these liars then, all of these are in the fire, the killers and those who were killed for they met [in combat] with their swords.

Obviously, it is incorrect to attribute the *hadith* to one who does not utter anything from his own desire but rather, [from] the revelation sent unto him. It is also, as we have previously pointed out, in conflict with logic and reason and contradicts the book of Allah and the *Sunnah* of His Prophet (s). The question that arises here is: "How could al-Bukhari and Muslim be so negligent of such lies and not be aware of them? Or did their school of thought believe in such narrations?"

Contradictions regarding virtues

Among the contradictory *hadiths* that you find in the "*Sahihs*" are those regarding the superiority of the Prophet of Allah (s) over all the Prophets and Apostles, and other traditions which elevate Moses to a level higher than him. I believe that the Jews, who converted during the times of 'Umar and 'Uthman like Ka'b al-Ahbar, Tamim al-Dari, and Wahb b. Munabbih, are the ones who fabricated those *hadiths*, attributing them to some companions who used to admire them such as Abu Hurayrah, Anas b. Malik and others. Al-Bukhari narrated in his *Sahih* in "The Book of *Tawhid*" in "The Chapter on Allah's words! 'And Allah spoke to Moses.'"

From Anas b. Malik, a long tale regarding the nocturnal journey (*isra'*) of the Prophet (s), then his ascent to the seven heavens, then to the remote tree (*al-sidrat al-muntaha*); and the story of the fifty obligatory prayers which were enjoined upon Muhammad and his *ummah,* and which, by the grace of Moses, were reduced to five applied [prayers]. In this [story] are clear lies and basest disbelief, like the all-Conquering Lord of Power drew close until He was two bow lengths or less away from the Prophet, and other fables. However, what is of importance to us here in this narration is that when Muhammad reached the seventh heaven, Moses, who had been elevated to the seventh [heaven] because of Allah's speaking to him, was there. Moses said: "My Lord! I did not think that anyone would be raised higher than me." Muslim reported in "The

Chapter 7: Concerning the Noble Hadith

Book of Faith," in "The Chapter On the Beginning of Revelation to the Prophet of Allah (s)," and al-Bukhari in his *Sahih* in "The Book of the Beginning of Creation," in "The Chapter of Accounts of the Angels" (peace be upon them), another anecdote which resembles the first; speaking of the nocturnal journey and ascension but states instead that Moses was in the sixth heaven, and Abraham in the seventh. What concerns us is the following section:

The Prophet of Allah (s) said: "We came to the sixth heaven. It was asked: 'Who is this?' It was said: 'Gabriel'. It was said: 'Who is with you?' He said: 'Muhammad (s).' It was said: 'Has revelation descended upon him?' He answered: 'Yes.' It was then said: 'Welcome to him! What a wonderful [person] has come!' I went to Moses and greeted him and he said: 'Welcome to my brother and Prophet.' When I went on, he wept. It was said: 'What has made you weep?' He said: 'O Lord! The followers of this youth who was sent after me will enter paradise in greater numbers than my followers.'"

Muslim reported in his *Sahih*, in "The Book of Faith" in "The Chapter [entitled] 'In the lowest of Paradise will be a House in It,'" from Abu Hurayrah, who said: "The Prophet of Allah (s) said: 'I am the leader of all mankind on the day of judgment, and do you know how that is? Those who came before and those who came after will be gathered in one area known as "al-Da'i". Their sight will be restored to them, then the Sun will descend and the men will encounter such sorrow and affliction that they will not be able to withstand it. The people will then say: 'Don't you see what has befallen you? Shall you not seek someone who will intercede for you with your Lord?' Whereupon some will say to the others: 'Go to Adam.' So they will go to Adam (as) and they will say to him: 'You are the father of mankind, Allah created you with His Hands and breathed His Spirit into you, and ordered the angels to prostrate before you. Intercede for us with your Lord. Don't you see our condition? Don't you see what has befallen us?' Whereupon Adam will say: 'Today my Lord got angry to a degree that He has never got before. After this day, He will never be so angered again. He prohibited me from the tree and I disobeyed Him. (I am) on my own! On my own! On my own! Go to someone else. Go to Noah.'"

The narration continues and it is very long (we always wish [to cite] a brief account). It goes on to state that the people go to Noah, then Abraham, then Moses then Jesus, and each of them said: "On my own! On my own! On my own!" Each relates his error or his sin, with the exception of Jesus who does not mention a sin but nonetheless says: "On my own! On my own! On my own! Go to someone else! Go to Muhammad!" The Prophet of Allah said: "So they come to me.

So I go forth and go under the throne, and fall in prostration before my Lord the Powerful and the Glorious, then Allah allows for me, out of his praises and beauty of adoration, something He had never allowed for anyone before me. Then it will be said: 'O Muhammad! Raise your head! Ask and you shall be given. Intervene and your intercession will prevail!' So I raise my head and I say: 'My *ummah* O Lord, My *ummah*, O Lord!' Then Allah will say: 'O Muhammad! I allow entry from your *ummah* those who have no reckoning upon them through the right gate of paradise. And they are to share with the others in the other gates besides this one.'" Then he said: "By He in whose hand is my soul! Indeed, what is between the levels of paradise is like what is between Mecca and Humayr or what is between Mecca and Basra."

In these *hadiths*, the Prophet of Allah (s) says that he is the leader of mankind on the Day of Judgment. And he says that Moses said: "O my Lord! I did not think that anyone would be elevated above me." And he says that Moses wept and said: "O Lord! The followers of this youth who was sent after me will enter paradise in greater numbers than my followers."

We adduce from these *hadiths* that all the Prophets and Apostles from Adam even Jesus through Noah and Abraham and Moses (upon them and upon our Prophet be the choicest of blessing and the purest of greetings) will not seek intercession with Allah on the day of reckoning, instead, Allah will restrict it to Muhammad (s) only. We believe in all of that and we attest too to his superiority (s)

Chapter 7: Concerning the Noble Hadith

over the rest of mankind. However, the "*Israiliyyun*"[12] and their helpers amongst the Umayyads could not tolerate this preference and superiority of Muhammad (s) and so they fabricated traditions on the superiority of Moses over him. We have already seen in a preceding discussion the words of Moses to Muhammad on the night of the nocturnal journey and *mi'raj* that when Allah enjoined upon Muhammad fifty prayers, Moses said to him: "I know the people more than you." This, though, was not sufficient so they invented other narrations speaking of his superiority, i.e., Moses over Muhammad by Muhammad himself. Following are some of these narrations:

Al-Bukhari reported in his *Sahih* in "The Book of *Tawhid*," in "The Chapter of Allah's Wish and Will and You do not Wish Anything except If Allah Wills it," from Abu Hurayrah, who said: "A Muslim man and a Jew quarreled, and the Muslim said: 'By Him who chose Muhammad over the universe' in an oath he took, whereupon the Jew said: 'By Him who chose Moses over the universe.' Upon this, the Muslim raised his hand and slapped the Jew. The Jew then went to the Prophet of Allah (s) and informed him of what had transpired between him and the Muslim. The Prophet (s) said: 'Do not give me preference over Moses for the people will be unconscious on the Day of Judgment, and I will be the first to recover. There will be Moses falling upon the side of the throne. I will not know whether he was among those who lost consciousness and recovered before I did, or if he was among those exempted by Allah.'"

In another narration of al-Bukhari, he said: "A Jew who had been slapped on the face came to the Prophet and said: 'O Muhammad! An Ansari companion of yours slapped me on my face.' The Prophet said: 'Call him.' So he called him. The Prophet said: 'Why did you slap his face?' The man said: 'O Prophet of Allah. I passed by the Jew and I heard him say: 'By him who chose Moses above all mankind.' I said: 'Over Muhammad?' So I became angry and I slapped him.

---

[12] i.e. those who had converted and spread the *"Isra'iliyyat"* (Jewish legends).

The Prophet said: 'Do not give me preference over the Prophets for the people will lose consciousness on the Day of Judgment and I will be the first to recover and I will be with Moses holding on to one of the pillars of the throne and I shall not know whether he recovered before me or if he was being compensated for his unconsciousness in the mountain.'"

Similarly, al-Bukhari has reported in "The Book of *Tafsir* of the Qur'an for *Surah* Yusuf (as)" in "The Chapter of His words: 'And when the Prophet came to him...'" from Abu Hurayrah, who said: "The Prophet of Allah said: 'May Allah bestow His Mercy on (Prophet) Lot. He wished he could have some powerful support; and if I were to remain in prison for the period Joseph had remained, I would surely respond to the call; and we have more right (to be in doubt) than Abraham. When Allah said to him: 'Don't you believe?' Abraham said: 'Yes, (I do believe) but [I ask] to be stronger in faith.'"

All these statements were not enough for them until they made the Prophet of Allah (s) doubt even his standing with his Lord. He had no [powers of] intercession, no praiseworthy position, and no preference over the Messengers and Apostles and no good tidings of Paradise for his companions, since he himself did not know his fate on the Day of Judgment. Read along with me this narration of al-Bukhari and think what you will of it.

Al-Bukhari reported in his *Sahih* in "The Chapter of The Funeral," in "The Book of Eclipses," in vol. 2, p. 71, from "Kharija b. Zayd b. Thabit, that Umm al-'Ala, a woman of the Ansar, pledged fealty to the Prophet (s) and told him that the Muhajirin cast lots (by throwing dice), and it fell on 'Uthman b. Maz'un, so we took him in our household. He became sick, an illness which caused his death. When he died and was bathed and shrouded in his clothes, the Prophet of Allah (s) came in and I said: 'May Allah have mercy upon you, O Abu al-Sa'ib for I bear witness that Allah has honored you.' The Prophet (s) said: 'How do you know that Allah has honored him?' I said: 'May my father be sacrificed, O Prophet of Allah, who then has Allah honored?' Whereupon he (as) said: 'As for him, death has come to him, and, by Allah, I wish him well. By Allah! I do not know what will be done to me, I, the Prophet of Allah.' I said: 'By Allah! Never will I ascribe purity to anyone after this.'"

This, by Allah, is an astonishing thing. If the Prophet of Allah swore by Allah that he does not know what will be done to him, what remains after this?

And if Allah, Glory be to Him, says: *"Every person is aware of his [own] self."* And if He has also said to His Prophet: *"We have bestowed upon you a clear victory! For Allah has forgiven your past sins and what may be done in the future to fulfill His blessing upon you and to guide you to a straight path and to aid you most honorably"* (48:1); and if the Muslims' entry into paradise depends upon following, obeying and believing him, how can we believe this *hadith* of which there is nothing more evil than it? We seek Allah's refuge from the creed of the Banu Umayyads who did not believe for even a day that Muhammad was truly the Prophet of Allah, but instead, used to believe that he was a king, having overcome the people by his intelligence and sagacity. This is what Abu Sufyan, Mu'awiyah, Yazid and other Caliphs and rulers of theirs have clearly said.

The Prophet contradicts science and medicine

Science has established by indubitable proofs that certain diseases are transmitted by infection. This is known to most people, even to those who are uneducated. However, if one were to say to university medical students that the Prophet of Allah (s) denied this, they would deride him and would find a point to defame the Prophet of Islam especially the German professors who are looking for such openings. Most unfortunately, the *hadith* that al-Bukhari and Muslim have reported support [the claim] against infection; yet in their books are others that support [claims for] infection. When we record these contradictions, under the heading "The Prophet Contradicts" we do not believe that he (s) contradicted himself even once in his words or deeds, but rather, [this is done] in accordance with normal practice and to attract the heart of the reader so that he might pay attention to the *hadiths* that were fabricated to disparage and defame the infallible bearer of the message. [This is also done] so that he might know that our goal in relating such *hadiths* is to exonerate the Prophet and to give him his [rightful] place in education which he precedes every modern scientist, for there is no true scientific theory which contradicts an authentic *hadith* of the Prophet. If they conflict or contradict, we know on the one hand that the *hadith* is falsely attributed to him (s) and, on the other hand, the *hadith* itself may be contradicted by other *hadith* which support the scientific theory. As is obvious, it would be necessary to accept the second *hadith* and discard the first one.

To cite an example, I shall use the *hadith* regarding infection. For it is important to the discussion and gives us a true picture of the disharmony amongst the companions, the narrators and the forgers. [It does not imply] contradiction in the bearer of the message (s), that is never possible.

Al-Bukhari related the two *hadiths* in his *Sahih*. I shall limit myself to his book, as it is regarded by the *Ahl al-Sunnah* as the most authentic book; also so that those interpreting from different schools should not say al-Bukhari thinks a *hadith* is authentic whilst another scholar (in another book) thinks the opposite [of the same *hadith*]. So the reader should note that in this chapter, I am restricting myself to al-Bukhari alone in the conflicting *hadiths*.

In "The Book of Medicine," in "The Chapter of no *Hama*," al-Bukhari in his *Sahih*, said that Abu Hurayrah reported: "The Prophet (s) said: 'There is no infection, nor *safar*, nor *hama*.'[13] A Bedouin stood up and said: 'Then what about my camels? They are like deer on the sand, but when a camel afflicted with scab comes and mixes with them, they all get infected with scab'. The Prophet said: 'Then who conveyed the disease to the first one?'"

Observe this Bedouin, how he is guided by his instinct to the nature of sickness of infection of all camels by a mangy camel

---

[13] A type of bird which preys at night.

Chapter 7: Concerning the Noble Hadith 317

when they mix. But the Prophet does not find a convincing answer to the Bedouin's question and instead says: "And who infected the first?" Thus he becomes the questioner.

This reminds me of the doctor who asked a mother who had brought her child suffering from measles. "Is there anyone at home or a neighbor who has this disease?" The mother replied: "No way." The doctor said: "Perhaps he caught it in school." The mother replied promptly: "Most certainly not. He has not yet entered school for he is not yet five." The doctor said: "In kindergarten therefore." The mother said: "No. He does not go to kindergarten." The doctor said: "Perhaps you took him to visit to your relatives or some relatives visited you who were carrying the germs." The mother denied this. At that, the doctor said to her: "Then the germs came through the air."

Certainly, the air carries the germs and infectious diseases, a whole village or entire city can be affected. For this reason, we have inoculations and prevention [shots], for the wind can carry deadly diseases such as epidemics and plague and others. How can this be not known to one who does not say anything of his desire? He is the Prophet of the Lord of the worlds. He from whom nothing is hidden, nothing in the heavens or the earth can be concealed, He who is the all hearing, the all knowing. Therefore, we reject this *hadith* and can never accept it. We instead accept the second *hadith* which al-Bukhari himself reported on the same page, the same chapter. And in the same *hadith* he says: "Abu Salama heard Abu Hurayrah say afterwards: 'The Prophet (s) said: 'Do not expose a sick person to a healthy one.' Abu Hurayrah denied the first *hadith*. We said: 'Did you not say there is no infection?' He spoke unintelligibly in Ethiopian. Abu Salama said: 'I have not seen him forgetting any other *hadith*."

The two *hadiths* are contradictory (no infection, do not expose a sick person to a healthy one). Muslim also reported them in his *Sahih* in "The Book of Peace," in "The Chapter of no Infection, no Evil Omen, no *Hama* no *Safar* no Star promising Rain, no *Ghoul* and the sick person should not be exposed to a healthy one."

From an examination of these *hadiths*, we know that the *hadith*: "Do not expose a sick person to a healthy one" is the true narration which the Prophet of Allah (s) said for it does not contradict science. As for the *hadith* of no infection, it is falsely attributed to him, for it is a saying of one who is ignorant of the natural facts. As a result, some of the companions understood that the two *hadiths* contradicted each other and opposed Abu Hurayrah, astonished at the first *hadith*. Abu Hurayrah found no escape from this predicament and exclaimed in Ethiopian. The commentator of al-Bukhari said: "He said in anger something which was not understood."

What increases our certainty that the Prophet of Allah (s) preceded what modern science has established, especially in infectious diseases, is that he used to warn the Muslims of plagues, leprosy and epidemics, etc.

As al-Bukhari has reported in his *Sahih* in "The Book of The Prophets", the chapter entitled: "Abu al-Yaman informed us..." and Muslim in his *Sahih* in "The Book of Peace" in "The Chapter on Plagues, ill omen and magic." From Usama b. Zayd who said the Prophet of Allah (s) said: "The plague is a calamity which was inflicted on a tribe of Banu Isra'il, or to those before you. So if you hear of it in a land, do not approach it; and if it afflicts a land in which you are, do not flee from there." In another narration: "Do not leave except to flee from it."

A *hadith* has been verified from him (s) in this meaning: "Flee from leprosy the way you would flee from a lion" and his saying: "If you drink, do not breathe in the utensil." And his saying: "If the dog licks your utensil, wash it seven times, once with earth." All of this [he said] so that he could teach his *ummah* cleanliness and health and prevention. He did not say to them: "If a fly falls in the drink of any one of you, immerse it completely." We have mentioned this *hadith* before for those who wish to refer to it.

We find clear contradictions, even in that which is specific to *al-hama*, which the Arabs used to regard as an evil omen. It is a famous bird flying at night. It is said it was an owl; this is the

Chapter 7: Concerning the Noble Hadith

explanation of Malik b. Anas. If the Prophet (s) said: "There is no *al-hama*," how could he then contradict himself and seek protection from it?

Al-Bukhari reported in his *Sahih* in "The Book of The Beginning of Creation," in "The Chapter of those who Walk in Haste" in vol. 4, p. 119, from Sa'id b. Jubayr from Ibn 'Abbas (r), who said: "The Prophet (s) used to seek refuge for al-Hasan and al-Husayn and would say: 'Your father used to seek refuge from it for Isma'il and Isaac. I seek refuge in Allah's complete words from every Satan, a *hama* and an evil eye.'"

In this chapter, we wanted to relate some examples of contradictory *hadiths* which were attributed to the Prophet of Allah (s) although he is innocent [of these].

There are hundreds of other conflicting *hadith* which al-Bukhari and Muslim have related in their two collections. We have devoted [special] pages for them as we have habituated the reader to present things concisely and with indicators. It is up to the researcher to study so Allah may purify through them the *Sunnah* of His Prophet (s) and reward them generously and become the means by which the truth is made manifest from falsehood. They can perhaps give to the new generation valuable dissertations that are an integral part of the message of Islam.

"O You who believe, do not be like those who harassed Moses. Verily Allah cleaned him of what they uttered against him; he was honored in the sight of Allah. O you who believe, fear Allah and be righteous of speech so that He may set your deeds right and forgive your sins. Whoever, obeys Allah and His Prophet has obtained the ultimate success" (33:71).

Chapter Eight

Concerning the two *Sahihs* of al-Bukhari and Muslim

These two collections are of such paramount importance to the *Ahl al-Sunnah wa'l-Jama'a* that they have become, for Muslims in general, the two principal references and primary sources in every religious research work. It has become difficult for some to report the absurd [traditions], contradictions and objectionable [things] they discover, so they accept them reluctantly. They do not reveal them to their people, either out of fear of them or fear for them. In their souls is instilled respect and veneration of these two books, when, in fact, al-Bukhari and Muslim never dreamt even for a day that they would get the veneration from the scholars or the general public.

If we begin to criticize and relate some refutations against them, this is only done so as to exonerate our Prophet (s) and to remove any scar on his infallibility. If some companions are not spared from this criticism and refutation and become targets of it, then surely al-Bukhari and Muslim are not better than those who were close to the bearer of the message.

Our goal is only the exoneration of the Arab Prophet (s) and to try our utmost to establish his infallibility and that he was the most knowledgeable and pious of all men. We believe that Allah, Glory be to Him, chose him to be a mercy for all the worlds and sent him to both mankind and the *jinn*. There is no doubt that Allah requires of us that we exonerate His Prophet [from any untruth], that we sanctify him, and that we do not tolerate abuses against him. As a result of this, we and every Muslim are obligated to refute anything opposing the exalted character which was his particular trait, and to disprove anything which contradicts his infallibility or his noble personality, regardless of whether that is from near or distant. The companions, the successors, the Imams, the *hadith* scholars, every Muslim, in fact all of mankind profess his superiority and outstanding qualities.

Those who criticize him oppose or those who are prejudiced will, as usual, be enraged against everything new. But the pleasure of Allah, Glory be to Him, is the goal; and the pleasure of His Prophet is our hope. That is the true dividend, treasury and our capital on the day when neither wealth nor children will be of benefit, except he who comes to Allah with a pure heart.

Despite all of this, it is upon us to please and console the true believers who realize the status of Allah and of His Prophet (s) before they know the power of the rulers, the Caliphs and the Sultans.

I recall having to endure stern objections so much so that I was accused of disbelief and having gone out of religion when I criticized al-Bukhari for his narration of the *hadith* of Moses slapping the angel of death and gouging out his eyes. It was said to me: "Who are you to criticize al-Bukhari?" There arose around me so much noise and commotion as if I had criticized a verse from Allah's book.

In reality, if a researcher were to free himself from the yoke of blind imitation and abject fanaticism, he would find in al-Bukhari and Muslim strange and astonishing things which reflect absolutely the outlook of the Bedouin Arab whose thinking is still stagnant, believing in some tales and legends. His thinking leans towards everything that is strange. This itself is not a fault, and we do not accuse him of mental deficiency for his early era was not the time of electronic technology, nor of television, the telephone or rocket.

However, we also do not desire that this be associated with the bearer of the message (s), for in this there is a huge and vast difference. He is the one whom Allah sent amongst the illiterate to recite to them His verses, to purify and to teach them the book and wisdom since he is the seal of the Prophets and Apostles, Allah

Chapter 8: Concerning the two Sahihs ...

bestowed him with the knowledge that came before and that which was to come.

We have to draw to the respected reader's attention that not everything in al-Bukhari is attributed to the Prophet of Allah (s) Al-Bukhari has related *hadith* of the Prophet (s), then attached the views of some companions. The reader assumes that the view or tradition is from the Prophet when, in fact, it is not his. Let me cite an example:

In "The book of Stratagems," in "The Chapter on Marriage," vol. 8, p. 62, al-Bukhari reported in his *Sahih*: "From Abu Hurayrah that the Prophet (s) said: 'The virgin is not to be married off until her permission is sought, and the non-virgin until she has been consulted.' It was said: 'O Prophet of Allah, how do we know of her permission?' He replied: 'If she stays silent.' Some of the people said: 'If the virgin's permission has not been sought, and she is not married, and a man her deceives by producing two false witnesses [to testify] that he has married her with her consent, and the Qadi rules on the validity of the marriage, then, although the man knows that the testimony is false, there is no harm if he consummates it for it is now a valid marriage.'"

Examine the narration of al-Bukhari (after the *hadith* of the Prophet (s)) "and some people said". Why [do we need] the speech of some people (and they are unknown) that marriage by false testimony is legal? The reader assumes that is the view of the Prophet, which is not true.

Another example, in "The Book of The Beginning of Creation," in "The Chapter on the Merits of the Muhajirun and their superiority" vol. 4, p. 203 al-Bukhari reports in his *Sahih* from 'Abd Allah b. 'Umar (r) who said: "During the time of the Prophet (s), we never took anyone to be equal to Abu Bakr, then after him 'Umar, then 'Uthman and after that we left the companions of the Prophet without according anyone superiority over the others." That is the view of 'Abd Allah b. 'Umar and no one is responsible for it except himself. Otherwise, how could 'Ali b. Abi Talib, who was the best of men after the Prophet of Allah, not be accorded any preference and 'Abd Allah b. 'Umar regarded him as the same as the other men? As a result, you find that 'Abd Allah b. 'Umar refused to give the pledge to the Commander of the Faithful and their master; one who did not take 'Ali as his master is not a believer.[1]

'Ali is the one of whom the Prophet said: "'Ali is with the truth and the truth is with 'Ali."[2] Instead, we find him (Ibn 'Umar) pledging allegiance to the enemy of Allah, His Prophet and the believers, al-Hajjaj b. Yusuf, the corrupt and immoral one. We do not wish to return to such topics, but we desire to make it clear to the reader the character of al-Bukhari and those of his type. He reports this *hadith* in the chapter on the merits of the Muhajirun, as if he is covertly implying to the readers that this is the Prophet's (s) view, whereas it is the view of 'Abd Allah b. 'Umar who declared Imam 'Ali to be an enemy.

We will prove to the discerning reader the position of al-Bukhari on everything concerning 'Ali b. Abi Talib and how he tried his utmost to hide his merits and disseminate any faults attributed to him.

Al-Bukhari reported in his *Sahih* in "The Book of the Beginning of Creation" in "The Chapter of al-Humaydi informed us": "Muhammad b. Kathir informed us that Sufyan informed him that Jami' b. Abi Rashid informed him that Abu Ya'la was informed by Muhammad b. al-Hanafiyya, who said: 'I said to my father: 'Who is the best of men after the Prophet of Allah (s)?' He said: 'Abu Bakr.' I said: 'Then who?' He said: 'Then 'Umar'. I was afraid now that he would say 'Uthman so I said: 'Then you.' He said: 'I am nothing but a man amongst the Muslims.'"

They attributed this *hadith* to Muhammad b. al-Hanafiyya, the son of Imam 'Ali b. Abi Talib. It is similar to that reported previously from Ibn 'Umar. The conclusion in the end is one; Ibn al-Hanafiyya feared that his father would say 'Uthman is the third [best person] but instead his father said: "I am nothing but a man

---

[1] *Al-Sawa'iq al-Muhriqa,* Ibn Hajar, p.107.

[2] *Sahih al-Tirmidhi* 5/297, al-Hakim, *Mustadrak*, 3/124.

Chapter 8: Concerning the two Sahihs ...

from amongst the Muslims;" this means then that 'Uthman is better than him for there is none amongst the *Ahl al-Sunnah* who says that 'Uthman is simply a man amongst the Muslims. Instead they say, as noted, that the best of men is Abu Bakr, then 'Umar, then 'Uthman and then we leave the rest of the companions of the Prophet (s) without giving preference to any of them, and all men after them are equal.

Are you not surprised at these traditions which al-Bukhari narrates? All lead to one goal, i.e., the denial of any merit to 'Ali b. Abi Talib. Is it not to be understood from this that al-Bukhari used to write everything which pleased the Banu Umayyads and the Banu 'Abbas and all the rulers who undertook to denigrate the *Ahl al-Bayt*? These are cogent arguments for whoever wishes to find the truth.

Al-Bukhari and Muslim relate anything which lauds Abu Bakr and 'Umar

In vol. 4, p. 149, al-Bukhari reported in his *Sahih* in "The Book of The Beginning of Creation" and in "The Chapter [entitled] 'Al-Yaman informed us'" which Muslim also reported in his *Sahih,* in "The Book on the Merits of the Companions" in "The Chapter On the Merits of Abu Bakr, the Truthful (r)": from Abu Hurayrah, who said: "The Prophet of Allah (s) prayed the morning prayer then faced the people and said: 'Once a man was leading a cow, rode on it and beat it whereupon it said: 'We were not created for this. We were created for tilling [the land].'

The people said: 'Glory be to Allah! A cow speaking?' He said: 'I believe in this, Abu Bakr and 'Umar also do.' They were not present. 'And once there was a man amongst his flocks, a wolf raided them and took a sheep. So the man pursued him until he came close to rescuing it. The wolf said: 'You are rescuing it from me and who will rescue it on the day of hunting when there will be no shepherd for it, but me?' The people said: 'Glory be to Allah, a wolf speaking?' He said: 'I believe in this, Abu Bakr and 'Umar also do.' The two were not present."

This *hadith* is manifestly difficult [to accept]; it is amongst the forged traditions on the merits of the two Caliphs. If not, how come the people belied it even though they were the companions of the Prophet of Allah (s)? What he told them he had to say twice: "I believe in this, Abu Bakr and 'Umar and I do." Then observe how the reporter reaffirms the absence of Abu Bakr and 'Umar on both occasions. These "merits" are laughable and have no meaning. But the people are like those engrossed by hashish. The forgers, when they cannot find an event or important occurrence to mention the two, create images of such merits. Most of these are dreams, imaginations or interpretations. They are not based on historical, logical or scientific proofs.

Al-Bukhari reported in his *Sahih* in "The Book of The Merits of the Companions of the Prophet (s)", in "The Chapter on the Saying of the Prophet 'Were I to take a sincere friend....'" as did Muslim in his *Sahih* in "The Book of The Merits of the Companions," in "The Chapter on the Merits of Abu Bakr al-Siddiq (r)" the following *hadith*: "From 'Amr b. al-'As that the Prophet sent him to the army of al-Salasil. So I ('Amr) came to him and said: 'Who is the most beloved of people to you?' He said: "A'isha'. I said: 'Amongst the men?' He said: 'Her father'. I said: 'Then who?' he said: "Umar b. al-Khattab, for he is a man.'"

This *hadith* was fabricated by forgers who realized that history has recorded that in the year 8 A.H. (i.e., two years before the death of the Prophet (s)), the Prophet sent an army in which were Abu Bakr and 'Umar under the command of 'Amr b. al-'As to the battle of al-Salasil. To deny the claim of anyone who might advocate the superiority of 'Amr b. al-'As over Abu Bakr and 'Umar, you see them fabricating this *hadith* and attributing this to 'Amr himself to affirm the superiority of Abu Bakr and 'Umar. They also involved 'A'isha to dispel any doubts on the one hand, and so that they could ascribe to her absolute superiority on the other.

As a result, you find that Imam al-Nawawi, in his explanation of *Sahih Muslim*, saying: "This is a clear statement regarding the overwhelming excellences of Abu Bakr, 'Umar and 'A'isha (r). In it is clear proof for the *Ahl al-Sunnah* on the superiority of Abu Bakr, then 'Umar over all the companions."

Chapter 8: Concerning the two Sahihs ...

This is like the rest of the absurd traditions which the swindlers did not hesitate to fabricate even attributing them to 'Ali b. Abi Talib himself; thereby negating, in their view, the argument of the Shi'as who claim the superiority of 'Ali b. Abi Talib over all the companions on the one hand, and to delude the Muslims into thinking that 'Ali was not oppressed and that he did not complain to Abu Bakr and 'Umar, on the other.

Al-Bukhari reported in his *Sahih* in "The Book of The Merits of the companions of the Prophet (s)" in "The Chapter on The Virtues of 'Umar b. al-Khattab Abu Hafsa", Muslim also narrated it in "The Book of The Merits of the Companions," in "The Chapter on the Merits of 'Umar (r)" thus: from 'Ali, from Ibn 'Abbas who said: "The body of 'Umar was put on his deathbed, the people gathered around him and invoked (Allah) and prayed for him before the body was taken away, and I was amongst them. Suddenly I felt somebody taking hold of my shoulder; it was 'Ali. He invoked Allah's mercy for 'Umar and said: 'You have not left behind you a person whose deeds I like to imitate and meet Allah with more than I like your deeds. By Allah! I always thought that Allah would keep you with your two companions, for very often I used to hear the Prophet saying: 'I, Abu Bakr and 'Umar went [somewhere] I, Abu Bakr and 'Umar entered [somewhere], and I, Abu Bakr and 'Umar went out.'"

This is a clear fabrication which smells of politics which played a role in distancing Fatima al-Zahra (sa) and causing her not to be buried near her father even though she was the first to join him. The narrator omitted to add here after his statement: "I went, Abu Bakr, 'Umar and I" and "I entered, Abu Bakr, 'Umar and I" and "I emerged, Abu Bakr, 'Umar and I" and I will be buried, I, Abu Bakr, 'Umar."

Don't those, who argue by such spurious traditions which are refuted by history and reality, not hesitate [to fabricate]? The books of the Muslims are replete with oppression against 'Ali and Fatima al-Zahra (sa) due to what Abu Bakr and 'Umar did during their lifetime.

Then reflect on the narration; you will observe the narrator presenting 'Ali as if he is a stranger coming to observe the funeral of a stranger and finds the people crowding around him and supplicating and praying for him. Whereupon he takes the shoulder of Ibn 'Abbas as if he wishes to whisper in his ear those words and then wishes to go away. It would be assumed that 'Ali would be in the forefront leading the people in prayers and not leaving 'Umar until he was placed in the ground.

The people during the Umayyad dynasty used to vie with one another in fabricating *hadith* as ordered by "the Commander of the Faithful" Mu'awiyah who wanted to elevate the status of Abu Bakr and 'Umar, in contrast to the merits of 'Ali b. Abi Talib.

The *hadiths* of the excellences are ridiculously laughable and contradictory in some cases, depending on the wishes of the narrator. Among these were al-Taymi who would never prefer anyone over Abu Bakr and amongst them was al-'Adwi who never preferred anyone over 'Umar. The Umayyads were fascinated by the personality of Ibn al-Khattab, for he was bold in front of the Prophet and employed harsh words without exercising caution against anything and feared nothing. They often praised him and fabricated traditions which made him superior to Abu Bakr.

Here, O reader, are some examples:

Muslim in his *Sahih*, in "The Book of the Merits of the Companions." in "The Chapter on the Merits of 'Umar" (r), as well as al-Bukhari in his *Sahih*, in "The Book of Faith", in "The Chapter of the Superiority of the Believers in the Performance of Deeds," from Abu Said al-Khudri: "The Prophet of Allah (s) said: 'When I was sleeping I saw some people presented to me, they wore shirts, some of which reached up to the breast, some were shorter than that. And then 'Umar b. al-Khattab was presented to me and he was wearing a shirt which was dragging [behind].' They said: 'How do you interpret that O Messenger of Allah?' He said: 'Religion.'"

If the interpretation of the Prophet (s) for this dream was religion,

Chapter 8: Concerning the two Sahihs ...

then 'Umar b. al-Khattab is better than everyone because, their religion hardly reached their breasts and didn't go past their hearts. 'Umar, however, was filled with religion from his head to the bottom of his feet and more than that for he was dragging it behind him as a shirt is dragged. Where is Abu Bakr, the Truthful one, whose faith is better than that of the entire *ummah*?

Likewise, al-Bukhari reported in his *Sahih*, in "The Book of Knowledge" in "The Chapter on the Superiority of Knowledge" while Muslim narrated it in "The Book of Merits of the Companions," in "The Chapter on the Merits of 'Umar":

From Ibn 'Umar, who said: "I heard the Prophet of Allah (s) say: 'While I was sleeping, I was given a jug of milk from which I drank until I observed its wetness coming through my nails. I gave the remainder to 'Umar b. al-Khattab.' The people said: 'How did you interpret that O Prophet of Allah?' He said: 'Knowledge.'"

I say, are those who know equal to those who do not know? If Ibn al-Khattab was superior to the entire *ummah* or all the people in religion and among them was Abu Bakr; then this narration manifestly shows his elevation over them in knowledge too, for he was the most knowledgeable of men after the Prophet (s).

There remains here another virtue, which people compete with each other to acquire. It is amongst those praiseworthy traits that Allah and his Prophet love and all mankind love and strive for it, i.e., bravery. It was necessary for the narrators to invent *hadiths* in favor of Abu Hafs - and they most surely did it!

Al-Bukhari reported in his *Sahih*, in "The Book of the Merits of the Companions of the Prophet" in "The Chapter on The Prophet's (s) saying 'If I were to take a sincere friend,'" and Muslim reported in his *Sahih*, in "The Book of The Merits of the Companions," in "The Chapter on the Merits of 'Umar": From Abu Hurayrah who said: "I heard the Prophet (s) saying: 'While I was sleeping, I saw myself at a well, on it there was a bucket. I drew water from it as much as Allah wished. Then Ibn Abi Quhafa (Abu Bakr) took the bucket from me and brought out one or two buckets (of water) and there was weakness in his drawing it. May Allah forgive him for his weakness. Then the bucket turned into a very big one and Ibn Al-Khattab took it over and I had never seen such a mighty person amongst the people as 'Umar in drawing water till the people drank to their satisfaction and watered their camels that knelt down there.'"

If religion is the centre of faith and Islam, piety and closeness to Allah, Glory be to Him, then 'Umar seized it until he dragged it behind him. The people did not receive their share except what reached their breasts, whilst the rest of their bodies were naked. Knowledge was restricted to 'Umar b. al-Khattab, he didn't leave anything for the rest of the people due to the grace of the Prophet (s) since he drank all that he (the Prophet) gave him. He didn't think of his friend Abu Bakr al-Siddiq - (no doubt, it is the knowledge which 'Umar used in changing the rulings of Allah after the Prophet (s) died. His *ijtihad* was by the grace of that knowledge).

Strength and courage were also the traits of Ibn al-Khattab after the weakness which overcame his companion, Abu Bakr and this is correct, for did Abu Bakr not say to 'Umar once: "I told you that you are stronger in this matter than I am, but you overruled me". May Allah forgive Abu Bakr for his weakness and his preceding him to the Caliphate. The supporters of 'Umar from the Banu 'Adi and the Banu Umayya did not see any hope or benefits, or spoils of war, or conquests as they saw during his time.

All of these were the virtues of 'Umar in this world. Obviously, it was necessary for them to guarantee him [a place in] heaven in the hereafter also, with a higher and superior status than his companion Abu Bakr and they did that [also].

In "The Book on the Beginning of Creation," in "The Chapter on the Description of Heaven and that it was Created", al-Bukhari reported in his *Sahih* a [*hadith*] which Muslim [also] related in his collection in "The Book on the Virtues of the Companions," in "The Chapter on the Virtues of 'Umar": "On the authority of Abu Hurayrah (r), who said: 'We were with the Prophet of Allah (s) when he said: 'While I was sleeping, I saw myself in paradise, and

Chapter 8: Concerning the two Sahihs ...

there was a lady performing the ablutions next to a castle. I asked: 'To whom does this castle belong?' They said: 'To 'Umar b. al-Khattab'. I then recalled his jealousy so I quickly retreated'. 'Umar wept and said: 'Would I be jealous against you O Prophet of Allah?'"

Dear reader, I think you will notice the [peculiar] systematic arrangement of these false traditions. I have underlined in each one of them a single expression [that is] common to all the narrations pertaining to the merits of 'Umar b. al-Khattab, i.e., the saying of the Prophet of Allah (s) (Allah forbid of course) "While I was sleeping." You will always find it in every report. "While I was sleeping, I saw people appearing before me; while I was sleeping I was given a cup of milk...; while I was sleeping I saw myself at a well...; while I was sleeping I saw myself in paradise." Perhaps the reporter of the *hadith* used to have many dreams or was in a confused state of mind, interpreting and inventing *hadiths* and attributing them to the Prophet of Allah (s). How many lies were attributed to him while he was in their midst? So how about after his death, when the *ummah* had deviated, fought each other and had become sects and factions, each party happy with what it had?

There remains one thing, however, which the historians as well as those companions who were 'Umar's supporters have recorded, i.e., the character which distinguished 'Umar - his harshness, crudeness and severity over the people as well as his violent nature. The people do not love one whose nature is such. Allah says: *"Were you to be harsh and hard of heart, the people would certainly go away from you"* (3:159).

Those fascinated by 'Umar turned the tables over, and they made his shortcomings and vices into virtues and merits. They resorted to the invention of *hadith* by extremely foolish, stupid and insane means [to tarnish] the nobility of the Prophet - whereas Allah, Glory be to Him, has born testimony that he was neither rude nor harsh. Rather, he was of an affable nature. "Due to Allah's mercy, you are lenient with them, and indeed, you are of the most exalted character, kind and merciful with the believers and a mercy to the entire universe." Let us listen to these fools [to see] what they say regarding him.

In "The Book of the Beginning of Creation" in "The Chapter on the Description of Satan and his forces," al-Bukhari reported a *hadith* in his *Sahih* that was [also] narrated by Muslim in "The Book on the Merits of the Companions," in "The Chapter on the Merits of 'Umar," from Sa'd b. Abi Waqqas, who said: "'Umar sought permission to visit the Prophet of Allah (s) while the latter was talking to some Qurayshi women. They were crowding him and raising their voices. When 'Umar sought permission, they stood up hastening to put on their veils. The Prophet of Allah (s) gave him permission [to enter], and began to laugh. 'Umar said: "Did Allah cause you to laugh so much, O Prophet of Allah?" He replied: 'I was surprised at these [women] who were with me. When they heard your voice, they grabbed their veils'. 'Umar said: 'But it is more proper they fear you, O Prophet of Allah.' Then he said: 'O enemies of yourselves. Do you fear me and not the Prophet of Allah (s)?' They replied: 'Yes, you are harsher and more severe than the Prophet of Allah (s).' The Prophet of Allah said: 'By He in whose hand is my soul! Satan will never meet you travelling on a road except that he will seek a path [different] from yours.'"

Grave indeed are the words that come out of their mouths, they utter nothing but lies. Look at the repulsive [nature of the] narration, and how the women were afraid of 'Umar and not afraid of the Prophet of Allah (s). They raised their voices above the Prophet's (s), did not respect him, nor wear their veils properly in his presence. At the mere sound of 'Umar's voice, they kept quiet and hastened to put on their veils. I am surprised, by Allah, at these fools who are not satisfied by all these [traditions], but now clearly state that he was of harsh and stern nature. These [become] meritorious attributes, as 'Umar was harsher and sterner than the Apostle of Allah (s). If they are virtues belonging to the Prophet then 'Umar is superior to him. If they are blemishes, how can the Muslims, with al-Bukhari and Muslim at the helm, accept these traditions?

They were not satisfied by all this; they made Satan play and rejoice in the presence of the Prophet (s), not fearing him. No doubt it was Satan who incited the women so that they raised their voices and abandoned their veils. Satan, however, fled and sought another path by the mere entry of 'Umar in the house of the Prophet.

Do you see, O concerned Muslim, how they value the Prophet (s)? How they say whatever they are aware or unaware of, that 'Umar is better than him? This is exactly what is happening today. When they speak of the Prophet of Allah, they enumerate his alleged mistakes and justify [them] by stating that he was mortal, not infallible, and that 'Umar often corrected his mistakes. They [also allege] that the Qur'an was revealed to support 'Umar on several occasions. They cite as proof *Surah 'Abasa*, the pollination of the date palms, and [the incident of] the prisoners of war at Badr and other instances. However, if you tell them that 'Umar erred in denying the share of those whose hearts were to be placated, or in forbidding the two *mut'as*, or in giving preference in the allocation of prescribed shares, you'll see them becoming furious and their eyes turning red. They will accuse you of going out of [the fold of] religion. It will be said to you: "Who are you, O so and so, that you can criticize our master 'Umar, the differentiator, one who differentiates between truth and falsehood?" You will have no choice but to submit, you cannot attempt to speak with them again otherwise you will come to harm.

Al-Bukhari forges hadith to preserve the honour of 'Umar b. al-Khattab

If a researcher studies the traditions of al-Bukhari, he will not understand many of them. Some appear defective or broken; he relates the same *hadith* with the same chains of narrators, but on every occasion, he cites different phrases in different chapters. All of this was due to his intense love for 'Umar b. al-Khattab. Perhaps this is what attracted the *Ahl al-Sunnah* to him and made them prefer it above all other books, even though Muslim is more accurate and his work is arranged according to chapters. Due to this and because he diminishes [the importance of] the virtues of 'Ali b. Abu Talib, al-Bukhari's work is deemed by them to be the most authentic book after the book of God. Al-Bukhari worked with a bias, that of disrupting a *hadith* and abridging it if it disparages the personality of 'Umar. He used the same method with the traditions which mention the merits of 'Ali b. Abi Talib. We will produce some examples of these presently, God willing.

Some examples of the interpolation of traditions containing realities which expose 'Umar b. al-Khattab

1. In "The Book of Menstruation", in "The Chapter on *Tayammum,*" Muslim, in his *Sahih,* reported: "A man came to 'Umar and said: 'I have become ritually impure and cannot find water.' 'Umar said: 'Do not pray.' Whereupon 'Ammar said: 'Do you not recall, O Commander of the Faithful, that you and I were on a campaign and we both became ritually impure and couldn't find water. As for you, you did not pray. But I rolled [myself] in the dust and then prayed. The Prophet (s) then said: 'It would have sufficed for you to have struck the ground with your hands and then blown upon them, then wiped your face and hands with them.' 'Umar responded: 'Fear Allah, O 'Ammar.' He said: 'If you so desire, I shall not mention [this *hadith*].'" This narration has been related by Abu Dawud in his *Sunan,* Ahmad b. Hanbal in his *Musnad,* al-Nas'ai in his *Sunan,* and al-Bayhaqi and Ibn Maja too.

Al-Bukhari betrayed the trust given [in the] transmission of *hadith*. To protect the stature of 'Umar, he distorted the *hadith* for it did not please him [to see] that the people should know about the ignorance of the Caliph in basic Islamic laws. Here is the report as it is transmitted in al-Bukhari. In the book "Of *Tayammum,*" in the chapter on "One who does *Tayammum,* can he blow [on his hands]" al-Bukhari reported in his *Sahih*: "A man came to 'Umar b. al-Khattab and said: 'I am ritually impure (*junub)* and I have not found any water.' 'Ammar b. Yasir said to 'Umar b. al-Khattab: 'Do you not recall that we were on a journey, you and I.....'"

The text, as you will have observed, has been edited by al-Bukhari. 'Umar said: "Do not pray" has been omitted for this is embarrassing. No doubt, al-Bukhari edited and expurgated it so that the people may not know the rulings of 'Umar which he formulated during the life of the Prophet of Allah (s) and that his judgments opposed the text of the Qur'an and *Sunnah.* [He also did not want

Chapter 8: Concerning the two Sahihs ...

the people to know] that 'Umar maintained this opinion even after he became the Commander of the Faithful. He began to spread his view amongst the Muslims. Ibn Hajar said: "This is a famous opinion of 'Umar." The proof that he used to strongly advocate his view is 'Ammar's address to him: "If you so desire, I shall not mention [this *hadith*]." So read and wonder!

2. Al-Hakim al-Nisapuri, in his *al-Mustadrak*, in vol. 2, p. 514, reported [the *hadith*] which al-Dhahabi authenticated in his *Talkhis*: "From Anas b. Malik who said: "Umar b. al-Khattab recited on the pulpit Allah's words: *'And we grow grain and grapes and herbs and the olives and date palms and dense gardens and fruits and herbage'(16:11),*
He said: 'We know all of this, but what is herbage (*al-ab*)?' Then he said: 'This, by Allah, is a problem; there is no blame upon you if you don't know what "herbage" is. Follow what His guidance has made clear for you in His book and act upon it. As for that which you do not know, eat it in [the name] of your Lord.'"

The narration that we have just mentioned has been transmitted by commentators in their books, and in commentaries on the *Surah* "'*Abasa*", among them are al-Suyuti in *al-Dar al-Manthur*, and al-Zamakhshari in *al-Kashshaf*, and Ibn Kathir in his commentary, also al-Razi in his *tafsir* and al-Khazan in his commentary.

However, al-Bukhari, as is his normal practice, deleted the *hadith* and never mentioned it so that the people would not realize the ignorance of the Caliph regarding the meaning of "*al-ab*". Instead, he related the *hadith* as follows:

Al-Bukhari in his *Sahih*, narrated in "The Book of Holding Fast to the Qur'an and the *Sunnah* in "The Chapter on what is Detested in [asking] many Questions, and overburdening [oneself] with what does not concern him, and Allah the most Exalted's words: *'Do not ask about things which, if they are made known to you, would trouble you.'"(5:101)* [On the authority of] Anas b. Malik: "We were with 'Umar and he said: 'We were forbidden from overburdening [ourselves].'" So this is how al-Bukhari deals with every *hadith* in which he smells [any trace of] denigration of 'Umar. How can a reader understand from this curtailed *hadith* the truth about things, for it conceals 'Umar's ignorance of the meaning of *al-ab* as it simply states that 'Umar said: "We have been forbidden to overburden [ourselves]?"

3. Ibn Maja, in his *Sunan*, vol. 2, p. 227, al-Hakim in vol. 2, p. 59 of his *Mustadrak*, Abu Dawud in vol. 2, p. 402 of his *Sunan*, al-Bayhaqi in vol. 6, p. 64 of his *Sunan*, Ibn Hajar in *Fath al-Bari*, and other reporters relate from Ibn 'Abbas, that he said: "A mad woman who had committed adultery was brought to 'Umar. He sought counsel from the people regarding her, and then ordered that she be stoned. 'Ali b. Abu Talib passed by her and asked: 'What is the matter with her?' The people said: 'She is a mad woman of such and such a tribe and has committed adultery, and 'Umar has ordered that she be stoned'. He said: 'Take her back;' then he went to him and said: 'Do you not know that the pen has been lifted from the mad person until he is sane, from the one asleep until he awakes, and from the child until he attains puberty?'

'Umar freed her and said: 'Had it not been for 'Ali, Umar would have perished.'" (Ibn al-Jawzi in his *al-Tadhkira*, p.75). But al-Bukhari was confused by this narration. How could he inform the people of 'Umar's ignorance regarding the penalties legislated in Allah's book, and which the Prophet of Allah (s) had explained? How could one assume the position of the head of the Caliphate if his condition was such? Furthermore, how could al-Bukhari narrate this narration, when it contains the merits of 'Ali b. Abu Talib who had resorted to teaching them what they did not know? Moreover, [how could he mention] 'Umar's admission "Had it not been for 'Ali, 'Umar would perished." Let us see how al-Bukhari distorted and tampered with the *hadith*.

Al-Bukhari reported in his *Sahih*, in "The Book of the Disbelievers and Apostates Against whom War is Waged," in "The Chapter on the Lunatic (male and female) are not to be Stoned," al-Bukhari reported without mentioning any chain of transmitters: "'Ali said to 'Umar: 'Do you not know that the pen is raised from the mad person until he attains sanity, from the child until he attains

Chapter 8: Concerning the two Sahihs ...

maturity, and from the one sleeping until he wakes up?'"

Here is a living example of al-Bukhari's treatment of *hadith*, and how he abridges a *hadith* if it disgraces 'Umar. He also tampers with the tradition if there is a merit or virtue of Imam 'Ali [mentioned] which he cannot reject.

4. In "The Book of Penalties," in "The Chapter on the Penalty of one who consumes Intoxicants," Muslim reported in his *Sahih* on the authority of Anas b. Malik who reported that a man who had drunk alcohol was brought to the Prophet (s). He ordered that he be whipped 40 lashes with two palm leaves. He (Anas) said: "Abu Bakr did likewise. When 'Umar was Caliph he sought the advice of the people and 'Abd al-Rahman b. 'Awf said: 'The most lenient punishment is 80 strokes,' so 'Umar ordered this."

Al-Bukhari, as is his usual practice, did not wish to reveal 'Umar's ignorance of rulings on penalties and how he sought the people's advice on a well-known penalty, which the Prophet of Allah (s) had acted upon, and which Abu Bakr after him had also practiced.

Al-Bukhari, in his *Sahih*, in "The Book of Penalties," in "The Chapter on what was Related regarding the Whipping of one who Consumes Intoxicants" reported on the authority of Anas b. Malik that the Prophet (s) ordered a penalty for [consuming] intoxicants, the whipping by date palm leaves, or shoes and Abu Bakr whipped 40 lashes.

5. The *hadith* scholars and historians have recorded the sickness and death of the Prophet (s), and how he asked to write for them a letter so that they would never go astray after him; this [episode] has been called the calamity of Thursday, 'Umar b. al-Khattab opposed it saying that the Prophet of Allah was hallucinating (God forbid).

Al-Bukhari, in his *Sahih*, in "The Book of *Jihad*," in "The Chapter on is Mediation to be sought from the *Ahl al-Dhimma* (the people of the book under Muslim protection) and how to deal with Them" in "The Book of Bequests" in "The Chapter on Exemption from he who does not have anything to Bequeath from." It is reported from Ibn 'Abbas that he said: "Thursday! What a Thursday!" Then he wept until the pebbles were wet with his tears. He said: "On Thursday, the Prophet's pain became more severe. He said: 'Bring a letter, so that I may write for you an epistle [due to which] you will never go astray.' They argued amongst themselves, it was not fitting that they argue in the Prophet's presence. They said: 'The Prophet of Allah is hallucinating.' He said: 'Leave me alone. [The situation] I am in is better than what you invite me to.' He bequeathed three [things] on his death: (1) Remove the polytheists from the Arabian Peninsula (2) To permit the delegations what I used to permit (3) I forgot the third."

Yes! This is the calamity of Thursday wherein 'Umar played a heroic role, he opposed the Prophet (s), prevented him from writing, using those vile words which contradict the book of Allah, i.e., when he said the Prophet was hallucinating. Al-Bukhari and Muslim transmitted it here with the proper words which 'Umar uttered, and did not change it as long as the name of 'Umar was not mentioned. The attribution of this vile saying to an unknown person did not harm [him].

However, when the name of 'Umar came up in the narration which mentions that he is the one who uttered [the words], it became difficult for al-Bukhari and Muslim to leave it as it was; for it disparages the Caliph and showed his real naked truth, uncovering the scope of his boldness with the position of the Prophet of Allah (s) and that he used to oppose him during his life in most matters. Muslim and al-Bukhari and those like them, knew that these words alone were enough to influence the feelings of every Muslim - even the *Ahl al-Sunnah* - against the Caliph, so they resorted to tampering with it. For this is their well known occupation in such matters. They therefore changed the word "hallucinate" to "overcome with pain" [so as] to do away with the evil expression. The following is what Muslim and al-Bukhari related regarding the same catastrophic incident:

"On the authority of Ibn 'Abbas who said: 'When death approached the Prophet of Allah, there were some men in [his]

Chapter 8: Concerning the two Sahihs ...

home, among them 'Umar b. al-Khattab. The Prophet said: 'Bring me paper so that I may write for you [so that] you will not go astray after it.' 'Umar said: 'The Prophet has been overcome by pain, you have the Qur'an, the book of Allah is sufficient for us.' The members of the household differed and argued. Among them were those who said: 'Bring it so that the Prophet may write for you a letter [due to which] you will never go astray.' There were those who said as 'Umar said. When the vain talk and differences intensified in the Prophet's presence, he said to them: 'Go away!' 'Abd Allah b. Mas'ud said: 'And Ibn 'Abbas used to say: 'Indeed the catastrophe of all catastrophes was what occurred between the Prophet of Allah's [wanting to] write for them that letter and their dissension and wrangling.'"[3]

Although Muslim took [the narration] from his teacher al-Bukhari, we say to al-Bukhari no matter how much you edited the words, and no matter how much you attempted to hide the facts, what you have reported is sufficient and a proof against you and your master 'Umar. Because the words "hallucinate" (and its meaning is delusion) or "overcome by pain" lead to the same conclusion; for he who researches carefully will observe that even today, people say "Poor fellow! He was overcome by fever until he became delirious."

Especially if we add his words "You have the Qur'an, and the book of God is sufficient for us;" this means that the period of [dependence on] the Prophet (s) had ended and his existence had become the same as his non-existence.

We dare any scholar who has conscience to study carefully this occurrence only without any preconceived commitments or hindrances; you will find him becoming furious with the Caliph who prevented the community from [attaining] guidance, and was the immediate cause for its straying.

---

[3] *Sahih al-Bukhari*, "The Book of Sickness" "The Chapter on the saying of the sick: 'Go away from me'", 7/9, and *Sahih Muslim*, "The Book of Bequests", "The Book of Rejection and Bequests", 5/76.

Why should we be afraid of speaking the truth as long as it is in the defense of the Prophet of Allah (s), and consequently the Qur'an and the complete Islamic view? Allah said: *"Do not fear people but fear me! And do not trade my signs for a small price. Whosoever does not judge by what Allah has revealed, these are the disbelievers" (5:44).* Why then do some scholars, even in this age of knowledge and enlightenment, try to cover the truth by inventing far-fetched interpretations which are devoid of any credibility?

This is what the scholar Muhammad Fu'ad 'Abd al-Baqi conjured up in his commentary of the book "*Al lu'lu' wa'l-Marjan fi ma ittafaqa 'alayhi al-Shaykhan* when he mentions the *hadith* of the calamity of Thursday.[4]

He said, commenting on the incident: "Bring me a paper," i.e., bring me the instruments of writing such as a pen and ink pot, or he meant by paper what could be used for writing on, such as paper or shoulder blades (of animals). It appears the letter he wanted [to write] was for the designation of Abu Bakr for the Caliphate. However, when they disputed and his sickness increased, he changed his mind, relying instead upon having nominated him to lead the prayer. (Then he started to explain the meaning of hallucinate). He said: "Hallucinate: Ibn Battal says it means to be confused. Ibn al-Tin says it means being delirious. But this is not in keeping with his exalted status. Perhaps it means that the Prophet of Allah (s) is leaving you, from the word "*al-hajar*" which is the opposite of [the word] "connection" as had been divinely inspired to him. Therefore he said in "The Highest companion," Ibn al-Athir said: 'It (the statement) is in an interrogative mode and the *alif* denoting the question was omitted, therefore, [the sentence means] 'Has his talk become delirious because of his sickness?'"

This is the best that can be said about it. The term should not be taken in the form of a statement. [If it is then] it will become either corrupt or hallucination. The one who uttered [the words] was

---

[4] *Al Lu'lu wa'l-Marjan*, on what the two shaykhs have agreed, 2/166.

Chapter 8: Concerning the two Sahihs ...

'Umar, so it cannot be imagined [he meant that]."

We, in response, O great, noble scholar, say to you that conjecture cannot avail against the truth. It is sufficient for us that you admit that he who uttered this evil talk was 'Umar. Who informed you that the Prophet of Allah (s) wanted to write about the Caliphate of Abu Bakr? Would 'Umar have gone against this? He was the one who constructed the pillars of the Caliphate of Abu Bakr and had coerced the people into it harshly and violently, even to the point where he threatened to burn the house of al-Zahra (sa). Is there anyone besides you, O great, noble scholar, who advocates this explanation?

What is known to both the past and contemporary scholars is that 'Ali b. Abi Talib was designated for the Caliphate by the Prophet (s) even if they did not accept the [clear] declaration for it. It is sufficient for you [to note] what al-Bukhari reported in his *Sahih*, in "The Book of Testament" in vol. 3 p. 186. He said: "They mentioned to 'A'isha that 'Ali (r) was the executor of the will. She said: 'When did he appoint him as his executor? I was supporting him on my chest, and he asked for a wash basin. I [made him] lean on my lap, I did not [even] realize that he had passed away, so when did he appoint him?'"

Al-Bukhari reported this *hadith* because in it is 'A'isha's denial of the successor ship and this pleases al-Bukhari. We say that those who mentioned to 'A'isha that the Prophet of Allah had appointed 'Ali were truthful, for 'A'isha did not refute them and did not herself deny the successor ship but rather asked as one having no knowledge: "When was he appointed?" We respond by saying that he was designated in the presence of those noble companions and in her absence. There is no doubt that those companions told her when he was appointed, but the ruling authorities forbade the mention of such proofs, in the same way as they proscribed the mention of the third testament and forgot it. Politics undertook to suppress this truth even though 'Umar himself related how he prevented the Prophet of Allah (s) from writing his bequest because of his knowledge that it specifically concerned the Caliphate of 'Ali. Ibn Abi'l-Hadid reported the conversation that took place between

'Umar b. al-Khattab and 'Abd Allah b. 'Abbas in which 'Umar said while questioning Ibn 'Abbas: "Is there anything in 'Ali's soul for the Caliphate?" Ibn 'Abbas said: "Yes." 'Umar said: "The Prophet of Allah wanted, during his illness, to clearly mention his name, but I prevented him from that, out of love and care for Islam."[5]

Why do you, O great scholar, run away from the reality? Instead of exposing the truth, after the period of oppression passed with the Banu Umayyads and Banu 'Abbasids, here you are adding to that oppression by covering and hiding, and preventing others from reaching and attaining the truth. If what you said was done with good intention, then I ask Allah, Glory be to Him, to guide you and to open your perception.

6. Al-Bukhari also did many things so as to change, tamper or mix up the Prophet's *hadiths* which he perceived had any [form of] disparagement or denigration of the statures of Abu Bakr and 'Umar in them. We see him in a famous historical incident wherein the Prophet of Allah (s) uttered a *hadith* that did not please Imam al-Bukhari, so he completely obliterated it, for it elevated the position of 'Ali at Abu Bakr's expense.

The scholars of the *Sunnah* such as al-Tirmidhi in his *Sahih*, al-Hakim in his al-*Mustadrak*, Ahmad b. Hanbal in his *Musnad*, Imam al-Nas'ai in his *al-Khasa'is*, al-Tabari in his *Tafsir*, Jalal al-Din al-Suyuti in *al-Dar al-Manthur*, Ibn al-Athir in his History, and the author of *Kanz al-'Ummal*, and al-Zamakhshari in *al-Kashshaf* and numerous other scholars have reported in their *Sahihs* and *Musnad* works the following:

"The Messenger of Allah (s) sent Abu Bakr (r) and ordered him to proclaim these words (i.e. Allah and His Prophet are exonerated....); then he sent 'Ali (r) and ordered him instead to proclaim it. So 'Ali (r), on the days of *tashriq* (the 12th, 13th and 14th day of any month), stood up and proclaimed: 'Indeed Allah

---

[5] *Sharh Nahj al-Balagha*, Ibn Abi'l-Hadid, 12/21. Ibn Abi'l-Hadid mentioned that the story was reported by Ahmad b. Tahir, the author of *The book of the history of Baghdad*, in his book *Musnad*.

Chapter 8: Concerning the two Sahihs ... 343

and his Messenger are exonerated of the polytheists. So go about in the land for four months, and after this year, no polytheist will be permitted to make the pilgrimage, or circumambulate the Ka'ba in a naked state.' Abu Bakr (r) returned and said: 'O Prophet of Allah was there something revealed concerning me?' He said: 'No! But Gabriel came to me and said: 'None shall do this for you but you or a man [related] to you.'"

Al-Bukhari, as is his usual custom, related the *hadith* in his well known abridged way. He reported in "The book of *Tafsir* of the Qur'an" in "The Chapter [entitled] 'So go about in the land for four months'": "Humayd b. 'Abd al-Rahman informed me that Abu Hurayrah (r) said: 'Abu Bakr sent me on that *hajj* with those who proclaim on the day of sacrifice to proclaim at Mina that after that year no polytheist could perform the pilgrimage nor circumambulate the Ka'ba whilst naked.' Humayd b. 'Abd al-Rahman said: 'Then the Prophet of Allah followed it up with 'Ali b. Abi Talib and ordered him to proclaim the verses of *al-bara'a* (exoneration)'. Abu Hurayrah said: "Ali proclaimed with us on the day of sacrifice for the people at Mina about *al-bara'a*, and that after that year, no polytheist would perform the *hajj*, nor circumambulate the Ka'ba while naked.'"[6]

See, O reader, how the act of distortion of the *hadith* and events was perfected to suit the goals and factional desires? Is there any similarity between what al-Bukhari related on this issue and what the other *hadith* scholars and commentators from the *Ahl al-Sunnah* reported on this matter?

Al-Bukhari makes Abu Bakr the one who sent Abu Hurayrah and those who proclaim to announce at Mina that no polytheist could perform the *hajj* after that year nor could they circumambulate the Ka'ba in a naked state. Then comes the narration of Humayd b. 'Abd al-Rahman that the Prophet of Allah followed it up with 'Ali b. Abi Talib and ordered him to proclaim the verses of renunciation. Then comes the speech of Abu Hurayrah once again, that 'Ali participated with them in the proclamation on the day of sacrifice

---

[6] *Sahih al-Bukhari*, 5/202, *Kitab Tafsir al-Qur'an, Surah al-Bara'a*.

that no polytheist could perform the *hajj* or circumambulate in a naked state henceforth.

In this way, al-Bukhari negated the excellences of 'Ali b. Abi Talib, in that he was the one whom the Prophet of Allah chose to proclaim the verses of *al-bara'a* after Gabriel had come to him and commanded him, on Allah's behalf, to remove Abu Bakr from this undertaking, saying to him: "None shall do this for you but yourself or a man from you". It was difficult for al-Bukhari [to relate] Abu Bakr's removal by a revelation from Allah and to prefer 'Ali b. Abi Talib over him. This is what al-Bukhari would never ever be pleased with, so he edited the *hadith* and distorted it as he did with other narrations.

How can the researcher not be aware of this distortion, this forgery, and this betrayal of academic trust especially when he reads that Abu Hurayrah says: "Abu Bakr sent me for the *hajj* with the proclaimers whom he sent on the day of sacrifice"! Was Abu Bakr in charge of affairs, even in the time of the Prophet of Allah (s)? How did the one who was sent become the sender, [he became] one who selects the proclaimers among the companions?

Pay careful attention to the style of al-Bukhari how he changed everything around so that 'Ali b. Abi Talib, who was sent by the Prophet (s) to undertake a task for which no one but he was qualified, became the participator along with Abu Hurayrah and the rest of the proclaimers; without any mention of the removal of Abu Bakr, nor of his returning to the Prophet in tears (as is reported in some narrations), nor any mention of the Prophet's words: "Gabriel came to me and said: 'None shall do this for you except yourself or a man (related) to you.'"

For this *hadith* is tantamount to a badge of honor that the Prophet (s) accorded to his cousin and his successor 'Ali b. Abi Talib and to his community. Furthermore, it clearly states that this was in accordance with what Gabriel had brought, according to the Prophet's narration. After this, there is no scope for interpreters like al-Bukhari [to claim] that it was the personal opinion of Muhammad (s) who was like any other man, liable to commit error

Chapter 8: Concerning the two Sahihs ...

like others. It would have been better for al-Bukhari to discard and abandon this narration completely from his enumeration [of traditions] as he discarded other [*hadiths*].

You see him reporting in his *Sahih*, in "The Book of Treaty," in "The Chapter on how it is written that this is how so and so has reconciled - the saying of the Messenger of Allah (s) to 'Ali b. Abi Talib: 'You are from me, and I am from you'" during the argument of 'Ali, Ja'far and Zayd over the children of Hamza in which Ibn Maja, al-Tirmidhi, al-Nas'ai, Imam Ahmad and the author of *Kanz al-'Ummal* all reported that the Messenger of Allah said: "Ali is from me and I am from 'Ali, and none can deliver [it] on my behalf except myself and Ali."[7] He said it at the farewell pilgrimage, but al-Bukhari refused to report it.

7. I add to that Imam Muslim reported in his *Sahih*, in "The Book of Faith," in "The Book of Proof that love of the Ansar and 'Ali is a sign of belief, and that Hatred of them is amongst the Signs of Hypocrisy." 'Ali said: "By he who split the grain and created the soul, it is according to the covenant of the illiterate Prophet (s) to me, that none but a believer will love me, and none but a hypocrite shall hate me."

The *hadith* scholars and authors of the *Sunans* have confirmed the saying of the Prophet (s) to 'Ali: "None shall love you except a believer, and none shall hate you except a hypocrite." This has been reported by al-Tirmidhi in his *Sahih*, al-Nas'ai in his *Sunan*, the *Musnad* of Imam Ahmad b. Hanbal, al-Bayhaqi in his *Sunan*, al-Tabari in "*al-Dhakha'ir al-Aqba*," Ibn Hajar in "*Lisan al-Mizan*". Al-Bukhari however, in spite of having confirmed the authenticity of this *hadith*, which Muslim also reported, and [despite the fact that] all the transmitters in the chain were verified as reliable, did not relate the *hadith* because he reflected and realized that the Muslims would perceive the hypocrisy of many companions who were close to the Prophet (s).

---

[7] *Sunan* Ibn Maja 1/44, *al-Jami' al-Sahih*, al-Tirmidhi, 5/300, *al-Khasa'is* by al-Nasa'i, p.20, Ibn Hanbal, *Musnad*, 5/30, al-Khawarizmi, *al-Manaqib* p.79, Ibn al- Jawzi, *Tadhkira al-Khawas*, p.36, Ibn Hajar, *al-Sawa'iq al-Muhriqa*, p.120.

Due to this sign, which was clarified by he who did not say anything from his own desires, rather, from the revelation sent unto him, the *hadith* shows the great superiority of 'Ali alone over the rest of mankind as, because of him, truth can be separated from falsehood, and faith distinguished from hypocrisy. For he is Allah's greatest sign and His greatest proof to this *ummah* and he is a test through which Allah examines the *ummah* of Muhammad (s) after it's Prophet. Hypocrisy is of the inner secrets which no one knows except He who knows the deception of the eyes and what the hearts hide. None knows it except one who knows the unseen, for Allah, Glory be to Him, [out of His] grace and mercy to this *ummah,* established signs for it [so that] those who are destroyed are destroyed after clear signs [come to them] and those who are saved are saved after clear signs [come to them].

I would like to point out an example of al-Bukhari's cunningness and shrewdness in this respect. I personally believe that the past [figures] amongst the *Ahl al-Sunnah* preferred and promoted him for this specialty through which he is distinguished above others. He tried his best [to ensure] the *hadiths* did not contradict the *madhab* he chose and embraced.

He reported in his *Sahih,* in "The Book of Gifts, its Merits, and the encouragement to Give," in "The Chapter on the Gift of a Man to his Wife, and a Wife to her Husband": He said: "'Ubayd Allah b. 'Abd Allah informed me that 'A'isha (r) said: 'When the Apostle of Allah became bedridden, and his illness increased, he sought the permission of his wives to be nursed in my home. They allowed it. He went out assisted by two men, with his feet dragging on the ground. He was between al-'Abbas and another man'. 'Ubayd Allah said: 'I related what 'A'isha said to Ibn 'Abbas and he said to me: 'Do you know who was the other man that 'A'isha did not mention?' I said: 'No.' He said: 'He was 'Ali b. Abi Talib.'"

Ibn Sa'd reported this *hadith* exactly [as above] in his *Tabaqat,* by an authentic chain, in vol. 2, p. 29. Similarly, the author of *al-Sira al-Halabiyya* and other authors of the *Sunan* works also reported that "Certainly, 'A'isha was not happy to hear good things [ascribed] to him."

Al-Bukhari, however, omitted this sentence through which it becomes clear that 'A'isha hated 'Ali, and that she could not mention his name. Yet in what he has reported there is sufficient and clear proof for anyone who is cognizant of the implications of [the usage of] words. Is it hidden to any researcher who reads history the special hatred the mother of the believers had towards her master and protector[8] 'Ali b. Abi Talib even to the point where, when the news of his death reached her, she prostrated out of thanks to Allah? In any case, may Allah have mercy upon the mother of the believers and forgive her out of honor to her husband. We do not seek to limit the scope of Allah's mercy which encompasses everything. However, we do wish that those wars, discords and calamities had not occurred for they caused our fragmentation, breaking of our unity and the destruction of our spirit to the extent that today we are prey for the hungry ones; the object for the colonialists and we are the victims of tyrants. There is neither power, nor strength but in Allah, the Highest, the most Powerful.

Narrations disparaging the Ahl al-Bayt please al-Bukhari

It is extremely regretful that Imam al-Bukhari chose his path and travelled his way amidst the schools of the Caliphs which were established by the ruling authorities or those schools chose al-Bukhari and others like him. They (the schools) constructed from them support, pillars and symbols to consolidate their power and to propagate their schools and market their views which became, during the Caliphates of the Umayyads and 'Abbasids, a circulating market and a profitable commodity for all scholars who competed and fought to assist the Caliphate by all forms of fabrications and interpolations which were in concordance with the prevalent

---

[8] Ibn Hajar in *al-Sawa'iq al-Muhriqa* reported on page 107 He said: "Two desert Arabs argued and presented themselves to 'Umar, he sent the case to 'Ali to juge. One of them said:"Is this one going to judge our case?" Whereupon Umar grabbed him and said:"Woe unto you, don't you know who is this! This is your master and the master of every believer. He who does not take him as a master is not believer".

politics. All this was done to gain the honor and rewards from the rulers. In doing so, they sold their hereafter for this world, their commerce was not profitable, and on the Day of Judgment they will regret and will be among the losers.

People are people and time is time; and you see today the same method, the same politics. How many a great scholar has been placed under house arrest and the people do not [even] know him. How many ignorant [scholars] have mounted the pulpit to deliver sermons, to be the Imams of the congregations, to judge the fate of the Muslims?

This is because he is of the close ones who obtained the pleasure and support of the authorities. Otherwise tell me, by your Lord, how can al-Bukhari's averseness towards the Prophet's household be explained, [those from whom] Allah has removed all filth and purified them completely? How do you explain al-Bukhari's animosity towards the rightly guided Imams, some of whom were his contemporaries and lived in his time?

He related nothing from them except spurious things to denigrate their elevated nobility and to blemish their proven infallibility which was confirmed by the Qur'an and *Sunnah*. We will provide examples on this.

Then, al-Bukhari turned towards the *Nasibis* (those who hate the *Ahl al-Bayt*) and the Khawarij who waged war against the *Ahl al-Bayt* and killed them. You see him narrating from Mu'awiyah, 'Amr b. al-'As, Abu Hurayrah, Marwan b. al-Hakam, from Muqatal b. Sulayman who was known as a swindler, from Imran b. Hatan, the enemy of the Commander of the Faithful and the enemy of the *Ahl al-Bayt*, the poet of the Khawarij, and their orator who used to sing the praises of Ibn Muljam Muradi for his killing of 'Ali b. Abi Talib.

Al-Bukhari used to cite as proofs [for arguments] the *hadiths* of the Khawarij, the Murji'a, the *Mujassima* (corporealists), and some unknown [persons] whose existence history has not [even] been recorded.

Chapter 8: Concerning the two Sahihs ...

In his *Sahih*, in addition to lies and forgery [inserted] from transmitters noted for these [traits], he has narrated some foolish and repulsive traditions. An example of this is what he related in his *Sahih* in "The Book of Marriage," in "The Chapter Who is Lawful and who is Unlawful amongst the Women" and Allah's verses "Your mothers are unlawful unto you.." to the end of the verse.

At the end of the chapter he said about Allah's words: ***"And permitted for you is all else other than those."*** Ikrima said on the authority of Ibn 'Abbas: "If a man commits adultery with his wife's sister, his wife is not forbidden for him. And it has been related from Yahya al-Kindi on the authority of al-Sha'bi and from Abu Ja'far, if someone fondles a little boy and has intercourse with him, then he cannot marry his mother."

The commentator of al-Bukhari has commented in the footnotes: "It is more in keeping with the status of scholars to disdain from writing or speaking such speech."

Al-Bukhari has also reported in his *Sahih* in "The Book of the Commentary of the Qur'an," in "The Chapter on Your women are a tilth unto You" on the authority of Nafi' who said: "When Ibn 'Umar (r) read the Qur'an, he used to not speak until he had finished. So I went to him one day and he read *Surah al-Baqara* until he stopped at a spot, and he said: 'Do you know concerning what it has been revealed?' I said: 'No.' He said: 'Concerning so and so..' Then he continued."

And from Nafi' from Ibn 'Umar: *"So approach your tilth from wherever you wish,"* he said: 'He approaches her in...'" The commentator added: "His words... by the deletion of the preposition, it is, in fact, an adverb, i.e. [signifying] the anus." It is said: "The author omitted this due to its repugnance; this is [how it appears] in the commentary."[9]

---

[9] *Sahih al-Bukhari*, 5/160.

One day, I was at the University of Sorbonne in Paris, speaking about the etiquettes of the Prophet (s), his exalted character which the Qur'an spoke about and that the Prophet (s) was famous for [the traits] even before the call to prophecy, for they called him "The truthful, trustworthy". The lecture lasted for about an hour. During the lecture, I explained that the Prophet did not initiate wars, he did not abuse human rights during the course of his life, nor [did he] impose his religion by force and coercion as some Orientalists have claimed.

During the discussion, in which a group of lecturers, doctors specialized in Islam and in Muslim history, most of who were Orientalists, were present, I emerged victorious to some extent over the adversaries who had raised some doubts. However, one of them, an Arab Christian of old age (I believe he was Lebanese), objected in a malicious and clever way, and he almost turned my victory into a shameful defeat.

This doctor said in pure Arabic that what I had mentioned in the lecture was filled with exaggeration, especially concerning the infallibility of the Prophet since the Muslims themselves do not agree upon that. Indeed, even Muhammad himself would not agree to that. For he said on innumerable occasions that he is mortal, permitted to err. The Muslims have recorded numerous mistakes which we have no need to describe here while the Muslim authentic and reliable books bear witness to it. Then he said: "As regards to the wars specifically, all the audience of the lecture have to do is to refer to history. In fact, it is sufficient to read the books of the expeditions which Muhammad undertook during his lifetime. And then the rightly guided Caliphs continued these after his death until they arrived at Poitier, a city in Western France. In every battle, they imposed their new religion on the people by coercion and the power of the sword."

The listeners accepted his words with applause and supported his speech. I attempted my best to convince them that what the Christian doctor had said was untrue, even if they had been recorded in the books of the Muslims. A great laughter arose in the hall deriding and mocking at me.

Chapter 8: Concerning the two Sahihs ...

The Christian doctor interjected again to state that what he had related was not from any questionable books, but was from the *Sahihs* of al-Bukhari and Muslim. I retorted that these books were deemed authentic by the *Ahl al-Sunnah* but that the Shi'as do not accord any weight to them, and that I was from them. He said: "We care not for the views of the Shi'a who are regarded as disbelievers by the majority of the Muslims. The Sunni Muslims are ten times more numerous than the Shi'as, they do not pay any heed to the views of the Shi'as." He added, saying: "If you Muslims understood each other and convinced each other of the infallibility of your Prophet, perhaps then you would be able to convince us" (he said this in a laughing, mocking manner).

He then turned towards me again and said: "And as regards the praiseworthy traits, I ask you to convince the listeners how come Muhammad, who had reached fifty four years of age, married 'A'isha who was only six years old?"

The mocking and laughter arose again and the people raised their necks to see what my reply would be. I tried my best to explain to them that marriage among the Arabs was performed in two stages - the first stage was the agreement and affirmation of the marriage, and the second stage was the living together and consummation. The Prophet (s) had married A'isha when she was six, but that he did not sleep with her until she was nine. I pointed out that this is what al-Bukhari says in case my opponent tried to argue with me by citing what was in it.

I personally doubt the authenticity of the report as the people in those days were not an established city community, and did not record the dates of birth or death. And even if we are to assume the validity of the narration, then 'A'isha attained puberty in her ninth year - for how many Russian and Romanian girls have we seen on the TV screens today performing gymnastics, their bodies fully developed, and you are amazed when their ages are announced that they are not even eleven years old. No doubt the Prophet (s) did not consummate his marriage until she had reached puberty and began to have a monthly period. Islam does not state that maturity [is attained] at reaching eighteen years as is the rule in France; instead, Islam considers maturity by the appearance of the menstrual cycle in women, and by the secretion of sperms in a male. And all of us know today that among the males are those who produce sperms even from the age of ten and that among the females are those who menstruate from an early age, sometimes when they are not even ten.

At this point, a lady got up and said: "On the assumption that what you have said is true - and it is scientifically possible - how can we accept the marriage of an old man advanced in his twilight years with a girl who was still in her first stage of life?"

I said: "Muhammad was the Prophet of Allah and would not do anything unless it was revealed from Allah. There is no doubt that there is wisdom in everything that Allah does even if I am personally not aware of that wisdom."

The Christian doctor said: "But the Muslims have taken that as an established practice. How many little girls have been married off by their fathers forcibly to men equal in age to him (the father)? Regrettably, this phenomenon has remained even to our present day." I seized this opportunity to say: "As a result of this, I left the *madhab* of the Sunnis and followed that of the Shi'as, for it gives the woman the right to marry herself to whomsoever she pleases, not to [one] whom her guardian forces upon her." He said: "Let us leave aside the matter of Sunnis and Shi'as and return to the subject of Muhammad's marriage to 'A'isha." He turned to the listeners saying with blatant mockery: "Muhammad was a Prophet and over fifty, and married to a small girl not cognizant at all of marriage. Al-Bukhari tells us that she was in her husband's house playing with dolls. This confirms the innocence of her infancy. Is this the exalted character through which the Prophet was distinguished?"

I attempted again to convince the listeners that al-Bukhari was not a proof [to be cited] against the Prophet (s) but without success. For this Lebanese Christian had played on their minds as he wished. There was nothing for me to do but stop the debate, pointing out that we were not talking on the same wavelength, for they sought to

Chapter 8: Concerning the two Sahihs ...

argue with me based on al-Bukhari, when I did not believe in everything he reported.

I emerged angry at the Muslims who had provided these people and the enemies of Islam and Muhammad (s) with an effective weapon which they used to fight against us and at the head of these was al-Bukhari. I returned to my home that day, sad; and began to read through *Sahih al-Bukhari* to find out what he mentioned about the merits of 'A'isha and her condition when lo! I had to say: "All praise is due to Allah who opened my eyes, otherwise, I would have remained perplexed regarding the personality of the Messenger of Allah (s) and perhaps doubt regarding him would have entered my mind, God forbid."

It is absolutely necessary that I relate some of the narrations that I came across during the debate so that it may be clear to the reader that the critics do not [criticize] emptily, but rather, have based their views on our own *Sihah* and have used them against us.

In "The Book of the Beginning of Creation", in "The Chapter on the Marriage of the Prophet to 'A'isha, and his arrival in Medina and his taking up residence with Her" al-Bukhari related: "From 'A'isha (r) who said: 'The Prophet married me when I was a girl of six (years). We went to Medina and stayed at the home of Banu al-Harith b. Khazraj. Then I got ill and my hair fell down. Later on, my hair grew (again) and my mother, Umm Ruman, came to me while I was playing on a swing with some of my girl friends. She called me and I went to her, not knowing what she wanted to do to me. She caught me by the hand and made me stand at the door of the house. I was breathless then, and when my breathing became all right, she took some water and rubbed my face and head with it. Then she took me into the house. There in the house I saw some Ansari women who said: 'Best wishes and Allah's Blessing and good luck.' Then she entrusted me to them and they prepared me (for the marriage). Unexpectedly Allah's Apostle came to me in the forenoon and my mother handed me over to him, at that time I was a girl of nine years of age.'"

I leave for you, O reader, to reflect upon such narrations.

Similarly, al-Bukhari reported in "The Book of Manners," in "The Chapter of Being Happy with the People": From 'A'isha (r) who said: "I used to play with some dolls in the presence of the Prophet, and I had some companions who played with me. When the Prophet of Allah entered, they would stop themselves [from playing], but he would instruct them to come to me, and they used to come play with me."

The commentator said: "Playing with dolls, means the images (of living things) which are called dolls: and "*yusaribihinna ilayya,* i.e., instruct and send them to me." When you read narrations such as these in *Sahih al-Bukhari*, does there remain any objection to the criticisms of the Orientalists, if you are objective?

Tell me, by your lord! When you read the words of 'A'isha to the Prophet of Allah: "I do not perceive your Lord except that he hastens [to fulfill] your desires"[10] does there remain in your mind any respect and veneration for a woman such as this, who doubts the Prophet's purity? Does that not make you feel that her behavior is that of an adolescent who is immature?

After this, can the enemies of Islam be rebuked, those who pose the [question of] the love of Muhammad for women, and that he was desirous [women]? If they read in al-Bukhari that Allah used to hasten [to fulfill] his desires, and they also read in al-Bukhari that he used to sleep with eleven wives in a single hour, and that he had the strength of thirty men, [can they be blamed]?

The blame is on those Muslims who accepted these legends and accepted them as being correct; in fact, they considered it like the Qur'an, which is not open to doubt. But these [Muslims] have been controlled in everything - even in their creed and there is no choice for them in anything. These books have been imposed on them from the earliest rulers. Let us relate now traditions from al-Bukhari

---

[10] *Sahih al-Bukhari,* 6/24, *Kitab Tafsir al-Qur'an*: "The Chapter on the saying of the Most High:'You may defer any one amongst them that you please and you may receive anyone that you wish, there is no blame on you whose turn you had set aside'".

Chapter 8: Concerning the two Sahihs ...

that denigrates the *Ahl al-Bayt.*

In "The Book of Campaigns," in "The Chapter on the Witnessing by the Angels at Badr" vol. 5 p.16, al-Bukhari reported: "From 'Ali b. al-Husayn, that al-Husayn b. 'Ali informed him that 'Ali said: 'I got a she-camel in my share of the war booty on the day [of the battle] of Badr, and the Prophet had given me a she-camel from the *khumus*. When I intended to marry Fatima, the daughter of Allah's Apostle, I had an appointment with a goldsmith from the tribe of Bani Qaynuqa' to go with me to bring *idhkhir* (i.e. grass of pleasant smell) and sell it to the goldsmiths and spend its price on my wedding party. I was collecting for my she-camels equipment of saddles, sacks and ropes while my two she-camels were kneeling down beside the room of an Ansari man. I returned after collecting whatever I collected to see the humps of my two she-camels cut off and their flanks cut open and some portion of their livers was taken out. When I saw that state of my two she-camels, I could not help weeping. I asked: 'Who has done this?' The people replied: 'Hamza b. 'Abd al-Muttalib who is staying with some Ansari drunks in this house.' I went away till I reached the Prophet, and Zayd b. Haritha was with him. The Prophet noticed on my face the effect of what I had suffered, he asked: 'What is wrong with you?' I replied: 'O Allah's Apostle! I have never seen such a day as today. Hamza attacked my two she-camels, cut off their humps, and ripped open their flanks, and he is sitting there in a house in the company of some drunks.' The Prophet then asked for his covering sheet, put it on, and set out walking followed by me and Zayd b. Haritha till he came to the house where Hamza was. He asked permission to enter, they allowed him and they were drunk. Allah's Apostle started rebuking Hamza for what he had done, but Hamza was drunk and his eyes were red. Hamza looked at Allah's Apostle and then he raised his eyes, looking at his knees, then he raised his eyes looking at his umbilicus, and again he raised his eyes and looked at his face. Hamza then said: 'Aren't you but the slaves of my father?' Allah's Apostle realized that he was drunk, so he retreated, and we went out with him.'"

Reflect, O reader, upon this transmission which is filled with lies and false charges, defaming the leader of the martyrs for he is the pride of the *Ahl al-Bayt*. How many times did Imam 'Ali (as) take pride in him in his poems saying: "And Hamza, the chief of the martyrs, is my uncle" and how often the Prophet took pride in him to the point that when he was killed, he was greatly saddened and he wept intensely for him and named him "the leader of the martyrs?"

Hamza was the uncle of the Prophet (s) through whom Allah had strengthened Islam. When some of the weak Muslims used to worship Allah in secrecy, he took his famous stand against the Quraysh and helped his nephew, declaring his Islam to the assembly of the Quraysh, not fearing anyone.

Hamza had emigrated before the Prophet and prepared for his nephew's coming on the famous day. Hamza was, with his nephew 'Ali, the hero of Badr and Uhud. Al-Bukhari himself related in his *Sahih* in "The Book of *Tafsir* of the Qur'an," in "The Chapter of these are two opponents who disputed with their Lord" vol. 5, p. 242: "[Narrated] from 'Ali b. Abi Talib (r) who said: 'I am the first of those who will kneel infront of the Merciful one for accounting on the day of judgement.'" Qays said that it is in their regard that "These were two opponents who disputed about their Lord" was revealed. He said: "They are the ones who fought on the day of Badr: 'Ali and Hamza and 'Ubayda, and Shaiba b. Rabi'a and 'Utba b. Rabi'a, and al-Walid b. 'Utba."

Al-Bukhari is pleased to relate such blemishes that destroy the pride of the *Ahl al-Bayt*, and the chain of falsifiers who concocted such narrations is long. Al-Bukhari said: "Abdan told us that 'Abd Allah informed him from Yunus, and Ahmad b. Salih told us that Anbasatu informed him from Yunus from al-Zuhri who reported from 'Ali b. al-Husayn.[11] There are seven persons from whom al-Bukhari reports before the chain reaches 'Ali b. al-Husayn, i.e., Zayn al-'Abidin, and the leader of those who prostrate. Is it proper that Zayn al-'Abidin should relate such lies, to the effect that the leader of the martyrs drank intoxicants after his accepting Islam, after his emigration, and shortly before his martyrdom for,

---

[11] *Sahih al-Bukhari*, 5/16.

Chapter 8: Concerning the two Sahihs ...

according to the narration, 'Ali b. Abi Talib was preparing the feast for his wedding with Fatima (sa) with whom he cohabited in 2 A.H. The Prophet (s) had given 'Ali his share from the booty the day of Badr. Now, is it proper for the chief of martyrs that he should have a prostitute singer singing to him and asking him to slaughter the two camels and that he did this without any concern?

Is it proper for the leader of the martyrs to eat forbidden meat without the [prescribed] slaughter, to cut open the hips and take the livers? Is it proper for the Prophet of Allah (s) to go and seek permission to see Hamza in that setting wherein there were intoxicants and immoral [things]? And for him to enter that place?

Does it behoove the leader of the martyrs to be red eyed and insult the Messenger (s): "You are nothing but slaves of my father?" Is it proper that the Apostle of Allah retreat back without any remonstration or rebuke when it is known about him that he used to get angry for Allah's sake?

I am absolutely convinced that this narration, were it (for argument's sake only, of course) to mention Abu Bakr, 'Umar, 'Uthman, or Mu'awiyah instead of Hamza, al-Bukhari would not have reported it due to its disgraceful [nature]. Had he reported it, he would have edited and expurgated it as was his practice. But what could be done, since al-Bukhari did not love those who refused to accept the school of the Caliphs? Even after the incident of Kerbala and their murdering all of them, none remained with the exception of 'Ali b. al-Husayn, to whom they falsely attributed the narration.

Why did al-Bukhari not relate any *fiqh* from the *Ahl al-Bayt* nor [anything] of their knowledge, traits, asceticism, nor their virtues which have filled books and which are abundantly [found] in the collection of the *Ahl al-Sunnah* before [they are found] in the collection of the Shi'as?

Let us look at another narration he recorded, slandering the *Ahl al-Bayt*, the apex in essence, since all the transmitters, among them al-Bukhari, could not find in 'Ali b. Abi Talib a single defect, nor could they record throughout his entire life a single lie, and did not know of a single wrong doing. If there was [even] one, they would have filled the earth with clamor and laments. Instead, they resorted to fabricating a *hadith* alleging that 'Ali would take the prayers lightly.

In "The Book of Eclipse" in "The Chapter on the Encouraging by the Prophet (s) of the Night Prayer and the Prophet's (s) knocking [on the door of] Fatima and 'Ali (as) at Night for Prayer," al-Bukhari reported in vol. 2, p. 43 of his *Sahih*: Abu'l-Yaman said to us that Shu'ayb reported from al-Zuhri who said: "'Ali b. al-Husayn informed me that al-Husayn b. 'Ali informed him that 'Ali b. Abi Talib informed him that the Prophet of Allah (s) knocked on the door of Fatima, the daughter of the Prophet (s) one night and said: 'Do you not pray?' I said: 'O Apostle of Allah, our souls are in the hands of Allah. When he wishes to awaken us, He does so.' He went away when we said this without replying anything to me. Then I heard him when he turned away, striking his thigh saying: 'Surely man argues in most things.'"

Fear Allah, O Bukhari! This is 'Ali b. Abi Talib we are discussing, the historians record that he would observe the night prayer growling, (in the battle of Siffin) having spread a mat and praying between the lines of battle while the archers and arrows fell around him, yet he was not frightened nor did he discontinue his night prayer.

'Ali b. Abi Talib was the one who explained to the people the principles of fate and divine decree and he enjoined upon human beings the responsibility of their [own] actions. Do you perceive him, in this narration, to be a fatalist believing in predestination and arguing based on this with the Prophet of Allah [using] the words: "Our souls are in the hands of Allah, if He wishes to awaken us, we do" meaning that if Allah wanted us to pray, we would have prayed. This is 'Ali, love for him is [a sign of] faith, and hatred for him is [a sign of] hypocrisy. Yet you describe him to be the most argumentative of creatures in most things? This is a disgraceful lie which even Ibn Muljim, the murderer of the Imam, or Mu'awiyah, who used to order the people to curse him, will not agree with. It is

Chapter 8: Concerning the two Sahihs ...

a cheap lie but you were tagging along many behind [you] since, by this, you pleased the rulers of your time and the enemies of the *Ahl al-Bayt*. They raised your stature in this transitory world, but you have angered your Lord by this stand against the Commander of the Faithful, the leader of those with distinctive marks of paradise, the one who will divide [people] between heaven and hell for he will stand on the day of judgement on the heights and everyone will be known by his marks[12] and he will say to the Fire: "This one is for me, and that one is for you."[13]

I don't know if your book on the Day of Judgment will be like your book of today which is adorned, [classified] in volumes, embellished so as to be the most magnificent adornment which a book can be known for.

Certainly it was difficult for al-Bukhari to show that his master 'Umar b. al-Khattab did not observe the obligatory prayer when there was no water and that he espoused this view even in his Caliphate and said: "As for me, I do not pray" thereby challenging the Qur'an and the *Sunnah*.

So al-Bukhari searched among the Satans and the falsifiers and they concocted for him this *hadith* which accuses the Commander of the Faithful, 'Ali b. Abi Talib (as), that he was lazy and did not pray the supererogatory night prayer. Assuming his tradition is authentic, there is no blame nor any sin nor wrong doing on 'Ali for

---

[12] *Shawahid al-Tanzil*, of al-Hiskani al-Hanafi 1/198 on the commentary of Allah's words:"And upon the heights are men, each known by his marks" Al-Hakim reported from 'Ali who said: "We will stand on the day of Judgement between heaven and hell and whosoever helped us, we will recognize him by his signs, and we will allow him into Paradise, and whosoever hated us, we will know him by his signs".

[13] Ibn Hajar in *al-Sawa'iq al-Muhriqa* page 101. He said: "It was reported from the Prophet (s) that he said: "O 'Ali! You are the divider between heaven and hell. And on the day of Judgement you will say to fire: 'This one is for me and that one for you'". Ibn Hajar added that Abu Bakr said to Ali (r): "I heared the Apostle of Allah say: 'None will be allowed on the path unless 'Ali gives him permission'".

it concerns the optional prayers, for which one receives rewards for performing but is not punished for not doing it. There can be no comparison between the action of 'Umar in leaving the obligatory prayer and 'Ali's leaving the optional prayers, if the narration is correct. But there is no way this tradition can be correct, even if it was reported in al-Bukhari's *Sahih*.

Al-Bukhari is regarded by the *Ahl al-Sunnah* as being authentic, and the *Ahl al-Sunnah* are the ones who supported the school of the Caliphate which was built on Umayyad and 'Abbasid politics. A researcher knows this fact, which is no longer a secret to anyone. The *Ahl al-Sunnah wa'l-Jama'a*, in following of the politics of the rulers who persisted on enmity and fighting the *Ahl al-Bayt* and anyone who befriended and followed them, became, without their knowledge, the enemies of the *Ahl al-Bayt* and their Shi'as as they befriended their enemies and were inimical to their friends. As a result, they raised the status of al-Bukhari to the degree of the highest honor. You therefore do not find with them any legacy of the *Ahl al-Bayt* nor any sayings of the twelve Imams mentioned not even from the door of the city of knowledge, he who was in relation to the Prophet (s) as Aaron was to Moses, that of a Prophet of his Lord.

The question that needs to be posed to the *Ahl al-Sunnah* is: "In comparison to the other *hadith* scholars, what is it that al-Bukhari preserved that [made him] attain this excellence for you?" I believe that the only answer to this question is that al-Bukhari:

1. Changed the *hadith* that touched on the honor of [some] companions, especially Abu Bakr, 'Umar, 'Uthman and Mu'awiyah. This is what Mu'awiyah and the rulers after him wanted.

2. Propagated the *hadith* that spoke against the infallibility of the Prophet of Allah (s), and portrayed him as an ordinary person subject to error. This is what the rulers wished at all times.

3. He reported false *hadith* in praise of the three Caliphs and he preferred them over 'Ali b. Abi Talib. This is precisely what Mu'awiyah wanted, to obliterate the mention of 'Ali's name, according to his [own] claim.

4. He related spurious *hadith* that denigrated the honor of the *Ahl al-Bayt*.

5. He related other *hadith* that supported fatalism, corporealism, fate and destiny regarding the Caliphate. These were what the Umayyads and 'Abbasids propagated so as to determine the fate of the community.

6. He related spurious *hadith* which resembled myths and fairy tales to scare the *ummah* and cause confusion. This is what the rulers wanted in al-Bukhari's time.

To cite an example; here, O reader is a narration:

Al-Bukhari reported in "The Book of The Beginning of Creation" in "The Chapter of the Days of Ignorance," vol. 4, p. 238: Al-Bukhari said: "Nu'aym b. Hammad informed me that Hushaym b. al-Husayn heard from Amr' b. Maymun, who said: 'I saw in the days of ignorance a monkey which had fornicated. [Other] monkeys gathered around her to stone her and I also stoned her along with them.'"

We say to al-Bukhari: "Perhaps Allah, Glory be to Him, out of mercy to the apes, abrogated the ruling of stoning which He had made obligatory upon them after their expulsion from heaven, and made fornication permissible for them during Islam after it was initially forbidden in the days of ignorance. As a result, no Muslim has ever claimed that he attended or took part in the stoning of a monkey since the prophethood of Muhammad (s) up to our present time."

CONCLUSION

After these tales, and others like this are abundant in al-Bukhari's [work], can the researchers, the scholars, free thinkers remain silent and not speak out?

Some will say: "Why this attack on al-Bukhari alone? There are in other *hadith* books more numerous [traditions] than in this [book]. This is correct, but we have analyzed al-Bukhari's work critically because this book has attained fame beyond comprehension; so much so that it has become like a holy book for the scholars of the *Ahl al-Sunnah,* as if no falsehood comes from the front nor from behind it, for everything in it is [deemed to be] true, not subject to any doubt. The fountain of this illusion and sanctity originated from the sultans and the kings, especially during the 'Abbasid dynasty, when the Persians took over the ruler ship in every part of the state and amongst them were ministers, advisers, doctors, and astronomers. Abu Faras said of that:

"Convey this message to the Banu 'Abbasid. They should not claim the ownership of this kingdom

Because the real kings are the non-Arabs,
What glorious qualities have remained in your houses
Because in it, the aliens are ruling and managing you"

The Persians tried their utmost, and used all their resources until the book of al-Bukhari occupied the highest position after the noble Qur'an and Abu Hanifa became the greatest Imam, above the other three Imams.

Had it not been for the Persian fear of Arab national agitation during the 'Abbasid caliphate, they would have raised al-Bukhari higher than the Qur'an itself, and they would have elevated Abu Hanifa above the Prophet (s), who knows?

I have read from some of them their attempts in this regard. They have said clearly that the *hadith* adjudicates the Qur'an, they mean the *hadith* of al-Bukhari of course. Similarly, they say that if the *hadith* of the Prophet (s) is at variance with the views and personal judgments of Abu Hanifa, it is necessary to give precedence to the judgments of Abu Hanifa. They justify [this by saying] that the *hadith* may have several meanings. This is if the *hadith* is of established authenticity; if however, there is doubt regarding its veracity, and then there is no problem.

The Islamic community has grown and increased gradually but its affairs have always been controlled, its fate directed by kings and sultans, by the foreigners, the Persians, the Mamlukes, the slaves, the Moghuls, the Turks, the French, the English, Italians, and Portugese colonialists.

Many scholars have persisted backing the rulers, and have sought to please them by issuing rulings, flattering them, and coveting their wealth and glory. They have always worked along the principle of "divide and rule". They did not allow *ijtihad* to anyone, nor to open that door which the rulers closed at the beginning of the second century, relying on the discord and war which occurred between the *Ahl al-Sunnah* - which is the majority that represented the governing body, and the Shi'a who were the neglected minority representing, in their (rulers) view, a dangerous opponent that had to be destroyed. The *'ulama'* of the *Ahl al-Sunnah* have busied themselves in the political games and plots, in criticizing and labelling the Shi'as as infidels, refuting their proofs by [using] all types of arguments and debates; so much so that thousands of books have been written, and thousands of innocent people have been killed for no other reason but because of their friendship to the progeny of the Prophet (s), and because of their rejection of those who ruled over the *ummah* by power and force.

Here we are today in the age of freedom, in the age of enlightenment, as they call it, a period of knowledge and competition of nations to conquer outer space and to control the earth. [Yet] any scholar who stands up and frees himself from the fetters of zeal and blind imitation and writes anything which smells of the following of the *Ahl al-Bayt*, they become furious and spend their efforts vilifying and labeling him as an infidel and [trying to] disgrace him. Not because of anything except that he has opposed what has been written by them. But if he was to write a book praising al-Bukhari and glorifying him, he would be seen as the most erudite of the learned, and they would heap honor and praise on him from every side, people whose prayer and fasting do not prevent them from flattery and falsity would bow at his doorstep.

When you think of all the factors which have led most of [Allah's] servants to deviate, and the reasons which have resulted in leading most of the people astray, the noble Qur'an informs you of its hidden secret during the conversation between the Lord of Honor and Majesty and the accursed devil.

He (the Lord) said: "What prevented you from prostrating when I ordered you to do so?" He (Satan) said: "I am better than him. You created me from fire and him from clay."

He said: "Go down from it, You cannot be arrogant here [in the garden] so begone! You are amongst the meanest of creatures."

He said: "Give me a respite until the day when they are resurrected."

He said: "You are amongst those who are given a respite."

He said: "As You have expelled me, I will lay in wait for them in your straight path, then I shall come from the front and from behind, from their right and left, and you will find most of them ungrateful to You". He said: "Get out abased and expelled! If any of them follows you, I shall fill the hell with all of you" (7:12-18).

"O Children of Adam! Do not let Satan corrupt you as he led to the expulsion of your parents from paradise, stripping them of their clothes to show them their nakedness. Surely he

(Satan) and his tribe see you from whence you perceive them not. We have made Satans the friends for those who do not believe.

If they commit an immoral [deed] they say we found our fathers doing it and Allah has ordered us to do it! Say to them: 'Certainly Allah never orders wrongdoing! Do you say of Allah what you do not know?' Say: 'My Lord has ordered me [to practice] justice and to fix your attention (to Him) at every place of prostration and to supplicate to Him in sincerity for, as He has brought you into being, so unto Him will you return. Some He has guided right, others have deserved to go astray, for they have taken Satans as their friends instead of Allah, they think that they are rightly guided'" (7:26-30).

I therefore say to all my Muslim brothers in general: "Curse the Satan and do not grant him any means of [approaching] you. Come together for an academic discussion which the Qur'an and the authentic *Sunnah* establish. Let us agree upon a common word between us and you that we will not use as proof except what is proven to be authentic to both you and us. We will leave aside what we differ on. Did the Prophet of Allah (s) not say "My *ummah* will not unite in (committing) a mistake?" Truth and what is right lies in what we, Sunnis and Shi'as, agree upon. Falsehood lies in what we differ in. If we erect this pillar, only purity, agreement and joy would envelope us, we would be reunited; the help of Allah and victory would come. From the earth and the skies blessings would rain upon us. For the time has come, and we do not have any more time to wait, before that day in which there is no barter and no transaction is allowed. We are all - Sunnis and Shi'as - awaiting the coming of our Imam al-Mahdi (as) for our books are replete with the tidings of his coming. Is this not sufficient proof of the oneness of our path? The Shi'as are nothing but your brothers, and the *Ahl al-Bayt* are not exclusive to them. For Muhammad (s) and the members of his household are the Imams of all Muslims. We, Sunnis and Shi'as, are in agreement on the veracity of the *hadith* of

Conclusion

the two weighty things, and the saying of the Prophet (s): "I have left with you something which, if you stick to, you will never go astray; Allah's book and my household."[1]

And the Mahdi is from his progeny. Is this not another proof? Now the time of tyranny and oppression during which no one was as oppressed as the *Ahl al-Bayt*, the progeny of the Prophet (s) were, has passed. They were cursed from the pulpits, killed, their women and children taken prisoners - all this within the sight and earshot of all the Muslims.

The time has now come to remove the acts of injustices from the members of the Prophet's household, for the *ummah* to return under their protective arms which are filled with affection and mercy to their flourishing group which is filled with knowledge and deeds. [It is time for the *ummah* to return] to the shadows of the lofty tree which is filled with merit and honor. Allah and His angels have sent blessings to them, and [He] has ordered the Muslims to do that in every prayer just as he has ordered us to love and befriend them.

The superiority of the *Ahl al-Bayt* then, is something which no Muslim denies; the poets have sung their praises with the passage of time. Al-Farazdaq said about them:

"If the pious men were enumerated, they would be their Imams. If it was asked who are the best of the people on earth, it would be said 'them'.

They are from that group, love for them is [true] religion. And hating them is infidelity

---

[1] We have explained in a previous discussion that this *hadith* in no way contradicts the *hadith* of "the book of Allah and my *sunnah*" for the book of Allah and the *Sunnah* of his Prophet are silent speeches, they need an interpreter and elucidator. The Prophet guides us in that the commentator and elucidator of the Qur'an and the *Sunnah* is his family, the Imams of *Ahl al-Bayt*; all Muslims bear witness that they take precedence over everyone in knowledge and acts.

And closeness to them is place of refuge and stronghold. Their remembrance has precedence after the remembrance of Allah in every good deed; and the talks are sealed with their remembrance."

And Abu Faras, the famous poet praised the *Ahl al-Bayt* and exposed the 'Abbasids in his well known elegy called *al-Shafi'a*. We quote here a bit from it:

"O wine sellers, stop your boasting [and submit to] those people who sell their lives in battles, leave the boasting for those who are the most knowledgeable when they are asked and the most accomplished implementers when they know

Those who do not become angry except for Allah's sake when they are angry

And do not abandon the law of the Lord when they judge.

In their houses the Qur'an is recited in the mornings and in your houses there are musical instruments and songs.

Their places are at *rukn al-Yamani* and the Ka'ba and its cover and Zam Zam and Safa' and the *hijr Isma'il* and the sanctuary.

There is no oath in the Qur'an which we know except they are, without any doubt, that oath."

Al-Zamakhshari, al-Bayhaqi and al-Qastalani have all narrated the following verses from Imam Abu 'Abd Allah Muhammad b. 'Ali al-Ansari al-Shatibi.

Some Christians have written numerous books on the qualities and excellences of 'Ali b. Abi Talib specifically, and of the *Ahl al-Bayt* in general. This is what al-Shatibi meant:

"I do not want to mention Banu 'Uday and Banu Taym in a derogatory manner.

But I am the lover of Banu Hashim, and when 'Ali and his family are mentioned For the sake of Allah, I do not care for the rebuke of critics. They say: 'Why do even Christians love them and also the people of intelligence whether Arabs or non-Arabs?' I say to them: 'I think that their love has penetrated into the hearts of all creatures, even the animals.'"

The author of "*Kashf al-Ghumma*" on page 20 of his book has quoted the sayings of some Christians in praise of the Commander of the Faithful 'Ali b. Abi Talib:

"'Ali is the Commander of the Faithful, definitely
And no other person can aspire for the Caliphate
He has the highest lineage, and he is the first in his Islam - and virtues
They all agree 'Ali is the best of the people and most pious and bravest of them all after the Prophet
If I were I to desire any religion other than my own,
I would not be anything but a Shi'a Muslim."

The Muslims are more fitting to show love and to befriend the *Ahl al-Bayt* of the Prophet; and the reward of having accepted the message is completely dependent on [our] loving them.

Perchance my call will reach [some] attentive ears, perceptive hearts and open eyes, and I hope that I will, by that, achieve happiness in this world and in the hereafter. I beseech Him, the most Glorious and Exalted, to make my effort sincere for His noble cause, to accept my effort and to forgive me and to make me a servant for Muhammad and his progeny (as) in this world and in the hereafter. For in service to them lies a great success. Indeed, with my Lord is the straight Path. My last prayer is that all praise is for Allah the Lord of all the worlds, and the choicest praises and blessings be for Muhammad and his progeny, the most cleansed and pure.

Muhammad Al-Tijani Al-Samawi

REFERENCE BOOKS

1. *Abqariyat Khalid* by Abbas al-'Aqqad
2. *Ahkam al-Qur'an* by Ibn al-Arabi
3. *Al-'Iqd al-Farid,* by Ibn 'Abd al-Rabbih
4. *Al-Bidaya wa al-Nihaya* by Ibn al-Kathir
5. *Al-Dur al-Manthur* by Jalaluddin al-Suyuti
6. *Al-Ghadir* by Allama Amini
7. *Al-Imama wa al-Siyasa* also known as *Tarikh al-Khulafa'* by Ibn Qutayba
8. *Al-'Iqd al-Farid* by Ibn 'Abd Rabbih
9. *Al-Isaba fi tamyiz al-Sahaba* also known as *al-Isaba* by Ibn Hajar al-'Asqalani
10. *Al-Isti'ab fi Ma'rifat al-Ashab* by Ibn Abd al-Barr
11. *Al-Jawhara al-Naira fi fiqh* by al-Hanafi
12. *Al-Kashshaaf* by al-Zamakhshari
13. *Al-Khasa'is* by al-Nasa'i
14. *Al-Manaqib* by al-Khawarizmi
15. *Al-Mu'jam al-Kabir* by Tabrani
16. *Al-Mufaqiyyat* (no author listed)
17. *Al-Riyad al-Nadira fi manaqib al-'ashara (*also known as *Al-Riyad al-Nadira)* by Muhibb al-Din al-Tabari
18. *Al-Sahih min sirat al-Nabi al-A'zam* by 'Allama Ja'far al-Murtada al-'Amili
19. *Al-Saqifa* by Abu Bakr Ahmad Ibn al-'Aziz al-Jawhari
20. *Al-Sawa'iq al-Muhriqa* by Ibn Hajar
21. *Al-Sira al-Halabiya fi Sirat al-Amin al-Ma'mun* by 'Ali Burhan al-Din Al-Halabi
22. *Ansab al-Ashraf* by Al-Baladhuri

23. *Asbab al-Nuzul* by Ali ibn Ahmad al-Wahidi
24. *Black Thursday* by Mohammad al-Tijani al-Samawi
25. *Ihya' 'Ulum al-Din* by Imam Ghazali
26. *Jami' al-bayan 'an ta'wil ay al-Qur'an* also known as *Tafsir al-Ṭabari* by Muhammad ibn Jarir al-Tabari
27. *Jami' Bayan al-ilm wa fadlih* by Ibn 'Abd al-Barr
28. *Kanz-al-'Ummal* by Ali al-Muttaqi al-Hindi
29. *Kitab al-Milal wa al-Nihal* by al-Shahrastani
30. *Kitab Tabaqat Al-Kubra* popularly known as *Tabaqat Ibn Sa'd* by Muhammad Ibn Sa'd Ibn Mani' al-Hashimi
31. *Lisan al-'Arab* by Ibn Manzur
32. *Masabih al-Sunnah* by Abu Mubammad al-Farra' al-Baghawi
33. *Muntakhab Kanz al-'Ummal fi Sunan al-Aqwal wa-al-Af'al* by Ahmad ibn Muhammad Ibn Hanbal
34. *Muruj al-Dhahab* by Ali Ibn Husayn al-Mas'udi
35. *Musnad* by Ibn Hanbal
36. *Musnad al-Sadiq* by Mohammad al-Tijani al-Samawi
37. *Mustadrak* by Imam al-Hakim
38. *Nahj al-Balagha*
39. *Rabi'al-Abrar* by Zamakhshari
40. *Sahih al-Bukhari*
41. *Sahih al-Tirmidhi*
42. *Sahih Muslim*
43. *Sharaf Ashab al-Hadith* by Khatib al-Baghdadi
44. *Sharh Nahj al-Balagha* by Ibn Abi'l-Hadid
45. *Sharh Nahj al-Balagha* by Muhammad 'Abduh
46. *Shawahid al-Tanzil,* by al-Hiskani al-Hanafi
47. *Sira Nabawiya (Al-Sira Dihlania)* by Ahmad Zaini Dahlan
48. *Sirr al-'Alamayn* by Imam al-Ghazali

49. *Sunan Abu Dawud*
50. *Sunan* al-Bayhaqi by Imam Bayhaqi
51. *Sunan al-Darimi* by `Abd Allah al-Darimi
52. *Sunan Ibn Maja*
53. *Tadhkira al-Huffaz* by Al-Dhahabi
54. *Tadhkirat al-Khawas min al-Umma fi Dhikr Khasa'is al-A'imma* by Sibt Ibn al-Jawzi
55. *Tafsir* al-Alusi also known as *Ruh al-Ma'ani* by Mahmud al-Alusi
56. *Tafsir al-Kabir* aka *Mafatih al-Ghayb* by Fakhr al-Din al-Razi
57. *Tafsir al-Kabir* by Imam al-Tha'labi
58. *Tafsir al-Qurtubi* by Imam Abu 'Abullah al-Qurtubi
59. *Tafsir al-Tahrir wa'l-Tanwir* by Muhammad al-Tahir ibn 'Ashur
60. *Tafsir al-Tustari* also known as *Ihqaq al-Haqq* by Qazi NurAllah Shushtari
61. *Takyid al-'ilm* by al-Baghdadi
62. *Talkhis al-Mustadrak* by Al-Dhahabi
63. *Tarikh Abul-Fida* by Abu al-Fida
64. *Tarikh al-Khulafa* by Jalaluddin al-Suyuti
65. *Tarikh al-Ya'qubi* by Ahmad Ibn Abi Ya'qub
66. *Tarikh Baghdad* by Khatib al-Baghdadi
67. *Tarikh Dimishq* by Ibn 'Asakir
68. *Tarikh Ibn al-Athir* by 'Izz al-Din Abi al-Hasan Ibn al-Athir
69. *Tarikh Tabari* by Muhammad Ibn Jarir al-Tabari
70. *Then I Was Guided* by Mohammad al-Tijani al-Samawi
71. *Yanabi al-Muwadda (The Fountains of Love)* by al-Qanduzi al-Hanafi

www.ingramcontent.com/pod-product-compliance
Ingram Content Group UK Ltd.
Pitfield, Milton Keynes, MK11 3LW, UK
UKHW041401150526
12504UKWH00028B/240